Career Paths in Telemental Health

Marlene M. Maheu • Kenneth P. Drude
Shawna D. Wright

Editors

Career Paths in Telemental Health

 Springer

Editors
Marlene M. Maheu
San Diego, CA, USA

Kenneth P. Drude
Kenneth P. Drude, Ph.D. LLC.
Dayton, OH, USA

Shawna D. Wright
Wright Psychological Services, LLC
Chanute, KS, USA

ISBN 978-3-319-23735-0   ISBN 978-3-319-23736-7   (eBook)
DOI 10.1007/978-3-319-23736-7

Library of Congress Control Number: 2016946372

Printed on acid-free paper

This Springer imprint is published by Springer Nature
The registered company is Springer International Publishing AG Switzerland

Foreword by L'Abate

Can a profession devoted to helping people make positive behavior changes, in turn, modify its own clinical practices? If the stages of change model can be applied to a profession, and the mental health profession in particular, the change is now taking place as witnessed in this new volume. Contributors to this volume who have meditated, processed, and thought about incorporating Internet technology in their work demonstrate here how they eventually had no choice but to embrace the Internet as the next medium of psychological help and healing in this century. The diverse paths these varied professionals took toward their use of technology highlight the many individual ways technology may be used to benefit people needing services.

In the 1970s under the influence of the late attorney, Dan McDougald, I started to use programmed writing as a way to change and improve behavior, especially with inmates. When I gave then a workshop about distance writing at a GPA annual meeting, only three colleagues attended and two left after my introductory remarks. At the time, the idea that you could change behavior through distance writing was anathema to all those trained in the primacy of personal presence. In fact, many of my GPA colleagues began to avoid me. I had experimental results from my own students and my laboratory to support this position, but evidence is not always convincing in the face of strong traditional beliefs.

With the many varied contributions of this volume, I do feel a sense of vindication. However, I feel we are still only at the beginning of a great change. In 1976 I argued that only structured, replicable interventions based on writing would result in an empirically based profession of clinical psychology. In my opinion, the clinical psychology profession has continued to practice as art rather than as an empirical science. This, in spite of the more recent movement toward evidence-based interventions. Here the basic steps to pre-post- and follow-up evaluation were completely forgotten: process was valued above outcome. However, as long as these empirically based interventions were based on face-to-face talk, there was no way to replicate them.

The clinical mental health professions, lacking any organizational limits, have continued to practice as artists, no initial baseline, no post-intervention evaluation, and no follow-up. Gaudiano and Scott Lilienfeld (reference here please) in their writings have emphasized how the public tends to view clinicians as artists rather than professionals. The medical model has been cited as the underlying rationale for this kind of practice, to urge defensive rebuttals to possible criticisms. The idea that a referral should be linked with a concrete and specific targeted treatment was frowned upon. Talk and personal presence seemed to be the magic formula without a specific strategy. Some would say that clinical success was measured by how many professionals were financially successful.

The contributors to this volume appear at a crucial point in the evolution from auditory-verbal psychotherapies to visually digital remote writing interventions. They reflect a question that faces the twenty-first century clinician as to whether they are going to use replicable, targeted programmed remote interactive interventions that have been validated with pre-post- and follow-up client by single client. Will they continue practicing online in the same manner as face-to-face psychotherapists, without internal or external controls? Or will they practice (as psychologists were trained to do) in a replicable and scientific manner that provides a baseline, a targeted treatment, and follow-up? Anything short of these three steps departs from the scientific realm and enters the artistic realm. If it is not replicable in evaluation and in treatment, it remains in the artistic realm. do not need to demonstrate the validity of their productions. The last time I counted, there were 23 different types of psychotherapy where eclecticism prevented the need for a model responsible for change. But with the use of technology, as reflected in the experiences of this book, we are on the brink of a newer, more precise and scientific approach to helping those with psychological problems.

Georgia State University   Luciano L'Abate
Atlanta, GA, USA

Foreword by Zimbardo

I remember vividly the very first time I became aware of how technology could transform my teaching in dramatic ways. I have taught large lecture classes at different universities and realized that a teacher in a large auditorium must become a performer. That means going well beyond simply delivering information, but also to captivate, motivate, and inspire students to want to know more about psychology and life. But at a simple level, these grand themes get reduced to getting the students to attend to what you are saying and showing, to hold that attention for nearly an hour, and also from time to time, to divert it from one topic to another.

I also always wanted to make my class unique and memorable among all the others that students were taking. To do so I relied upon technologies of the time: I began my class with warm-up music, played through a CD player connected to big speakers; presented the outline of my lecture on an overhead transparency; showed 60–100 slides on the carousel slide projector; and showed 16 mm films on a separate film projector. In addition, I also would regularly do class demonstrations and many experiments.

One day, in the middle of teaching a lecture on mental illness and its treatment, a student in the front row began to giggle loudly. I tried to simply stare her down to stop, which stifled the sound, but not the negative headshaking. I could not understand what was funny about some of the tragic cases I was presenting of severe mental illness. I asked her to remain after class, which she did, and to explain what was so funny.

"*You* are funny, running around the stage like a madman turning one device after another, on and off, into the audience to start the film, back to overhead transparency, reveal revealing line by line moving a piece of cardboard marker!"

I asked her: "How else is it possible to operate all those AV-devices, without doing what I was doing, and have been doing for years?"

"DIGITIZE."

"What does that mean," I asked puzzled.

She, Cindy Wang, asked me to let her demonstrate how to do so, rather than try to explain. She then asked me to give her all my AV materials. I reluctantly shared them, but was open to any new gimmick that might make my teaching better and easier.

The next day Cindy came to my office and exchanged the two slide trays, music CD, overhead transparency, and 16 mm film reel for one little disk, something called a DVD. She had somehow transferred all that analog information and input into a digital format that could be burned to a disk, which could be all played through a computer—at one station with no frantic antics. It was sheer magic. Of course, I hired her as my tech TA for the next few years, and together we reprogrammed my class lectures and also my research-colloquium lectures. My life got easier, and my lectures became "dazzling" as I learned how to use PowerPoint, Keynote, and now Prezi performance programs for combining audio, video, and information.

In my next class lecture following the one on mental illness, I was discussing different forms of therapy and raised the issue of various barriers and obstacles that prevented someone who needed help to actually go to a therapist's office for the therapy he or she had available for clients. I had started the first therapy center in the world at Stanford University focused entirely on treating extremely shy people. However, many shy people were unable to call our office phone to make an initial appointment, so we had to provide a mailing address in order for some of them to do that. That experience sensitized me to the many reasons potential clients do not become actual clients. Among them are living in a rural or remote area, lack of transportation, lack of sufficient funds to pay for the service, language barriers, and appointment timing issues, such as can't take off from work during daytime office hours, among others.

So how can these barriers be converted to challenges that can be adequately handled by technology? If potential clients simply had access to a computer, iPad, or smartphone, they cannot only make appointments, but the therapeutic session itself would be available on those services. Thinking in this way is the equivalent to my earlier lesson to simply "digitize." This is such a simple idea but one with enormous positive consequences. Fortunately, many professionals in mental health domains now have available such services provided by the wedding of information technology with the future-oriented thinking of the editors of this unique volume, along with its many talented contributors.

The bottomline of my introduction is to alert you, the reader, along with all professionals with mental health degrees about the revolution that is happening in the world of telehealth. Why should you care?

First, there will be ample and rewarding employment in the information technology (IT) industry. Four introductory chapters discuss the importance of technology and what's going on that impacts behavioral and mental health. They focus on healthcare reform, legal and regulatory changes, education, and mental health. These introductory chapters are followed by 30–35 short chapters each written by educators, counselors, or psychologists who started out in behavioral health and now works in somewhere in this new tech sector.

From my perspective, it is not only my colleagues in psychology that I want to alert about this exciting new adventure so they can be in the forefront of this movement, but all behavioral scientists should know about and appreciate fully this revolution that combines the wisdom of ages of effective therapies with new technologies that hold the promise of delivering these strategies to so many more people whose lives can be enhanced by such easy and always available treatment options.

Stanford University   Philip Zimbardo, Ph.D.

Preface

As dreamers who know they are dreaming, most of us realize that we are in the midst of unprecedented change, even as we engage in the minutia of everyday life. Relatively mundane tasks such as buying our groceries or pumping our gas are now often dependent on technology. Sleek, hip, and oh-so-convenient, our mobile phones bring a world of computing to our hip pockets.

Our youth have adapted to this change in ways that leave many of us in awe. Young people, even very young people, now have the capacity to dazzle and amaze us with their technical prowess. They reverse the teacher-student roles quietly, as they help us untangle our email or bring our PowerPoints to life with video and audio effects that flip and whiz. Professors cannot teach without being aware that any student can take a picture of the professor's every gesture, facial expression or body stance at any time, to post YouTube with a particularly humorous or scathing comment. For those in the behavioral health field, it is apparent that technology increasingly offers new opportunities for delivering professional services. However, these opportunities, no matter how promising, remain elusive to many. This is uncharted territory, and how and where to begin or where to go can be a daunting experience.

Welcome to the future. This book on technology in behavioral health aims to provide real insights into how one can envision a career that is fully integrated with the technological environment. It is intended to inspire both graduate students and experienced behavioral and mental health professionals by offering perspectives on emerging, nontraditional career paths that derive from the current technology revolution. Based on personal histories, it illustrates how some professionals have successfully embraced technology to the benefit of their careers and their clients' health. It is readily apparent that, for many of our chapter authors, inspiration and the excitement of exploration have led to new ways of contributing to our respective fields. Themes of rigorous discipline, adversity, ingenuity, wisdom, and plain good luck are evident through various age groups, disciplines, employment settings, and continents represented by our authors. From young and old; from hospital administrators, physicians, lawyers, and psychiatrists to social workers, psychologists, nurses, counselors, and in between; from hospitals to universities; from private and group practices to corporate settings; and from various countries, our authors were all eager to share their stories of carving a personal career path by embracing new technology.

They are a new breed of behavioral and mental health professionals who can serve as models who point the way for others to follow. While fascinating and often engrossing, the specifics of the stories you will read in this book are *not the way*. Rather, the editors of this text encourage you to look beyond the individual stories of the chapter authors whose stories are offered. You are encouraged to consider the experiences described herein to help you to plot your own path toward your technology-related career and professional goals. Although it can be challenging to adapt to the emerging 21st Century landscape, behavioral health professionals are optimally equipped for engaging in change rather than just theorizing, lecturing, researching or guiding others to weather such difficult processes. Luckily for you, the many different authors of this book's chapters have made unprecedented leaps of faith to get to where they are now. As a reader then, you are in the fortunate position to benefit from an inside glimpse of their successes, failures and words of wisdom regarding how to get from a bahavioal health degree to a satisfying career in a technology-related field.

Five introductory chapters were invited to provide a real-world, practical context for the individual stories of the pioneering adventurers whose experiences are depicted in the main body of this book. The five chapters defining the perimeter of the area include general advances in the age of health care reform; technology-related healthcare law; behavioral technology professional education and training; integrated healthcare; and technology overuse and gaming disorders.

The subsequent chapter authors then offer their personal accounts of how they are using different technologies in their work, taking sometimes unique and often serendipitous routes to reach their sometimes undefined goals. They include thoughtful evaluations of their decisions related to immersing themselves in technology in lieu of "settling" for traditional behavioral health care careers. Readers will note that the authors' training and experiences vary considerably, as do their choices related to which technology to adopt, or develop, or research.

At indentifiable points, their divergence from traditional formal training backgrounds becomes palpable. The reader will sense the grit, the resolve and the occasional tears of many authors as they re-count episodes of self-questionning about their futures. The reader will also recoil upon reading of the frequent discouragement and occasionally, mistreatment by traditional colleagues to tried to dissuade the authors from making their "risky" career choices. Yet, these brave explorers persisted courageouly, steadfastly, and as if driven to tolerate the disapproval until they met with the success that they knew awaited. Clearly their stories demonstrate that there are many creative and exciting routes to developing personally satisfying and financially successful careers in behavioral health and technology, but that such an explorer must be willing to weather the inevitable storms that are part of the voyage. Hopefully, this anthology of pioneering spirits will excite the reader into plotting his or her own course into this exciting new world.

This book then, is a testimony to professionals in the behavioral fields as they adapt to worldwide economic forces that are creating new challenges and new opportunities. A willingness to take risks, seek or develop the needed training, try and fail only to try again, and to create their own community are common characteristics of this assembly of creative and persistent explorers. Perseverance is illustrated in repeated creative manifestations of a "can do" and "will do" attitude that will not (and possibly cannot) tolerate attempts at suppression.

Each chapter begins with an inspirational quote that the authors felt relevant to their work. Such quotes are followed by a vignette depicting a "moment in time" during their tech-related day, or an example of someone using their technology. Authors next describe their formal training and work experiences as a backdrop to illustrate from whence they came. So as to more clearly describe how they managed to traverse the chasm between their traditional and nontraditional worlds. Next, they outline some of the perceived pros and cons relevant to their chosen behavioral technology-related work. Lastly, the authors provide references to clearly demonstrate that their work has an evidence base, and is thus replicable. Each chapter is freestanding and can be independently read.

The editors wish to acknowledge and express gratitude to the eminent psychologists, Drs. Luciano L'Abate and Philip Zimbardo, who graciously agreed wrote the book forewords. Both of these mentors have taken the time to express perspectives that are pivotal for the future of behavioral telepractice. Dr. L'Abate's emphasis on developing and using empirical methods with the use of technology is crucial for establishing a strong evidence base for telepractice. The late Dr. L'Abate has not only been an advocate for the use of technologies for more than two decades, but he has been steadfast in his focused assertion that professionals have a responsibility to develop and follow specific, effective and replicable routes to creating change. The foreword provided by Dr. Zimbardo points to the need to remain humble and open to new ways of delivering the services that many professionals have spent decades perfecting. As he humorously described, much can be learn from the younger generations. Beyond doubt, technological innovation is needed to help the many people who are still unserved or underserved by the professional behavioral health community.

The editors appreciate the time and effort that the chapter authors took in writing about their experiences with technology in a personal rather than academic style. The editors also also thank their families, the Coalition for Technology in Behavioral Science (www.CTiBS.org), and Sharon Panulla at Springer Science for their steadfast support and encouragement. Lastly, they thank the many professionals who could not write a chapter for the current book, but who wholeheartedly supported their efforts to offer this compendium of insights to share with the interprofessional community at large.

San Diego, CA, USA   Marlene M. Maheu, PhD
Dayton, OH, USA   Kenneth P. Drude, PhD
Chanute, KS, USA   Shawna D. Wright, PhD

Contents

About the Editors

Marlene Maheu, Ph.D. Consultant, trainer, author, and researcher, Marlene M. Maheu, Ph.D., is the Executive Director of the *TeleMental Health Institute, Inc.*, where she has overseen the development and delivery of professional training in telemental health via an eLearning platform that serves thousands of clinicians seeking professional training and consultation from more than 39 countries worldwide.

For more than 20 years, Dr. Maheu's focus has been on the legal and ethical risk management issues related to the use of technologies to better serve behavioral health clients and patients. She has served on a dozen professional association committees and task forces related to establishing standards and guidelines for telehealth. She has written dozens of peer-reviewed articles and is lead author of multiple telehealth textbooks.

Dr. Maheu is a technology developer and lectures internationally on the subject of best practices in the use of various technologies. She is a staunch advocate for technological change to reach more people, reduce healthcare costs, and improve the quality of care via self-help, wireless technologies, and telepractice.

Kenneth P. Drude, Ph.D. has a doctorate in counseling psychology from the University of Illinois. His telemental health interests include the ethics, standards, guidelines, policy and regulation of telemental health practice, and interprofessional relations. He chaired an Ohio Psychological Association committee that developed the first psychological association telepsychology guidelines in the United States in 2008. Dr. Drude served on the Ohio Psychological Association governing board for 28 years in various capacities and as editor of *The Ohio Psychologist*. He currently is the president of the Ohio Board of Psychology. He was a member of the Association for State and Provincial Psychology Board's Telepsychology Task Force that developed an interstate psychology compact. He currently provides outpatient psychological services in a general private practice in Dayton, Ohio.

Shawna Wright, Ph.D. is a licensed psychologist in Kansas and Nebraska who works in private practice as a telepsychologist. She obtained her graduate training in clinical psychology from Texas Tech University specializing in child and family treatment. She has worked for over a decade in community mental health in southeastern Kansas as outpatient therapist. In 2011, she completed a comprehensive telemental health certificate training program through the TeleMental Health Institute and initiated a private practice providing telepsychology services to residents of rural nursing facilities. Dr. Wright has a keen interest in working to develop standards, training, and resources to assist psychologists who are interested in telepsychology careers. She is the membership chair for the Coalition for Technology in Behavioral Sciences (CTiBS) and maintains aspirations of sharing her professional experience to help advance professional resources for telepsychology through educational endeavors and consultation.

About the Authors

Stephen Agboola, MD, MPH is a Research Scientist at the Center for Connected Health, Partners Healthcare, and Harvard Medical School. His research is focused on finding innovative strategies to support healthcare delivery by creatively engaging patients, caregivers, and care providers using technology for objective data collection and personalized feedback. He seeks to employ technology to improve access to quality care as well as promote wellness, prevent disease, and limit the complications due to chronic diseases. At the Center for Connected Health, he leads efforts in designing and implementing rigorous research methodologies to evaluate new mobile health interventions in clinical trials.

Sara Smucker Barnwell, Ph.D. is a licensed clinical psychologist whose research and clinical interests center on the development and dissemination of empirically based treatments in telehealth. She provides workshops and trainings on a diversity of technology-related topics, including telehealth, ethics in technology use, and others. Dr. Smucker Barnwell also delivers telehealth consultation to large-scale providers (e.g., hospital systems, corporations) as well as individual practitioners. Dr. Smucker Barnwell is a Clinical Professor in the Department of Psychiatry and Behavioral Sciences at the University of Washington and the former Director of Telehealth Training and Education for VA Puget Sound Health Care System. She is the former Chair of the Washington State Psychological Foundation. Dr. Smucker Barnwell served on the Joint APA/ASPPB/APAIT Telepsychology Taskforce. She delivers evidence-based outpatient telehealth and in-person care through independent practice in Seattle, WA.

Olivia C. Boyce is a telebehavioral health advocate, a communications professional, and the editor-in-chief of the *InSight Bulletin*, a behavioral health wellness blog.

Steven Bucky, Ph.D. is a Founder, Distinguished Professor, and Director of Professional Training at the California School of Professional Psychology at Alliant International University-San Diego. He is also the Chair of the Ethics Committee, has served as Chair of the AIU Faculty Senate, Executive Director of the Addictions Institute, and the Interim Systemwide Dean as well.

Dr. Bucky was on California Psychological Association's ("CPA") Board of Directors from 1996 to 2000, on CPA's Ethics Committee from 1990 to 1997 and 2012 to Present, and President of CPA in 1997. Dr. Bucky has published more than 60 papers, presented at major conventions, and has edited three books. He is a Fellow of the American Psychological Association, the California Psychological Association, and the San Diego Psychological Association.

Dr. Bucky also maintains a private practice that focuses on children, adolescents, families, substance abuse, forensics, and the assessment and treatment of professional and college athletes.

Joanne E. Callan, Ph.D., A.B.P.P. who earlier was Dean and then Provost at the California School of Professional Psychology-San Diego, is a Distinguished Professor in both the Clinical Ph.D. and Clinical Psy.D. Programs at CSPP-SD of Alliant International University. She holds a Clinical Associate Professor appointment (Voluntary) in the University of California—San Diego's Department of Psychiatry and is also a Training and Supervising Analyst at the San Diego Psychoanalytic Center. A Diplomate in Clinical Psychology (American Board of Professional Psychology), she was the first Executive Director of the American Psychological Association's Education Directorate. Her presentations and publications focus on professional ethics, professional education and training of psychologists, women's professional issues, and applications of attachment and object relations theories in professional development and practice.

Norah Chapman, Ph.D. is an assistant professor at Spalding University in Louisville, Kentucky. Her primary research interests are in evaluating components of psychotherapy process and outcome, both in person and via telepsychology, to develop evidence-based practices that increase the access to and quality of mental healthcare amongst underserved populations.

Robert N. Cuyler, Ph.D. is president of Clinical Psychology Consultants Ltd., LLP. His consulting practice focuses on planning, developing, and refining behavioral health telemedicine services. His extensive telemedicine activities have included clinical, public policy, project planning, and business development. Dr. Cuyler previously served as interim chief executive officer of JSA Health, a Houston-based emergency telepsychiatry company. He was senior vice president of Diamond Healthcare and cofounded Heritage Health Services, a behavioral health management company, where he served as COO and clinical director until Heritage was acquired by Diamond. He is author (with Dutch Holland, Ph.D.) of the book *Implementing Telemedicine: Completing Projects on Target on Time on Budget.*

Andrew P. Doan, M.D., Ph.D. Andrew P. Doan, Kathryn Yung, Paulette Cazares, and Warren P. Klam work in the US Navy in the Department of Mental Health at the Naval Medical Center in San Diego. They have an interest in how technology, the Internet, and video games affect the mind and behavior in children and adults. Their research is focused on the benefits of these technologies in medicine and behavioral health, as well as why these technologies are objects of abusive behavior in some individuals. Dr. Klam is the director of the Department of Mental Health. Dr. Cazares is the department head at the Substance Abuse Rehabilitation Program at the Naval Medical Center in San Diego. Dr. Doan is the coauthor of *Hooked on Games: The Lure and Cost of Video Game and Internet Addiction.*

Matt J. Gray, Ph.D. is a professor of psychology at the University of Wyoming. He is the developer and founder of the Wyoming Telehealth Trauma Treatment Clinic. He trained at the National Crime Victims Research and Treatment Center and the National Center for PTSD. His primary research interests include intimate partner violence and sexual violence treatment and prevention.

Donald M. Hilty, M.D. is a scholar in psychiatry, education, faculty development, and telemedicine to rural primary care. He is vice-chair of education, director of Medical Student Education, and a clinical scholar at the USC Keck School of Medicine. His research involves public health, consultation-liaison models, mood disorders, and genomics in underserved medical populations. He is co-investigator of an Agency for Healthcare Quality and Research (AHRQ) randomized controlled trial that compares synchronous and asynchronous telepsychiatry. He is also the former director and developer of the 5-year MD/MPH UC Davis Rural Program in Medical Education. Dr. Hilty's specific educational interests include pedagogy, evaluation, and distance education. Dr. Hilty has authored over 170 articles, chapters, book reviews, and/or books. He has participated in over 100 peer-reviewed presentations as a member of the Association for Academic Psychiatry (AAP), the Academy for Psychosomatic Medicine, the American Telemedicine Association, and the American Psychiatric Association (APA). He chaired or vice-chaired the annual meetings of the APA, AAP, and AAMC scientific program committees. He recently joined the American College of Psychiatry, and he is currently a member of a treatment guideline writing group in a project of the American Psychiatric Association and Institute of Medicine.

Eva Hudlicka, Ph.D., M.S.W., L.I.C.S.W. has a dual career in affective computing (Ph.D., Computer Science/Artificial Intelligence; University of Massachusetts-Amherst) and psychotherapy (M.S.W.; Simmons College School of Social Work). She is currently a psychotherapist in private practice in Western Massachusetts and a Principal Scientist and President of Psychometrix Associates in Amherst, MA. She is also a Visiting Lecturer at the School of Computer and Information Sciences at the University of Massachusetts-Amherst, where she teaches courses in Affective Computing and Human-Computer Interaction. Prior to founding Psychometrix Associates in 1995, she was a Senior Scientist at Bolt Beranek & Newman in

Cambridge, MA. Her interests in telemental health focus on the use of advanced technologies to improve client engagement and outcomes. She has authored over 50 journal and conference papers and numerous book chapters.

Kamal Jethwani, M.D., M.P.H. leads the research and program evaluation initiatives at the Center for Connected Health. His research is focused on technology-based models of health delivery and the use of behavior change as a tool for preventive and supportive care in a tertiary healthcare setting. His work at the Center for Connected Health has spanned from designing and implementing clinical trials to leading efforts in predictive modeling using behavioral parameters.

Dr. Jethwani is also responsible for shaping the research roadmap for the Center, leads the evaluation of all on-going programs, and contributes to efforts at program development and scaling. His research has evolved over time to include exploration of newer health delivery models, like employer-based health programs and electronic social network-based programs. Dr. Jethwani is also exploring newer tools to deliver feedback to patients, like simple text message-based platforms, applications for smart phones, etc.

Dr. Jethwani is currently an Assistant in Dermatology at Massachusetts General Hospital and Instructor at Harvard Medical School.

Deborah Jones, Ph.D. earned her doctorate in clinical psychology from the University of Georgia, completed her clinical internship at the Brown University Clinical Psychology Training Consortium, and did a postdoctoral fellowship at the University of Pittsburgh. She is currently a Professor in the child and family track of the clinical psychology training program in the Department of Psychology and Neuroscience at the University of North Carolina at Chapel Hill. Dr. Jones' basic and applied research have long focused on understanding variability in risk and resilience in underserved families. This work really sparked Dr. Jones' interest in the capacity for increasingly available innovations in technology to bridge the research-to-practice gap, particularly for families who may need, yet be least likely to have access to and/or benefit from, evidence-based mental healthcare. Dr. Jones' research in this area has been consistently funded by the National Institute of Mental Health and also allows her the added benefit of actively participating in clinical supervision and training, which she enjoys greatly.

Thomas J. Kim, M.D., M.P.H. has worked as a telehealth practitioner, developer, educator, investigator, strategist, and advocate. His efforts have focused on collaborative care models, vulnerable populations, disaster preparedness, public policy, and service sustainability and scalability. From academia and government to private industry and nonprofits, Dr. Kim has engaged a wide variety of organizations toward understanding how best to apply technology to healthcare.

Dr. Kim received his BA in philosophy from Georgetown and MD/MPH from Tulane University. Dr. Kim continued at Tulane to complete a combined residency in internal medicine and psychiatry and general medicine fellowship in health services research.

Keely Kolmes, Psy.D. is a licensed private practice psychologist in San Francisco. Dr. Kolmes is serving her second term on the Ethics Committee of the California Psychological Association. She is Founder and President of Bay Area Open Minds, a group of over 170 mental health professionals who work with sexual and gender diversity. Dr. Kolmes is coauthor of the fifth revision of Ed Zuckerman's The Paper Office for the Digital Age. She is a pioneer in the development of digital ethics for clinicians on social media. Her Social Media Policy has been internationally taught and adapted across health disciplines. She writes, does research, and provides consultation and training on clinical and ethical issues related to social networking and technology. She has published a *New York Times* Op-Ed on the challenge of consumer reviews of mental health services and developed Getting Better, a product to help clinicians track treatment outcomes and address client satisfaction on the Internet. Dr. Kolmes has been quoted in the Washington Post, BBC News, HuffPost Live, Forbes, and Fox News. Website: www.drkkolmes.com Twitter: @drkkolmes.

Geoff Lee, Ph.D. has a doctorate in counseling psychology from the University of Florida. He is a clinical assistant professor and serves in the role of digital services coordinator at the University of Florida Counseling and Wellness Center. His work focuses on using technology to make mental health resources more accessible for college students. He served as the clinical development lead and clinical coordinator for the Therapist Assisted Online (TAO) treatment developed at the University of Florida. He currently serves as a consultant on the Higher Education Mental Health Alliance (HEMHA) Distance Counseling Guide for colleges and universities.

Susan C. Litton, Ph.D. holds degrees in both the mental health and IT fields and is actively engaged with careers in both. In mental health, she's a clinical psychologist in private practice. As an IT professional, she's the creator and driving force behind PSYBooks (www.psybooks.com), an online practice management system (EHR) and telemental health portal for mental health professionals.

Steven Locke, M.D. is a thought leader in the field of behavioral informatics and primary care. Dr. Locke is a founder and Chief Medical Officer of iHope Network, a Boston-based behavioral telehealth company that uses clinician-delivered and technology-guided Cognitive Behavioral Therapy (CBT) via smartphone and secure video therapy to integrate behavioral health into primary care. Dr. Locke also is a primary care psychiatrist both in private practice and at the Beth Israel Deaconess Medical Center where he is a member of the primary care telepsychiatry consulting team. He is Associate Clinical Professor of Psychiatry at Harvard Medical School, a Distinguished Life Fellow of the American Psychiatric Association, a Life Fellow of the Society of Behavioral Medicine, and a Past-President of the American Psychosomatic Society. Dr. Locke serves on the editorial boards of *Cyberpsychology, Behavior, and Social Networking*, the *American Journal of Health Promotion*, and *Population Health Management*.

Joseph P. ("Joe") McMenamin, M.D., J.D. is a physician-attorney in Richmond, Virginia. Both his law practice and his consultancy concentrate on and benefit from his 20 years' experience in telemedicine. Joe advises institutional and individual telehealth service providers, remote monitoring services, trade associations, telehealth platform companies, private equity firms, and telecoms on a broad array of medico-legal questions arising from distance care. He also publishes extensively and lectures widely on these and related matters.

Before being admitted to the Bar in 1985, Joe had been a university-trained internist and a practicing emergency physician. For many years he represented an array of healthcare clients at a large international law firm before striking out on his own in 2013 to found MDJD, PLC, and McMenamin Law Offices, PLLC.

Joe presently serves as general counsel to the Virginia Telemedicine Network. He is an associate professor of Legal Medicine at Virginia Commonwealth University, and a member of the Board of Advisors of the Medical Information Technology Law Report and of the Legal Resource Team of CTeL, the Center for Telemedicine and eHealth Law. He is board certified in Legal Medicine and a Fellow of the American College of Legal Medicine.

Mark R. McMinn, Ph.D. is professor of clinical psychology at George Fox University. He is a licensed psychologist in Oregon; a fellow and former president of APA's Division 36, Society for the Psychology of Religion and Spirituality; and board certified in clinical psychology through the American Board of Professional Psychology. His research interests include the integration of psychology and Christianity, positive psychology, clergy-psychology collaboration, and technology in psychological practice.

Mindy Mueller, Psy.D. received her Psy.D. in Clinical Psychology from Antioch New England Graduate School, her Master's in Counseling Psychology at Boston College, and her Master's in Child and Family Development at Syracuse University. She is a licensed psychologist in California and has been working for the past 8 years on Catalina Island as a Program Manager, Clinical Supervisor, and therapist for The Guidance Center, a multidisciplinary community mental health center. Dr. Mueller has an extensive background in providing mental health services to children, adolescents, and adults within a variety of settings. She also has a background in evaluation and research focusing on the provision of mental health in rural communities and the development of community coalitions. Since 2009, Dr. Mueller has devoted her energy and expertise to developing sustainable telemental health programs in rural areas with her business partner, Dawn Sampson, of TeleConnect Therapies.

Max M. North, Ph.D. is a tenured professor of management information systems in the Business Administration Department. He has been teaching, conducting research, and providing community service for Computer Science and Information Systems Departments at higher education institutions for more than 20 years. He holds a master's degree in computer science with a concentration in management information systems and a Ph.D. in counseling psychology/psychological services with concentration in cognitive and behavior sciences. Dr. Max North has been successfully involved in the research of human-computer interaction/interface, information security and ethics awareness, and virtual reality technology. Dr. Max North is the director of the Visualization and Simulation Research Center. Additionally, Dr. Max North has several published books, book chapters, and a number of technical referred scholarly articles. He has served as principal/co-principal investigator on a number of research grants sponsored by the Boeing Company, the US Army Research Laboratory, the National Science Foundation, and the National Security Agency. Dr. Max North's major contribution to the scientific community is his discovery and continuous research activities in the innovative area of virtual reality technology, which have received international attention and coverage in the scientific community and popular media.

Sarah M. North, Ph.D. is a faculty member of the Computer Science Department at Kennesaw State University. Dr. Sarah North has been teaching, conducting research, and providing community service in computing for over 20 years at higher education institutions. Dr. Sarah North's graduate work is on computer science with a concentration in programming languages, while her doctoral work is on educational technology and leadership and administration with a concentration in information cyber technology. Dr. Sarah North has been successfully involved in the research in the areas of information security education, human-computer interaction, cognitive science, and virtual reality therapy/technology. Additionally, Dr. Sarah North has several book chapters and a number of technical referred scholarly articles nationally and internationally. She also served as principal/co-principal investigator on a number of research grants sponsored by the Boeing Company, National Science Foundation, and National Security Agency.

Gerald R. Quimby, Psy.D., M.A., M.S. holds a bachelor's degree in computer science, master's degrees in counseling and in psychopharmacology, and a doctorate in clinical psychology. He completed a 2-year health psychology fellowship at Tripler Army Medical Center and is currently a behavioral health consultant in the family practice clinic at the Naval Health Clinic at Pearl Harbor. Dr. Quimby is also on the faculty of the American School of Professional Psychology. He has been active in telemental health issues since 1996. Recently, he was recognized by the Navy Bureau of Medicine and Surgery for his database which identifies diagnostic trends and program needs used throughout the Navy healthcare clinics.

Robert J. Reese, Ph.D. completed his doctoral degree in counseling psychology at Texas A&M University. He is a professor and chair in the Department of Educational, School, and Counseling psychology at the University of Kentucky. Dr. Reese's research interests are psychotherapy process/outcome, psychotherapy supervision and training, and telehealth. His current research is focused on investigating the process of client feedback and the use of technology to provide psychological services to underserved populations. He is a licensed psychologist in Kentucky.

Wayne Roffer, Psy.D. is a licensed psychologist in Pennsylvania, working at the Lebanon VA Medical Center, Lebanon, PA. Dr. Roffer specializes in the treatment of comorbid post-traumatic stress disorder (PTSD) and substance use disorders (SUDs). Dr. Roffer has completed Department of Veterans Affairs' trainings in cognitive processing therapy (CPT) and prolonged exposure therapy (PE) for PTSD, as well as clinical video telehealth (CVT). Dr. Roffer is proficient in the delivery of CVT and provides education and consultation to other behavioral health professionals in the areas of telemental health clinical practice, HIPAA, and telepsychology legal/ethical issues. In his spare time, he enjoys outdoor activities such as camping, hiking, and biking.

After graduation from Middlebury College in 1982, Susan Landgren's first professional activities were as a science educator. In 2000, following a year as a technician in a molecular genetics laboratory, Susan entered the master of science program in genetic counseling at Brandeis University. Since obtaining her M.S. degree in 2002, Susan has provided genetic counseling services from Billings, Montana. She was certified by the American Board of Genetic Counselors in 2005. Many of her patients live in Wyoming and North and South Dakota. In 2009, Susan initiated a program providing genetic counseling services to patients over the Eastern Montana Telemedicine Network, which coordinates its services with neighboring systems. That effort was supported by a generous grant from the Mountain States Genetics Regional Collaborative.

Dawn Sampson, M.S.W., L.C.S.W. received her Master of Social Work degree from the University of Southern California and is licensed as a Clinical Social Worker in California. Dawn was the Director of Social Services for the Catalina Island Medical Center, a rural Critical Access Hospital, for 26 years. During this time she obtained grants and developed programs to serve the community, including a successful telehealth program. In 2009 Dawn and Dr. Mindy Mueller started a partnership, TeleConnect Therapies, which provides telemental health services to clinics in rural areas throughout California. They have presented on telehealth and telemental health topics for the American Psychological Association, the California Association of Rural Health Clinics, the California State Rural Health Association, the California Telehealth Network, and the TeleMental Health Institute. Over the course of her career, Dawn has provided clinical therapy services to individuals, groups, and families, in areas both urban and rural, and has been providing clinical telemental health services to patients in rural clinics for the past 7 years.

Marcia Scherer, Ph.D., M.P.H., F.A.C.R.M. is a rehabilitation psychologist and founding president of the Institute for Matching Person & Technology. She is also a professor of physical medicine and rehabilitation at the University of Rochester Medical Center and project director at Burton Blatt Institute in Syracuse University. She is a past member of the National Advisory Board on Medical Rehabilitation Research of the National Institutes of Health and is editor of the journal *Disability and Rehabilitation: Assistive Technology*. She has authored, edited, or coedited ten books. She has published over 60 articles on disability and rehabilitation in peer-reviewed scientific journals and over 25 book chapters; she has been cited over 2500 times by others.

Laura Schopp, Ph.D., A.B.P.P. is a board-certified clinical neuropsychologist and Professor in the Department of Health Psychology at the University of Missouri. She has directed over $5 M in federal grants as Principal or Co-Principal Investigator, largely in health services delivery for primary, secondary, and tertiary prevention using a variety of telehealth strategies. She served on and chaired the American Psychological Association (APA) Committee on Rural Health, as APA's representative to the Health Resources and Services Administration's federal rural mental health shortage area designation committee, as Co-Chair of APA's Early Career Presidential Task Force, as a member of the APA Telehealth Implementation Work Group, and chaired the Scientific Affairs Committee of the Missouri Psychological Association. She has provided expert testimony to the Missouri legislature on the use of telehealth strategies to meet the needs of rural patients with neurologic disorders.

Brian M. Shaw, Ph.D. is a clinical assistant professor in the Counseling and Wellness Center at the University of Florida. He holds a doctorate in Counselor Education from Old Dominion University. He is a Licensed Professional Counselor in the state of Georgia and a Licensed Mental Health Counselor in the state of Florida. In his current position, Dr. Shaw provides counseling services for college students and supervision to counselors in training. Drawing on his prior training and experience as a software engineer, Dr. Shaw enjoys exploring applications for the use of technology to enhance the quality and delivery of counseling services. He was involved in the development of the first therapist-assisted online counseling intervention for college students.

Jay Shore, M.D., M.P.H. is the Native Domain Lead for the VA Office of Rural Health's Veterans Rural Health Resource Center, Salt Lake City. He is an Associate Professor of Psychiatry at the University of Colorado, Anschutz Medical Campus, Department of Psychiatry and Centers for American Indian and Alaska Native Health. He also serves as Director of Telemedicine at the University's Helen and Arthur E Johnson Depression Center. Dr. Shore's career has focused on telepsychiatry creating, implementing, and administering services and conducting evaluation and research with federal, state, university, and tribal organizations. His worked has centered around increasing access and quality of care for native, military, and rural populations. He has served in leadership positions for telepsychiatry in the American Psychiatric Association and American Telemedicine Association.

Sarah Steinmetz, M.S. is a doctoral student in clinical psychology at the University of Wyoming. Her research interests include sexual violence prevention and treatment, intimate partner violence, and post-traumatic stress and adjustment. She is presently the lead therapist for the Wyoming Telehealth Trauma Treatment Clinic which is funded with generous support from the Verizon Foundation.

Joseph Ternullo, J.D., M.P.H. is chief operating officer of Pulse Infoframe, a global healthcare data analytics company, and president-elect of the Society for Participatory Medicine. Mr. Ternullo is also a senior advisor to the Consulate of Canada—Boston. Previously, Mr. Ternullo served as associate director of Partners HealthCare's Center for Connected Health. He founded the Connected Health Symposium, a prominent two-day international annual event, and co-founded Continua Health Alliance, a standards and interoperability organization now associated with HIMSS. Mr. Ternullo has sat on several boards and on HHS's American Health Information Community Chronic Care Workgroup and a US Commerce Department International Trade Advisory Committee. An attorney and certified public accountant, Mr. Ternullo holds degrees from Boston College, Bentley University, Boston University School of Law, and Harvard T.H. Chan School of Public Health.

Carolyn Turvey, Ph.D. received her Ph.D. in Clinical Psychology from Yale University in 1994 and her M.S. in Epidemiology from the Harvard School of Public Health in 1996. She is a Research Health Scientist at the Iowa City VA Health Care System and a Professor in the Department of Psychiatry at the University of Iowa. Since 2000, Dr. Turvey has conducted clinical trials, validity studies, and usability studies of psychological interventions delivered through technology ranging from telephone-based psychotherapies to the use of interactive voice response to screen for depression in Medicaid populations. Since 2008, Dr. Turvey has been interested in personal health records and their effectiveness in promoting health while reducing cost. She is currently conducting a nationwide, multi-site study that trains veterans to use the Blue Button feature of My HealtheVet to share health information with their non-VA providers.

James R. Varrell, M.D. is the founder and medical director of the CFG Health Network and InSight Telepsychiatry. Dr. Varrell is American Board certified in psychiatry and neurology and certified by the American Academy of Child and Adolescent Psychiatry with a specialty in autism. Fifteen years ago, Dr. Varrell provided the nation's first commitment via telepsychiatry. He has since been one of the nation's top advocates for the appropriate use of telepsychiatry. Dr. Varrell regularly educates policy makers and the medical community on telepsychiatry best practices. Today, Dr. Varrell still serves consumers via telepsychiatry and oversees 200+ prescribers who treat consumers in 19 states.

Kristofer Vernmark is a clinical psychologist and a Ph.D. student. He has been specializing in Internet-based treatment since 2004 doing research, educating and supervising Internet therapists, creating CBT/ACT treatment programs for online use, and helping the healthcare sector implement those programs into primary care settings.

Mr. Vernmark is the author of the first book in Swedish on Internet therapy (*Internetbehandling med KBT—en praktisk handbok*). He is also the published author of the first randomized controlled study on CBT-based email therapy.

Mr. Vernmark is conducting his research at Linköping University where he investigates the effectiveness of different treatment modalities, and the role of alliance, when delivering online treatment for depression. He is the business area manager of digital psychology in the private company Psykologpartners that delivers several services in the psychology market. At Psykologpartners he is involved in large-scale implementation projects, assisting Swedish county councils in the process of making Internet-based CBT/ACT an integrated part of their regular care.

Karen Wall, Ed.D., R.N.-B.C. has a doctorate in counseling psychology from Argosy University and a bachelors in nursing from York College of Pennsylvania. She is a psychiatric-mental health nurse with the VA, in the role of Dementia Care Coordinator. Her telemental health interests include competencies, app review, interdisciplinary standards development, application of technology, and mobile apps in the VA and with the elderly. She served on the steering committee, app review team, and competency task force for the Telemental Health Technology and the Coalition for Technology in Behavioral Science. Dr. Wall serves as the co-chair of the VA Palo Alto Dementia Committee and on the VA Office of Nursing Service Geriatric Field Advisory Committee. She has a private practice under supervision as a Marriage and Family Therapy Registered Intern in San Leandro, CA. She has used mobile apps extensively in the acute inpatient psychiatric setting with veterans experiencing various psychiatric illness, including PTSD, depression, anxiety, and cognitive and memory care.

Part I
Introduction

Chapter 1
Tackling Changes in Mental Health Practice: The Impact of Information-Age Healthcare

Joseph L. Ternullo and Steven E. Locke

"I slept and dreamt that life was joy. I awoke and saw that life was service. I acted and behold, service was joy."

—*Rabindranath Tagore, the first Asian to receive the Nobel Prize in Literature (1913).*

Wherever you are in your journey, a career focused on mental health draws upon the noblest of human instincts—serving others, relieving suffering, rendering compassionate care, and pursuing knowledge. The field is dynamic and, especially now, for reasons summarized in this chapter, change is occurring rapidly. Employment opportunities are expanding and projected to outpace those of other fields. With the advent of a plethora of affordable and reliable enabling technologies coupled with a rapidly evolving regulatory landscape, traditional boundaries to practice are falling and brand-new electronic avenues of care are opening. For those seeking enriching and high-impact careers, there is no better time to pursue a career in the mental health professions. Cutting across all aspects of humanity, the profession draws upon the tension and complexities of our contemporary world and increasingly incorporates elements of technical savvy, team collaboration, and continuous learning.

This chapter summarizes the mental health marketplace dimensions and regulatory landscape, explores the evolution of enabling technologies and the changing nature of care, and identifies barriers to telemental health and career trends and

J.L. Ternullo, J.D., M.P.H. (✉)
Chief Operating Officer of Pulse Infoframe, 1377 Main St., Lynnfield, MA 1940, USA
e-mail: jternullo@post.harvard.edu

S.E. Locke, M.D.
iHope Network, Inc., Wenham, MA, USA

Primary Care Telepsychiatry Service, Beth Isreal Deaconess Health Care, Boston, MA, USA

Harvard Medical School, Boston, MA, USA
e-mail: slockemd@verizon.net

© Springer International Publishing Switzerland 2017
M.M. Maheu et al. (eds.), *Career Paths in Telemental Health*,
DOI 10.1007/978-3-319-23736-7_1

pathways. Later in this book, you will find a brief compendium of representative governmental, professional society and trade association resources consistent with the themes of this chapter.

Market Landscape

Mental health, as defined by the World Health Organization, is "a state of well-being in which every individual realizes his or her own potential, can cope with the normal stresses of life, can work productively and fruitfully, and is able to make a contribution to her or his community." (WHO, 2014) The term "behavioral health," which appears often in published literature, increasingly is used in the profession as a modern incarnation of the term "mental health" and carries the same meaning.

According to the National Alliance on Mental Illness, one in four adults in the USA experiences a mental health disorder annually, and one in ten children in the USA has a serious mental or emotional disorder. While US annual expenditures on mental health services exceed $110 billion, published data indicate that most people suffering from a mental health disorder do not receive care.

The cadre of professionals delivering or contributing to the delivery of mental health services includes psychiatrists, psychologists, psychiatric/mental health nurse practitioners, psychiatric/mental health nurses, social workers, licensed professional counselors, and peer specialists. Each profession has its own education and training requirements and focal areas of expertise. The US Department of Labor's Bureau of Labor Statistics reports that there are over 552,000 mental health professionals practicing in the USA today whose main focus is the treatment and/or diagnosis of mental health or substance abuse concerns (Grohol, 2011). Social workers, who often work with patients and families around mental health issues, account for another 642,000 jobs in the USA (Grohol, 2011).

It is intuitive that well-being and mental health are inextricably linked, and it is almost certainly the case that well-being is more about mental health than physical health. The combination of (a) a growing and aging population, (b) a world of ever-increasing complexities and stressors, and (c) a substantial underserved population suggests that for the foreseeable future, the field will remain a much needed and stable area of employment.

Those drawn to the field out of abiding feelings to serve others and motivated to render compassionate care and relieve suffering will find substantial unmet need, a welcoming community of professionals and peers, and an inner need and professional obligation to keep current and pursue a commitment to lifelong learning. All of that is what this book is about.

Regulatory Landscape

In the USA, healthcare is subject to growing federal and state government regulation and cost-containment programs. Increasing per capita healthcare consumption has accelerated healthcare reform with an aim to reduce overall healthcare spending and improve the quality of care. Today, there is great emphasis on expanding access to primary care accompanied by preventive practices and technologies that improve outcomes. Further, metrics for healthcare success increasingly involve factors such as cost-effectiveness, efficiency, and accountability. The concept of "pay for performance," commonly referred to as P4P, is changing the healthcare landscape. We are entering an era where payment incentives rewarding quality rather than quantity of care are becoming the norm. Healthcare reform has created internal and external market imperatives to shift care closer to home, to less expensive settings, and increase focus on prevention and management of chronic disease. This progress in our evolving healthcare system is creating opportunities for technology innovation that extend into behavioral health and is changing practice.

In chapter "The Law of Telemental Health" in this book, our colleague, attorney Joseph McMenamin, dedicates the entire chapter to legislative and regulatory change. Because of this extensive coverage, we have opted to limit the regulatory remarks contained in this chapter.

In the last several years, we have witnessed the greatest overhaul of US healthcare since the enactment of Medicare and Medicaid in 1965. This has occurred principally through three pieces of legislation and their related regulations: (a) the American Recovery and Reinvestment Act ("ARRA"), (b) the Patient Protection and Affordable Care Act (the "ACA"), and, in the context of a discussion of behavioral health, (c) the Mental Health Parity and Addiction Equity Act.

Signed into law in February 2009 as an economic stimulus package, ARRA provided substantial economic incentives for providers to shift from paper to electronic medical records and economic penalties for non-adoption and nonuse. A major driver for the legislation was a comprehensive 2005 RAND study concluding that the US healthcare system could save more than $80 billion annually and improve the quality if it were to broadly adopt computerized medical records (Hillestad et al., 2005). Beginning in 2015, clinicians who do not adopt and successfully demonstrate "meaningful use" of a certified electronic health record technology will see their Medicare reimbursement for professional services adjusted downward by 1 % each year.

Commonly called "Obamacare," the ACA was signed into law in March 2010. The goal of the law was to increase healthcare quality and affordability and reduce the cost of care for individuals and government. It dramatically increased the number of individuals who are likely to access the healthcare system and expanded required mental health services. In addition, the implementation of the Mental Health Parity Act in 2014 guarantees greater insurance coverage for mental disorders by requiring that benefits be comparable with those provided to patients with medical and surgical conditions. An estimated 32 million, previously uninsured,

Americans will gain access to mental health services as a result of Obamacare. Further, the ACA mandates the integration of mental health services into standard health plans. Among the list of mandated preventive services is depression screening for adults and adolescents, without charging customers a co-payment or coinsurance. As a result of these legislative actions, there is every reason to believe that there will be a significant influx into the system of individuals seeking care for mental disorders. Community health centers and primary care practices will almost certainly be the entry portal for those seeking such care.

Our educational and service delivery programs need to anticipate the impact of the expansion resulting from the aggregate effects of the government effort to move toward electronic records, expand patient access to care, and mandate mental health screening. In the behavioral health field, while welcome from the standpoint of enabling individuals in need of care to receive care, these new requirements also represent challenges to the extent that they exacerbate the underserved population and have the effect of increasing provider shortages. Collectively, these changes highlight the need for innovation in providing multiple avenues for accessing evidence-based mental healthcare.

Evolution of Enabling Technology

Traditional mental health service delivery involves an in-person, real-time, face-to-face encounter between a clinician and a patient, typically in a clinical setting such as the mental health caregiver's office.

Telemental health, a subset of telemedicine, is the use of telecommunication technology to deliver mental health services remotely. "Tele," a Greek prefix meaning "at a distance," implies separateness. In the context of healthcare, the term is intended to convey facilitating access and bringing geographically separated parties together.

Multiple demonstration projects and pilots have proven that enabling technologies can successfully facilitate remote mental health service delivery and create new pathways to accessing care for patients. In the context of this book, it seems intuitive that the combination of new technologies, new pathways to accessing care, and the aforementioned legislative changes portend expanded career opportunities across the profession. We hasten to add that the "tele" phenomenon does not signal the impending obsolescence of traditional mental health service delivery. To the contrary, it represents progress, thrusts the field into the modern world of telecommunications and social media, and opens up new avenues of access to care. Telemental health:

- Enables the provision of care to geographically isolated and/or underserved communities
- Fosters patient choice and enables "convenient care" options
- Facilitates shared decision-making and enriched clinician/patient interactions

- Creates a platform for social support to promote patient engagement and to access and mobilize social networks
- Makes possible the use of lower-cost providers by leveraging clinician-delivered computer-guided care
- Allows clinical caregivers to practice at the top of their license

The American Telemedicine Association (ATA), the leading international resource promoting the use of advanced remote medical technologies, defines telemedicine as the use of medical information exchanged from one site to another via electronic communications to improve a patient's clinical health status and encompassing, among others:

- Patient consultations via video conferencing
- Transmission of still or video images
- e-Health including patient portals (i.e., web pages linking patients with their electronic records and providers and educational or self-assessment resources)
- Remote monitoring of vital signs and other physiological parameters
- Educational resources for professionals, patients, and families
- Consumer-focused wireless applications ("m-health")
- Nursing call centers (ATA, 2014)

Historically, telemedicine and telemental health were grant-funded demonstration and pilot programs. Many were funded through the US Health Resources and Services Administration's Office for the Advancement of Telemedicine or the US Department of Agriculture's Distance Learning and Telemedicine Loan and Grant Program. The primary purpose of these programs was to connect underserved patients living in remote, geographically isolated locations with clinicians. The programs were about proof of concept, technical connectivity, and access. Generally, they were not financially self-sustaining as that was not the objective. When the grant funds dried up, frequently the program did too. Although telemedicine services were developed for at-risk populations for whom access was a barrier, there were few federal programs that provided telemedicine or telemental health services to urban communities, underserved or not. Nonetheless, those federally funded grant programs resulted in valuable experience that is being leveraged to build an improved twenty-first-century US healthcare system.

Innovative applications of affordable, enabling technologies that can facilitate patient-centered care and shared decision-making make it possible to shift the locus of care to the patient. There are a variety of data sources for use in communication between patients and clinicians. Because much of this data involves protected health information, systems designed to facilitate sharing must address the specific requirements outlined in the federal and state laws and regulations that address privacy, confidentiality, and security of personal health information. The following chart illustrates how technology tools can be incorporated into behavioral health interactions:

Data sources	Asynchronous	Synchronous	Clinical applications
Writing	• Secure email • Text messages • Blogs • Bulletin board postings	• Chat room/live chat • Text messaging • Collaborative document sharing	• Patient education • Interactive self-assessment • Social support
Speaking	• Voicemail • Attached voice files • Webcast	• Telephone/speakerphone • Webcast • Web-based audio conference	• Group therapies • Support groups • Telephonic treatment ("CBT-T")
Still images	• Instagram • X-rays, images • jpeg, pdf, gif, etc.		• Assessing emotion
Video	• YouTube • Video attachments to email	• Videoconferencing • Skype, WebEx, FaceTime, etc.	• Group therapies • Support groups • Telephonic treatment ("CBT-T") • Abnormal movements • Affect
Physiological measures	• Scale • Blood pressure • Holter monitor • Motion analytics	• EKG, EEG • Telemetry • Voice analytics • Motion analytics	• Depression detection • PTSD detection • Comorbidity detection • Adverse events/ side effects • Measure progress

The chart above, which does not even address the potential utility of apps on the fields, is illustrative of the dynamic nature of the introduction of technologies to facilitate new methods of clinician/patient interaction. As we have witnessed in the last 20 years, technology comes and goes, with increasing frequency! As new technologies emerge, healthcare innovators will respond to the opportunities that they present. Some innovations will disrupt traditional methods of care and change the care landscape. Successful innovations that improve quality and efficiency will eventually replace older methods.

Each method of interacting has its advantages and disadvantages. For example, patients are more likely to disclose information of a private and sensitive nature to a computer interview than a human interviewer (Locke et al., 1993). Thus, the computer interview can be a useful adjunct to face-to-face interviewing by enabling patients to more easily share sensitive information (e.g., risky behaviors, trauma, and substance use) with less risk of shame and embarrassment. The ability of well-written computer-based interviews will not replace the need for skillful interviews delivered by clinicians.

By intent, the chart above does not present a comprehensive catalog of new and emerging telemental health media. Instead, it presents an array of telecommunication tools with the goal of meeting the behavioral health needs of patients in a compassionate and patient-centered manner, freer of traditional time and geography constraints. More than ever before, technology has the capability of bringing telemental health resources to the point of need and matching the right provider informed by the right information who can engage in the right treatment with the appropriate patient.

Changing Nature of Care

The demands of information-age medicine require the ability to use knowledge bases (e.g., PubMed, UpToDate), search engines (e.g., Google) and decision support tools (e.g., PHQ-9, drug interaction checker). The explosive growth of new clinical knowledge compels clinicians to change how they practice. This means that for modern-day practitioners, the ability to keep current must be available at the point of care, changing the nature of the clinical encounter. Indeed, a thriving industry of organizations offering tools and knowledge resources has developed. Vendors are being challenged to integrate these assets into the electronic medical record.

The idealized twentieth-century image of a family doctor as portrayed on television has become obsolete. His twenty-first-century counterpart is a tech savvy, compassionate "cyberdoc," a skilled clinician who is adept at integrating knowledge systems and decision support tools into routine practice and clinical communications. Such a clinician is likely to carry a tablet computer into the exam room to capture important information, provide just-in-time education using multimedia educational resources, share progress with the patient, and prescribe treatment.

Innovative technologies have always presented challenges to clinicians because of the threat that they may interfere with an empathic connection during the clinical encounter. Consider the loss of intimacy experienced by Laennec's patients when instead of pressing his ear to the patient's chest, he used a primitive stethoscope to auscultate the heart. Progress in medical technology is relentless. Some disruptive innovations can have an adverse impact on the doctor-patient relationship. When technology innovation diminishes the human connection, then we must find ways to compensate for it.

For generations, mental health professionals in private practice in the USA have been paid on a fee-for-service basis. This has meant that clinicians primarily bill for their time—the traditional 50-min hour. Now that more Americans have mental health insurance benefits and as new mental health parity regulations take hold, a greater proportion of patients will have improved access to, and lower out-of-pocket costs for, mental health services. When behavioral health clinicians practice in group or institutional settings, increasingly their revenue will be predicated on bundled payments and risk-bearing contracts. This means that more and more behavioral health clinicians will receive predetermined fixed amounts to care for a population of patients. Quality measures will be used to confirm that clinical performance targets are being met. Consequently, payments no longer will be determined by time spent but by the outcomes achieved. In the case of risk-bearing contracts, payments will be adjusted up or down based upon the quality of care provided. This further incentivizes clinicians to provide the best care possible in the most efficient manner and to document their work accordingly. Consequently, there is an opportunity to use technology to improve both the quantity and quality of care provided.

Growing recognition of the prevalence of mental disorders in primary care populations, especially among the elderly and those with chronic medical conditions, has led to a movement toward *integrated care*. In the integrated care model, psychiatrists, as well as other mental health clinicians, practice in a manner that acknowledges that the mind and body are inseparable. Psychiatrists prescribing medications now are expected to check for drug-drug interactions, perform medication reconciliations, measure blood pressures, and take comprehensive medical histories. In short, psychiatrists now must practice like other physicians, no longer only as psychotherapists. This has led to the growth of the subspecialty of psychosomatic medicine and its cousin, primary care psychiatry. This has been incentivized by reimbursement policies that have rewarded psychiatrists for conducting more thorough medical and biopsychosocial evaluations and allowing them to use "E & M" (evaluation and management) CPT coding that more accurately reflects the procedures and clinical activities they perform during an office visit. By rewarding the integrated model with greater reimbursement based on the new rate schedules for E & M codes in mental health, the behavior of psychiatrists is being shaped toward practicing in more of a medical model. The likely outcome in a generation will be a shift in psychiatry toward the biopsychosocial model advocated by Engel in his seminal paper, *The Clinical Application of the Biopsychosocial Model* (Engel, 1980).

These changes in healthcare financing along with the associated emphasis on objective clinical outcomes have spawned a growing industry of behavioral health analytics that uses newly required quality measures to assess the performance of healthcare organizations and even individual clinicians.

Another fundamental aspect of integrated care is the concept of *collaborative care*, described by Katon et al. (1995). This model recognizes that the complexity of care needed to manage chronic conditions requires a team-based approach and that behavioral health specialists and psychiatrists are essential members of the team. Integrated and collaborative care models that leverage telemedicine capabilities can facilitate greater care coordination among behavioral health specialists and other clinicians.

An additional transformation in clinical practice intended to improve quality of clinical outcomes is the current emphasis on evidence-based treatment ("EBT"). Integration of EBT principles into behavioral health practice supports the development and implementation of standardized treatments that have been proven effective in randomized clinical trials. EBTs, when applied to telemental health modalities, can lead to new clinical guideline development and create opportunities for (1) efficient dissemination of behavioral treatments in a variety of populations and settings and (2) psychologists and other behavioral health specialists to participate in guideline development and consequently to shape payment policies that depend upon EBT. EBTs that can be manualized lend themselves both to delivery by computer-guided clinicians and to adoption as self-directed computer-based treatment delivered over the Internet using e-Health and m-Health platforms.

Barriers to Telemental Health

In the banking, airline, and other industries, nowadays consumers transact business remotely; it has become the norm, perhaps even a meme. With the advent of services such as Peapod, even the ordering and home delivery of groceries can be arranged remotely. Technological advancements enabling remote interactions have existed for more than 40 years and become mainstream in the past 20. Despite this, in healthcare, remote care is the exception, not the rule. The promise of telemental health service delivery, while it does occur, is still in its infancy. The telemental health barriers presented in three groupings below are adapted from Magan (2013). As you peruse these, consider whether there is something fundamentally different about mental healthcare that represents an enduring obstacle to the growth of telemental healthcare delivery models or whether these barriers, with time, can and will be overcome.

Barrier: Rapport Building and Adherence Challenges. Many mental health clinicians have expressed concern that telemental health solutions interfere with the ability to build a positive, intimate, and influential relationship of trust with their patients. They worry that this could translate into less effective treatment and reduced patient adherence to their treatment plans. Essentially, some clinicians believe that computer-guided or tele-delivered treatment will be superficial. Behaviorally oriented practitioners are likely to be more comfortable with rapport building, treatment planning, and progress monitoring via video than their psychoanalytically oriented counterparts. As telemental health is integrated into population health management to provide better mental healthcare, it will facilitate the delivery of structured, behavioral treatments as well as psychodynamic treatment.

Barrier: Impact on Workflow, Productivity, and Office Cost. In discharging their day-to-day clinical responsibilities, clinicians rely on routine and proven processes. They wonder how the introduction of telemental health service delivery into their daily practices will affect office routine and require workflow changes and how productivity would be impacted as they accommodate both face-to-face and telemental health patient encounters. Practitioners face additional demands of understanding the technology options so as to make informed purchasing decisions and acquiring the knowledge to master and maintain the hardware and software for telemental health practice.

Barrier: Licensure, Credentialing, and Reimbursement. Telemental health practitioners need to be licensed in the state where they physically practice as well as in the state where each patient resides. Further, they must be credentialed in each hospital or clinic where they see patients. State laws differ, and navigating through a complex web of state and federal credentialing regulations can be confusing, expensive, and time consuming. Legislation and regulation governing telemedicine practice are undergoing active review in most states. The dynamic nature of the regulatory environment imposes an insurmountable burden to the individual practitioner. For that reason, membership in organizations such as the American Telemedicine Association, the American Association for Technology in Psychiatry, and the TeleMental Health Institute to keep current is quite useful for those interested in the field and those anticipating and preparing for modern practice.

The barriers relating to reimbursement are twofold. First, there is a bewildering array of different reimbursement policies for remotely delivered care among public and private payers. Second, parity for reimbursement of face-to-face mental health treatment and tele-delivered mental health treatment does not exist. The vast majority of traditional in-person mental health consultations are not reimbursable if recast as telemental health consultations. There is also the barrier among some payers that video consultation will be reimbursed but not treatment delivered by telephone without video. The lag in recognizing the value of tele-delivered mental health services by public and private payers is the most formidable barrier to telemental health adoption and expansion.

Because of stigma, cost, and inconvenience, there is pent-up demand for mental health services that have been out of reach for many, especially the poor and under/uninsured. Now that we have the ability to efficiently deliver evidence-based treatments (e.g., for depression), to the home or other convenient sites, the potential exists for extending care to a large portion of previously underserved individuals suffering from mental illness. The US Preventive Services Task Force has already identified depression as a target for annual screening as a part of routine preventative care for all patients. What seems so surprising is how difficult it has proven to meet this challenge, and it begs the question of who stands to benefit from restraining the delivery of mental health treatment in such a convenient and affordable manner.

As these barriers fall, new opportunities will emerge for careers for forward-looking psychologists and other mental health clinicians who seek to prepare themselves for the future.

Careers and Pathways

Telemental health can deliver behavioral healthcare in a variety of ways and settings. Through the power of technology, clinical expertise can overcome time and distance and be brought right to the point of need to remotely assess patients, educate them, intervene with Internet-delivered therapies, use mobile platforms, monitor care and quality metrics, and provide individual or aggregate reports for guiding care or health policy. There are a variety of settings in which this care may be delivered and be a potentially useful disruptive innovation. These include:

- Nursing homes
- Correctional institutions
- Rural hospitals
- Schools (colleges, universities, and specialty schools)
- Specialty hospitals (children, hospice, pain, chronic disease)
- Integrated care practices (i.e., behavioral specialist who is part of team)
- Veterans Administration
- Military
- Extreme environments (undersea, polar research stations, space, ocean-going ships)
- Industry (workplace mental health, EAPs)
- Working for insurance panels who serve an Internet
- Small group and private practitioners migrating known clients to the Net
- The home and any other location where a patient in need may be

For those readers interested to explore employment in telemental health in any of these careers, the chapters that follow will provide guidance about the training and experience needed to direct you along a career path in that niche.

Conclusion

Telemental health is an emerging career resulting from the confluence of healthcare reform, innovative technologies, and evidence-based medicine. Spurred by the need to address healthcare disparities and the encumbrance of stigma and barriers to access, the Affordable Care Act has set the stage for the reintegration of behavioral health into primary care and the prevention and management of chronic medical conditions.

References

American Telemedicine Association. (2014). *What is telemedicine.* Retrieved January 28, 2014, from http://www.americantelemed.org/about-telemedicine/what-is-telemedicine#.VtSOcfkrLs1
Engel, G. (1980). The clinical application of the biopsychosocial model. *The American Journal of Psychiatry, 137*(5), 535–544.
Grohol, J. (2011). Mental health professionals: US statistics. *Psych Central.* Retrieved on January 28, 2014 from http://psychcentral.com/lib/mental-health-professionals-us-statistics/0009373
Hillestad, R., Bigelow, J., Bower, A., Girosi, F., Meili, R., Scoville, R., & Taylor, R. (2005). Can electronic medical record systems transform health care? Potential health benefits, savings, and costs. *Health Affairs, 24*(5), 1103–1117.

Katon, W., Von Korff, M., Lin, E., Walker, E., Simon, G., Bush, T., ... Russo, J. (1995). Collaborative management to achieve treatment guidelines impact on depression in primary care. *Journal of the American Medical Association, 273*(13), 1026–1031.

Locke, S., Slack, W., Safran, C., Cotton, D., Popovsky, M., & Hoff, R. (1993). Screening blood donors by computer interview—Reply. *Journal of the American Medical Association, 269*(12), 1505–1506.

Magan, G. (2013). *3 Sets of barriers and guidelines for telemental health.* Retrieved from https: // www.leadingage.org/3_Sets_of_Barriers_and_Guidelines_for_Telemental_Health.aspx

World Health Organization. (2014). *Mental health: a state of well-being.* Retrieved January 28, 2015, from http://www.who.int/features/factfiles/mental_health/en/

Chapter 2
The Law of Telemental Health

Joseph McMenamin

This chapter touches on some of the main legal issues pertinent to the provision of mental healthcare at a distance.

Licensure

Traditionally, the states have regulated healthcare through licensure. Although licensing requirements state to state tend to address common topics (professional education and training, continuing education, ethics, confidentiality, advertising, professional self-governance, etc.), details vary. In no way does a license to practice psychology in State A authorize the bearer to practice in State B; State A is without authority to confer such a privilege. States tend to be rather restrictive in their readings of relevant statutes, partly for quality control—state boards see it as their role to police the profession to protect the public—partly to protect their own licensees, and partly to vindicate state sovereignty.

For a practitioner proposing to offer services across state lines, multistate licensure is a perfectly lawful approach, but it can be costly and cumbersome. Each state has different requirements, and a licensee failing to meet one in a particular state is likely to lose his license there. Keeping up with the requirements is both an administrative headache and a significant financial burden. For a professional who wishes to concentrate on only a couple of states, however, it may be a relatively simple, cost-effective solution.

Portions of this chapter are taken from an unpublished paper prepared in aid of the writer's verbal remarks at the Roundtable on Legal Impediments to Telemedicine, held at the University of Maryland School of Law in Baltimore on 16 April 2010.

J. McMenamin, M.D., J.D. (✉)
10617 Falconbridge Drive, Richmond, VA 23238, USA
e-mail: mcmenamin@medicalawfirm.com

© Springer International Publishing Switzerland 2017
M.M. Maheu et al. (eds.), *Career Paths in Telemental Health*,
DOI 10.1007/978-3-319-23736-7_2

Whether a behavioral health professional wants to practice in a single state or in 50, it is necessary to become acquainted with at least the general contours of the relevant law in each such state. Recognize, though, that laws change. Statutes are enacted, amended, and repealed; new regulations are written; and courts construe legislative language, or previous decisions, sometimes in ways not easily anticipated. Hence, one must not only have a working knowledge of the law in each state where one practices, but one must also make reasonable efforts to stay current with legal requirements as they evolve.

APA published a 50-state survey of laws pertinent to telepsychology, specifically those most pertinent to licensure, and reportedly current as of October 2013. See http://www.apapracticecentral.org/update/2013/10-24/telepsychology-review.aspx. For each state, the survey specifies whether there are telehealth or telepsychology statutes or regulations, whether the practice of psychology is defined to include distance care specifically, whether there is a telehealth coverage mandate, what provisions exist for temporary or guest practice, and what penalties can be imposed for practicing psychology without a license. Some states are plainly more amenable to accommodating out-of-state practitioners than others. With the law in flux, full licensure is still the safest course, except in special circumstances. For example, the military and the VA generally recognize a valid license issued by any state in the union. The private practice world is not so accommodating.

In at least one state, the physician disciplinary authority has declared that treatment via the Internet or over the phone will be held to the same standard as is applied in traditional face-to-face settings (Illinois Medical Disciplinary Board, "Guidelines for the Appropriate Use of Internet/Telephonic Communication in Medical Practice" (2003), cited in John D. Blum, "Internet Medicine and the Evolving Status of the Physician-Patient Relationship," 24 *J. Legal Med.* 413, 445 (2003)). In some states, legislation now provides that, at least as to physicians, the standard of care at a distance is to be the same as that of care in person. See, e.g., Colo. Rev. Stat. § 10-16-123(2), Haw. Rev. Stat. § 453-1.3(d), and 22 Tex. Admin. Code § 174.8(b). Although these authorities govern the practices of physicians, and not of psychologists, they are nevertheless instructive. Our legal system reasons by analogy, and there is a good possibility that boards focused on other branches of the healing arts may be influenced by these and similar legal developments.

For better and for worse, we will likely see some, perhaps substantial, erosion of the power and influence of State Boards in the future. Numerous proposals are pending to create a system similar to that for drivers' licenses, or to create a federal licensing system, or to expand reciprocating arrangements, or to invent a mechanism to license those whose work is limited to distance care. FSMB has developed an Interstate Medical Licensure Compact (http://www.licenseportability.org), effectively a contract between states, which in some particulars resembles the Compact the nurses have had for years (https://www.ncsbn.org/nlc.htm). Counselors have been working toward licensure portability in their 20/20 project. See http://www.counseling.org/knowledge-center/20-20-a-vision-for-the-future-of-counseling/statement-of-principles. In February 2015, the Board of Directors of the Association of State and Provincial Psychology Boards (ASPPB) introduced the Psychology

Interjurisdictional Compact (PSYPACT), designed to facilitate telehealth as well as temporary in-person psychology practice across jurisdictional boundaries (http://www.asppb.net/news/217917/Psychology-Interjurisdictional-Compact-PSYPACT-Announced.htm). As with the compacts developed by other health disciplines, this one requires buy-in from state legislatures. It sets up a Psychology Interjurisdictional Compact Commission, responsible for articulating the rules governing cross-border psychology practice. To practice in a state other than her own, the psychologist must among other things subject herself to the Board in the patient's state, obtain a certificate called an "E. Passport" to be further defined when the Commission is in place, and comply with any other Commission rules.

It is difficult to predict what the final form of licensing will be in a country as large and diverse as ours. Increasingly, however, the emphasis on state borders will be seen as an anachronism. It will grow easier to provide services not only where you hang your hat but where you send your electrons. Over time, that will probably also be true of international practice, as to some extent is already true in the EU, for example. If seven states enact the PSYPACT, it will become valid for practitioners in those states. As of this writing, however, that has not yet occurred.

For now, then, caution is the watchword. State boards have plenary power over a practitioner's license. The best course continues to be to obtain and maintain a license in each state where your patients live. Doing so entails expense, administrative chores, complying with varying continuing education requirements, and, of course, subjecting yourself to the jurisdiction of a board that may be far from home. The alternatives, however, are worse.

A California patient asked an online pharmacy for a refill of fluoxetine, prescribed to manage his depression. Identifying himself as a California resident, the patient filled out an online form, eliciting answers to questions pertinent to medical history, and sent it to a pharmacy in cyberspace. The Internet pharmacy sent the request, and the form, to a server in Texas, which relayed the documentation to Christian Hageseth, MD, a physician licensed and working in Colorado. On the basis of the information submitted, Dr. Hageseth concluded the refill was indicated and sent a prescription back to the Texas server, which in turn sent it to a bricks-and-mortar pharmacy in Mississippi. That pharmacy shipped the actual product to the patient, who died a suicide 2 months later from carbon monoxide poisoning. Although the patient had fluoxetine on board at the time, there was no evidence the drug caused the death; the patient was also inebriated. Finding that there had been no in-person evaluation, the California Board of Medicine concluded that between Dr. Hageseth and the patient, a true doctor–patient relationship had not been established, so it referred the case for prosecution to the state authorities. California took the position that Dr. Hageseth had engaged in the unauthorized practice of medicine there, a felony under § 2052 of the California Business and Professions Code. Dr. Hageseth had never been present in California, nor had he sought patients there. Moreover, another professional, under a separate license, actually filled the script. Dr. Hageseth therefore denied that California had jurisdiction. The California Courts of Appeal, however, held that California authorities could cross state lines to pursue criminal charges against the defendant (*Hageseth v. Superior Court*, 150 Cal.

App. 4th 1399, 59 Cal. Rptr.3d 385 (2007)). Dr. Hageseth was sentenced to 9 months in jail, which he was permitted to serve in Colorado. He also was ordered to pay $4200 to reimburse the California Medical Board for investigation costs.

There do not appear to be any published cases in which a psychologist licensed in one state was criminally prosecuted for caring for a patient electronically in another state. Moreover, the law in California is just that: the law of a single state, not of all 50. *Hageseth*, though, remains instructive. As noted, courts often reason by analogy, and at least until the law changes appreciably, mental health professionals should go to school on Dr. Hageseth's experience.

In a more recent case, the Oklahoma Medical Board disciplined a pain physician, mainly for what it saw as excessively liberal prescribing of controlled substances. The board also sanctioned the licensee, however, for using Skype to communicate with patients, because that approach failed to protect privacy, and for failing to keep adequate records and to perform proper examinations (*State of Oklahoma ex rel. Oklahoma Board of Medical Licensure and Supervision v. Thomas Edward Trow, M.D.*, License No. 10255, case No. 11-11-4439 (12 September 2013). Although this, too, was a medical case, the board's concerns about privacy and record-keeping are not peculiar to physicians.

Privacy

The protection of patient/client privacy is among the best-established obligations of healthcare professionals, dating at least to the time of Hippocrates. In no branch of the healing arts is privacy more important than it is in mental health, concerned as it is with the patient's most sensitive and personal information. The duty to protect patient privacy is reflected in statutes, regulations, and case law, and it applies regardless whether care is provided in-person or at a distance.

By no means can traditional paper-based records guarantee privacy. In telehealth, however, data move from one place to another by electronic means vulnerable to mishap or to intentional invasion. And with so many health professionals now enthusiastically utilizing a wide array of mobile devices and with the continual blurring of the line between our personal and professional lives, the risks of inadvertent disclosures are high and increasing. Scarcely a week goes by without some news report of another breach of healthcare privacy.

HIPAA

The Health Insurance Portability and Accountability Act (HIPAA), Pub. L. No. 104-191, 110 Stat. 1936 (1996), gave rise to the privacy rule, 45 CFR Part 160, and to the security rule, Subparts A and E of Part 164. HIPAA was enacted primarily to permit workers switching jobs to transfer and continue health insurance coverage.

Its elaborate array of rules to protect health information privacy, however, is what HIPAA is best known for. These rules were developed in large part to allay the understandable misgivings of patients fearing that, with the increasing influence of third-party payers, the waning authority of healthcare professionals, the digitization of data of all kinds, and the depersonalization of what used to be the intensely personal exchange between treater and patient, confidence that privacy will be protected was no longer justified.

HIPAA applies only to covered entities (CEs) and business associates (BAs), defined below. For CEs, the HIPAA Privacy and Security Rules govern healthcare records, including, of course, mental healthcare records, and they apply to distance care just as they do to in-person care. As HHS puts it, "the HIPAA Privacy Rule establishes national standards to protect individuals' medical records and other personal health information…[It] requires appropriate safeguards to protect the privacy of personal health information ["PHI"], and sets limits and conditions on the uses and disclosures that may be made of such information without patient authorization. The Rule also gives patients rights over their health information, including rights to examine and obtain a copy of their health records, and to request corrections" (http://www.hhs.gov/ocr/privacy/hipaa/administrative/privacyrule/). The HIPAA Privacy and Security Rule requires CEs and BAs acting on their behalf to implement administrative, physical, and technical safeguards if engaged in the transmission or storage of PHI. 45 C.F.R. §§ 164.302–318. See http://www.hhs.gov/ocr/privacy/hipaa/administrative/securityrule/.

Health insurers, healthcare clearinghouses, and healthcare providers who transmit information in electronic form in connection with a transaction governed by an HHS standard are all CEs. "BA" is a broad term and includes entities needing routine access to the CE's PHI to provide data transmission services to it,[1] entities offering personal health records on a CE's behalf, subcontractors (other than mere conduits) of BAs handling PHI for it, and anyone who creates, receives, maintains, or transmits PHI on behalf of a CE (including entities storing electronic PHI). The list of affected BAs may include vendors, contractors, or consultants, such as those providing professional services, e.g., lawyers, accountants, marketers, and software vendors. Under HIPAA, a CE engaging a BA must enter into a contract with the BA, a "business associate agreement" (BAA), imposing on the BA by contract substantially the same obligations the CE shoulders by operation of law. Under the Health Information Technology for Economic and Clinical Health (HITECH) Act, enacted as part of the American Recovery and Reinvestment Act of 2009 (ARRA), BAs are obliged to protect PHI just as CEs are, not just because through BAAs they are contractually bound to do so, but directly under federal law. See 45 C.F.R. § 160.103; 42 USC § 17921(2).

Mental health professionals in particular should remember that patients who pay for services out of pocket can request that their health information not be disclosed to others, including their third-party payers.

---

[1] The definition of a BA excludes mere conduits of such data, such as telecommunications concerns and Internet carriers. The HITECH Act defines a "conduit" as an entity that transports information, but does not access it except on a random or infrequent basis as necessary to perform the transportation services.

The Final Omnibus Rule

The HIPAA Omnibus Rule (Final Rule), 78 (17) Fed. Reg. 5566-5702, published by HHS on 25 January 2013 pursuant to the Genetic Information Nondiscrimination Act of 2008 (GINA), Pub.L. 110–233, 122 Stat. 881, and to the HITECH Act, 42 USC §§ 17931–39, imposed a compliance deadline of 23 September 2013 on all BAAs entered into after 25 January 2013. All BAAs entered into before then had to be updated and brought into compliance by 23 September 2014. The Final Rule made the legal requirements for PHI privacy and security even more onerous than they were before.

By changing the definition of a breach, the Final Rule lowered the threshold for a finding of liability, simultaneously shifting the burden of proof from the government to the accused. Originally, a breach was defined to mean a compromise of the security or privacy of PHI that posed significant risk of financial, reputational, or other harm to an individual — the so-called "harm" standard. The Final Rule, however, abandoned that standard. A breach is now defined as "impermissible use or disclosure of PHI." Such a use or disclosure "is presumed to be a breach unless an entity demonstrates and documents a low probability PHI was compromised." To show breach, patients need no longer prove "harm"; they need but show unauthorized viewing of patient records, without more.

The Final Rule expands the definition of BA to include health information organizations, e-prescribing gateways, certain personal health record (PHR) providers, patient safety organizations, data transmission service providers with access to PHI, and contractors handling PHI. BA liabilities for HIPAA infractions are substantially identical to those to which covered entities themselves are vulnerable. The Final Rule also provides that a contract between a BA and its subcontractor is required; it must be as stringent as a BAA. Broader exposure for BAs is not tantamount to diminished risk for CEs; they remain liable for their own breaches, just as they were before the Final Rule was promulgated.

The Final Rule also imposes new notification rules triggered when breaches are discovered. Within 60 days of such discovery, CEs (or, under a BAA, the BA) must notify patients in writing, supplying a "brief description of the breach, a description of the types of information that were involved in the breach, the steps affected individuals should take to protect themselves from potential harm, a brief description of what the covered entity is doing to investigate the breach, mitigate the harm, and prevent further breaches, as well as contact information for the covered entity (or BA, as applicable)." If the BA is responsible for the breach, it must notify its CE. The CE or the BA must notify the Secretary of HHS of all such breaches annually. When a breach affects more than 500 patients in a given jurisdiction, notification must also be made through prominent media outlets within that jurisdiction and to the Secretary (HHS, Breach Notification Rule, http://www.hhs.gov/ocr/privacy/hipaa/administrative/breachnotificationrule/). HHS now posts a list of such breaches at https://ocrportal.hhs.gov/ocr/breach/breach_report.jsf.

The HIPAA Final Rule also changes the HIPAA Enforcement Rule to incorporate the HITECH Act's higher civil monetary and criminal penalties. Even in cases when a CE did not know it was committing a HIPAA violation and would not have known it even by exercising reasonable diligence, civil penalties can range from $100 up to—for willfully negligent breaches—$50,000 per violation with a maximum of $1,500,000 per section violation. Pre-HITECH HIPAA fines, in contrast, were capped at $100 per violation, with an aggregate limit of $25,000.00 per year.

HIPAA provides for severe criminal penalties as well. Under the Final Rule, up to 1 year of imprisonment can be imposed for violations done unknowingly or with reasonable cause to believe they were not violations. A person who knowingly uses, obtains, or discloses individually identifiable health information with the intent to sell, transfer, or use the information for commercial advantage, personal gain, or malicious harm, however, shall be fined not more than $250,000 and/or imprisoned for up to 10 years (42 USC 1320d-6). To understand the gravity of these sanctions, consider the Florida nursing assistant sentenced to 3 years in prison and to a $12,000 fine for stealing and selling, at but meager profit, PHI that included Social Security numbers, birth dates, and other data (Tim Mullaney, "Nursing assistant faces 3 years in prison for HIPAA crime," http://www.mcknights.com/nursing-assistant-faces-3-years-in-prison-for-hipaa-crime/article/318745/ (31 October 2013)).

Risk Analyses

CEs that want to transmit PHI must conduct a risk analysis. Such an analysis consists of "an accurate and thorough assessment of the potential risks and vulnerabilities to the confidentiality, integrity, and availability of electronic protected health information held by the covered entity" (HIPAA Administrative safeguards, §164.308 (a)(1)(ii)(A)). All CEs, including one-person practices, and all providers who want to receive EHR incentive payments, even those with certified EHRs, must perform such a risk analysis. An outside consultant can help, but is not required. A checklist can also help, but may not be sufficient. Moreover, a single risk analysis is not enough. A CE must continue to review, correct or modify, and update security protections over time. Risks need not be mitigated immediately. OCR has issued Guidance on Risk Analysis Requirements of the Security Rule (http://www.hhs.gov/ocr/privacy/hipaa/administrative/securityrule/rafinalintro.html).

Enforcement

The HHS Office for Civil Rights (OCR) has initiated the vast majority of HIPAA enforcement ever since HITECH's 2009 enactment, resulting in imposition of civil penalties and corrective action plans (CAPs).

The settlements the government has entered into with CEs demonstrate the seriousness of HIPAA violations. In 2009, CVS Pharmacies agreed to pay $2.25 million for PHI violations. In 2012, the Alaska Department of HHS paid a $1.7 million penalty, the Massachusetts Eye and Ear Infirmary settled a fine for $1.5 million, and BlueCross BlueShield of Tennessee settled a HIPAA claim for $1.5 million. Another fine of $4.3 million was imposed on Cignet Health of Prince George's County, Maryland.

Rarely if ever do covered entities defend HIPAA charges in court. The imbalance in power between OCR and the CE is such that the defendant usually sees settlement as the best resolution. At http://www.hhs.gov/ocr/privacy/hipaa/enforcement/examples/, HHS presents, in reverse chronological order, a list of recent enforcement actions resulting in settlements. Payments typically are in the 6–7-figure range. The list is not comprehensive, but it is illustrative. In 2014, for example, OCR settled with Anchorage Community Mental Health Services, New York, and Presbyterian Hospital, Concentra Health Services, and Skagit County, Washington. In 2013, OCR settled with, among others, Idaho State University, WellPoint, and Affinity Health Plan, a not-for-profit managed care plan. These agreements demonstrate that both provider and payer CEs, large and small, private and public, are at risk.

It is also instructive to consider the array of fact patterns that give rise to exposure. The commonest breaches are attributable to human error: unencrypted laptops or thumb drives left on trains or in unlocked cars, microfiches left undestroyed, misplaced paper records, or failing to follow one's organization's own policies and procedures. In the 2014 *Parkview* settlement, OCR reported that

...Parkview took custody of medical records pertaining to approximately 5,000 to 8,000 patients while assisting [a] retiring physician to transition her patients to new providers, and while considering the possibility of purchasing some of the physician's practice. On June 4, 2009, Parkview employees, with notice that the physician was not at home, left 71 cardboard boxes of these medical records unattended and accessible to unauthorized persons on the driveway of the physician's home, within 20 feet of the public road and a short distance away from a heavily trafficked public shopping venue. (http://www.hhs.gov/news/press/2014pres/06/20140623a.html)

Not all the breaches, however, arise from human carelessness; some are caused by deliberate misdeeds such as malware, disabled firewalls, or scam sales of x-rays (ostensibly to recover their silver).

Settlements are not limited to payments. OCR typically imposes a corrective action plan upon the CE. These vary with the circumstances, but often requires new risk analyses and risk management plans that OCR must review and approve. Usually, the CE must also report any HIPAA violations to OCR within a defined period, often 30 days.

HHS has published a list of problems that most often lead to formal investigations:

Impermissible uses and disclosures of PHI
Lack of safeguards for PHI
Lack of patients' access to their own PHI
Uses or disclosures of more than the minimum necessary PHI
Lack of administrative safeguards of electronic PHI (US Department of Health & Human Services)

HHS has also identified the CEs most frequently required to take corrective action to achieve compliance:

Private practices
General hospitals
Outpatient facilities
Health plans
Pharmacies (*id.*)

Practitioners should bear in mind that under Section 13410(e) of the HITECH Act, enforcement of the HIPAA Privacy Rule, though a federal law, is not limited to OCR. State Attorneys General are authorized to do so as well and have. See, e.g., http://www.ct.gov/ag/cwp/view.asp?A=2341&Q=462754. OCR even provides training to state AGs for just this purpose. See http://www.hhs.gov/ocr/privacy/hipaa/enforcement/sag/.

HIPAA, Privacy, and Federal Agencies

There may be no better evidence of the force and power of HIPAA than its use against federal agencies.

In November 2013, the HHS Office of Inspector General (OIG), which "fights waste, fraud and abuse in Medicare, Medicaid and more than 300 other HHS programs" (http://oig.hhs.gov/about-oig/about-us/index.asp), completed an audit of the OCR Security Rule oversight and enforcement from 2009 to 2011 (OIG, Audit (A-04-11-05025), https://oig.hhs.gov/oas/reports/region4/41105025.asp). OCR is the very office "responsible for enforcing the Privacy and Security Rules" (http://www.hhs.gov/ocr/privacy/hipaa/enforcement/). OIG concluded that, in its oversight and enforcement of the HIPAA Security Rule, OCR did not meet all federal requirements. OIG found 39 of 60 selected records were missing one or more documents needed for security violation investigations. OCR had not "assessed the risks, established priorities, or implemented controls for its HITECH requirement to provide for periodic audits of covered entities to ensure their compliance with Security Rule requirements." OIG found that the OCR investigation files

> did not contain required documentation supporting key decisions because its staff did not consistently follow OCR investigation procedures by sufficiently reviewing investigation case documentation. OCR had not implemented sufficient controls, including supervisory review and documentation retention, to ensure investigators followed investigation policies and procedures for properly initiating, processing and closing Security Rule investigations.

OIG also found that for its information systems used to process and store investigation data, OCR had not fully complied with federal cybersecurity requirements included in the National Institute of Standards and Technology (NIST) Risk Management Framework (http://csrc.nist.gov/groups/SMA/fisma/documents/risk-management-framework-2009_bw.pdf). OIG concluded that "by not complying with Federal cybersecurity requirements, OCR increased the risk that it might not identify or mitigate system vulnerabilities." OIG noted that not following the federal cybersecurity requirements could "increase the risk of unauthorized disclosure or destruction of ePHI" in OCR's possession.

As is customary, OCR was given an opportunity to respond to OIG's recommendations. One such was: "Provide for periodic audits in accordance with HITECH to ensure Security Rule compliance at CEs." OCR stated: "While OCR agrees with the recommendation that the HITECH audit program represents an effective tool, no monies have been appropriated for OCR to maintain a permanent audit program" (OIG, "The Office for Civil Rights Did not Meet all Federal Requirements in its Oversight and Enforcement of the HIPAA Security Rule" (November 2013), https://oig.hhs.gov/oas/reports/region4/41105025.pdf). Those in private practice can relate.

Another dispute with a federal agency, though not pursued under HIPAA, illustrates the risks involved when privacy is not sufficiently protected. The ACLU claims that in response to a FOIA request, it procured a copy of a 2009 *Search Warrant Handbook* from the IRS Criminal Tax Division's Office of Chief Counsel. ACLU quotes the *Handbook* as saying "the Fourth Amendment does not protect communications held in electronic storage, such as email messages stored on a server, because internet users do not have a reasonable expectation of privacy in such communications." ACLU indicates that it also procured other evidence that the IRS has reached this conclusion (Nathan F. Wessler, "New Documents Suggest IRS Reads Emails Without a Warrant," https://www.aclu.org/blog/technology-and-liberty-national-security/new-documents-suggest-irs-reads-emails-without-warrant).

A California CE, identified merely as John Doe Company, filed a putative class action in the Superior Court of California against the IRS in March 2013, accusing 15 IRS agents of seizing 60 million medical records from 10 million patients. The complaint, available at http://www.scribd.com/doc/142305534/John-Doe-Company-et-al-vs-John-Does-1-15-IRS-Seized-60-Million-Personal-Medical-Records#scribd, alleged that the agents took, for example, psychological and gynecological counseling data and sexual/drug treatment and other medical treatment data on California state judges, members of the Screen Actors Guild, and Major League Baseball players, among many others. It claimed: "No search warrant authorized the seizure of these records; no subpoena authorized the seizure of these records; none of the 10,000,000 Americans were (*sic*) under any kind of known criminal or civil investigation and their medical records had no relevance whatsoever to the IRS search." In addition to punitive damages for constitutional violations, the complaint sought $25,000 in compensatory damages "per violation per individual."

"HIPAA-Compliant" Technologies

Purveyors of telehealth equipment or technology sometimes promote their products as "HIPAA-compliant." Many of these are highly useful. But no technology is "HIPAA-compliant." CEs and BAs are compliant, or are not. The use of technology—any technology—cannot ensure that a CE is "HIPAA-compliant." HIPAA demands more than reliance on devices or technologies with privacy-protective features or technical specifications. Certain features may indeed help a CE comply with the rules. For example, a telehealth software program may permit encryption, or the technology might require use of passwords. Such features, though valuable, provide mere tools to help a CE comply; they do not ensure compliance and cannot substitute for an organized, thoughtful, documented set of security practices.

Text Messaging

SMS text messaging is quick, convenient, and feasible on ordinary cell phones. One need not be technically proficient to use it. Text4baby, for maternal and child health, and Text2Quit, for smoking cessation, have probably benefited tens of thousands. Historically, text messaging was risky. Such messages were unencrypted, neither party could authenticate the other, and the PHI could remain stored on the individual's device and, for unpredictable periods, on telecommunications company servers as well. The Joint Commission, originally deemed it unacceptable for "physicians or licensed independent practitioners to text orders for patients to the hospital or other healthcare setting[s]" (Standards, FAQ Details, http://www.jointcommission.org/standards_information/jcfaqdetails.aspx?StandardsFaqId=401&ProgramId=1). With improving technology, however, especially widespread use of encryption the risk is now much lower. In fact, the joint Commission recently reversed itself and now approves text messaging for transmission of physician orders. See, "Update: Texting Orders 36(5) Joint Commission Perspectives 15 (May, 2016), https://www.jointcommission.org/assets/1/6Update_Texting_Orders.pdf.

The Cloud

Using the cloud is also risky. Dropbox, for example, one of the most popular and perhaps one of the most well developed of the cloud storage providers, discusses its security and privacy features and identifies standards and regulations it complies with, at https://www.dropbox.com/help/238/en. It makes no claim, however, that it complies with HIPAA. Nor could it. Dropbox keeps metadata, including the file name, which is not secure. It also lacks the audit controls that HIPAA demands. It is possible that, with technological advances and evolution in the law, the cloud may gradually become a legally responsible place to stou PHI. At present practitioners should be leery of using the cloud for communicating about PHI.

Future

There is no reason to believe that HITECH enforcement will relent in 2016 or beyond, especially because the HITECH Act authorized the transfer of funds collected through civil monetary penalties or monetary settlements for HIPAA violations to OCR to support enforcement efforts.

HHS has published a notice of proposed rulemaking, proposing to amend the Privacy Rule to permit certain CEs to disclose the minimum necessary demographic and other information for National Instant Criminal Background Check System (NICS) reporting purposes. NICS determines whether a potential firearms purchaser is statutorily prohibited from possessing or obtaining a firearm. That category includes those who have been (1) involuntarily civilly committed; (2) found incompetent to stand trial or found not guilty by reason of insanity; or (3) otherwise determined, through a formal adjudication, to have a severe mental condition that makes the individual a danger to himself or others, or incapable of managing his own affairs. As of this writing, the final rule has not yet been published. See https://www. federalregister.gov/articles/2014/01/07/2014-00055/health-insurance-portability-and-accountability-act-hipaa-privacy-rule-and-the-national-instant.

Private Claims

Under HIPAA, there is no private right of action. That is, although a CE violating the law is vulnerable to a variety of governmental penalties, the patient whose records were compromised finds no basis in HIPAA to sue the CE. That does not mean that plaintiffs have not tried to sue over breaches of privacy or security of their private information. First, such a patient might well have an avenue of recovery under state law, independent of any asserted HIPAA violation. Second, in a handful of cases, courts have permitted state law claims supported in part by alleged HIPAA violations and pleaded as claims such as "negligence per se." Negligence lies for harms resulting from a failure to act as a reasonable person in like circumstances would act. Under negligence per se theory, a court may find a defendant who has violated a statute, ordinance, or regulation negligent as a matter of law.

On 11 December 2009, AvMed, a Florida-based health insurer, reported the theft from a locked conference room of two laptops containing unencrypted personal information on more than 1.2 million customers, including names, Social Security numbers, and other PHI. Patients brought a putative class action in Florida federal court, alleging that in failing to secure its computers or encrypt their data, AvMed violated federal health privacy rules, industry standards, and its own stated consumer protections. The Southern District of Florida dismissed plaintiffs' claims, in part because the complaint failed to allege cognizable injury. In *Resnick v. Avmed, Inc.*, 693 F. 3d 1317 (11th Cir. 2012), however, the appellate court reversed the trial court's dismissal of all but two claims. It held that the plaintiffs had properly alleged an injury in fact that was fairly traceable to the theft by alleging that they had been careful with their own PHI, that they were victims of identity theft, and that their identities were stolen only after the AvMed incident. The ensuing settlement was the first to offer financial remuneration to class members who did not themselves suffer identity theft. The settlement not only provided monetary damages for customers who can show they actually experienced identity theft but also provided for a $3 million fund from which current and former members can make claims for $10 for every year they were AvMed customers, thereby recouping the part of their premiums that plaintiffs claimed should have been used on data security. AvMed also agreed to implement data security measures consistent with HIPAA regulations, including mandatory security awareness training, new password protocols, upgrades to laptop security systems, facility security upgrades, and updates to security policies and procedures.

On 29 January 2013, a putative class action was filed in New Jersey federal court against Horizon Blue Cross for a data breach allegedly affecting 840,000 enrollees. Over a weekend, thieves stole computers cable-locked to workstations, gaining access to names, addresses, dates of birth, clinical information, and Social Security numbers. The complaint is available at http://www.garfunkelwild.com/ NJHLBulletin/NJHLPDF/2014/DataBreachSpring2014.pdf. On 31 March 2015, the case was dismissed, because, said the court, an injury sufficient to confer standing was not proved. Standing refers to a party's ability to demonstrate to the court sufficient connection to and harm from the action challenged to support that party's participation in the case. Specifically, plaintiffs were unable to show that they had been or would be harmed. See Elizabeth Snell, "Data Breach Lawsuit Against Horizon BCBS Dismissed," *HealthITSecurity* (7 April 2015), http://healthitsecurity. com/news/data-breach-lawsuit-against-horizon-bcbs-dismissed.

The States

With the understandably heavy emphasis on HIPAA, state statutes are too often overlooked. Every state has some form of legislated protection of the privacy of health records, and those laws retain their vitality despite HIPAA's enactment. An exhaustive treatment of the topic would exceed the scope of this chapter, but an example or two may be illustrative.

Eleven years before HIPAA was enacted, a plaintiff successfully sued a plastic surgeon for posting patient-identifiable before-and-after photographs on TV and in a department store promotion of aesthetic surgery. Although photos could be a legitimate part of a medical record, said the court, public display without patient consent was actionable as a breach of privacy (*Vassiliades v. Garfinckel's, Brooks Bros.*, 492 A.2d 580 (D.C. App. 1985)). In a more recent case, however, the court held that violation of California's Confidentiality of Medical Information Act, Civil Code § 56-56.07, requires "more than an allegation of loss of possession by the health care provider." Rather, a plaintiff must prove that "the confidential nature of the plaintiff's medical information was breached as a result of the health care provider's negligence" (*Regents of the University of California v. Superior Court*, No. B249148, 2013 WL 5616775 (Cal. Ct. App. 15 October 2013) at *12). See also *Sutter Health et al. v. The Superior Court of Sacramento County*, C072591 (Cal. 3d App. Dist. 2014) (absent an allegation that a protected medical information thief actually viewed the stolen data, mere theft without more does not give rise to a cause of action for nominal damages under the California Confidentiality of Medical Information Act (CMIA) (Cal. Civ. Code, § 56 *et seq.*, http://www.cmanet.org/files/assets/news/2014/07/sutter-health-v-superior-court-july-21-2014.pdf)). On the other side of the country, by a statute passed unanimously in January 2015, New Jersey required health insurers to encrypt their health data. Violations entail imposition of a fine of up to $10,000 for a first offense and up to $20,000 for a subsequent offense; treble damages and a court order to pay the costs of adversely affected parties are also available. See http://www.njleg.state.nj.us/2014/Bills/S1000/562_R1.PDF. These examples illustrate the need for health professionals to understand and abide by not only federal but also state legal requirements in their practices.

Informed Consent

The standard of care for informed consent varies with the state. For a general discussion, see Paula Walter, "The Doctrine of Informed Consent: To Warn or Not to Warn," 71 *St. John's L. Rev.* 543, 545–49 (1997). Some states, such as California, have enacted specific statutes governing informed consent in telemedicine (Cal. Bus. Prof. Code § 2290.5 (2009)). Other examples include Oklahoma, which not only has developed statutory authority on informed consent but has expressly identified information that must be disclosed. See discussion of *Trow,* supra. See also 22 Tex. Admin. Code § 174.5(b).

Most states, however, have no legislation directly on point. In those states, the analysis of informed consent allegations in telemedicine cases will probably proceed along lines pertinent to informed consent generally.

The requirement to obtain informed consent derives from the unremarkable proposition that each of us is entitled to control what is to happen to his own body. Legal recognition of this principle has been black letter American law for at least a century. See *Schloendorff v. Society of New York Hospital*, 211 N.Y. 125, 105 N.E. 92 (1914). Although traditionally most closely linked to invasive procedures, in principle informed consent covers substantially everything a provider does for and with a patient, even if the body is not invaded at all.

The states follow one of three general approaches to the standard of care for obtaining consent. The approach most favorable to the provider is to require him to disclose only that information which reasonably prudent practitioners in the same field would reveal in similar circumstances. Considerably less provider-friendly is a requirement to reveal that which a reasonable person in the patient's shoes would want to know. The harshest standard, fortunately limited to only a couple of outlier states, is to demand that the professional reveal whatever this particular patient claims he wanted to know. In case of a dispute, it would not require an especially active imagination to anticipate that the patient's description of his desire for information as expressed to his clinician at the time of care, and his description of those wishes to a jury some years later, may or may not be the same.

Assuming the plaintiff patient can prove that the provider failed to divulge information obligatory under the standard of care, he must next show what the consequences were. On this question, states typically ask one of two questions: (1) what would a reasonable patient have done had she been advised of the allegedly omitted information? or (2) what would this particular patient have done had she been advised of the allegedly omitted information? This second formulation is vulnerable to the same manipulation as is the third iteration of the consent standard of care above.

In the absence of much case law to guide us, the best course for a telemental health professional to follow is to advise the client/patient that distance care may entail not only all the risks of in-person care but also those peculiar to distance care, such as power interruption. One risk to mention is that, since telehealth is still fairly new, practitioners may not even know of all the risks that patients might be exposed to.

Professional Liability

Malpractice is a form of negligence and thus a type of tort. A tort is a civil wrong. It is distinguished from a crime (an offense against the state) and a breach of contract (a failure to fulfill obligations voluntarily assumed). Professional liability in tort arises not because the practitioner committed a crime, nor because he broke his word, but because the patient was harmed because the professional failed to do as a reasonably prudent practitioner in his field would have done in similar circumstances at the time the case arose. Professional liability claims are numerous. Probably because telemedicine still has but limited market penetration, few reported cases describe claims against professionals providing this service. The plaintiffs' bar, however, is wily and persistent. Some of their number are trolling the Internet, advertising for patients, just as they do for individuals asserting asbestos claims or those hurt in auto accidents. It is naïve to imagine that distance care will be spared.

Jurisdiction

In all litigation, a fundamental issue is whether the court where the matter was brought has legal authority to entertain the claim. If it does not, it should dismiss the case for want of jurisdiction: the court lacks power to rule. The claim may be valid, but it has to be heard, if at all, somewhere else.

Historically, in malpractice litigation, jurisdiction was usually not a major issue. Doctor and patient were typically citizens of the same jurisdiction, and since malpractice cases are heard where the tort was committed, the local court typically had jurisdiction. In telehealth, of course, therapist and patient need not be in the same jurisdiction. In fact, they need not even necessarily be in the same country. Whether a court has jurisdiction, then, depends on where, in contemplation of law, the tort was committed. In the current state of the law, when clinician and patient are not in the same jurisdiction, there is no definitive answer. The conclusion most commonly reached is that the tort occurred where the patient is, so jurisdiction lies in that jurisdiction. In some states, this principle has been established as a matter of law, e.g., 225 Ill. Stat. 60/49.5 (an out-of-state physician "providing a service … to a patient residing in Illinois through the practice of telemedicine submits himself or herself to the jurisdiction of the courts of this state." Id. at 60/49.5(e)); http://www.ilga.gov/legislation/ilcs/fulltext.asp?DocName=022500600K49.5 (*Accord*, Ga. Code Ann. 43-34-31). Some have argued for the opposite conclusion, however. Since a clear answer is not yet established, it is probably best to (1) assume a case would be heard in the patient's jurisdiction and (2) comply insofar as possible with the laws of both jurisdictions.

Creating the Relationship

The first leg of the analysis needed to assess a possible malpractice claim is whether the defendant owes the plaintiff a duty. If no duty exists, there can be no breach of duty; where there is no breach, there is no case. Whether a physician–patient relationship exists is a question of law for the court (*Reynolds v. Decatur Mem'l Hosp.*, 660 N.E.2d 235, 238 (Ill. App. 1996), citing *Kirk. v. Michael Reese Hosp. & Med. Ctr.*, 513 N.E.2d 387 (Ill. 1987) but see, Mackey v. Sarroca, 35 NE 3d 631 Ill. Ct. App. 2015, (duty arises only when physician-patient relationship has been expressly established or there is a special relationship such as when one physician asks another to provide a service to the patient).

Determining whether a duty exists is ordinarily very straightforward: If X is Y's therapist, X owes Y a duty. To some extent, however, the analysis can be more complex when professional and patient are not in the same room. Physical contact between doctor and patient is not necessary to create a doctor–patient relationship (*Bovara v. St. Francis Hosp.*, 298 Ill. App. 3d 1025, 700 N.E.2d 143, 147, 233 Ill. Dec. 42 (1988) (determining which patients were angioplasty candidates)). But see *Adams v. Via Christi Reg'l Med. Ctr.*, 270 Kan. 824, 835 (2001) (no relationship arises until doctor undertakes some affirmative action). A telephone call may suffice to form a doctor–patient relationship (*Reynolds v. Decatur Mem'l Hosp., supra; Bienz v. Central Suffolk Hospital*, 163 A.D. 2d 269. 270, 557 N.Y.S.2d 139, 140 (2d Dep't 1990)). In fact, such a relationship can arise even where the physician and patient have not spoken with each other (*Kelley v. Middle Tennessee Emergency Physicians, P.C.*, 133 S.W.3d 587, 596, 2004 Tenn. LEXIS 333 (Tenn. 2004)) (whether a physician–patient relationship arose between covering cardiologist consulted by phone about a patient he never saw, nor was ever asked to see, was a question of fact for the jury).

Nonmedical advice to a patient's provider creates no professional relationship between the provider's adviser and the patient. A licensed clinical social worker whose practice employs a life coach does not assume a provider–patient relationship with the coach's client by advising the coach to report suspected child abuse; doing so is "giving non-medical professional advice" to the coach. The same is true of a psychiatrist employed by the same practice and giving similar advice to the same coach (*Wolf v. Fauquier County Bd. of Supervisors*, 555 F.3d 311, 321, 2009 US App. LEXIS 2256 (4th Cir. 2009)).

In the current state of the law, what is needed to establish a duty in a telehealth context is thus not always clear, especially in jurisdictions that require a physical exam to create a doctor–patient relationship. In the right circumstances, a physician defendant may deny that between himself and the plaintiff, any doctor–patient relationship even existed, since prevailing on that theory would defeat the claim. In telemental health, however, such a defense will probably be more difficult to mount, because the physical separation between treater and patient is of less consequence.

The Standard of Care

Assuming a duty exists, the question then becomes whether that duty was breached. To answer, the finder of fact must determine what the standard of care is in the circumstances and whether the defendant did or did not comply therewith. The standard of care in telemedical malpractice is often said to be that which obtains in conventional, in-person care. See, e.g., Fed'n State Med. Bds., Model Policy for the Appropriate Use of Telemedicine Technologies in the Practice of Medicine (2014) (http://www.fsmb.org/pdf/FSMB_Telemedicine_Policy.pdf). In some jurisdictions, that principle is enshrined in law. See, e.g., Haw. Rev. Stat. § 453-1.3(d) (Supp. 2012). As with so many other issues in telemedical malpractice, however, few if any courts have actually addressed the issue. See *Roush v. Southern Arizona Ear, Nose & Throat*, 2CA-CV 2008-0049, Unpub. LEXIS 1167 (Ariz. App. Div. 2, 2009) (in defamation claim arising from defendant's statement that plaintiff's supposed ear problem was "all in his head," ENT providing telemedicine services to inmate was entitled to summary judgment). For an argument that, where "telemedical procedure and traditional-medical procedures are distinctive" and not, as with teleradiology, substantially identical, "the standard of care for telephysicians should be higher than the applicable standard for traditional physicians"; see Lisa Rannefeld, "The Doctor Will E-Mail You Now: Physicians' Use of Telemedicine to Treat Patients Over the Internet," 19 *J.L. & Health* 75, 100 (2004/05).

The genius of the common law is its ability to adapt to change. In most states, the standard of care is time-sensitive. One is judged by how one's peers would act under similar circumstances at the time the case arose. See, e.g., Va. Code Ann. § 8.01-581.20; N.C. Gen. Stat. 90-21.12.[2] On occasion, a failure to adopt new approaches

---

[2] For a discussion of pertinent case law, see Carter L. Williams, "Evidence-Based Medicine in the Law Beyond Clinical Practice Guidelines: What Effect will EBM Have on the Standard of Care?" 61 *Wash. & Lee L. Rev.* 479, 508–12 (2004).

can be a breach, even where the care complained of comports with prevailing professional practice (*Helling v. Carey*, 519 P.2d 981, 985 (Wash. 1974) (ophthalmologist held liable for failing to diagnose glaucoma in young patient even though reasonably prudent ophthalmologists did not test for it then); *Washington v. Wash. Hosp. Ctr.*, 579 A.2d 177, 180 (D.C. Cir. 1990) (hospital held liable for failing to use continuous oximetry during anesthesia); *Nowatske v. Osterloh*, 543 N.W.2d 265, 272 (Wis. 1996); *Burton v. Brooklyn Doctors Hosp.* 452 (N.Y.S.2d 875 (N.Y. App. Div. 1982)).

An issue that providers, and eventually juries, will nonetheless need to consider is whether and to what extent a professional could be held liable for <u>failing</u> to utilize distance care technologies. The best case for such a theory may be in telestroke. Given the impressive therapeutic benefit of consulting distant specialists via technology, now rather well recognized, it would not be surprising to see a claim brought by or on behalf of an ischemic stroke patient denied thrombolytics based on the theory that had the clinician sought a telestroke consult, a diagnosis could have been timely made and paved the way to treatment. There do not yet appear to be any plainly analogous circumstances in telemental health, but as distance care services become more widely available to emergency departments, for example, that might change. See Patricia Kuszler, "Telemedicine & Integrated Healthcare Delivery: Compounding Malpractice Liability," 25 *Am. J.L. & Med.* 297, 316 (1999) (hereinafter "Kuszler"); Angela Holder, "Failure to 'Keep Up' as Negligence," 224 *JAMA* 1461, 1462 (1973). See also Donald E. Kacman, "The Impact of Computerized Medical Literature Databases on Medical Malpractice Litigation: Time for Another *Helling v. Carey* Wake-Up Call?" 50 *Ohio St. L. J.* 617, 621 (1997).

Insurance

Given the risks inherent in all forms of healthcare and given in particular our country's obsession with litigation, clinicians need insurance coverage to avoid, or at least reduce the risk of, financial ruin. Most malpractice insurance policies, however, cover care provided by the insured within the state where he is licensed to practice only (Medical Malpractice and Liability, Telehealth Resource Centers, http://www.telehealthresourcecenter.org/toolbox-module/medical-malpractice-and-liability). Before offering distance care services, clinicians need to determine whether they are adequately protected.

Some carriers decline coverage altogether for telehealth care (S.N. Singh and R.M. Wachta, "Perspectives on Medical Outsourcing and Telemedicine: Rough Edges in a Flat World?" 358 (15) *New Engl. J. Med.* 1622, 1625 (2008); Kip Poe, "Telemedicine Liability: Texas & Other State Delve into the Uncertainties of Healthcare Delivery via Advanced Communications Technology," 20 *Rev. Litig.* 681, 698 (2001)). Besides identified risks for which there is relatively little experience on which to base underwriting judgments, there may be risks thus far not identified. Carriers may have particular difficulty in assessing risk of suit in locales distant from the insured's. See Robert F. Pendrak and R. Peter Ericson, "Telemedicine May Spawn Long-Distance Lawsuits," *Nat'l. Underwriter*, Nov. 4, 1996, at 44. There is a possibility that litigation would entail product liability claims in addition to conventional professional negligence claims; that would tend to both complicate the litigation and increase the stakes. If, for example, a defect were alleged in a medical imaging device, its manufacturer or distributor or both could be codefendants. See, e.g., Fran O'Connell, "Telemedicine Creates New Dimensions of Risks," *Nat'l. Underwriter*, 18 September 1995, at 44; J.P. McMenamin, "Does Product Liability Litigation Threaten Picture Archiving and Communication Systems and/or Telemedicine?" 11 (1) *J. Dig. Imaging* 21–32 (1998). That risk may be relatively unlikely, however (Robert F. Pendrak and R. Peter Ericson, "Telemedicine May Soon Spawn Long-Distance Lawsuits," *National Underwriter Life & Health Financial Services Edition*, Nov. 4, 1996, at *4).

These problems do not mean that insurance is unavailable. They do suggest that for the telemental health professional, a careful, prepurchase examination of any proposed policy is in order. The best course is to obtain in writing the carrier's representation that, up to the policy limits, it will insure the provider not only for in-person care but for distance care as well.

Malpractice Claims in Telemental Health: What Lies Ahead?

It's hard to make predictions, especially about the future.

—Yogi Berra[3]

For the most part, malpractice claims in a telehealth setting will probably mirror those asserted in ordinary, in-person care. After all, telehealth is not a specialty; it is simply another way for professionals to provide their services. In most branches of medicine, we might expect to see a somewhat higher prevalence of failure-to-diagnose claims, since even with high-resolution video and peripherals, the technology does tend to limit the scope of physical examination. In mental healthcare, however, physical examination is less central to diagnosis, and so such an increase might be less likely there. Similarly, highly visual specialties, such as radiology and pathology, labor at no particular disadvantage whether examining images or microscope slides inches away or miles away. One aspect of distance care that might be relatively telehealth-specific, admittedly, is liability associated with technology failures (Kuszler, supra, 25 *Am. J.L. & Med.* at 317–18 (1999)).

The current emphasis on apologies will probably continue. See, e.g., Joe Cantlupe, "Doctors: 'I'm Sorry' Doesn't Mean 'I'm Liable'" (2011) (http://www.healthleadersmedia.com/page-1/PHY-265488/Doctors-Im-Sorry-Doesnt-Mean--Im-Liable##). The first time a plaintiffs' lawyer manages to get such an apology

---

[3] Spoilsport scholars actually attribute this bit of wisdom to an unknown Dane (http://quote investigator.com/2013/10/20/no-predict/). Pshaw.

admitted into evidence—and that will happen in due course—growth of this phenomenon will be checked temporarily. It will resume, however, as soon as carriers recognize that the occasional disaster is offset by consistent savings.

The current push to publish practice guidelines, both in distance care and in in-person care, will probably also continue. Texas, for example, has codified guidelines into regulations. See 22 Tex. Admin. Code §§ 174.1–.12. Most states have not gone that far, but more and more organizations are publishing guidelines for use by practitioners generally and distance care practitioners specifically. In May 2013, ATA published its *Practice Guidelines for Video-Based Online Mental Health Services* (http://www.americantelemed.org/docs/default-source/standards/practice-guidelines-for-video-based-online-mental-health-services.pdf?sfvrsn=6). In July 2013, the American Psychological Association (APA) published an extensive bibliography on *Standards and Guidelines Relevant to Telemental Health*, prepared by Kenneth Drude, PhD (http://www.apadivisions.org/division-31/news-events/blog/health-care/standards-telehealth.pdf).[4] Evidence-based guidelines for clinical practice are gaining increasing legal recognition. See Agency for Healthcare Research & Quality, The National Guideline Clearinghouse (http://www.guideline.gov). For a discussion of the place of clinical guidelines in medicine, see Institute of Medicine, *Leadership by Example* (2004). The IOM has taken the position that a provider's compliance with clinical guidelines is the best indicator of quality care (Institute of Medicine, *Patient Safety: Achieving a New Standard of Care*, (2004) at 5–6).

Guidelines such as these are intended to improve the quality of care, introduce a measure of standardization, and decrease liability exposure. Though the sincerity and expertise of the developers are clear, and while there is some merit in each of these objectives, a contrarian viewpoint deserves to be aired.

First, human biology is almost infinitely variable. The wisest of graybeards, with limitless resources and the best of intentions, would have difficulty developing guidelines that could cover every clinical situation and that could be applied to all comers in all circumstances. Second, lawyers are in the word business. They are trained to scrutinize words, phrases, and sentences to spot ambiguities, inconsistencies, and weaknesses. Over time, they become proficient in these skills and can use even carefully crafted language against its author. Finally, like textbooks, guidelines can become obsolete rapidly. It takes time to assemble the author team, it takes time to debate and write the guidelines, and, even in the Internet age, it takes still more time to edit and publish them. During all that time, new discoveries are being made, new papers are being published, and new approaches to management of clinical problems are getting developed. The guideline writers are necessarily shooting at a moving target.

---

[4] In April 2012, the American Psychiatric Association recommended that the VA's Office of Mental Health Services (OMHS) "work more closely with VA's Office of Rural Health (ORH) on best practices in meeting the mental health needs of rural veterans and in hiring and retaining rural psychiatrists and expanding telepsychiatry."

In an effort, perhaps, to cope with clinical complexity, multiple guidelines may be available for a given condition or procedure. See Lori Rinella, "The Use of Medical Practice Guidelines in Medical Malpractice Litigation – Should Practice Guidelines Define the Standard of Care?" 64 *UMKC L. Rev.* 337, 353 (1995); Troyen Brennen, "Practice Guidelines and Malpractice Litigation: Collision or Cohesion?" 16 *J. Health Polit. Policy Law* 67–85 (1991). The effort to accommodate the variations inherent in human biology tends to diminish the ability of guidelines to create bright-line tests of compliance or noncompliance with the standard of care. Moreover, for some guidelines, there is little or no scientific foundation (Rinella at 354). It would be ironic indeed if, in this *Daubert*[5] era, advocates for the health professions or for tort reform more generally relied upon guidelines tending to defeat the courts' relatively new and highly welcome effort to police the effort to pass off junk science for the genuine article.

There is good reason to doubt that practice parameters will diminish the prevalence of substandard care and defensive medicine (D. Garnick, A. Hendricks, and T. Brelinan, "Can Practice Guidelines Reduce the Number and Costs of Malpractice Claims?" 266 *JAMA* 2856 (1991)). Guidelines cannot replace medical judgment; hence, they may provide a feeble defense. And, of course, plaintiffs may be able to use them to advantage. See Michelle M. Mello, "Of Swords and Shields: The Role of Clinical Practice Guidelines in Medical Malpractice Litigation," 149 *U. Pa. L. Rev.* 645 (2001) (arguing against the use of guidelines because, inter alia, they are not in fact generally followed in actual practice). To the extent guidelines are drafted to control costs of care, for example (see, e.g., C. Havinghurst, "Practice Guideline for Medical Care: The Policy Rationale," 34 *St. Louis Univ. L. Rev.* 777 (1990)), plaintiffs will attack their use and, more importantly, will sing the familiar strains of their favorite hymn (*Profits Over People*). Moreover, the finder of fact typically remains at liberty to consider other evidence and to reject practice parameters as establishing the standard of care (Edward Hirshfeld, "Should Practice Parameters be the Standard of Care in Malpractice Litigation?" 266 *JAMA* 2886 (1991) (arguing against national implementation of guidelines to set the standard of care)).

The faith that guidelines will provide the shield needed to protect providers from the slings and arrows of outrageous lawsuits may be misplaced. According to Hyams et al., "Practice guidelines and malpractice litigation: A 2-way street," 122 *Ann. Int. Med.* 450–55 (1995), clinical practice guidelines are used in an inculpatory fashion twice as often as they are used to exculpate (54% v. 23%). See also Mehlman, M.J., "Medical Practice Guidelines as Malpractice Safe Harbors: Illusion or Deceit?" 40 *J.L. Med. & Ethics* 286 (2012). When guidelines are used to exonerate the defendant provider, however, the evidentiary value was usually sufficient for dismissal.

Hence, guidelines ought not be rejected out of hand. But they need to be developed with the clear understanding that the adversaries of healthcare professionals will attempt to use them not as shields but as swords. At times, they will succeed.

---

[5] *Daubert v. Merrell Dow Pharmaceuticals*, 509 U.S. 579 (1993), a case restricting what expert testimony will be accepted into evidence in federal and some state courts.

Clinicians should not assume that good faith efforts to comply, nor even slavish adherence to the very best of guidelines, will prevent claims, or even successful claims.

Reimbursement

Reimbursement for distance care remains limited. The government fears overutilization and so has imposed severe restrictions on its reimbursement for telehealth of all kinds. Historically, private carriers have generally followed in the footsteps of CMS, but in recent years increasing number of commercial carriers have begun offering coverage when Medicare does not.

There has been considerable, if gradual, liberalization of reimbursement rules, and that is likely to continue and probably to accelerate. First, although telemedicine was not initiated to further the ACA goal of expanded emphasis on outpatient care, it is nonetheless beautifully designed for that purpose. If we are serious about saving costs by decreasing our reliance on inpatient management, and institutionalized care, then we will need to provide enhanced communication between providers and patients. In a lot of ways, telemedicine is simply a communications mechanism. Second, popular demand will require expansion of telemedical services. We use the Internet to chat, buy and read books, secure hotel and travel reservations, watch movies, order dinner, and purchase medications, among numerous other functions. We will demand healthcare services in the same way, and Medicare will eventually pay for it. Third, reimbursement is apt to increase as we continue to wander farther from fee-for-service care.

In certain circumstances, Medicare does pay for telemental health services now. The patient must reside in a designated rural health professional shortage area or in a county outside of a metropolitan statistical area. Except in federal pilot programs in Hawaii and Alaska, the patient must be located at a healthcare facility, such as a community mental health center, and engage in real-time, interactive communication with his provider. Under current law, distance care of a patient at home generally cannot be reimbursed. Nor is store-and-forward technology a covered service. The practitioner, however, is eligible for reimbursement irrespective of his location. Not every type of provider is eligible for reimbursement, though most are, including psychologists (42 C.F.R. §410.78).

Several new developments have expanded the opportunities for Medicare reimbursement: a modification of "regulations describing eligible telehealth originating sites to include health professional shortage areas (HPSAs) located in rural census tracts of metropolitan statistical areas" and the addition of two new codes. Codes 99495 and 99496 are used to report transitional care management (TCM) services. Code 99490 is used to report care coordination services, and all of these, subject to various limitations, can be reimbursed when provided at a distance. For a description of Medicare's approach, see http://www.cms.gov/Outreach-and-Education/Medicare-Learning-Network-MLN/MLNMattersArticles/Downloads/MM8553.pdf.

The commentary sheds some additional light on the meanings of these Codes:

- CPT Code 99495

  - Transitional care management services with the following required elements: Communication (direct contact, telephone, electronic) with the patient and/or caregiver within 2 business days of discharge
  - Medical decision making of at least moderate complexity during the service period
  - A face-to-face visit, within 14 calendar days of discharge

- CPT Code 99496

  - Transitional care management services with the following required elements: Communication (direct contact, telephone, electronic) with the patient and/or caregiver within 2 business days of discharge
  - Medical decision making of high complexity during the service period
  - A face-to-face visit, within 7 calendar days of discharge

Transitional care management, then, means one in-person visit within a specified period post-discharge, in combination with services not in person that may be performed by the physician or other qualified healthcare professional and/or licensed clinical staff under his direction.

In 2013, CMS modified the definition of "rural" under Section 332(a)(1)(A) of the Public Health Service Act (PHSA). Originally, CMS interpreted "rural" under Section 1834(m)(4)(C)(i)(I) of the PHSA to mean "an area that is not located within a metropolitan statistical area (MSA)." Its final rule modified the definition of "rural" to include "geographic areas located in rural census tracts within MSAs." As ATA puts it, the government is thus beginning to pay for telehealth at "the fringes of metropolitan areas." CMS is also adding coverage (CPT codes 99495 and 99496) for patient–physician communications in transitional care management and chronic care and is slightly increasing telehealth reimbursement for physicians from $24.43 to $24.63, up from $20 in 2011. "Transitional care management services" can be reimbursed for those "whose medical and/or psychosocial problems require moderate or high complexity medical decision making during transitions in care from an inpatient hospital setting (including acute hospital, rehabilitation hospital, long-term acute care hospital), partial hospitalization, observation status in a hospital, or skilled nursing facility/nursing facility, to the patient's community setting (home, domiciliary, rest home, or assisted living)."

The emphasis on rural care creates a need to determine what geographic regions qualify. Population growth and demographic shifts can render any given determination obsolete. Providers need to check demographic data periodically. CMS is developing an online rural HPSA analyzer and will announce its availability on the CMS Medicare telehealth web page. See http://www.ers.usda.gov/data-products/rural-urban-commuting-area-codes.aspx#.UdxUEUHVDw9. To avoid mid-year interruptions, CMS will make the determinations on 31 December of the prior year.

On Jan. 1, 2015, the Medicare program began making payments under CPT code 99490 for management and care coordination services provided virtually rather than in-person. Under the rule, providers managing patients with chronic illness may delegate part of the work to nurses. CMS will allow providers to count the time they spend reviewing data towards the 20-minute monthly minimum time required to bill the chronic care management code. Reimbursement is available for service rendered to patients in their homes, a first under the program On April 11, 2016. CMS announced its comprehensive Primary Care Plus (CPC+) model, expanding opportunities for reimbursement through a policy that more nearly approximates capitations. As is true with the chronic care management scheme, CPC+ imposes new and significant burdens on providers, but provides an opportunity to expand distance care service. The probability is good that further liberalization of coverage and payment will gradually increase over time.

Another advance toward broader reimbursement is found in the 2014 National Defense Authorization Act (https://www.govtrack.us/congress/bills/113/hr1960/text). Under section 704, service members transitioning to civilian life are eligible to receive 180 days of health insurance coverage for services provided through telehealth.

The Mental Health Parity and Addiction Equity Act, Pub.L. 110–343, 122 Stat. 376, is also pertinent here. Although not specific to distance care, the Departments of HHS, Labor, and Treasury jointly issued a final rule implementing the Paul Wellstone and Pete Domenici Mental Health Parity and Addiction Equity Act (MHPAEA) in November 2013. See https://www.federalregister.gov/articles/2013/11/13/2013-27086/final-rules-under-the-paul-wellstone-and-pete-domenici-mental-health-parity-and-addiction-equity-act. The MHPAEA prohibits group health plans and health insurers from imposing financial requirements such as co-pays, deductibles, and treatment limitations applicable to mental health and substance use disorder benefits that are more restrictive than the limitations applied to medical and surgical benefits.

State Approaches to Reimbursement

At least 48 state Medicaid programs, and the District of Columbia reimburse in some form for telemedicine, though no two state laws are alike and reimbursement policies vary considerably, because each state sets its own. Center for Connected Health Policy, "Telehealth Medicaid and State Policy (2015), cchpca.org. The only states that at this writing *do not* cover telemedicine under Medicaid are Connecticut and Rhode Island. AJA," State Telemedicine Gaps Analysis: Coverage and Reimbursement (May, 2015).

Effective 1 October 2013, Texas Medicaid approved procedure code 99090 for deploying vital sign monitors into the home for a reimbursement of $50. Using this code with modifier GQ yields $9.45 a day for patient monitoring. Physicians also receive new reimbursement under code 99444. This new code pays $57.20, to review the patient's vitals once every 7 days. None of this is directly relevant to reimbursement for telemental health services. It may presage, however, a new willingness to acknowledge the value of distance care. If so, reimbursement may become more widely available in future.

A development in recent years that continues to show signs of vitality is the movement toward telehealth parity. As of this writing, some 29 states have enacted legislation providing that, when a carrier reimburses for a service done in-person, it must also reimburse when that same service is provided remotely. See Brian Dolan, "Delaware's telehealth parity bill becomes law as Congress re-floats nationwide version," *MobiHealth News* (8 July 2015), http://mobihealthnews.com/45124/delawares-telehealth-parity-bill-becomes-law-as-congress-re-floats-nationwide--version/. These states include Arizona (partial), California, Colorado (partial), Delaware, the District of Columbia, Georgia, Hawaii, Indiana, Kentucky, Louisiana, Maine, Maryland, Massachusetts, Michigan, Minnesota, Mississippi, Missouri, Montana, Nevada, New Mexico, New Hampshire, New Mexico, New York, Oklahoma, Oregon, Tennessee, Texas, Vermont, and Virginia.

The likelihood seems good that, over time, both public and private reimbursement for telehealth services will grow more generous. At the same time, the cost of connectivity may well fall. Once the financial barriers are lowered, or perhaps overcome entirely, the benefits of distance care will become both more widespread and more obvious.

Chapter 3
Technology: Revolutionizing the Delivery of Health Behavior Change Interventions with Integrated Care

Stephen O. Agboola and Kamal Jethwani

Introduction to Integrated Care

In 2005, estimates suggest that 50 % of United States (US) adults have at least one form of chronic disease (Centers for Disease Control & Prevention, 2014), of which the leading causes are cardiovascular disease, cancer, obesity, arthritis, and chronic pulmonary obstructive disease. Chronic diseases account for 70 % of deaths in the USA; about one-fourth of people affected have one or more daily activity limitations and cost the economy about $1.3 trillion annually (Centers for Disease Control & Prevention, 2014; DeVol & Bedroussian, 2007; Anderson, 2004). Although most of these diseases are preventable, yet their incidence is rising. This is attributable to interplay between genetic predisposition and modifiable behaviors like physical inactivity, poor diet, excessive alcohol consumption, and smoking (Centers for Disease Control & Prevention, 2014). These behaviors constitute a health risk and pose significant public health threat in today's society. Worldwide, overweight and obesity, due to energy imbalance in the amounts consumed in the diet and expenditure in daily activity, are leading risks for morbidity and mortality. According to the World Health Organization (WHO), obesity rates have more than doubled since 1980 (WHO, 2014). However, there is overwhelming evidence that demonstrates that behavior modification significantly reduces risks, morbidity, and mortality

S.O. Agboola, M.D., M.P.H. (✉) • K. Jethwani, M.D., M.P.H.
Partners Connected Health, 25 New Chardon St., Suite 300, Boston, MA, USA

Massachusetts General Hospital, Boston, MA, USA

Harvard Medical School, Boston, MA, USA
e-mail: sagboola@mgh.harvard.edu

© Springer International Publishing Switzerland 2017
M.M. Maheu et al. (eds.), *Career Paths in Telemental Health*,
DOI 10.1007/978-3-319-23736-7_3

associated with chronic diseases. For example, within 2–5 years of smoking cessation, the risk of stroke reduces to the same as that of a nonsmoker, and the risk for lung cancer decreases by 50 % within ten years of quitting (Ambrose & Barua, 2004). Similarly, weight loss is associated with significant reductions in blood pressure (Harsha & Bray, 2008).

The rise in chronic disease burden, coupled with population growth and aging, imposes a great strain on the healthcare system and has led to a disequilibrium in the demand and supply of healthcare services. In the USA, for example, it is estimated that 52,000 additional primary care physicians (PCPs) will be needed to meet increased demands by 2025 (Petterson et al., 2012). This shortage of PCPs may even be further pronounced with the recent healthcare reforms implemented to increase national access to care. As a result, innovative care delivery models that can increase access to high-quality, cost-effective care are being implemented.

Currently, the timely and exponential growth of technological innovations is proving to be a key factor in revolutionizing healthcare delivery. For example, it is estimated that by the end of 2014, mobile phone subscriptions will reach about seven billion worldwide, i.e., about 96 % penetration rate (International Telecommunication Union, 2014). Therefore, this near global ubiquity of mobile phones coupled with the low cost of text messaging and ease of scalability makes it logical that a huge majority of healthcare interventions are being delivered via telephones and other connected technologies. Thus far, integrated care results have been promising; and interest is growing among patients, providers, payers, policy makers, and in academia on the use of connected technologies in healthcare.

Terminologies for Technology-Based Health Interventions

A number of terminologies have been used to describe technology-based health interventions. According to the American Telemedicine Association, telemedicine refers to *the use of medical information exchanged from one site to another via electronic communications to improve a patient's clinical health status*, whereas telehealth refers to *a broader definition of remote healthcare that does not always involve clinical services*, but they are often used interchangeably (American Telemedicine Association, 2014). Another broad terminology used is eHealth which refers "to health services and information delivered or enhanced through the Internet and related technologies" (Eysenbach, 2001). On the other hand, mobile health (mHealth) is a more recent and more specific term describing interventions delivered via mobile technologies, i.e., "wireless devices and sensors (including mobile phones) that are intended to be worn, carried, or accessed by the person during normal daily activities" (Kumar et al., 2013). Finally, a broader, more encompassing terminology for all these family of technology-based interventions is Connected

Health for which Caulfield et al. proposed a definition. They defined Connected Health as encompassing *terms such as wireless, digital, electronic, mobile, and tele-health and refers to a conceptual model for health management where devices, services or interventions are designed around the patient's needs, and health related data is shared, in such a way that the patient can receive care in the most proactive and efficient manner possible. All stakeholders in the process are 'connected' by means of timely sharing and presentation of accurate and pertinent information regarding patient status through smarter use of data, devices, communication platforms and people* (Caulfield & Donnelly, 2013).

Modifiable Risks Behaviors and Health

Health as defined broadly by the WHO is the *state of complete physical, mental and social well-being and not merely the absence of disease or infirmity.* Today, evidence abounds that behavior, which Gochman defined as "something that people do or refrain from doing, although not always consciously or voluntarily" could positively or negatively impact health (Gochman, 1997). He further defined health behaviors as *those personal attributes such as belief, expectations, motives, values, perceptions and other cognitive elements; personality characteristics including affective and emotional states and traits; and overt behavior patterns, actions and habits that relate to health maintenance, to health restoration and to health improvement* (Gochman, 1997).

The impact of five major modifiable health behaviors affecting public health and chronic diseases are described below.

Physical Inactivity

Physical inactivity is one of the two key drivers of the obesity epidemic. Current estimates suggest that more than half (52 %) of US adults do not meet the recommended physical activity levels, and less than 30 % of high school students get at least 60 min of physical activity every day (Centers for Disease Control & Prevention, 2014). However, it is now widely accepted that regular physical activity generally improves the overall quality of life and increases one's chances of living longer. It is estimated that about 7 h of physical activity per week is associated with a 40 % reduction in risk of dying early compared with less than 30 min of physical activity per week (Centers for Disease Control & Prevention, 2014). Other benefits of physical activity include weight control and reduction in risks for cardiovascular diseases, type 2 diabetes, metabolic syndrome, and some cancers (Centers for Disease Control & Prevention, 2014).

Nutrition

Another vitally important driver of the global obesity epidemic is unhealthy diet. Initially considered a problem of developed nations but now many Third World countries are also facing an obesity epidemic in addition to the infectious disease burden resulting in what the WHO calls a "double burden of disease" (WHO, 2014). Nowadays, while there's an increase intake of foods high in calories, saturated fats, sodium, added sugars, and refined grains, there's also been a concomitant decrease in the consumption of fruits and vegetables. For example, it is estimated that 90 % of US adults consume too much salt (Cogswell et al., 2012); and the average person consume 1.1 servings of fruits/day and 1.6 servings of vegetables/day compared to the recommended 5–13 servings of fruits and vegetables/day depending on caloric intake (National Center for Chronic Disease Prevention & Health Promotion, 2013).

Tobacco Use

Globally, tobacco use has a devastating impact on public health. It is the leading cause of preventable deaths, accounting for about six million deaths annually (WHO, 2014). It increases the risk of coronary heart disease and strokes by two fourfold and mortality from chronic obstructive pulmonary diseases by 12- to 13-folds (Centers for Disease Control & Prevention, 2014). It causes lung cancer and increases the risk for cancer in other parts of the body. Sadly, not only smokers are directly affected; the adverse effects of secondhand smoke in nonsmokers are well documented (WHO, 2014). Estimates suggest that about 600,000 nonsmokers die annually as a result of exposure to secondhand smoke (WHO, 2014). In spite of these startling statistics, still, one of five American adults is a current smoker (US Department of Health & Human Services, 2014).

Excessive Alcohol Use

Excessive alcohol use is defined for women as four or more drinks at a single occasion (binge drinking) or ≥ 8 drinks per week (heavy drinking) and for men as five or more drinks at a single occasion or ≥ 15 drinks per week (Centers for Disease Control and Prevention, 2014). US data reports that about 38 million people report binge drinking an average of four times a month (Kanny, Liu, Brewer, & Lu, 2013). Excessive alcohol use is associated with many acute and long-term detrimental health effects and accounts for annual deaths of about 3.3 million globally (World Health Organization, 2014). Short-term health effects include injuries from motor vehicle accidents or violence, alcohol poisoning, risky sexual behaviors, etc, whereas long-term effects include cardiovascular diseases, liver diseases, mental health problems, and some cancers.

Self-Care Practices

While not a health risk behavior per se, self-care behaviors are essential for the management of chronic diseases. This is so because most chronic diseases require a long-term commitment to management protocols which are performed by patients. Therefore, the onus is on patients to participate actively in self-managing the disease. A working group of the WHO defined self-care as "the ability of individuals, families and communities to promote health, prevent disease, and maintain health and to cope with illness and disability with or without the support of a healthcare provider" (World Health Organization, 2009). There is abundant evidence demonstrating that self-care practices are essential to improved outcomes.

Connected Technologies and Lifestyle Modification Interventions

The medical literature is replete with evidence that adopting healthy behaviors can significantly reduce the burden of chronic diseases. Hence, the increasing number of interventions is targeted at lifestyle modification. A number of factors are driving the current proliferation of health behavior change interventions on connected technologies. First is the ubiquity and popularity of modern technologies which make them suitable to deliver these interventions. Interestingly, it is purported that the average person checks their phones about 150 times in a day (Meeker & Wu, 2013). In addition to this is the potential of technology to make care delivery more cost-effective. For example, remote monitoring has been utilized in many disease management programs to replace routine clinic visits to monitor data like blood pressure, blood glucose, international normalized ratio (INR) testing, etc. Also, low-cost interventions like text messaging could be used to deliver more effective bite-size, actionable, and just-in-time education. Another compelling reason for the rapid adoption of technology to deliver care is the capability of these modern technologies to capture a wide variety of time-sensitive personal data, which was hitherto unthought of, with minimal interference with daily life.

Depending on the need, settings, user demographics, and available resources, a number of connected technologies have being used to creatively engage patients to deliver care in a variety of settings. These include but are not limited to desktop and laptop computers, tablets and other personal digital devices, web-based applications, telephones, sensing devices, and personal health technologies. Today, mobile technologies are generally preferred because of their portability and ease of use. The functions commonly used on these devices to deliver various intervention contents include Short Message Service (SMS), Multimedia Messaging Service (MMS), video, automated voice response, software applications, etc. Intervention content could be delivered synchronously (real time) or asynchronously (store and forward). In all, modern technologies offer the potential to improve access to care and deliver more relevant, dynamic, and highly personalized interventions in real time.

Application of Behavior Change Theories/Models in Technology-Based Interventions

Given the proliferation of technology-based lifestyle interventions, it is therefore imperative to implement evidence-based strategies in designing interventions to optimize treatment effects. Previous studies have shown that compared with non-theory-based interventions, theory-based interventions tended to be more effective in changing behaviors as they can allow for tailoring of intervention to the individual due to enhanced engagement (Painter, Borba, Hynes, Mays, & Glanz, 2008). Although some researchers have questioned the effectiveness of these theories (Ogden, 2003), they have however traditionally guided the development and delivery of most health behavior change interventions. The most commonly used of these theories include Social Cognitive Theory, Transtheoretical Model, Theory of Reasoned Action/Planned Behavior, Health Belief Model, and Learning theories.

A review of literature evaluating the use of health behavior models in mobile-based interventions by Riley et al. reported that these theories are inadequately applied in many mobile interventions. While most smoking cessation and weight loss intervention report a theoretical basis—largely Social Cognitive Theory—most of the treatment adherence and disease management studies did not (Riley et al., 2011). While there is evidence that interventions designed based on these theoretical models could better help tailor the intervention to the individual, improve engagement, and enhance treatment effects, some researchers question the suitability of these theories in designing technology-based interventions. This is based on the fact that these theories are more relevant in evaluating static baseline between person factors and may not be suitable for dynamic intraindividual data which are currently being captured by modern technologies (Riley et al., 2011). The volume of data and capability of modern technologies to deliver highly customized real-time and dynamic content add complexity to intervention design for which some of the older models may be inadequate. Therefore, to maximize the potential of modern technologies, Riley et al. recommend more research into developing adaptive behavioral theories that can adequately evaluate the complex time-varying data captured by modern technologies.

An example typifying this challenge, as well as opportunity for development of adaptive behavior change models, is the Text to Move program, a 6-month intervention designed at the Partner Healthcare Center for Connected Health to improve physical activity behaviors in patients with type 2 diabetes (Agboola et al., 2013). The program was based on the Transtheoretical Model and Social Cognitive Theory; it combined physical activity monitoring, captured by wearable activity monitors, with daily tailored text messaging on any regular mobile phone. At baseline, participants were categorized into stages of change based on the Transtheoretical Model. Afterward, participants then received tailored text messages based on this staging, objective physical activity data over the past 24 h, and other prespecified baseline factors for the next one month after enrollment. At the end of each month, specialized algorithms automatically reevaluated participants' stage on the Transtheoretical Model to guide the content of messages that participants received in the succeeding month. Text messages included both one-way and two-way interactive messages to foster engagement; and the content was designed to provide general education about physical activity and diabetes self-management and assess physical health and psychological and motivational states which were in turn used to reengage participants. Compared with usual care controls who receive only the activity monitors, participants who received the intervention were more active and achieved greater weight loss at the end of the six-month program.

Questions remain about the timing and frequency of the reassessments of the stage of behavior change used in the Text to Move program and also about opportunities to prompt participants to engage in physical activity if the activity monitor detects inactivity at times when they are usually active. This could even be more complicated in intervention design for more complex behaviors like smoking or other addictive behaviors that could be triggered by social influences (location, companions, activities, etc.) and physical or psychological states which have daily temporal patterns of variation. The MOMENT intervention designed to reduce marijuana use in youths exemplifies this challenge (Shrier, Rhoads, Burke, Walls, & Blood, 2014). This intervention combined mobile self-monitoring of the desire to use and actual use of marijuana on a personal digital assistant (PDA) with real-time messaging based on responses to preprogrammed promptings to identify momentary contextual factors that trigger use. The feedback to momentary reports contained supportive messages to build self-efficacy to reduce use and prompted them to consider coping strategies in the presence of the reported trigger.

Currently, there are a number of technology-based lifestyle modification interventions that apply behavior change techniques based on these established behavior change theories. However, the techniques applied in these interventions are diverse and are not adequately reported in the literature. Abraham and Michie in their seminal work proposed a taxonomy of 26 various behavior change techniques used in behavior modification interventions which was later refined to be more specific and more comprehensive to 40 items in the CALO-RE taxonomy for interventions aimed at increasing physical activity and healthy eating behaviors (Abraham & Michie, 2008; Michie et al., 2011). The top ten most commonly used of these techniques in mHealth technology interventions based on a systematic review by Free et al. are listed in Table 3.1 with definitions and examples of interventions utilizing each technique (Free et al., 2013). While tailoring was included as a technique in the ranking by Free et al., it is excluded from this list based on Michie et al.'s CALO-RE taxonomy argument that tailoring in itself is not a technique but rather a specification of when and how a particular technique is to be applied to individuals or groups of people (Michie et al., 2011).

Table 3.1 Rankings of commonly used behavior change techniques in mHealth behavior change interventions

	Behavior change techniques	Definition	Example of application
1	Provide feedback on performance	Providing data about a participant's recorded behavior or commenting on the person's behavioral performance either in relation to personal set goals or other people's performance	Provided type 2 diabetic patients feedback on their physical activity levels over the previous 24 h via text messaging. Physical activity was monitored objectively captured via sensor-enabled activity monitors (Agboola et al., 2013)
2	Provide information on consequences of behavior in general	Information about the relationship between the behavior and its possible or likely consequences in the general case, usually based on epidemiological data, and not personalized for the individual	Educational information delivered via text messages to improve treatment adherence in adolescents and adults with atopic dermatitis (Pena-Robichaux, Kvedar, & Watson, 2010)
3	Goal setting (behavior)	The person is encouraged to make a behavioral resolution (e.g., take more exercise next week). This is directed toward encouraging people to decide, change, or maintain change	Childhood obesity prevention intervention delivered via handheld computer (PDA) targeting fruits, vegetables, and sugar-sweetened beverage intake and screen time. Participants were prompted real time to set goals related to the target behaviors (Nollen et al., 2014)
4	Prompt self-monitoring of behavior	The person is asked to keep a record of specified behavior(s) as a method for changing behavior	Mobile phone-enabled intervention to reduce youth marijuana use. Participants were prompted 4–6 times per day to report their current desire to use and actual use of marijuana (Shrier et al., 2014)
5	Prompt barrier identification/ problem solving	The person is prompted to think about potential barriers to performing planned behavior and identify the ways of overcoming them	Intervention designed to increase consumption of vegetables and whole grains in healthy adults delivered via a handheld device (i.e., personal digital assistant, PDA). The PDA was programmed to evaluate barriers that make it difficult to eat vegetables and whole grains (Atienza, King, Oliveira, Ahn, & Gardner, 2008)

(continued)

Table 3.1 (continued)

	Behavior change techniques	Definition	Example of application
6	Action planning	This involves detailed planning of what the person will do including, as a minimum, when, in which situation, and/or where to act	Web-based intervention designed to prevent weight gain by inducing small changes in dietary and physical behaviors. Participants were guided to set goals and plan ahead of time where, when, and how to make the behavior change (van Genugten, van Empelen, & Oenema, 2014)
7	Goal setting (outcome)	The person is encouraged to set a general goal that can be achieved by behavioral means but is not defined in terms of behavior (e.g., or lose/ maintain weight), as opposed to a goal based on changing behavior as such engaging in regular physical activity	Android-based smartphone application for weight loss. The app allows users to set a weight loss goal and track daily calorie intake toward achieving the goal (Carter, Burley, Nykjaer, & Cade, 2013)
8	Prompt self-monitoring of behavioral outcome	The person is asked to keep a record of specified measures expected to be influenced by the behavior change, e.g., blood pressure, blood glucose, weight loss, and physical fitness	Mobile phone-based text message and Multimedia Message Service intervention designed to help overweight individuals achieve and maintain weight loss over four months. Participants were instructed to monitor their weight on a weekly basis (Patrick et al., 2009)
9	Provide instruction on how to perform the behavior	This involves telling the person how to perform behavior or preparatory behaviors, either verbally or in written form	Mobile phone text messages to enable smokers to successfully quit smoking. Messages provided information on how to quit smoking and maintain the positive behavior change (Free et al., 2011)
10	Use of follow-up prompts	The intervention components are gradually reduced in intensity, duration, and frequency over time, e.g., letters or telephone calls, instead of face to face and/or provided at longer time intervals	Text message reminders via cell phones for prompting participants to apply sunscreen to reduce the risk of developing skin cancer. An electronic monitoring device was used to capture adherence data in real time (Armstrong et al., 2009)

Emerging Challenges in Practice

While the interest in the use of technology to deliver care is increasing, a number of challenges are emerging in practice. First is the problem of reimbursement for technology-based health services. As of today, there are no comprehensive coverage policies across all payers; and not all technology-based services are covered. Factors used to determine the scope of coverage include location of provider (has to be in a health professional shortage area), type of service (reimbursement covers real time but not store-and-forward consultations), etc. (Telehealth n.d.). Similarly, there is the problem of regulations concerning cross-state practices. Most states require providers to be licensed to practice within a given state which places some practice restriction across state lines (Telehealth n.d.). Another challenge is the logistics of working with multiple data sources. Therefore, systems to aggregate and integrate device data into existing workflows could go a long way in facilitating healthcare provider adoption and engagement. In addition, concerns still remain about maintaining the integrity and confidentiality of personal data. These however could be achieved by strict compliance to the Health Insurance Portability and Accountability Act of 1996 (HIPAA) and by adequate data encryption (Kumar et al., 2013). Finally, there is also the problem of lack of standard data collection procedures and intervention designs. Currently, there are increasing calls to standardize data collection procedures and improve the design and reporting of clinical trials to be able to demonstrate convincing evidence of the effectiveness of technology-based healthcare interventions (Kumar et al., 2013).

References

Abraham, C., & Michie, S. (2008). A taxonomy of behavior change techniques used in interventions. *Health Psychology, 27*(3), 379–387.

Agboola, S. O., Searl, M., Havasy, R., Lopez, L., Kvedar, J. C., & Jethwani, K. (2013). Text to Move (TTM) Study—A randomized controlled trial exploring the effect personalized text messages and physical activity monitoring in T2DM patients. *Journal of Mobile Technology in Medicine, 2*(4S), 8.

Alcohol [Internet]. (2014) Geneva, Switzerland: World Health Organization [updated May; cited October 30, 2014]. Retrieved from http://www.who.int/mediacentre/factsheets/fs349/en/

Alcohol and public health [Internet]. (2014). Atlanta, GA: Centers for Disease Control and Prevention [updated August 19; cited October 30, 2014]. Retrieved from http://www.cdc.gov/alcohol/fact-sheets/alcohol-use.htm

Ambrose, J. A., & Barua, R. S. (2004). The pathophysiology of cigarette smoking and cardiovascular disease: An update. *Journal of the American College of Cardiology, 43*(10), 1731–1737.

Anderson, G. (2004). *Chronic conditions: Making the case for ongoing care*. Baltimore, MD: John Hopkins University.

Armstrong, A. W., Watson, A. J., Makredes, M., Frangos, J. E., Kimball, A. B., & Kvedar, J. C. (2009). Text-message reminders to improve sunscreen use: A randomized, controlled trial using electronic monitoring. *Archives of Dermatology, 145*(11), 1230–1236.

Atienza, A. A., King, A. C., Oliveira, B. M., Ahn, D. K., & Gardner, C. D. (2008). Using hand-held computer technologies to improve dietary intake. *American Journal of Preventive Medicine, 34*(6), 514–518.

Carter, M. C., Burley, V. J., Nykjaer, C., & Cade, J. E. (2013). Adherence to a smartphone application for weight loss compared to website and paper diary: Pilot randomized controlled trial. *Journal of Medical Internet Research, 15*(4), e32.

Caulfield, B. M., & Donnelly, S. C. (2013). What is connected health and why will it change your practice? *QJM, 106*(8), 703–707.

Chronic diseases and health promotion [Internet]. Atlanta, GA: Centers for Disease Control and Prevention; 2014 [updated May 9; cited October 30, 2014]. Retrieved from http://www.cdc. gov/chronicdisease/overview/index.htm

Cogswell ME, Zhang Z, Carriquiry AL, Gunn JP, Kuklina EV, Saydah SH, ..., Moshfegh, A. J. (2012). Sodium and potassium intakes among US adults: NHANES 2003-2008. *The American Journal of Clinical Nutrition, 96*(3), 647–657.

DeVol, R., & Bedroussian, A. (2007). *An Unhealthy America: The economic burden of chronic disease*. Milken Institute (2007) Santa Monica, California [cited October 30, 2014]. Retrieved from http://assets1b.milkeninstitute.org/assets/Publication/ResearchReport/PDF/chronic_disease_report.pdf

Eysenbach, G. (2001). What is e-health? *Journal of Medical Internet Research, 3*(2), E20.

Free, C., Knight, R., Robertson, S., Whittaker, R., Edwards, P., Zhou, W., ... Roberts, I. (2011). Smoking cessation support delivered via mobile phone text messaging (txt2stop): A single-blind, randomized trial. *Lancet, 378*(9785), 49–55.

Free, C., Phillips, G., Galli, L., Watson, L., Felix, L., Edwards, P., ... Haines A. (2013). The effectiveness of mobile-health technology-based health behaviour change or disease management interventions for health care consumers: A systematic review. *PLoS Medicine, 10*(1), e1001362.

Gochman, D. S. (1997). *Handbook of health behavior research I*. New York, NY: Springer.

Harsha, D. W., & Bray, G. A. (2008). Weight loss and blood pressure control (pro). *Hypertension, 51*(6), 1420–1425. discussion 1425.

Kanny, D., Liu, Y., Brewer, R. D., & Lu, H. (2013). Centers for Disease Control and Prevention (CDC) Binge drinking—United States, 2011. *MMWR Surveillance Summaries, 62*(Suppl. 3), 77–80.

Kumar, S., Nilsen, W. J., Abernethy, A., Atienza, A., Patrick, K., Pavel, M., ... Swendeman, D. (2013). Mobile health technology evaluation: The mHealth evidence workshop. *American Journal of Preventive Medicine, 45*(2), 228–236.

Meeker, M., & Wu, L. (2013). *Internet trends 2013*. All things D D11 conference 2013; May 28–30, 2013; California [cited October 30, 2014]. Retrieved from http://www.kpcb.com/insights/2013-internet-trends

Michie, S., Ashford, S., Sniehotta, F. F., Dombrowski, S. U., Bishop, A., & French, D. P. (2011). A refined taxonomy of behaviour change techniques to help people change their physical activity and healthy eating behaviours: The CALO-RE taxonomy. *Psychology & Health, 26*(11), 1479–1498.

National Center for Chronic Disease Prevention and Health Promotion. (2013). *State Indicator report on fruits and vegetables* [cited October 30, 2014]. Retrieved from http://www.cdc.gov/nutrition/downloads/State-Indicator-Report-Fruits-Vegetables-2013.pdf

Nollen, N. L., Mayo, M. S., Carlson, S. E., Rapoff, M. A., Goggin, K. J., & Ellerbeck, E. F. (2014). Mobile technology for obesity prevention: A randomized pilot study in racial- and ethnic-minority girls. *American Journal of Preventive Medicine, 46*(4), 404–408.

Obesity and overweight [Internet]. Geneva, Switzerland: World Health Organization; 2014 [updated August; cited October 30]. Retrieved from http://www.who.int/mediacentre/factsheets/fs311/en/

Ogden, J. (2003). Some problems with social cognition models: A pragmatic and conceptual analysis. *Health Psychology, 22*(4), 424–428.

Painter, J. E., Borba, C. P., Hynes, M., Mays, D., & Glanz, K. (2008). The use of theory in health behavior research from 2000 to 2005: A systematic review. *Annals of Behavioral Medicine, 35*(3), 358–362.

Patrick, K., Raab, F., Adams, M. A., Dillon, L., Zabinski, M., Rock, C. L., ... Norman, G. J. (2009). A text message-based intervention for weight loss: Randomized controlled trial. *Journal of Medical Internet Research, 11*(1), e1.

Pena-Robichaux, V., Kvedar, J. C., & Watson, A. J. (2010). Text messages as a reminder aid and educational tool in adults and adolescents with atopic dermatitis: A pilot study. *Dermatology Research and Practice, 2010,* 6. doi:10.1155/2010/894258. Epub 2010 Sep 1.

Petterson, S. M., Liaw, W. R., Phillips, R. L., Jr., Rabin, D. L., Meyers, D. S., & Bazemore, A. W. (2012). Projecting US primary care physician workforce needs: 2010–2025. *Annals of Family Medicine, 10*(6), 503–509.

Physical activity [Internet]. Atlanta, GA: Centers for Disease Control and Prevention; 2014 [updated July 14; cited October 30, 2014]. Retrieved from http://www.cdc.gov/physicalactivity/

Riley, W. T., Rivera, D. E., Atienza, A. A., Nilsen, W., Allison, S. M., & Mermelstein, R. (2011). Health behavior models in the age of mobile interventions: Are our theories up to the task? *Translational Behavioral Medicine, 1*(1), 53–71.

Shrier, L. A., Rhoads, A., Burke, P., Walls, C., & Blood, E. A. (2014). Real-time, contextual intervention using mobile technology to reduce marijuana use among youth: A pilot study. *Addictive Behaviors, 39*(1), 173–180.

Smoking & tobacco use [Internet]. Atlanta, GA: Centers for Disease Control and Prevention; 2014 [updated February 6; cited October 30, 2014]. Retrieved from http://www.cdc.gov/tobacco/data_statistics/fact_sheets/health_effects/effects_cig_smoking/index.htm

Telehealth [Internet]. (n.d.). Health Resources and Services Administration, U.S. Department of Health and Human Services [cited October 30, 2014]. Retrieved from http://www.hrsa.gov/healthit/toolbox/RuralHealthITtoolbox/Telehealth/

The world in 2014: ICT facts and figures [Internet]. Geneva, Switzerland: International Telecommunication Union; 2014 [cited October 30, 2014]. Retrieved from http://www.itu.int/en/ITU-D/Statistics/Documents/facts/ICTFactsFigures2014-e.pdf

Tobacco [Internet]. Geneva, Switzerland: World Health Organization; 2014 [updated May; cited October 30, 2014]. Retrieved from http://www.who.int/mediacentre/factsheets/fs339/en/

US Department of Health and Human Services. (2014) The health consequences of smoking—50 years of progress: A report of the Surgeon General. Atlanta, GA: US Dept of Health and Human Services, Centers for Disease Control and Prevention [cited October 30, 2014]. Retrieved from http://www.surgeongeneral.gov/library/reports/50-years-of-progress/full-report.pdf

van Genugten, L., van Empelen, P., & Oenema, A. (2014). Intervention use and action planning in a web-based computer-tailored weight management program for overweight adults: Randomized controlled trial. *JMIR Research Protocols, 3*(3), e31.

What is telemedicine? [Internet]. Washington, DC: American Telemedicine Association [cited October 30, 2014]. Retrieved from http://www.americantelemed.org/about-telemedicine/what-is-telemedicine#.VFKcj2fEfe0

World Health Organization. (2009). *Self-care in the context of primary health care Report of the Regional Consultation Bangkok, Thailand, 7–9 January 2009.* India: World Health Organization. Report No.: SEA-HSD-320 [cited October 30, 2014]. Retrieved from http://www.searo.who.int/entity/primary_health_care/documents/sea_hsd_320.pdf?ua=1

Chapter 4
Internet Gaming Disorder and Internet Addiction Disorder: Future Careers in Research, Education, and Treatment

Andrew P. Doan, Kathryn Yung, Paulette Cazares, and Warren P. Klam

"It is easier to build strong children than to repair broken men."—Frederick Douglass

Introduction

Technology and the Internet facilitate robust advances in science, medicine, and business. We estimate that mental health careers involving technology will grow, and the need for mental health professionals who can recognize, assess, and treat disordered behaviors associated with technology use will also increase. There will be opportunities as treatment providers and as educators. Given the vast expansion and accessibility of technology, it is important that mental health professionals study, understand, and when appropriate, apply evidenced-based approaches to increase benefits and reduce risks to their patients. Chapters in this book provide

The views expressed in this article are those of the author(s) and do not necessarily reflect the official policy or position of the Department of the Navy, Department of Defense, or the US government.

A.P. Doan, M.D., Ph.D. (✉)
Department of Ophthalmology, Naval Medical Center San Diego,
Bldg 2, 34800 Bob Wilson Drive, San Diego, CA, USA

Department of Mental Health, Naval Medical Center San Diego, San Diego, CA, USA

Substance Abuse Rehabilitation Program, Naval Medical Center San Diego,
San Diego, CA, USA
e-mail: andy@andrew-doan.com

K. Yung, M.D. • P. Cazares, M.D., M.P.H. • W.P. Klam, M.D.
Department of Mental Health, Naval Medical Center San Diego, San Diego, CA, USA

Substance Abuse Rehabilitation Program, Naval Medical Center San Diego,
San Diego, CA, USA

numerous examples of benefits, of technology in behavioral health careers and to the healthcare delivered to patients. It is our hope that mental health professionals incorporate technology and leverage technology in their careers. Worldwide Internet connectivity provides many advantages to communication, education, and health. The applications of technology and video games have research-proven physical and emotional benefits such as improved vision, increased hand-eye coordination, enhanced mental processing skills, and even development of prosocial skills. Alternatively, instant and constant access to information, gaming, communication, and many other online activities activate brain reward systems and arousal of neuroendocrine systems in the body (Chaput et al., 2011; Hebert, Beland, Dionne-Fournelle, Crete, & Lupien, 2005). Without the proper knowledge of the current research literature on Internet gaming disorder (IGD) and Internet addiction disorder (IAD), the mental health provider may not recognize these problems in their patients and may miss an opportunity to provide services in a rapidly growing field of mental health. As of the publication of this book, both IGD and IAD are not recognized disorders by the *DSM-5*. Therefore, an approach utilizing an established definition of addiction is necessary to inform providers so that they may provide the best care possible for their patients. This chapter will equip scientists and healthcare providers for new career opportunities related to excessive use and abuse of video games, the Internet, and other technological devices that facilitate access to online activities.

With the growing cases of IGD and IAD, consider the following vignette. A mental health provider is evaluating a young man who is sleep deprived and distracted, does not make eye contact, and appears to have a blunted affect. The young man has significant problems with insomnia, and the provider prescribes sleep medication. After several months, the patient shows no change in symptoms, appearing to have sleep medication-resistant insomnia. During a clinic visit, the provider asks about Internet gaming habits, and the patient perks up with excitement, becomes animated, and engages in the discussion. Upon further questioning, the provider discovers that the patient endorses playing 30 to 60 h of Internet gaming a week in addition to maintaining full-time work (Eickhoff et al., 2015).

This vignette is becoming more common in the mental health setting. It is estimated that the average child 8–18 years of age is using a digital screen for entertainment purposes an average of 7 h 38 min daily (KaiserFamilyFoundation, 2010). On the other hand, the benefits of moderate use of video games have been well documented, such as improving hand-eye coordination, facilitating prosocial behaviors, and enhancing emotional stability (Przybylski, 2014). Children that play 1 h or less of video games daily exhibit higher satisfaction with life, prosocial behavior, and lower externalizing and internalizing of problems than children who do not play video games. The opposite was found for children playing 3 h or more daily (Przybylski, 2014). The excessive use of video games is a growing problem and can manifest as severe emotional, social, and mental dysfunction in multiple areas of daily living (Tao et al., 2010). In the areas of IGD and IAD, additional research is necessary. Here we approach IGD and IAD with an addiction model so that healthcare providers are informed and equipped with knowledge to provide the best addiction care possible for their patients who now live in the digital age. Career opportunities in clinical treatment and in research are anticipated in the near future with rich possibilities in many fields, ranging from developmental pediatrics to behavioral addictions to basic neuroscience.

In order to begin treating IGD and IAD, the healthcare professional should have training in behavioral addictions and mental health. It is our goal to provide some educational background; however, it will be likely necessary for the reader to do additional research and perhaps seek additional training. Both IGD and IAD are not yet recognized diagnoses in the current *Diagnostic and Statistical Manual of Mental Disorders* However, we anticipate that the demand for providers in the field of IGD and IAD will grow with time because children and adolescents may be more affected by IGD and IAD than adults, which will in turn create a growing population of patients with impairments that may prevent them from reaching their full human potential. Dr. Donald Hebb, a Canadian neuroscientist, described the basic mechanism for synaptic plasticity in 1949 (Hebb, 1949): a simple phrase that characterizes this mechanism is "neurons that fire together, wire together" (Doidge, 2007). A corollary to this mechanism is "use it or lose it." The brain is organized into numerous cortical columns. These columns change via neuronal plasticity, mediated by immediate early genes (IEGs), such as *c-myc*, *c-fos*, and *c-jun*. These IEGs are transcription factors mediating expression of proteins involved in synaptogenesis and neuronal connections. Repeated behaviors strengthen the neuronal pathways associated with the behaviors, while neuronal pathways associated with less utilized behaviors are not strengthened.

Human beings practice who they want to become, and individuals must be careful what they practice and how they program their brains. When a young child spends too much time in Internet gaming or Internet activities, there can be significant problems. We propose an analogy to clarify how a child's nervous system may develop when exposed to excessive time engaging in Internet gaming or other Internet activities. Observe your left hand. The thumb will represent the cortical areas associated with all the benefits of video gaming and use of technology: quick analytical skills, improved hand-eye coordination, and perhaps improved reflexes. The index finger will represent the cortical areas associated with communication skills. The middle finger will represent behaviors associated with social bonding with family and friends. The ring finger will represent the capacity to recognize emotions of both self and others (empathy). Lastly, the little finger will represent the cortical areas associated with self-control. While these higher executive functions are biologically based, they are not fully expressed without proper practice and feedback. When a child spends on average of 7 h 38 min in front of a digital screen for entertainment, that child is exceeding the recommended daily dosage for healthy screen time (Przybylski, 2014). Folding the fingers into the palm of your hand represents this situation. As the brain matures, the possible end product is a young adult who is *all thumbs* in their thinking: possessing quick analytical skills and quick reflexes, but not as developed in communication skills, having few bonds with people, exhibiting little empathy, and showing minimal self-control.

The term "addictive" is often used colloquially to refer to excessive and impairing focus on what is popular, pleasing, or fun. In spite of the common use of this term for numerous activities, the scientific definition of addictive behaviors focuses on dysfunction associated with excessive use of activities. We present a neuroendocrine model that may explain why behavioral addictions, also referred to as process addictions, become both psychologically and physiologically addicting.

Initially, Dr. Ivan Goldberg coined IAD as a joke in 1995, and to date, IAD is not recognized in the *Diagnostic and Statistical Manual of Mental Disorders* (DSM). Internet gaming disorder is noted in the *DSM-5* as a condition for further study (DSM-5, 2013):

> In the fifth edition of the Diagnostic and Statistical Manual of Mental Disorders (DSM-5), Internet Gaming Disorder is identified in Section III as a condition warranting more clinical research and experience before it might be considered for inclusion in the main book as a formal disorder. The Internet is now an integral, even inescapable, part of many people's daily lives; they turn to it to send messages, read news, conduct business, and much more. But recent scientific reports have begun to focus on the preoccupation some people develop with certain aspects of the Internet, particularly online games. The "gamers" play compulsively, to the exclusion of other interests, and their persistent and recurrent online activity results in clinically significant impairment or distress. People with this condition endanger their academic or job functioning because of the amount of time they spend playing. They experience symptoms of withdrawal when pulled away from gaming. Much of this literature stems from evidence from Asian countries and centers on young males. The studies suggest that when these individuals are engrossed in Internet games, certain pathways in their brains are triggered in the same direct and intense way that a drug addict's brain is affected by a particular substance. The gaming prompts a neurological response that influences feelings of pleasure and reward, and the result, in the extreme, is manifested as addictive behavior. Further research will determine if the same patterns of excessive online gaming are detected using the proposed criteria. At this time, the criteria for this condition are limited to Internet gaming and do not include general use of the Internet, online gambling, or social media. By listing Internet Gaming Disorder in DSM-5 Section III, APA hopes to encourage research to determine whether the condition should be added to the manual as a disorder.

While the *DSM-5* classification of IGD does not include other Internet activities in general, recent work by research teams primarily in China and South Korea and Dr. Young in the United States provides evidence that both IGD and IAD are clinical problems associated with severe emotional, social, and mental dysfunction in multiple areas of daily activities (Fu, Chan, Wong, & Yip, 2010; Tao et al., 2010; Young, 1996, 1999). Research studies have estimated that IAD is growing and affects 1 % of the general population and as much as 4 % of youths exhibiting dysfunction with daily activities associated with Internet use (Rumpf et al., 2013). On the other hand, because diagnostic criteria have not yet been standardized, other studies have shown that IAD rates range from 0.8 % in Italy to 26.7 % in Hong Kong (Kuss, Griffiths, Karila, & Billieux, 2014).

Douglas Gentile at Iowa State University estimates that IGD rates worldwide are about 8.5 % of children and adolescents (D. Gentile, 2009; D. A. Gentile et al., 2011). In the United States, it is estimated that IGD affects about three million children between 8 and 18 years of age. The clinical term "addiction" implies behaviors associated with particular dysfunction in occupational, social, emotional, and physical realms. The desire to continue to engage in the behaviors despite profound negative consequences is a key feature of an addiction. Based on research estimates, there are approximately 300,000 Americans suffering with IGD reaching adulthood annually who exhibit emotional, social, and mental dysfunction associated with their pathological use of video games. With each passing year, the number of individuals with IGD will grow. The medical community will ultimately need to recognize the presence of IGD and IAD. Without intervention and prevention measures, within a decade, over three million people may be suffering from IGD and IAD; this will come with a significant cost in lost productivity and mental health expenses. The cost for residential treatment at a unique IAD rehabilitation program (reSTART) in Fall City, Washington, is more than $20,000 per patient. Rehabilitation for three million people with IAD could potentially be more than a $70 billion problem.

Providers entering this field will find large numbers of patients needing help and will find opportunities to make a significant difference in the quality of patients' lives. Alternatively, without an official *DSM* diagnosis of IGD or IAD, the providers will be limited to cash-paying patients because insurance companies will not reimburse for therapy until there is a reimbursable clinical diagnostic code. In addition, with increasing Internet speeds, accessibility, and mobile computer devices, both IGD and IAD are emerging global problems. Smartphone use is becoming more prevalent as 1.75 billion people are expected to use smartphones in 2014. One out of two people in the United States own a smartphone (Smith, 2013). The accessibility of mobile computing devices has facilitated increasing use of video games and digital screens for entertainment.

Why are IGD and IAD considered addictive disorders? According to the American Society of Addiction Medicine, "Addiction is a primary, chronic disease of brain reward, motivation, memory and related circuitry. Dysfunction in these circuits leads to characteristic biological, psychological, social and spiritual manifestations. This is reflected in an individual pathologically pursuing reward and/or relief by substance use and other behaviors. Addiction is characterized by inability to consistently abstain, impairment in behavioral control, craving, diminished recognition of significant problems with one's behaviors and interpersonal relationships, and a dysfunctional emotional response. Like other chronic diseases, addiction often involves cycles of relapse and remission. Without treatment or engagement in recovery activities, addiction is progressive and can result in disability or premature death" (asam.org, 2011).

Brain reward appears tied to the mesolimbic dopamine pathway with subsequent neuroendocrine arousal and enhanced sympathetic nervous system tone. According to research at Stanford University, the elements that make video games highly attractive and pleasurable include immersive environments, in-game achievements, and social play (Yee, 2006). The commonalities between books and movies stop at immersion in regard to video games. Video games provide achievements and social connections through Internet gameplay. Individuals with IGD exhibit release of prefrontal cortex dopamine in the brain similar to people with substance addictions (Ko, Liu, Yen, Chen, et al., 2013; Ko, Liu, Yen, Yen, et al., 2013). Pleasure and excitement associated with video games involve physiological arousal and stimulation of the hypothalamic-pituitary-adrenal axis, resulting in increased heart rate, blood pressure, and sympathetic tone (Chaput et al., 2011). Video games building on the principles of social interactivity, increased immersion, and seemingly endless achievements are postulated to be neurologically and physiologically arousing. Built-in music adding to the immersive environment of the video game is shown to stimulate the hypothalamic-pituitary-adrenal stress response and release of cortisol (Hebert et al., 2005). Playing the game *Tetris* competitively with human opponents results in higher levels of testosterone in men (Zilioli & Watson, 2012).

Video games have been shown to suppress pain perception in pediatric patients and during routinely painful burn treatments (Das, Grimmer, Sparnon, McRae, & Thomas, 2005; Gold, Kim, Kant, Joseph, & Rizzo, 2006; Haik et al., 2006). Visual distraction and neuroendocrine arousal induced by video games provide plausible explanations for why patients feel less pain during painful medical and burn treatments. Additional research utilizing video games in clinical pain management may provide non-pharmacological alternatives during medical procedures. Determining the *digital potency* of different forms of digital media and video games to reveal their efficacy in reducing pain and stress in patients is another area open for study (Gilman et al., 2015). Clinical applications could range from virtual reality pain control during allergy skin testing, stress and pain control during labor, and pain control after battlefield trauma.

Because video games are stimulating to the brain via the dopaminergic-reward pathways and physiologically arousing through the hypothalamic-pituitary-adrenal axis, video gaming can be abused by those with a propensity for addictive behaviors, emotional dysregulation, and co-occurring mental illness. Individuals with IGD and IAD share behavioral similarities with patients struggling with substance abuse disorders, exhibiting psychological triggers, cravings, and addiction-seeking behaviors (Yung, Eickhoff, Davis, Klam, & Doan, 2014). It is not uncommon for addictive behaviors to be co-occurring (Pettinati et al., 2008), and patients with IGD and IAD can possess comorbid, underlying neuropsychiatric disorders (Ko, Yen, Yen, Chen, & Chen, 2012; Spada, 2014). Similarly, substance addictions can co-occur with mental disorders (Osher & Drake, 1996). For instance, a patient suffering from obsessive-compulsive disorder (OCD) who also abuses alcohol is a person with OCD and alcohol use disorder. Therefore, a person with OCD who abuses Internet gaming is an individual with OCD and IGD.

Both IGD and IAD manifest hyperarousal behaviors associated with minimal refractory periods. Things that are pleasurable in life are usually associated with rest periods between events, i.e., the refractory period. For example, sexual intercourse is associated with a refractory period. When male rats were allowed to copulate with a single female rat until 30 min had elapsed, they were very unlikely to engage in copulation when a second female was introduced 24 h later (Beach & Jordan, 1956). On the other hand, when a second female was introduced immediately after the male's 15-min refractory period, the male rat would rapidly copulate with the second female rat. By continuing to change the female rats after the male's 15-min refractory period, Fisher was able to double or triple the number of copulations (Fisher, 1962). Fisher stated that "… there is a critical period immediately following a series of ejaculations during which it is easier to reactivate sexual mechanisms than it will be for a number of days following." This phenomenon is also known as the Coolidge effect.

The mind prefers variation to both visual and physical stimuli. If we extrapolate the Coolidge effect to Internet gaming and Internet visual stimuli, it makes sense that these stimuli are arousing and why IGD and IAD are real problems (Wilson, 2014). The seemingly endless provocative images, stimulating game plays, and engagements via social media provide brain reward and physiological arousal that can be abused by certain individuals, because these individuals find the reward and arousal irresistible. The stimuli provided through the Internet via gaming and online connections are associated with minimal refractory periods. Similar to the male rat in the Coolidge effect, the individual is able to provide multiple rewarding stimuli via clicking a technological device in rapid succession with little rest periods between rewards, leading not only to the development of addiction but also to the physical sequelae of near constant enhanced sympathetic tone seen in IGD and IAD (Chaput et al., 2011).

Conclusions

With the widespread use of smartphones, the Internet, and video games, future research is necessary not only to examine the relationship between video game use and pain suppression but also to explore the potential adverse health outcomes of excessive gaming and Internet use. Furthermore, research is warranted to determine if pain reduction is a reason some individuals play video games excessively or manifest problems with IGD and IAD. Mental health providers with the understanding of IGD and IAD discussed in this chapter will have opportunities to contribute to patients in this rapidly growing area of behavioral addictions. Additionally, professionals who use, apply, or recommend technology in their interventions have responsibility for understanding the potential risks for patients and for educating patients about these risks.

Acknowledgment   No financial support was used for this research. No investigational or off-label use of drugs.

References

asam.org. (2011). Chevy Chase, MD: American Society of Addiction Medicine. http://www.asam.org/about.html

Beach, F. A., & Jordan, L. (1956). Effects of sexual reinforcement upon the performance of male rats in a straight runway. *Journal of Comparative Physiology and Psychology, 49*, 105–110.

Chaput, J. P., Visby, T., Nyby, S., Klingenberg, L., Gregersen, N. T., Tremblay, A., ... Sjodin, A. (2011). Video game playing increases food intake in adolescents: A randomized crossover study. *The American Journal of Clinical Nutrition, 93*, 1196–1203.

Das, D. A., Grimmer, K. A., Sparnon, A. L., McRae, S. E., & Thomas, B. H. (2005). The efficacy of playing a virtual reality game in modulating pain for children with acute burn injuries: A randomized controlled trial [ISRCTN87413556]. *BMC Pediatrics, 5*, 1.

Doidge, N. (2007). *The brain that changes itself* (p. 427). New York, NY: Viking Press.

DSM-5. (2013). *Gaming Disorder Fact Sheet.pdf*. http://www.dsm5.org/Documents/Internet

Eickhoff, E. E., Yung, K., Davis, D. L., Bishop, F., Klam, W. P., & Doan, A. P. (2015). *Excessive video game use, sleep deprivation, and poor work performance among United States marines treated in a military mental health clinic: A case series*. Mil Med. *180*(7):e839–843. doi: 10.7205/MILMED-D-14-00597.

Fisher, A. E. (1962). Effects of stimulus variation on sexual satiation in the male rat. *Journal of Comparative Physiology and Psychology, 55*, 614–620.

Fu, K. W., Chan, W. S., Wong, P. W., & Yip, P. S. (2010). Internet addiction: Prevalence, discriminant validity and correlates among adolescents in Hong Kong. *The British Journal of Psychiatry, 196*, 486–492.

Gentile, D. (2009). Pathological video-game use among youth ages 8 to 18: A national study. *Psychological Science, 20*, 594–602.

Gentile, D. A., Choo, H., Liau, A., Sim, T., Li, D., Fung, D., & Khoo, A. (2011). Pathological video game use among youths: A two-year longitudinal study. *Pediatrics, 127*, e319–e329.

Gilman, L., Cage, D., Horn, A., Bishop, F., Klam, W. P., & Doan, A. P. (2015). *Candy crushed tendons: Tendon rupture associated with excessive smartphone gaming*. JAMA Intern Med. *175*(6):1048–1049. doi: 10.1001/jamainternmed.2015.0753.

Gold, J. I., Kim, S. H., Kant, A. J., Joseph, M. H., & Rizzo, A. S. (2006). Effectiveness of virtual reality for pediatric pain distraction during i.v. placement. *Cyberpsychology & Behavior, 9*, 207–212.

Haik, J., Tessone, A., Nota, A., Mendes, D., Raz, L., Goldan, O., ... Hollombe, I. (2006). The use of video capture virtual reality in burn rehabilitation: The possibilities. *Journal of Burn Care & Research, 27*, 195–197.

Hebb, D. (1949). *The organization of behavior*. New York, NY: Wiley and Sons.

Hebert, S., Beland, R., Dionne-Fournelle, O., Crete, M., & Lupien, S. J. (2005). Physiological stress response to video-game playing: The contribution of built-in music. *Life Sciences, 76*, 2371–2380.

KaiserFamilyFoundation. (2010). *Generation M2: Media in the lives of 8- to 18-year-olds*. http://kff.org/other/event/generation-m2-media-in-the-lives-of/

Ko, C. H., Liu, G. C., Yen, J. Y., Chen, C. Y., Yen, C. F., & Chen, C. S. (2013). Brain correlates of craving for online gaming under cue exposure in subjects with Internet gaming addiction and in remitted subjects. *Addiction Biology, 18*, 559–569.

Ko, C. H., Liu, G. C., Yen, J. Y., Yen, C. F., Chen, C. S., & Lin, W. C. (2013). The brain activations for both cue-induced gaming urge and smoking craving among subjects comorbid with Internet gaming addiction and nicotine dependence. *Journal of Psychiatric Research, 47*, 486–493.

Ko, C. H., Yen, J. Y., Yen, C. F., Chen, C. S., & Chen, C. C. (2012). The association between Internet addiction and psychiatric disorder: A review of the literature. *European Psychiatry, 27*, 1–8.

Kuss, D. J., Griffiths, M. D., Karila, L., & Billieux, J. (2014). Internet addiction: A systematic review of epidemiological research for the last decade. *Current Pharmaceutical Design, 20*, 4026–4052.

Osher, F. C., & Drake, R. E. (1996). Reversing a history of unmet needs: Approaches to care for persons with co-occurring addictive and mental disorders. *American Journal of Orthopsychiatry, 66*, 4–11.

Pettinati, H. M., Kampman, K. M., Lynch, K. G., Suh, J. J., Dackis, C. A., Oslin, D. W., & O'Brien, C. P. (2008). Gender differences with high-dose naltrexone in patients with co-occurring cocaine and alcohol dependence. *Journal of Substance Abuse Treatment, 34*, 378–390.

Przybylski, A. K. (2014). Electronic gaming and psychosocial adjustment. *Pediatrics, 134*(3), e716–e722.

Rumpf, H. J., Vermulst, A. A., Bischof, A., Kastirke, N., Gurtler, D., Bischof, G., ... Meyer, C. (2013). Occurrence of Internet addiction in a general population sample: A latent class analysis. *European Addiction Research, 20*, 159–166.

Smith, A. (2013). *Smartphone ownership 2013*. Washington, DC: Pew Research Internet Project.

Spada, M. M. (2014). An overview of problematic Internet use. *Addictive Behaviors, 39*, 3–6.

Tao, R., Huang, X., Wang, J., Zhang, H., Zhang, Y., & Li, M. (2010). Proposed diagnostic criteria for internet addiction. *Addiction, 105*, 556–564.

Wilson, G. (2014). *Your brain on porn: Internet pornography and the emerging science of addiction.* Richmond, VA: Commonwealth Publishing.

Yee, N. (2006). Motivations for play in online games. *Cyberpsychology & Behavior, 9,* 772–775.

Young, K. S. (1996). Psychology of computer use: XL. Addictive use of the Internet: A case that breaks the stereotype. *Psychological Reports, 79,* 899–902.

Young, K. S. (1999). The research and controversy surrounding internet addiction. *Cyberpsychology & Behavior, 2,* 381–383.

Yung, K., Eickhoff, E., Davis, D. L., Klam, W. P., & Doan, A. P. (2014). Internet addiction disorder and problematic use of Google Glass in patient treated at a residential substance abuse treatment program. *Addictive Behaviors, 41c,* 58–60.

Zilioli, S., & Watson, N. V. (2012). The hidden dimensions of the competition effect: Basal cortisol and basal testosterone jointly predict changes in salivary testosterone after social victory in men. *Psychoneuroendocrinology, 37,* 1855–1865.

Chapter 5
Crisis in the Behavioral Health Classroom: Enhancing Knowledge, Skills, and Attitudes in Telehealth Training

Joanne E. Callan, Marlene M. Maheu, and Steven F. Bucky

Introduction

Advances in technology in the last several decades have created a sea change in almost all aspects of contemporary life. Certainly, this is so in regard to education and training at all levels, from the first grade to the 12th grade (as reflected in a recent TIME article, "The paperless classroom is coming" Scherer, 2014) and in undergraduate and graduate programs. As well, in advanced education and training for professionals, the use of computers and other technologies has grown remarkably in recent years. Moreover, this impact likely pales in comparison to what is on the horizon.

Of eight major shifts or developments that have contributed to marked change between 1960 and 2013 in the education and training of women in clinical and counseling psychology (as noted by Callan, 2014), the influence of the various technological advances emerging in that 50-year period has impacted the learning experiences and performances of men as well as women and faculty as well as students, in all behavioral health training. More specifically, not only have these advances impacted *how all graduate students are taught*, but they also have changed *how students and trainees carry out their scholarly endeavors*. By extension, these advances have also impacted *how all contemporary mental health trainees and*

J.E. Callan (✉)
Alliant International University, 10455 Pomerado Road, Daley Hall, #103, San Diego, CA 92131, USA
e-mail: jcallan@alliant.edu

M.M. Maheu
5173 Waring Rd., San Diego, CA 92120, USA

S.F. Bucky
California School of Psychology at Alliant International University, 10455 Pomerado Rd., DH 213-A, San Diego, CA 92131, USA

© Springer International Publishing Switzerland 2017
M.M. Maheu et al. (eds.), *Career Paths in Telemental Health*,
DOI 10.1007/978-3-319-23736-7_5

most, if not all, practitioners carry out and provide clinical services. Moreover, because it can be safely predicted that new advances will continue to emerge, it is imperative that both current and future needs for telemental health training (TMHTr) be addressed.

Crisis in the Classroom

In March of 2014, the Pew Research Center published a study called, "Digital Life in 2025," in which they reported their conclusions after canvassing 2558 "experts and technology builders" to identify common views of where we will be with technological development's impact on life in 2025. The report captured the overall view of the respondents with this statement:

> In their responses, these experts foresee an ambient information environment where accessing the Internet will be effortless and most people will tap into it so easily it will flow through their lives "like electricity." (p. 1)

In the report, the team delineated a series of 15 "striking patterns" that have relevance for how future behavioral and mental health training can be considered. The following quick outline presents their conclusions:

> Information sharing over the Internet will be so effortlessly interwoven into daily life that it will become invisible, flowing like electricity, often through machine intermediaries.
> The spread of the Internet will enhance global connectivity that fosters more planetary relationships and less ignorance.
> The *Internet of Things*, artificial intelligence, and big data will make people more aware of their worlds and their own behavior.
> Augmented reality and wearable devices will be implemented to monitor and give quick feedback on daily life, especially as tied to personal health.
> Political awareness and action will be facilitated, and more peaceful change _and_ public uprisings like the Arab Spring will emerge.
> The spread of the 'Ubernet' will diminish the meaning of borders, and new 'nations' of those with shared interests may emerge and exist beyond the capacity of current nation-states to control.
> The Internet will become 'the Internets' as access, systems, and principles are renegotiated.
> An Internet-enabled revolution in education will spread more opportunities, with less money spent on real estate and teachers.
> Abuses and abusers will 'evolve and scale' (p. 1).—Human nature isn't changing; there's laziness, bullying, stalking, stupidity, pornography, dirty tricks, and crime, and those who practice them will have new capacity to make life miserable for others.
> Pressured by these changes, governments and corporations will try to assert power— and, at times, succeed—as they invoke security and cultural norms.
> People will continue—sometimes grudgingly—to make tradeoffs favoring convenience and perceived immediate gains over privacy; and privacy will be something only the upscale will enjoy.
> Humans and their current organizations may not respond quickly enough to challenges presented by complex networks.

Most people are not yet noticing the profound changes today's communications networks are already bringing about; these networks will be even more disruptive in the future.

1. Foresight and accurate predictions can make a difference: "The best way to predict the future is to invent it."

Students and professionals, alike, already are challenged to be conversant with concepts, language, and skills to work with the technology-enabled clients and patients they see. Regardless of the accuracy of the above predictions, one thing is certain: students will be even challenged in the near future with yet newer technologies. How will graduate and postgraduate training best equip clinicians for changes of the magnitude suggested above?

Today, clinicians need to be aware of and compliant with laws, regulations, and ethics as required by various governing bodies and professional organizations and adhere to the evidence base of clinically sound, validated protocols for interventions. They need to learn how to responsibly employ everyday technologies that clients and patients use for daily functioning and relating. Moreover, with the dramatic uptake in healthcare automation, clinicians will be expected to be more transparent and accountable than ever imagined heretofore when seeking reimbursement. Difficult decisions will need to be made for when healthcare will be delivered by less expensive and more easily controlled robots and avatars as opposed to expensive and often more difficult to manage human beings. Such stark realities force yet more questions. Who will be properly trained to make these difficult, yet necessary, decisions? Who will oversee their implementation? How will *they* be trained? Who will guide them in that training? Will these decision-makers emerge from our traditional disciplines, or will hybrid teams be assembled and by whom?

In this book chapter, then, the authors draw on a combined experience of more than 100 years in teaching and supervising both graduate students in professional psychology and postgraduates across the behavioral and mental health professions, in order (1) to provide a context from which then (2) to assert the urgent need for TMHTr by providing relevant and specific examples and (3) to present critical values and views regarding such training.

Historical Context

To demonstrate the dramatic reach of today's technology, several earlier practices in the education and training of behavioral health professionals and how they have changed are presented as historical context. Behavioral health educators as well as behavioral health professionals have moved from practices in the fifties, sixties, seventies, and eighties, when, outside of face-to-face interactions, the landline telephone and United States Postal Service provided the only real means of communication between teachers/supervisors and their students and between therapists and patients. Copies of scholarly works (e.g., grant proposals and dissertation drafts)—which, by the way, had to be made by carbon paper, mimeograph, or multilith processes—were either hand delivered or sent by regular post and, thus, required considerable time, both for completing reviews and for efforts to correct or enhance written documents (Callan, 2014). Insurance forms and other patient records were also exchanged in person or were forwarded by post and, only later, by facsimile. Compare these former means of sharing and providing information with the more immediate ways in which information is shared today—e.g., as by email, Internet, and large cloud-based portals accessed by mobile health (mHealth) tools, such as smart tablets and mobile phones.

As a specific example, psychological test results can be scored today by computer, often in just minutes, then copied by high-definition copying machines, and scanned, after which they can be emailed or faxed—all accomplished in much shorter time periods than in earlier years when hand scoring was required and postal service was the only means to forward the results. For over a decade, psychological tests have been conducted via telecommunication and other technologies (Maheu et al., 2004). Current telemental health systems allow tests to be taken and results given to the patient within the same week and occasionally the same day (Luxton, Pruitt, & Osenbach, 2014). As another example, statistical analyses can be conducted today in minutes, sharply contrasting with the months required several decades ago to accomplish the same results (Callan, 2014).

The Urgent Need for Telemental Health (TMH) Training

Although the changes noted just above reflect the impressive progress that has been made via various technological advances, the overall impact of these advances on actual behavioral health instruction and practice is even more impressive. Indeed, descriptions noting the effects of various technologies on behavioral health practices (Godleski, Darkins, & Peters, 2012; Hilty et al., 2013; Maheu, Pulier, Wilhelm, McMenamin, & Brown-Connelly, 2004) and also ones predicting needs for future TMHTr have been fully articulated by a number of behavioral health professionals, including those by Maheu (2003); Maheu, Pulier, McMenamin, and Posen (2012); and Colbow (2013).

In addition, national professional associations, such as the American Counseling Association (2014), the American Psychological Association (2002, 2013), and the American Telemedicine Association (2009, 2013, 2014), among others—all recognizing the pervasive influence of technology on today's behavioral health practices—have (a) advocated appropriate guidelines for the use of various technologies (e.g., the Internet) and (b) emphasized the need for advancing knowledge and skills of those still in training and for those already in practice. To reiterate, these national professional associations strongly assert the urgency to provide learning experiences that facilitate the acquisition of telemental health and other technology-related knowledge and skills. We, as teachers of behavioral health trainees and professionals, enthusiastically endorse this assertion and provide the following discussion to support our endorsement.

Curricular and Instructional Needs for Telemental Health (TMH) Education and Training

Because several authors (e.g., Colbow, 2013) have already developed comprehensive proposals designed to include and integrate TMHTr into the curricula designed for different behavioral health professional groups, our next focus is on *six selected needs* we view as deserving particular attention in their education and training. These examples are based on our collective, shared, and independent teaching and supervisory experiences, and they are informed by the views of a good number of other colleagues who teach students/trainees. This next discussion begins with a brief statement on the basic or fundamental needs of behavioral health trainees and then turns to the six selected training needs.

Basic or Fundamental Needs. Arguably, in both graduate and postdoctoral behavioral health education and training, several fundamental reasons compel us to value the use of specific technologies. Among the most obvious ones are cost and time efficiencies. As examples (and as noted in the introductory comments above), the use of email, scanning, and facsimile for correspondence supporting student/trainee learning saves both time and money. Possibly even more important, though, it provides a model for education, one that not only allows for greater inclusion (as in the use of online surveys) but also promotes immediacy and proximity in the learning that occurs between teacher and student/trainee.

Selected TMHTr Curricular and Instructional Needs: Knowledge, Attitudes, and Skills. Beyond these fundamental and overarching advantages, however, are ones related to curricular components, i.e., to the specific dimensions/areas of behavioral health education and training that can be significantly enhanced by the teaching of technological understanding and applications. One approach is considering these advantages—beyond identifying and briefly discussing them—to observe the taxonomy suggested in *standards and evaluation in the education and training of professional psychologists* (National Council of Schools of Professional Psychology (NCSPP, 1987—now the National Council of Schools and Programs of Professional Psychology). The reader is referred also to Bloom (1956) for his presentation of educational objectives and to Gagne (1985) for his subsequently published and expanded focus on educational objectives. In the NCSPP publication, Jones (1987, p. 77) noted the following necessary components of applied training: "… (1) a basic scientific level or core; (2) a generic professional common to all or most service—provision programs; and (3) the specific techniques that comprise day-to-day practice in an area." The editors of that publication noted the following three dimensions/areas— or, as they described them—"… the tripartite conception of the role of a professional psychologist: *knowledge, skills, and attitudes*" (Bourg, 1987).

As noted above, the six training needs discussed below have been identified by the authors as ones that deserve further attention in behavioral health training. They include TMH therapy, case conceptualization and mechanisms of change, cognitive neurosciences, ethics and professional guidelines, governing laws and rules pertinent to mental health practice, and professional communications and record keeping.

They are presented to illustrate the learning advantages to be gained through a TMHTr approach. As well, the positive outcomes of such training are related to the tripartite model of professional learning noted above—specifically, as they relate to the acquisition of knowledge, skills, and attitudes relevant in TMHTr.

Telemental Health Therapy (TMHT)

Training needs to include information on evidence-based therapeutic technique, on relevant technical requirements of the technology or group of technologies chosen by the clinician, and on relevant ethics. Training focusing on the various telepractice modalities must be enhanced, if current and future trainees are to be prepared to meet the increasing demand (e.g., Backhaus et al., 2012; Colbow, 2013; Maheu et al., 2004; Maheu, Pulier, McMenamin, & Posen, 2012). Telepractice modalities include, but are not limited to, video teleconferencing (VTC), telephone, email, text messaging, and the informed use of a growing variety of apps. Ethics can be further divided into:

- Standards (requirements)
- Guidelines (aspirational suggestions)
- Competencies

Competencies are observable or measurable behaviors that encompass the knowledge, skills, and attitudes that define acceptable levels of work performance. The need for well-articulated competencies in training was identified by the US Institute of Medicine (2001) in a concerted effort across healthcare disciplines to close the gap between training and practice.

One of the earliest forms of competencies identified in the telepractice literature was the online clinical practice management (OCPM) model published by Maheu (2001, 2003) and Maheu and colleagues in 2004. Maheu thereby provided an early "roadmap" of the following seven competency areas to be addressed:

1. Training
2. Referral practices
3. Client education
4. Legal issues
5. Intake and assessment
6. Direct care
7. Reimbursement procedures

In 2010, that distillation of legal and ethical competencies has been further defined by the TeleMental Health Institute.

The Ohio Psychological Association (2013) encouraged both telepractitioners and telesupervisors to conduct a self-assessment of:

1. Knowledge and skills of technology approaches
2. Knowledge and skills of clinical telepractice

3. Knowledge and skills for establishing, maintaining, and terminating the teleprovider and client relationship
4. Supervisor and supervisee knowledge and skills of technology approaches
5. Knowledge and skills for establishing, maintaining, and terminating supervisor and supervisee relationship
6. Ongoing professional development requirements: continuing education to maintain current knowledge and skill competencies in telepractice

In 2014, the Coalition for Technology in Behavioral Science (CTiBS) initiated an effort to develop telemental health competencies in a task force led by Maheu. Their efforts led to not only an interprofessionally-derived grid of telemental health competencies, but also a series of journal articles describing the rationale, process and competencies themselves (Hilty, Maheu, Drude, Wall, Hertlein, Long, 2016), published by the Journal of Technology in Behavioral Science (JTiBS).

Other Training Opportunities. Another required, ethical focus for TMHTr was identified by Gifford, Niles, Rivkin, Koverola, and Polaha, in 2012, highlighting cultural competency as an area of particular need when using telehealth systems. In developing a telepractice model for behavioral telehealth providers working in rural Alaska with culturally diverse clientele, this research team reported unique aspects of telemental health training needed when using video and emphasized the need for both clinicians and patients to be taught to adapt the limitations of the video screen by identifying the ingredients of developing a "telepresence." Colbow thereafter further delineated overall telepractice competencies for professional training (2013). The Health Service Psychology Education Collaborative also published a "blueprint" for behavioral telepractice education and training in 2013.

Models for Telepractice. Clinical providers may also seek out onsite and online training opportunities at private institutes or other postgraduate opportunities specific to evidence-based best practices in telemental health. For less rigorous opportunities, individuals may pursue training through technology-related groups associated with their broader professional organizations by attending in-person workshops featuring telemental health leaders at annual state, provincial, or national conventions or through behavioral health groups within broader technology-focused professional groups (e.g., the telemental health special interest group through the American Telemedicine Association or the Society of Behavioral Medicine).

Webinars are also increasing in popularity because of their convenience and affordability online. They can easily serve as introductory samples of training for specific topic areas without requiring that trainees be graduates of any advanced training. On-demand libraries of such specialized webinar recordings are also available online from a variety of sources (see online search engines) for easy listening and viewing through any mobile device.

Several technology-related associations have formed for behavioral professionals interested in technology, including the Coalition for Technology in Behavioral Science at www.ctibs.org. Their missions vary in focus, but these groups can also offer a variety of experiences for professionals seeking to meet others with whom to share resources. Online communities of like-minded professionals are also available through TMH training institutes and a variety of social media websites such as LinkedIn.

Although not yet included in many graduate training programs, telepractice also offers exciting training opportunities for predoctoral trainees, particularly as training programs strive to train behavioral health students in reaching out to underserved populations. For example, behavioral health trainees must be apprised of research findings and recommendations on how to use available technology—that is, what works best and what doesn't (e.g., observing the American Telemedicine Association's recommendations [2013]). Such training would certainly address two of the tripartite components, knowledge and skills, and it could be designed to address trainees' attitudes as well.

Enhanced Learning and Mechanisms of Change

A second area of need that can be addressed effectively through TMHTr involves enhancing learning about case conceptualization and, relatedly, mechanisms of change. Although a substantial portion of today's psychotherapy literature and research focuses on the importance of evidence-based treatment, such that behavioral health training programs give considerable attention to introducing these modalities to trainees and to teaching them how to conduct these therapies, the instruction on these two key aspects of effective treatment—case conceptualization and mechanisms of change—is insufficient, based on our observations and dialogue with other senior faculty. As a result, trainees may err by determining too early the therapeutic approach best to take with a patient/client—i.e., before they have fully assessed an individual and, thus, before they have a solid understanding of that person, one they can articulate with precision and then use in treatment planning. Exacerbating this lack of attention and commitment to adequately conceptualizing each case/patient/client is the lack of understanding as to what brings about behavior change—i.e., the mechanisms of change.

Gabbard (2005) has discussed specific mechanisms of change in expressive psychodynamic treatment. Through years of clinical teaching, research, and practice, Blatt (2004, 2008) identified two different types of patients who respond differentially to different therapeutic approaches, specifically to different mechanisms of change. Given that entire classes or cadres of trainees can be exposed to more patients and to a greater variety of psychological problems and needs through distance learning, it seems clear that such TMHTr holds much promise in this regard, as it would clearly provide learning in both knowledge and skills and, again, could be designed to address trainee attitudes as well. An example of the latter would include helping trainees understand their contributions to a positive therapeutic relationship, one of the most important mechanisms of change (Beuler, 2006; Gabbard, 2005).

Yet, once graduates leave the hallowed halls of their training institutions where technology use may not be part of their curriculum, technology-based employers offer jobs with a noticeably different focus. Many online employers of licensed behavioral and behavioral health professionals simply ask professionals to provide evidence of licensure and then point them to an eager consumer public that readily pays a small fee in order to ask quick questions. While several online employers prepare their licensed professionals with well-grounded theory and practice technique for telemental health service delivery, the majority do not. To unknowing consumers, they may offer clinicians who practice over state lines, use nonsecured technologies, fail to provide a full informed consent process, do not develop emergency plans, operate without diagnosing or developing a treatment plan, don't follow evidence-based telemental health protocols, fail to contact other involved professionals, are uninformed as to the client or patient's local community resources or emergency services, and do not provide continuity of care (Shore et al., 2014; Maheu & Gordon, 2000).

Rather, many online therapy companies have launched successful businesses in the belief that they are offering an innovative service that meets the needs of consumers who do not want to label themselves as behavioral health patients. Coined by Clayton Christensen (2003), the term "disruptive innovation" refers to the improvement of a product or service in unexpected ways, often by being designed for an emerging and less expensive market and subsequently becoming so popular that it lowers prices in the traditional market. The advent of $40 online therapy sessions by licensed clinicians who are available 24/7 might be such "innovation."

On one hand, advantages of low-cost, immediately available Internet services delivered by desktop computer or mobile device can include access to an unprecedented array of behavioral specialists, widespread affordability, immediacy, lack of stigmatization, and the convenience of a few simple clicks from one's home or even when seated under a tree in a park. On the other hand, disadvantages can include lack of knowledge of, or adherence to, established education and training requirements for such clinicians; minimization of legal and ethical standards due to poor enforcement of mandates, across state, provincial, and national borders; lack of credentialing; and lack of insurance reimbursement among other factors (Maheu et al., 2012). These new services also can include anonymity for the client/patient, thereby making it impossible for clinicians to serve as mandated reporters for abuse as required in all US states. Anonymity also can make it impossible to comply with reporting laws for homicide threats as required in many states. See the Tarasoff decision by the Supreme Court of California in 1974 for details of what happened when a therapist failed to inform an intended victim of a homicide threat (Paul, 1977).

How else are these professional issues crystallizing to impact both students and professionals? One simply has to go to any Internet search engine to see immediate repercussions. To the dismay of some licensed professionals, a new wave of online therapy employers have been hiring licensed professionals to sell their coaching services over state lines, despite the vast majority of state laws prohibiting such practice in the absence of a professional holding licensure or registration in the foreign jurisdiction. While other online therapy or counseling services do not hire licensed professionals to deliver coaching, their business models are built on the hiring of minimally trained paraprofessionals. Doing so allows them to survive in the tumultuous world of Internet start-ups and perhaps deliver much needed care to many people who otherwise would not approach a fully licensed professional for care. The question for many has to do with the quality of such care.

However, rather than assuming that the gold standard in defining the best "treater" at the lowest cost rests with traditional training and licensing structures, however, proponents of minimally trained paraprofessionals are adamant that outcomes should determine value. For instance, the recent appearance of "mental health first aid" has challenged the assumptions of traditional behavioral training programs and their graduates. Such first aid programs offer 12 h of training to paraprofessionals to prepare them to work with people who are developing a mental illness or are in crisis. It is noteworthy that developers of this program have reported repeated success (Kitchener & Jorm, 2002, 2004), and it seems to be proliferating with thousands of graduates.

The ultimate worth of traditional versus innovative approaches to healthcare then will be in outcomes to consumers. Christiansen and his followers point to business and healthcare models when describing disruptive innovation (2008), but their theories may have profound implications for training in the behavioral health classroom as well. In these times of rapid technological advancement and ensuing change, it would be wise for all academics to consider their responsibilities to the next generations of behavioral care professionals and at least for a moment consider the delivery of care from the perspective of these and similar models which are sure to emerge as challenges to the status quo.

Cognitive Neurosciences

Findings from the cognitive neurosciences constitute another curricular area that deserves further attention via TMHTr. Although existing literature (e.g., Damasio, 2012; Montgomery, 2013; Schore, 2012) asserts the necessity to know neuroscience bases of human functioning as it informs the conduct of psychotherapy, graduate programs, in general, have not been including sufficient emphasis on relevant neuroscience findings in their clinical curricula. Through its use of telecommunications, not only could TMHTr provide such instruction to larger numbers of trainees, potentially taught by leading neuroscientists, and, arguably, it could do so with greater cost and time efficiencies. Clearly, such TMHTr instruction could contribute to knowledge and skills acquisition among behavioral health trainees, but also it could address some of the relational issues that potentially would contribute to more positive attitudes on the part of clinicians.

Ethics and Professional Guidelines

Given the array of technologies now available to behavioral health trainees for the use in learning, practice, and research endeavors, it is imperative that both students and licensed professionals be instructed on relevant ethics (see above) as well as on professional practice guidelines related to the use of their chosen technologies (i.e., telephone, text messaging, email, video). Such ethical standards and guidelines have been developed and recommended by each of the large professional groups representing physicians, psychologists, social workers, and counselors. The authors of the current chapter have all taught, consulted, and/or published on professional ethics, with particular focus on telehealth or professional psychology. From these experiences, we argue for the provision of ethics instruction and guidance on the proper use of various technologies in all professional endeavors among all behavioral health disciplines.

Although considerable literature exists which cautions behavioral health trainees and professionals about potential gray areas and possible conflictual situations associated with the use of different technologies in both the academic and professional worlds (Maheu et al., 2004; Prentice & Dobson, 2014), the need for continuing and ongoing exposure to relevant ethics education and also to current guidelines is compelling. The telepractice faculty member may consider supporting students with readings, such as national guidelines (Grady, Myers, Nelson, et al., 2011; APA, 2013; ATA, 2013), review articles (Gros et al., 2013), summary articles on issues related to the safe delivery of service to "unsupervised settings" such as the home (Luxton, Sirotin, & Mishkind, 2010) or more intensive textbooks, handbooks, or manuals (Myers & Turvey, 2012; Maheu et al., 2004; Luxton, Nelson, & Maheu, 2016).

Many large professional behavioral health associations have recently addressed social media as part of their ethical standards (ACA, 2014; AMA, 2011). Aware of such needs in the area of social media, the California School of Professional Psychology/Alliant International University Committee on Ethical and Professional Standards has developed an unpublished set of excerpts (2014), as based on an earlier publication by Stolberg et al. (2008) that present the following five recommendations for behavioral health professionals with respect to online use of social media: (1) Do not mix professional and private uses of any online sites; (2) Always set the privacy setting to the most conservative available choice; (3) Before posting anything, ask yourself if you would mind that one of your patients, students, or colleagues had access to the content; (4) Be suspicious *[or cautious]* if a request is made to use a private site; and (5) Consider developing a professional website.

Making practice guidelines known to trainees as well as to members of behavioral health professions can certainly be facilitated through TMHTr. Indeed, such instruction can be designed and then provided in ways that are timely and convenient for the trainee/learner and, furthermore, can have potential for reaching a much larger number of learners (Maheu et al., 2004). The merits of such ongoing instruction are obvious—for the trainee, by enhancing both knowledge and attitude and, importantly, for those to whom trainees provide professional services.

Governing Laws and Rules Pertinent to Mental Health Practice

Among the plethora of state as well as national governing rules (e.g., laws, acts, statutes, and regulations) pertinent to behavioral and mental health practices, two more recently enacted ones reflect an area of special need with respect to the training of these health professionals: The Health Insurance Portability and Accountability Act (HIPPA) (US Department of Commerce, National Institute of Standards and Technology, 2008) and The Affordable Care Act (Department of Human & Human Services, 2010). Because of their complexity as well as the reach of their authority, these acts require an ongoing review by behavioral health trainees and professionals so that they are sufficiently informed in order to observe best practices. Furthermore, departures from the guidance and requirements they provide can lead to serious consequences. Accordingly, ongoing TMHTr offers an effective approach to providing such ongoing review. Such TMHTr could provide not only the required knowledge content, but also could contribute to the development of appropriate attitudes surrounding the delivery of behavioral health services. These two examples point to what is likely an increasing area of need—i.e., more such complex rules that require ongoing familiarity among behavioral health professionals can be expected to emerge with increasing rapidity.

Enhancing Professional Communications and Record Keeping

Today's behavioral health trainees are exposed to myriad experiences that request, if not require, their responses. Some of these are professional ones, some are academic in nature, and others are more social in nature. Understandably, students/trainees have varying reactions to these different kinds of technology-based responses.

As examples, in an informal and unpublished survey (Bucky, 2014), graduate students in clinical psychology programs (both PhD and PsyD) reported on their attitudes toward technology. They noted the following 13 assets or advantages they associated with the use of technology in their lives: (1) Access to information (e.g., journals and textbooks) (2) Ease of sharing information (3) Word processing capabilities (e.g., organizational aspects and tracking options) (4) Access to online courses and training (5) Communication options (e.g., email, Facebook, LinkedIn) (6) Options for professional presentations (7) Online applications to APA/APPIC/CAPIC internships (8) Real-time presence options (9) Psychological assessments and analyses (10) Time efficiencies (11) Ready availability/accessibility (12) Record keeping options including practice management software and electronic health records (EHRs) (13) Ability to multitask (related to time efficiencies).

As well, they identified the following ten liabilities or disadvantages associated with the use of technology: (1) privacy concerns; (2) technological failures, as contributing to loss of productivity; (3) loss of information; (4) being constantly "connected" (as in being "on-call"); (5) personal safety concerns; (6) lack of human interaction; (7) requirements to be online for extended times (as required by some programs/courses); (8) slow responses from others (e.g., from faculty); (9) difficulty in remembering passwords; and (10) battery limitations (as with laptops, tablets, smartphones). It seems likely that providers of TMHTr could improve programmatic endeavors by knowing what trainees like and find useful about technology and what they don't like and don't find useful.

Another example of recent developments that impact behavioral and mental health trainees involves changes in the process of applying for admission to graduate programs and also that for applying for training experiences (e.g., practica and internships). Since 2009, graduate students in psychology have been required to submit their applications for APA, APPIC, and CAPIC internships online. This process necessitates getting all relevant information, including letters of recommendation from faculty and supervisors as well as approval/recommendation from their directors of training into an online communication form (Scott, 2014). Even though students seem to be *getting the hang* of packaging and then submitting online such a large set of application materials, it seems reasonable that they could profit from online instruction designed to facilitate and assure complete as well as sophisticated packages of the required information as well as to achieve some uniformity across applications.

Similarly, behavioral health trainees could benefit from TMHTr that focuses on best practices of record keeping (Nicholson, 2011) as well as those for filing third-party reimbursement. Because the various practices and requirements for these activities not only are different for various kinds of practices (e.g., inpatient vs. outpatient and adult vs. children and adolescents) but also change fairly often in the world of professional practice, training could provide updated information (i.e., knowledge) and also help trainees in developing the skills they need to carry out these functions appropriately and accurately.

Given the focus on healthcare reform in both the USA and worldwide and its broad-based attack on decreasing the US healthcare "spend," it is also imperative that students as well as professionals be aware of, and know how to effectively use, the electronic health record (EHR). It is equally important that graduate students understand how such EHRs will soon play a foundational role in reimbursement, as the USA shifts from a payment system based on time allocation of services to one that is not only based on outcomes. Outcomes will soon need to be significantly more documented and in compliance with proper billing codes and the scientific evidence base. In other words, delivering care and getting reimbursed are just about to become more difficult for the average clinician seeking third-party reimbursement. This shift has been systematized through the adoption of the electronic health records (EHRs). Although allied health professionals have not yet accepted the EHRs in daily practice as widely as medical professionals, financial pressures will soon come to bear as the USA and other countries attempt to reduce costs and improve care (Hillestad et al., 2005).

By developing a sense of ownership and accomplishment in carrying out these functions among learners and trainees at all levels, practitioners might concurrently experience a greater sense of professionalism and membership in the emerging team approach to health management as currently seen with integrated care and patient-centered models. Those choosing to deliver direct care will also be fully reimbursed for the services they deliver.

Faculty Training

While focusing on the needs of graduate students and practicing professionals is given, that of educating faculty members on the changing marketplace for their graduates is also essential. As mentioned earlier in the discussion of accelerating change in educational environments (Christiansen, Johnson, & Horn, 2010), such innovation is beginning to be felt at the graduate level. Graduate schools are encouraged to train their faculty about legal, ethical, and evidence-based approaches to telepractice training and supervision techniques that yield outcomes on par with, or better than, in-person care. Without the cooperation and leadership of existing faculty, our next generations of otherwise highly trained clinicians will be at a disadvantage when compared to coaches and mental health first aid paraprofessionals. Faculty members could be encouraged to understand that telepractice, when conducted properly, is not "half" service but approximates all key elements of best ethical onsite care.

The role of faculty in training students through telesupervision is also worthy of discussion. With more than 500 evidence-based articles on telesupervision alone (Shore et al., 2014), the faculty in our training institutions would do well to consider telesupervision to be a viable, evidence-based service rendered by professionals.

Behavioral health clinicians, particularly those who work in independent practice, can experience feelings of isolation and burnout, given the variety of specialization needed. Especially for those working in remote areas, clinical experts may benefit from "teleconsultation" as well as telesupervision. Teleconsultation is a traditional telehealth model that involves providing access to a distance specialist via video teleconferencing technologies for assessment and treatment. Accessing both telesupervision and teleconsultation via videoconferencing can also help alleviate these potential pressures (Luxton, Nelson & Maheu, 2016).

Conclusion

Without doubt, advances in technology have already had major impact on the education and training, as well as the practice, of behavioral health professionals, and it is apparent that other such advances are forthcoming. It is also the case that behavioral health service needs are likely to increase, emanating, for example, from an overall increase in the world's populations and from related competitions for resources, increasing numbers of elderly populations in some countries, globalization and immediacy of information dissemination/communication, and the complexity of relationships between and among different races, ethnic groups, and cultures and across the globe.

Telemental health training has much promise for facilitating the education and training of the professionals who will be providing the behavioral health services required to meet this increasing demand. The inclusion of such learning experiences for behavioral health trainees will depend, first, on teaching basic skills on the use of different technologies. Probably most important, though, such inclusion requires consideration of existing curricula, so that the added telemental health emphases are relevant to existing, as well as anticipated future, instructional content. For example, ethics courses must emphasize the ethical use of different technologies in teaching, research, and practice, including information illustrating possible dangers and pitfalls, as noted above. Postgraduate education will also need to provide some basic skills training in the use of available technologies—at least for a few more years—but certainly will need to provide learning experiences related to the actual delivery of telemental health services. As a caveat, faculty teaching in graduate and postgraduate programs, including continuing education, will have to buy into the importance of adding these learning experiences to existing (and sometimes packed) curricula.

The authors hope that this discussion will support telemental health training that responds not only to the six needs selected for discussion here but also to the many other training needs for which TMHTr programs and approaches have special potential to address.

References

American Counseling Association. (2014). *2014 ACA Code of Ethics*. Retrieved from http://www.counseling.org/Resources/aca-code-of-ethics.pdf

American Medical Association. (2011). Opinion 9.124—Professionalism in the use of social media. Retrieved from http://www.ama-assn.org/ama/pub/physician-resources/medical-ethics/code-medical-ethics/opinion9124.page?

American Psychological Association. (2002). Ethical principles of psychologists and code of ethics. *American Psychologist, 57*(12), 1060–1073. Washington, DC: American Psychological Association.

American Telemedicine Association Practice Guidelines for Videoconferencing-Based Telemental Health. (2009). Retrieved from http://www.americantelemed.org/docs/default-source/standards/practice-guidelines-for-videoconferencing-basedtelemental-health.pdf?sfvrsn=6. Accessed 1 May 2016.

American Psychological Association. (2013). *Guidelines for the practice of telepsychology.* Washington, DC: American Psychological Association.

American Telemedicine Association Practice Guidelines for Video-based Online Mental Health Services (2013). Retrieved from http://www.americantelemed.org/docs/defaultsource/standards/practice-guidelines-for-video-based-online-mental-health-services.pdf?sfvrsn=6. Accessed 1 May 2016.

American Telemedicine Association Telemental Health Group (2014). A lexicon of assessment and outcome measures for telemental health. Retrieved from http://www.americantelemed.org/resources/telemedicine-practice-guidelines/telemedicine-practiceguidelines/a-lexicon-of-assessment-and-outcome-measurements-for-telemental-health#.VvqE2BESPw8. Accessed 1 May 2016.

Backhaus, A., Agha, Z., Maglione, M. L., Repp, A., Ross, B., Zuest, D., et al. (2012). Videoconferencing psychotherapy: A systematic review. *Psychological Services, 9*, 111–131. doi:10.1037/a0017924.

Beuler, L. (2006). *Principles of therapeutic change that work*. New York, NY: Oxford University Press.

Blatt, S.J. (2004). Experiences of depression: Theoretical, clinical, & research perspectives. Washington, DC: American Psychological Assoc ISBN-10: 1591470951, ISBN-13: 978–1591470953.

Blatt, S.J. (2008) Polarities of experiences: Relatedness & self-definition in personality development, psychopathology, and the therapeutic process. Washington, DC: American Psychological Assoc. ISBN-10: 1433803143, ISBN-13: 978–1433803147.

Bloom, B. (1956). *Taxonomy of educational objectives, Vol. 1 (or Handbook I)*. New York, NY: David McKay Co.

Bourg, E. F. (1987). The evaluation of knowledge. In E. F. Bourg, R. J. Bent, J. E. Callan, N. F. Jones, J. McHolland, & G. Stricker (Eds.), Standards and evaluation in the education and training of professional psychologists: Knowledge, attitudes, and skills (pp. 51–54). Norman, OK: Transcript Press.

Bucky, S. (2014). Pros and cons of technology for doctoral-level psychology graduate students. Unpublished manuscript.

Callan, J. E. (2014). The education and training of women in clinical and counseling psychology programs: Then and now—1960–2013. *Women and Therapy, 37*, 122–134. doi:10.1080/02703149.2014.850340.

Christiansen, C., Grossman, J. H., & Hwang, J. (2008). *The innovator's prescription: A disruptive solution for health care*. New York, NY: McGraw-Hill.

Christensen, C. M. (2003). *The innovator's dilemma: The revolutionary book that will change the way you do business*. New York: HarperCollins.

Christiansen, C., Johnson, C., & Horn, M. (2010). *Disrupting class: How disruptive innovation will change the way the world learns* (2nd ed.). New York, NY: McGraw-Hill.

Colbow, A. J. (2013). Looking to the future: Integrating telemental health therapy into psychological training. *Training and education in professional psychology, 7*(3), 155–165. doi:10.1037/aoo33454. Washington, DC: American Psychological Association.

Damasio, A. R. (2012). *Self comes to mind: Constructing the conscious brain*. New York, NY: Pantheon Books.

Gabbard, G. O. (2005). *Psychodynamic psychiatry in clinical practice* (4th ed.). Washington, DC: American Psychiatric Association.

Gifford, V., Niles, B., Rivkin, I., Koverola, C., & Polaha, J. (2012). Continuing education training focused on the development of behavioral telehealth competencies in behavioral healthcare providers. *Rural and Remote Health, 12*(4), 2108.

Godleski, L., Darkins, A., & Peters, J. (2012). Outcomes of 98,609 U.S. Department of Veterans Affairs patients enrolled in telemental health services, 2006–2010. *Psychiatric Services, 63*(4), 383–385.

Grady, B., Myers, K. M., Nelson, E. L., Belz, N., Bennett, L., Carnahan, L., et al. (2011). Evidence-based practice for telemental health. *Telemedicine Journal and e-Health, 17*, 131–148. doi:10.1089/tmj.2010.0158.

Gros, D. F., Morland, L. A., Greene, C. J., Acierno, R., Strachan, M., Egede, L. E., et al. (2013). Delivery of evidence-based psychotherapy via video telehealth. *Journal of Psychopathology and Behavioral Assessment, 35*(4), 506–521. doi:10.1007/s10862-013-9363-4.

Hillestad, R., Bigelow, J., Bower, A., Girosi, F., Meili, R., Scoville, R., et al. (2005). Can electronic medical record systems transform health care? Potential health benefits, savings and costs.

Health Affairs, 24, 1103–1117. doi:10.1377/hlthaff.24.5.1103. Retrieved from http://content. healthaffairs.org/content/24/5/1103.full.

Hilty, D. M., Ferrer, D. C., Parish, M. B., Johnston, B., Callahan, E. J., & Yellowlees, P. M. (2013). The effectiveness of telemental health: A 2013 review. *Telemedicine and e-Health, 19*(6), 444–54. doi:10.1089/tmj.2013.0075.

Hilty, D. M., Maheu, M., Drude, K., Wall, K., Hertlein, K., & Long, R. (2017). *The need for telemental health competencies: an approach based on competency frameworks and common themes across behavioral disciplines*. Springer.

Institute of Medicine. (2001). *Crossing the quality chasm: A new health system for the 21st century*. Washington, DC: Author.

Jones, N. F. (1987). A model for defining the knowledge base in professional psychology. In E. F. Bourg, R. J. Bent, J. E. Callan, N. F. Jones, J. McHolland, & G. Stricker (Eds.), *Standards and evaluation in the education and training of professional psychologists: Knowledge, attitudes, and skills* (pp. 75–80). Norman, OK: Transcript Press.

Kitchener, B. A., & Jorm, A. F. (2002). Mental Health First Aid training for the public: Evaluation of effects knowledge, attitudes and helping behavior. BMC Psychiatry, 2(10), 1–6. Retrieved from http://www.ncbi.nlm.nih.gov/pubmed/12359045

Kitchener, B. A., & Jorm, A. F. (2004). Mental Health First Aid training in a workplace setting: A randomized controlled trial. *BMC Psychiatry, 4*(23), 1–8. Retrieved from http://www.ncbi.nlm. nih.gov/pubmed/15310395.

Luxton, D. D., Pruitt, L. D., & Osenbach, J. E. (2014). Best practices for remote psychological assessment via telehealth technologies. *Professional Psychology: Research and Practice, 45*(1), 27–35. Retrieved from http://dx.doi.org/10.1037/a0034547.

Luxton, D., Sirotin, A., & Mishkind, M. (2010). Safety of telemental healthcare delivered to clinically unsupervised settings: A systematic review. *Telemedicine and e-Health, 16*(6), 705–711. doi:10.1089/tmj.2009.0179. Retrieved from http://online.liebertpub.com/doi/abs/10.1089/ tmj.2009.0179.

Luxton, D., Nelson, E., & Maheu, M. (2016). *Telemental health best practices*. Washington, DC: American Psychological Association.

Maheu, M. M. (2003). The online clinical practice model. *Psychotherapy: Theory, Research, Practice, Training, 40*, 20–32. doi:10.1037/0033-3204.40.1-2.20.

Maheu, M. M., & Gordon, B. (2000). Psychotherapy on the Internet: Legal, ethical and practice issues. *Professional Psychology: Research and Practice, 31*(5), 484–489.

Maheu, M., Pulier, M., Wilhelm, F., McMenamin, J., & Brown-Connolly, N. (2004). *The mental health professional and the new technologies: A handbook for practice today*. Mahwah, NJ: Erlbaum.

Maheu, M., Pulier, M., McMenamin, J., & Posen, L. (2012). The future of telepsychology, telehealth, and various technologies in psychological research. *Professional Psychology: Research and Practice, 43*, 613–621.

Montgomery, A. (2013). *Neurobiology essentials for clinicians: What every therapist needs to know*. New York, NY: W.W. Norton.

Myers, K., & Turvey, C. (2012). (Eds.), pp. 171–195. Telemental health: Clinical, technical and administrative foundations for evidence-based practice. NY: Elsevier.

Nicholson, I. (2011). New technology, old issues: Demonstrating the relevance of the Canadian Code of Ethics for psychologists to the ever-sharper cutting edge of technology. *Canadian Psychology, 52*(3), 215–224.

Ohio Psychological Association. (2013). Areas of Competence for Psychologists in Telepsychology. Retrieved from March 2, 2015 at http://www.ohpsych.org/about/files/2012/03/FINAL_ COMPETENCY_DRAFT.pdf. Accessed 1 May 2016.

Paul, R. (1977). Tarasoff and the duty to warn: Toward a standard of conduct that balances the rights of clients against the rights of third parties. *Professional Psychology, 8*, 125–128.

Prentice, J. L., & Dobson, K. S. (2014). A review of the risks and benefits associated with mobile phone applications for psychological interventions. *Canadian Psychology/Psychologie Canadienne, 55*(4), 282–290. Retrieved from http://psycnet.apa.org/journals/cap/55/4/282/.

Scherer, M. (2014). The paperless classroom is coming. *TIME, 184*(15), 36–38. New York, NY: Time, Inc.

Schore, A. N. (2012). *The science of the art of psychotherapy.* New York, NY: W.W. Norton.

Scott, private communication, May, 2014.

Shore, J. H., Mishkind, M. C., Bernard, J., Doarn, C. R., Bell, I., Jr., Bhatla, R., et al. (2014). A lexicon of assessment and outcome measures for telemental health. *Telemedicine and e-Health, 20*, 282–292. doi:10.1089/tmj.2013.0357.

Stolberg, R., Murphy, J., Bucky, S., Dalenberg, C., Obegi, J., Swift, E., et al. (2008). Ethics corner: Maintaining professionalism within online communities. *San Diego Psychologist, 23*(3), 1.

The Patient Protection and Affordable Care Act, 124 Stat. 119-1025, Pub. L. No. 111-148. (March 23, 2010).

U.S. Department of Commerce, National Institute of Standards and Technology. (2008). *An introductory resource guide for implementing the Health Insurance Portability and Accountability Act (HIPPA) Security Rule.* Washington, DC: Author.

Part II
Special Topics and Personal Perspectives

Chapter 6
Making iCBT Available in Primary Care Settings: Bridging the Gap Between Research and Regular Health Care

Kristofer Vernmark

I'm just taking one step at a time. I could zigzag one way, but it's not usually on purpose.

Beck Hansen

Vignette

Alex is feeling depressed. He's been reluctant to seeking help, feeling ashamed about not being able to handle his problems. One day he reads online that it's possible to get effective treatment for depression by working with an online solution. He gathers courage and applies through the website of his local primary care setting. He gets an answer the same day that says he needs to answer some questions online and then meet up with a health-care professional for an assessment that makes sure that this type of treatment is right for him. He gets the option to come to the clinic or do the assessment through video. Alex chooses the video assessment, which confirms that he needs help and is suitable for an online therapy for depression. He gets all the information he needs to start his treatment the same day. Alex is really surprised by how quickly he gets access to help! He starts his depression program the very same evening. Over the course of 10 weeks, Alex works with his online program, sometimes through his smartphone, other times through his tablet or home computer. The program reminds him when to do his homework and rewards him when he does. Beforehand, he was a little bit afraid that there would be a lot of text to read since he's having a hard time concentrating on reading for longer periods of time. But he notices that his fears are ungrounded as he learns about depression

K. Vernmark, M.S. (✉)
Psykologpartners W&W/Linköping University, St Larsgatan 30,
582 24 Linköping, Sweden
e-mail: kristofer.vernmark@psykologpartners.se

© Springer International Publishing Switzerland 2017
M.M. Maheu et al. (eds.), *Career Paths in Telemental Health*,
DOI 10.1007/978-3-319-23736-7_6

83

and how to get better through the videos, animations, pictures, and short text materials (which also has voice-over) that he goes through every week. Alex is starting to really see the connection between his mood and his actions, which is even further clarified through graphic features provided by the program. He also gets feedback from his therapist who sends short messages and encourages him to keep up the good work. Sometimes, when he's stuck or needs help, he sends a message to the therapist who quickly replies, most of the time even the same day. It really feels like the therapist is dedicated to his treatment, and he feels he's not alone in this, which was a concern of his going into this. After 10 weeks, he and the therapist have another video meeting where they go through the progress that Alex has achieved over the time period of the program and decide some of the important changes that Alex keeps on working with he's done for a couple of more months. Even though he still has things to do to keep on feeling better, Alex is satisfied with the quick access to help, the user-friendly online program and the support from his online therapist. It really helped him in his struggle with depression.

Background

There's a lack of psychologists and other health-care professionals providing psychotherapy in the Swedish primary care. This means that a large percentage of patients in need of effective treatment for their psychological problems have to wait, or will never get access, to that kind of help. This is alarming. Doctors prescribe medications, even though a majority of patients prefer psychotherapy, because they don't want to leave their patients waiting for an appointment to a psychologist.

Many individuals in the need of help don't even contact their primary care setting because they're ashamed, are afraid, or don't think there's any help for them.

From an international perspective, it's even worse. The WHO estimates that in some countries, the amount of individuals getting effective help is as low as 10%.

What we need is tools that help us be quicker at delivering effective treatment to more individuals, without loosing quality. And this is where comes iCBT into the picture.

In 2006 we did our first two projects of implementing iCBT in primary care. We used programs that had been tested in earlier Swedish studies led by Gerhard Andersson and Per Carlbring. These programs were basic, but effective, consisting of text on a webpage and a secure system for communication.

What we realized immediately was that it's not about the effect size of your treatment program; it's about the context you're trying to implement it in. We had issues with the patients being remitted to us for iCBT, patients not knowing what to expect from this type of treatment, having psychiatric conditions that didn't match our treatment programs, us being unsure of what we were doing, prejudice about what iCBT was ("it's a quick fix secondhand alternative and can never work as good as a face-to-face solution"), and economic decisions affecting strategies for implementation. We learned a lot, that's for sure.

In parallel with this, I was in charge of developing a new platform for delivering iCBT (and iACT). Our goal was to make an interactive platform that would appeal to more patients and be an option for those in need of help, not only those who wanted their therapy online. It consisted of a technical framework developed especially for iCBT and also contained movies, images, voice-over, animation, registrations, and other bits and pieces that would make the platform itself motivating to work with. In 2009, we had our first two programs ready, Oroshjälpen® (Help with worry) and Depressionshjälpen® (Help with depression).

Att känna sig deprimerad

Känslan av att vara deprimerad är förstås olika från person till person. I filmen till höger får du ta del av ett exempel på hur det kan se ut för någon som känner sig deprimerad.

(Above is a picture from the program—Help with Depression)

We were confident that we had developed a solution that was as ready as it could be. In 2010 we started two new collaborations in primary care. Our goal was to get this boat sailing as soon as possible. Unfortunately, we experienced problems with low compliance and therapists working with the program being unsure of how to deliver and motivate patients in the best possible way. We also noticed that economic aspects affected the amount of programs being delivered and thereby never reaching a baseline of patients that would be enough for the therapist to learn and remember how to deliver the treatment as it should be done. So we had to take one step back again. At the same time, a large research project started that we got involved in—delivering iCBT for depression in primary care. It was called PRIMnet. Our program Depressionshjälpen® was used, but otherwise we had a small impact when it came to how the study was to be done. It turned out to be much more time-consuming than what everyone thought it would be, but in the end showing that iCBT for depression was as effective as TAU (treatment as usual being, e.g., CBT, antidepressant, and other psychotherapy) in a primary care setting. Again, the issue here was not the effectiveness of the program—it worked (as we could show in a randomized controlled study done at the same time). It was the insight into what it takes to implement new methods in an existing system and how much thought, energy, and willpower you have to put in it in order to be successful.

In 2013, I had finished the first Swedish book on Internet therapy, *Internetbehandling med KBT—en praktisk handbok* (translation: *Internet Therapy with CBT—A Practical Handbook*), together with my colleague Jonas Bjärehed. Its existence was a result of the work we had done implementing Depressionshjälpen® (and other iCBT programs) in primary care and other health-care settings, where we had observed the need for information and guidelines to what the method was really about and how it should be used. The main goal was to reach out to therapists, other health-care professionals, and decision makers, to make them understand and have the right information to move on with their work with iCBT. A whole chapter in this book was dedicated to implementation, because that's what we believed was crucial to achieve success when delivering iCBT in primary care and other health-care settings.

Having been part of more than 30 implementation projects trying to start-up iCBT in different health-care settings, it has been incredibly interesting and has forced me to change and develop my perspective on iCBT as a method and how we should use it in regular care. It's not quick and cheap. It's a way of delivering evidence-based psychotherapy to more people with them knowing exactly what they get.

Things we can't live without nowadays when implementing iCBT are, e.g., creating a workgroup for the implementation, creating goals and visions, going through checklists for change work in organizations, educating therapists (and only using those with a certain level of education and competence in CBT/ACT), supervising therapist, making sure they know the program their using, and much more. Thought before action is essentially crucial. We know iCBT works—and we soon know how to use it in the best possible way. Of that I'm certain.

But there's no thought and action without a solid foundation. That's why we've always tried to do as much research as possible along the way, as the large and slow wheels of health care have opened up for iCBT. As part of a private company, you have to be creative and open to what comes along. And that's been my way of approaching research collaborations. It has lead to almost 20 studies/evaluations, from pilot projects to large randomized controlled studies. Qualitative and quantitative aspects are covered, all in the name of data.

Training

I began as a psychology student with an interest in digital tools and did my master thesis with Professor Gerhard Andersson as my supervisor at Linköping University in Sweden. It was the first, to my knowledge, randomized controlled trial on email therapy. And it worked. After graduating I started working for a private psychology company named Psykologpartners. Almost 10 years later, that's still my place of work. I've learned how to develop digital tools through the openness of the company for new ideas and a willingness to explore new solutions. Without that, it would not have been me writing this chapter.

I've attended plenty of conferences, like the first International Society for Research on Internet Interventions (ISRII) meeting and Health 2.0 in San Francisco and learned a lot from colleagues and collaborators in the area of iCBT and digital health solutions. Also, always reading articles and keeping up with the latest research has been extremely important.

Being part of studies and collaborating closely with universities in Sweden have made me always having one foot in research and the other in the clinical world, which I think has been an advantage.

Since the possibilities to educate oneself in the area of Internet therapy have been limited, the solution has been to be the one educating others and also thereby creating the first specialist course in Internet therapy in Sweden for psychologists.

Pros and Cons

There are pros and cons working in the area of digital psychology, just like in any line of work. On the upside, it's rewarding to be able to create and deliver solutions that make psychological treatment and help for psychological distress more accessible. Also, combining technology with psychology is a promising area that is in its start-up. I feel proud to be part of this development and working with great researchers and colleagues.

On the flipside, change takes time. And time makes technology grow old. Changing the way health care deliver psychological treatment is a long-term commitment. It takes a lot of deep breaths and great people around you to make the time and effort worthwhile. As health care moves slow, technology moves faster than ever. It's sometimes frustrating and worrisome to be part of technological development in such a context.

Evidence Base

A lot of research has been done in the area of iCBT. Fifteen years of studies show a firm evidence base for delivering psychological treatment online. Sweden has been an international leader when it comes to producing studies of high quality, and lots of them. It's really been a great opportunity, and probably a necessity, for my own career that collaboration with leading researchers in the field has been possible. The first study I was part of in 2004–2005 was made possible by Gerhard Andersson and Per Carlbring (and of course fellow students making an amazing effort). It was after this study that I was confident in moving on together with Psykologpartners to develop an alternative technological framework for delivering iCBT. Without the research being done on our treatment programs together with Swedish universities, it would not be possible to offer evidence-based treatment to the Swedish healthcare sector the way we do now. Research has been crucial, no doubt about it.

What's lacking is the research on implementation of these methods in regular care. I mentioned one of these studies that I've been part of that's recently published, but there's only a handful of them out there, and only a few of them are in a primary care setting.

There's a need for more studies in clinical settings and treatments being delivered within the health-care context when evaluating them. I hope that this is a direction that research will take in the next years to come. Sweden can once again lead by example and let research go hand in hand with the implementation process of iCBT that is taking place in the Swedish health-care sector right now.

References

Andersson, G., Bergström, J., Holländare, F., Carlbring, P., Kaldo, V., & Ekselius, L. (2005). Internet-based self-help for depression: A randomised controlled trial. *British Journal of Psychiatry, 187*, 456–461.

Andersson, G., & Hedman, E. (2013). Effectiveness of guided Internet-delivered cognitive behaviour therapy in regular clinical settings. *Verhaltenstherapie, 23*, 140–148.

Andrews, G., Cuijpers, P., Craske, M. G., McEvoy, P., & Titov, N. (2010). Computer therapy for the anxiety and depressive disorders is effective, acceptable and practical health care: A meta-analysis. *PLoS One, 5*(10), e13196.

Carlbring, P., Hägglund, M., Luthström, A., Dahlin, M., Kadowaki, Å., Vernmark, K., & Andersson, G. (2013). Internet-based behavioral activation and acceptance-based treatment for depression: A randomized controlled trial. *Journal of Affective Disorders, 148*, 331–337.

Carlbring, P., Nilsson-Ihrfelt, E., Waara, J., Kollenstam, C., Buhrman, M., Kaldo, V., ... Andersson, G. (2005). Treatment of panic disorder: Live therapy vs. self-help via Internet. *Behaviour Research and Therapy, 43*, 1321–1333.

Kivi, M., Eriksson, M., Hange, D., Petersson, E.-L., Vernmark, K., Johansson, B., & Björkelund, C. (2014). Internet-based therapy for mild to moderate depression in Swedish primary care: Short term results from the PRIM-NET randomized controlled trial. *Cognitive Behaviour Therapy, 43*, 289–298.

Vernmark, K., Lenndin, J., Bjärehed, J., Carlsson, M., Karlsson, J., Öberg, J., ... Andersson, G. (2010). Internet administered guided self-help versus individualized e-mail therapy: A randomized trial of two versions of CBT for major depression. *Behaviour Research and Therapy, 48*, 368–376.

Chapter 7
Technology Use in Behavioral Medicine Health

Karen M. Wall

"Any sufficiently advanced technology is indistinguishable from magic"

-Arthur C. Clarke

Evidence-Based Practice Using Mobile Applications (Apps)

The Scene: *The nurse was working with one of her veteran patients who had recently been deployed in Afghanistan and suffered from PTSD and sleep disturbance (APA, 2012). She noted that when he had flashbacks or felt "closed in," he would become panicked and start to escalate, unable to calm himself without needing a benzodiazepine, which then oversedated him. Being a veteran herself, she had several mobile apps on her phone that were developed by various Department of Defense (DoD), Veterans Health Administration (VHA), and Federal agencies specifically for veterans to use as part of their treatment. One of the apps, Tactical Breather (Center for Telehealth & Technology (T2), (Grossman, 2012), teaches a person how to do controlled breathing "by the numbers" or "tactically" in the military vernacular. She met with the veteran and asked him to try a practice session with the app under her supervision. He agreed and within a few minutes he noticed he was feeling better and breathing normally. The nurse met with him for a few more sessions so that he could ingrain the technique in his mind since he could not have his cell phone on the unit. Later that day, the nurse was walking down the hall and noticed this veteran sitting with his peers showing them what he had learned, and they were all sitting in a group practicing tactical breathing. A few days later, the veteran was having an anxiety attack, and he was able to begin his breathing exercise and calm himself down without needing medications or other interventions. The nurse had observed*

K.M. Wall, Ed.D., R.N.-B.C., B.S.N. (✉)
Department of Veterans Affairs Palo Alto, 3801 Miranda Ave, Palo Alto, CA 94304, USA
e-mail: logos68540@gmail.com

© Springer International Publishing Switzerland 2017
M.M. Maheu et al. (eds.), *Career Paths in Telemental Health*,
DOI 10.1007/978-3-319-23736-7_7

him sitting in his room, doing his breathing exercise. He called it "magic breathing." He was discharge a couple days later with the app downloaded to his cell phone and has not been readmitted since that time.

The 1970s were a time in my life when "portable technology," as I like to call computers that are not attached to a building mainframe, began to come into schools. During my junior year in high school, I needed a math class for the semester, but I hated math. I noticed a new class was being offered for learning about computers. My mother has always told me I was not the child who could sit and look at something all day; rather, I needed to manipulate everything with which I came into contact. Manipulating a computer sounded like a good deal—and *NO* math formulas to ruin my life! That was the start of my journey into the world of technology. The first computer I ever used was known as the TRS-80, a "clunker" of a machine, but it did the job. Somehow I managed to receive an award for my computer skills at the year-end assembly—a hint of things to come. I graduated from high school, and the TRS-80, to college and eventually the "mainframe" system in the 1980s during my graduate studies for my Education Degree. The first Macintosh computers were introduced to the world—colorfully packaged monitors that put together looked like a bunch of gumballs.

Training Needed for Specific Technology-Related Positions

I was most immersed in the use of technology after I became a registered nurse (RN) in the military. When I was first exploring technology in healthcare, and especially in behavioral healthcare, not many of my colleagues were familiar with what was available, nor were they proficient in accessing available technology. I learn best by doing, and as the World Wide Web, aka Internet, evolved, I learned to search the web quite proficiently for education materials for my patients to take home when they were discharged from the hospital. I got used to hearing "Go ask Karen. She can find it" on a daily basis. Through my own experience with learning technology, I have identified some knowledge and training necessities needed for various technology-based positions:

(a) "Learn by doing"—take the time to seek out the latest technology and just play with it. Anytime you, a colleague, or a client needs information, be the one to find the information by using the available technology. Learn how to research and utilize the latest technology when doing any kind of patient care or education.
(b) Take classes offered either at your workplace or through various organizations that teach novice users how to navigate and gain optimal use of technology.
(c) Get involved with professional organizations that utilize technology in their daily operations and clinical practices.
(d) If you are not a "technology native" (most baby boomers and older), interact with younger users and let them show you the skills they possess.

Pros and Cons of Using Mobile Applications

While serving in the military, I was using technology in the field as a way to do my job while away from the conveniences of a fixed facility. The mobility of the military requires resources to be available at any time regardless of the location. There still were no laptops in existence, and mobile phones were the size of a woman's purse, so I followed the progress of technology over the years in how the military delivered care to soldiers in the field and in garrison. Eventually, the resources improved, and technology became more portable. My first laptop spent the majority of its time at work with me sitting with my patients and showing them helpful websites for their recovery from their psychological problems. When we found a site that the patient wanted to use, I went to my desktop at the nurses station and pulled up the site's homepage and printed it out so the soldier could take it home and get it on his or her own computer. This was what the early days of "mobile apps" looked like.

I had been doing my graduate work in behavioral health and counseling psychology since 2008, an active time for innovation in the healthcare industry for the use of technology. I have identified some pros and cons of using mobile applications based on my own experience in the field:

Pros:

(a) Mobile technology enables the clinician in the field to be physically present with the soldier/veteran to do therapy and help the soldier find mobile apps for his or her own use without having to find a stationary computer (Epstein & Bequette, 2013).

(b) A clinician is able to interact with the soldier/veteran remotely using HIPAA-compliant mobile apps that transmit the soldier's data to the clinician's secure office to be included in their chart (Anthony, Nagel, & Goss, 2010).

(c) Mobile apps go everywhere with the soldier/veteran, so they are able to "check in" between appointments or whenever they feel the need for support (Epstein & Bequette, 2013). Their provider has selected appropriate mobile apps for them to help manage their specific symptoms (Epstein & Bequette, 2013).

(d) Thousands of mobile applications—"apps"—have already been developed for ease of use on one's cell phone or tablet anytime, anywhere. They do not require Wi-Fi in order to be used.

(e) Mobile technology allows veterans to be in the field, on post, at home, anywhere, to use wellness tools to help with their stress and anxiety related to their service.

(f) Mobile technology also allows veterans to have a connection to their healthcare team, a sort of transitional object (Lopez, 2013) (Kazdin & Blase, 2011).

Cons:

(a) Mobile applications require the individual to have some type of mobile device (i.e., phone, tablet) on which to download the apps. Not everyone has a "smartphone" or tablet due to various reasons, including cost, personal reasons, job reasons, and psychological reasons (Epstein & Bequette, 2013).

(b) Not all mobile apps are available on every brand of device; therefore, a patient who has an Android phone would not be able to download a good app that is only found on iPhones.

(c) Some apps have a steep learning curve, making it difficult, at times almost impossible, for patients with traumatic brain injuries (TBI) or other neurocognitive dysfunctions to be able to comprehend the steps to use the app.

(d) The intended app user may not speak English, which is the primary language used in most mobile apps (Anthony, Nagel, & Goss, 2010). There are a few companies beginning to develop and offer multilingual apps; however, purely clinical apps are mainly in English.

(e) Many patients still prefer the "face-to-face" experience of the clinician-patient meetings (Anthony et al., 2010).

(f) Mobile devices must be able to access an internet connection in order to use or download many of the apps.

One of the industries having the biggest growth in mobile app development is the healthcare, and especially behavioral health, field. Since retiring from the military, I have been with the VA as a psychiatric nurse in acute inpatient psychiatry and outpatient behavioral health areas. Since 2001, when the wars started in Iraq and Afghanistan, the veterans coming home from combat zones are experiencing many obstacles to mental healthcare access and other resources to use for self-care (Lopez, 2013). The use of technology on the battlefield has grown exponentially, to the point where a soldier in Afghanistan can text her family back home or send an email on a field-safe laptop. Mobile phones are even being used to help artillery find targets and units to find their troops. Case in point, Mike Murphy, killed in action, saw his soldiers were under heavy fire. He had his cell phone with him but no reception from where he was taking cover. He walked out into the open and called his command on his cell phone to tell them where to fire rounds and where to pick up his men. Right before he died of his wounds, he was heard to say into the phone, "Yes sir, thank you." Technology in the palm of his hand saved his men.

The Department of Defense and the VA are the largest developers and users of mobile technology from early in the history of healthcare (Sloan, Marx, & Keane, 2011) (Author, 2014). Technology has been at the core of my work since the first cell phone was introduced to the public. My cell phone is never out of reach and has as many apps downloaded as it can hold so that I can just pull up an app at any time. When I have a veteran who is in need of learning resources for coping skills or relaxation from his or her symptoms of PTSD or some other psychiatric diagnosis, I need to be able to give them something to take with them everywhere they go. We veterans like our care quick, convenient, and discreet-like mobility in combat. My work with the VA involves educating patients and nurses about mobile technologies in mental health. As a nurse educator, I teach nurses how to access and use technology in their everyday practice to help their patients be more involved in their care. Patients who can access a mobile app to keep in touch with what they learned in the hospital feel empowered to stay well and stay connected to the system.

Having access to several agencies' resources at anytime makes what I do enjoyable, manageable, and relevant. Many of the apps I have downloaded, either for my patients, my nurses, or even myself, have been developed by the National Center for PTSD, the Center for Deployment Health, the National Center for Telehealth & Technology (T2), and other well-known agencies specializing in developing mobile apps for veteran mental healthcare (O'Brien, 2013). Each time I search for an app in the Apple App Store or the Google Play Store, I am building my knowledge base for the future of mental health. I know that when I get to work, I have the acceptance of my colleagues and managers to be part of bringing the facility into the ever-evolving world of healthcare technology. Many times I will meet with a veteran while in the hospital and share an app I have on my phone with them. I am able to let them try the app with my supervision, and if they like the app, I am able to either give them the info for them to download it at home or help them download it onto their phone or tablet before they leave the hospital. The most popular apps used by veterans are the apps that teach breathing techniques and help with sleep, two prominent issues associated with exposure to combat and military training. I feel I have high credibility because I am a veteran and know firsthand the stresses of military duty and combat exposure. I use the apps myself, which helps me vouch for the efficacy of the app when I introduce it to another veteran. Recently, I began researching and reviewing mobile apps for our Veteran Health Education council, after noticing there was not a readily available listing of mobile apps developed for mental health in veterans. This is another opportunity for me to influence the quality of care given to the veterans by their providers. With everything positive, there must be a downside, in this case, reluctance by mental health clinicians to accept and integrate mobile technology or internet resources into their treatment and discharge plans for patients under their care. I find it frustrating and sometimes disillusioning to know that I have a mobile app that could help a veteran avoid readmission, yet the clinician feels it is an "unrealistic" plan and does not follow through with talking about it. My hope is that my knowledge and influence in the organization would eventually show the clinicians the value of providing their patients with the ability to practice self-care at home. Being able to have a follow-up or "check-in" session with a veteran through the use of an app that is privacy protected and provides remote communication between veteran and clinician in real time saves the veteran time, money, and stress of travel and increases flexibility of scheduling (Luxton, McCann, Bush, Mishkind, & Reger, 2011).

References

American Psychiatric Association (2012). Diagnostic and statistical manual of mental disorders (5th Ed.). Washington, DC: American Psychiatric Publishing.

Anthony, K., Nagel, D. M., & Goss, S. (Eds.). (2010). *The use of technology in mental health: Applications, ethics and practice.* Springfield, IL: Charles C. Thomas.

Author. (2014). *California veterans use mobile technology.* Retrieved from http://www.paloalto.va.gov

Epstein, J., & Bequette, A. (2013). Smart phone applications in clinical practice. *Journal of Mental Health Counseling, 35*(4), 283–295.

Grossman, D. (2012). On combat: The psychology and physiology of deadly conflict in war and in peace (3rd Ed.). Milstadt, IL: Human Factors Research Group, Inc. Publications.

Kazdin, A., & Blase, S. (2011). Rebooting psychotherapy research and practice to reduce the burden of mental illness. *Perspectives of Psychological Science, 6*(1), 21–37.

Kemp, J. (2014). *Using technology to improve access to mental health care*. Retrieved from http://www.va.gov

Lopez, A. (2013). *Social presence & therapeutic demands: The role of technology in the therapeutic alliance* (Doctoral dissertation, University of Denver, Denver, CO). Retrieved from http://proquest.com

Luxton, D. D., McCann, R. A., Bush, N. E., Mishkind, M. C., & Reger, G. M. (2011). mHealth for mental health: Integrating smartphone technology in behavioral healthcare. *Professional Psychology: Research and Practice, 42*(6), 505–512. http://dx.doi.org/10.1037/a0024485.

The National Center for Telehealth & Technology (T2). Retrieved from "https://t2health.dcoe.mil/"https://t2health.dcoe.mil.

O'Brien, C. (2013). *mPeer: A mobile health approach to monitoring PTSD in veterans* (Doctoral dissertation, Marquette University, Milwaukee, WI). Retrieved from http://proquest.com

RTI International. (2012). *Behavioral health roundtable: Using information technology to integrate behavioral health and primary care: Summary report of findings*. The Office of the National Coordinator for Washington, DC: The Center for the Advancement of Health Information Technology.

Sloan, D. M., Marx, B. P., & Keane, T. M. (2011). Reducing the burden of mental illness in military veterans: Commentary on Kazdin and Blase. *Perspectives on Psychological Science, 6*(5), 503–506. http://dx.doi.org/http://dx.doi.org/10.1177/1745691611416995.

Chapter 8
New Adventures in Independent Practice: Leveraging Technology to Treat Underserved, Rural Populations in Skilled Nursing Facilities

Shawna Wright

> When you get to the end of all the light that you know and it's
> time to step into the darkness of the unknown, faith is knowing
> that one of two things shall happen: either you will be given
> something solid to stand on, or you will be taught how to fly.
>
> Edward Teller

Ms. Smith was a 68-year-old, widowed woman who sat in front of the televideo camera for the first time explaining "I just want to die. I'll never walk again." Her depression was severe, and her self-care was minimal after suffering a stroke. She was hopeless about her future and was devastated by the belief that people "come to nursing homes to die." Being a retired nurse with negative, preconceived beliefs about her future, she was struggling with her rehabilitation program. She was not demonstrating gains from physical therapy. Ms. Smith's depression was impeding her recovery to the point that her worst fear was being realized: living in a nursing facility and "waiting to die." With no mental health services readily available in her rural area, Ms. Smith agreed to engage in telemental health treatment. As her depressive symptoms were addressed and she was guided in regaining a voice to advocate for herself, she began to demonstrate physical gains. Within 2 months she was walking with a walker, and psychotherapy engaged her in challenging her thoughts and plans for the future. She had a loving family, whose members valued her quality of life and supported her in moving to an assisted living apartment. Three months after transitioning to an assisted living apartment, Ms. Smith reached out to her former telemental health provider with an update on her progress. She was successfully maintaining her health and was even volunteering weekly at the local nursing home by playing piano for the

S. Wright (✉)
Wright Psychological Services, LLC, P.O. BOX 226, Chanute, KS 66720, USA
e-mail: shawna@wrightpsychological.com

© Springer International Publishing Switzerland 2017
M.M. Maheu et al. (eds.), *Career Paths in Telemental Health*,
DOI 10.1007/978-3-319-23736-7_8

95

residents. She was thriving and was even helping others who were facing similar circumstances, which had seemed overwhelming to her just a few short months ago.

Background

What motivates a psychologist who has adamantly avoided independent practice to change career paths, and not only build an independent practice but to forge into the great unknown of telemental health? It turns out that my background is not different from many of the mental health providers I have met along this journey. I am a clinically trained psychologist who specializes in child and family treatment. For the first decade of my career, I worked at a community mental health center in rural Kansas. While providing treatment in a community mental health center setting is rewarding, working in rural and impoverished areas also presents many career limitations. The high demand for mental health providers coupled with a declining economy meant working in a setting that provided minimal, dare I say absent, opportunity for professional growth and advancement (i.e., waiting for those in leadership positions to retire or move) and annual cuts to employee benefits (e.g., reduced number of paid holidays, reductions to medical benefits, cuts to continuing education funds). The professional limitations and frustrations I faced led me to explore telemental health as a career alternative because uprooting my family was not feasible. Initially, I was unnerved by the web-based mental health services I found online. Websites offered to pair therapists with clients who were charged by the minute, and some patients were treated anonymously. It was difficult to discern which providers were trained and licensed. I searched for training and professional supports in telemental health and came upon the Telemental Health Institute (TMHI), an online training platform for mental health providers. As I engaged in formal training for telemental health provision and built a network of colleagues, the aspects of independent practice that had seemed daunting were easier to address and resolve. I have also learned how telemental health practice can enhance productivity for practitioners who are already in independent practice.

Training

As with other mental health specialties, treating professionals who aspire to provide telemental health services will need to consider many factors to ensure that they have the background and training to be professionally and financially successful. Minimal requirements would be an advanced degree in a mental health field (e.g., psychiatry, psychology, social work, counseling). Additional training needs can be defined by reimbursement, target populations, and the modality of treatment provision.

Mental health practitioners interested in providing telemental health treatment should consider and study models of financial reimbursement. For example, while Medicare and Medicaid programs typically reimburse for in-person and telemental health services, they are selective about which professionals they will reimburse. Currently, Medicare will only reimburse mental health services provided by psychiatrists, nurse practitioners, clinical psychologists, and clinical social workers. Medicaid programs often follow suit, but this may vary depending upon state programs and regulations. Third-party insurance payors define which mental health practitioners qualify for reimbursement, and it is prudent to be aware of which professions are reimbursed for mental health services in the area you wish to practice prior to selecting an advanced degree field. There are alternatives to fee-for-service and insurance reimbursement models such as contracting directly with skilled nursing facilities, rural hospitals, schools, or prisons for blocks of time or number of patient seen. Contractual agreements and reimbursement for services with institutions and health-care organizations can eliminate the need to bill directly for services. However, health-care organizations are likely to require that contractual mental health providers are licensed and credentialed regardless of professional degree and background.

Special populations and practice niches should also direct educational focus and training. Prior to my work with skilled nursing facilities, my educational background and training focused on child and family treatment, and my professional background was in community mental health. As I prepared to build an independent telepractice with residents of skilled nursing facilities, I dedicated my continuing education endeavors to older adult and geriatric mental health treatment (as historically this population only comprised approximately 5 % of my caseload). However, upon building a telemental health caseload through skilled nursing facilities, I found this population to be far more diverse than I had anticipated. My youngest patient is 23 years old, and my oldest is 92 years old. To my surprise, a little more than 30 % of my caseload is under the age of 55. In addition to treating geriatric patients, I provide treatment to patients with diverse medical and mental health problems, including multiple sclerosis, traumatic brain injuries, debilitating consequences of heart attacks and strokes, and the severely and persistently mentally ill. While my background in community mental health was useful in treating patients with some of these ailments, I also relied on consultation and additional continuing education opportunities to enhance my therapeutic skills and treatment approach with the skilled nursing population. Specialty niches for telemental health populations are abundant (e.g., prison populations, school districts, rural hospitals, employer assistance programs), and mental health professionals are advised and encouraged to seek training to best meet the needs of the populations they choose to treat.

Telemental health is an emerging field, and technology-based mental health careers, interventions, and applications are growing exponentially. However, having earned an advanced mental health degree alone is unlikely to prepare mental health providers for the challenges associated with telemental health-care provision. Given that telemental health services represent a specialized mode of treatment provision, mental health practitioners are wise to seek education, training, and consultation prior to endeavoring into telemental health practice. Given my novice status and the professional risks associated with telemental health provision, I enrolled in and completed a 40-h continuing education program through the Telemental Health Institute (for full disclosure, I am currently a faculty member for the Telemental

Health Institute). As the demand for telemental health services continues to grow, a variety of training programs and opportunities are available to interested mental health practitioners. As a practicing telepsychologist, I would recommend that professionals interested in telemental health careers seek focused training in the following areas as they apply to ethics, legal and regulatory requirements, reimbursement, technology, patient authentication, special populations, crisis intervention, and informed consent. Given that the subsequent list may be longer than expected, let me briefly discuss the relevance of each element.

Ethics—Given that telemental health can be distinguished as a unique mode of treatment delivery, it stands to reason that telepractitioners should study and understand ethical standards and challenges associated with telemental health provision. Telemedicine and telemental health ethics are crucial to safe, appropriate, and effective service provision. Ethical issues and problems abound in a rapidly growing field, and many professional associations and organizations are just now identifying and publishing ethical standards for telemental health providers. Telepractitioners, particularly those who are new to the field of telemental health, are encouraged to be diligent in understanding ethical standards and challenges associated with telemental health provision.

Legal and Regulatory Requirements—Mental health providers are typically aware of the legal and regulatory requirements of their professions; however, telemedicine adds another layer of guidelines, standards, and regulations. The American Telemedicine Association (ATA; americantelemed.org) is a valuable resource for telemedicine providers. The ATA offers a wealth of information regarding federal regulations as well as the ever-changing and ever-developing legal and regulatory requirements at the state level. Telemental health laws and regulations vary by state, and it is important that mental health providers understand the laws and regulations of every state in which they hold a license and practice. A legal issue that can easily be overlooked by telemental health providers is that most states would consider it illegal to practice across state lines (e.g., if you are licensed in state X and you provide telemental health treatment to a patient who resides in state Y where you are not licensed, state Y could charge you with practicing without a license). Federal and state laws and regulations may also specifically define who can bill Medicare, Medicaid, and third-party payors for telemental health services. The Health Insurance Portability and Accountability Act (HIPAA) and the Health Information Technology for Economic and Clinical Health (HITECH) Act speak not only to patient records and transmission of patient information but also to the privacy and security of technology-based treatment and communication with patients (e.g., tele-video, e-mail). Having a working knowledge of the legal and regulatory issues related to telemental health is essential for maintaining a successful and compliant telemental health practice.

Reimbursement—As noted earlier, there are several models for telemental health reimbursement. The Internet appears to be flooded with companies that offer to "rent" space and platforms to clinicians who want to move their practices online or grow their current caseloads by adding telemental health patients to their in-person services. Mental health providers may elect to establish self-pay or fee-for-service options, which may include online fee collection (e.g., using electronic shopping carts or platforms such as PayPal). A more conservative approach would be to seek reimbursement through contracting with facilities or agencies for clinical time or patients. Other reimbursement options exist for practitioners who can bill Medicare and Medicaid; however, there are guidelines and regulations regarding the location of the patient (e.g., currently a patient must be seen in a qualified originating site; Medicare does not reimburse for telemental health services to the home) and the location of the provider (e.g., the provider must have an identified distant site/place of service). Telemental health providers need to understand the ins and outs of telemental health billing and reimbursement schemes in order to develop a sustainable business plan.

Technology—Telemental health professionals are not required to be technology gurus. Partnering with or hiring a competent technology staff can suffice in developing a telemental health practice. However, telemental health professionals should be well versed on the equipment they implement (e.g., HIPAA/HITECH/Medicare technology requirements; how to effectively and appropriately choose and use technology/equipment, how to assist patients in choosing and using technology/equipment). There are technology companies that specialize in telemedicine and can provide secure connections between providers and patients, and many ensure that IT staff are available 24 h per day. Yet, ultimately, the telemental health provider is responsible for ensuring that the equipment and services they provide or recommend to patients meet legal, regulatory, and ethical standards. Telepractitioners are encouraged to understand basic fundamentals of technology and technology applications as well as how to ensure that any technology company or service they utilize complies with applicable laws and regulations.

Patient Authentication—Undoubtedly, there are a multitude of individuals who would like to seek mental health treatment anonymously. However, telemental health providers who provide treatment to anonymous patients bear the brunt of great risk to their career and to the patient. Additionally, telepractitioners who bill Medicare and third-party payors are required to authenticate their patients to avoid fraudulent billing practices. Patient authentication can be more complex for telemedicine providers, who need to be aware of challenges and strategies for success.

Special Populations—Most, if not all, mental health professional associations recommend that treating professionals study and demonstrate competency with any special population they serve. The growth and expansion of telemental health allow for providers to reach and serve distant areas and populations and increase the importance of cultural and diversity training. Additionally, telepractitioners should also be aware of how special and diverse populations respond to and interact with technology. For example, in my work with patients of skilled nursing facilities, I expected geriatric patients to be resistant to using the technology. However, what I learned through my interactions with geriatric patients and review of the literature was that they were receptive to technology as long as the implementation was not complicated. Televideo sessions that are initiated by the staff or available with the touch of a single button (as compared to starting a computer, choosing a program, logging on, etc.) were widely accepted. Furthermore, the placement of equipment as well as the types of microphones that are used in skilled nursing facilities should be selected based upon the physical needs of the patients. The overwhelming response to telemental health services with the geriatric population has been positive.

Crisis Intervention—Managing mental health crises can be stressful and demanding for any mental health professional. However, the risks and stressors associated with crisis management can increase exponentially for telemental health providers. Before initiating telemental health services with any patient, telepractitioners should study and understand the complex issues associated with remote crisis intervention and have a tentative crisis response plan (that is further developed with the patient). Crisis intervention and planning for telemental health providers and patients require extra attention to detail and identification of resources local to the patient.

Informed Consent—In addition to obtaining informed consent for treatment, tele-mental health providers are also called to provide their patients with informed consent regarding the technology that is used in treatment. This is not limited to televideo equipment and platforms, but also to any other form of technology or communication (e.g., voice mail, e-mail, text messaging, instant messaging, mobile applications). In order to define and provide appropriate informed consent to tele-mental health patients, practitioners should be aware of legal and regulatory require-ments, which may vary by state. Consultation and training in regard to informed consent are strongly encouraged for telepractitioners to ensure that their patients are informed of and understand the risks, benefits, and limitations of technology-based treatment.

As I embarked on my telemental health career and sought professional training, I found that the more I learned, the more I did not know. In developing a training and educational plan, it may be helpful for mental health professionals to first identify the populations they wish to serve and determine in which settings they will reach their population in order to design an appropriate educational/training plan.

Pros and Cons of Independent Telemental Health Practice

As with any other mental health career, independent telepractice yields benefits and challenges to both the provider and the patient. For the most part, I have been very satisfied with my work in telemental health. On a personal level, the most obvious benefits to initiating an independent telepractice included professional growth, net-working with like-minded colleagues, and a sense of control over my professional destiny. Focusing on telemental health allowed me to establish an office in my home, which eliminated the overhead associated with renting and maintaining a brick-and-mortar office. Furthermore, I could have a home office without inviting patients into my home. The telemental health practice model assuaged many of my fears and preconceived notions about the risks associated with independent practice. The start-up costs for independent telepractice were minimal as the equipment I needed for start-up was basic and affordable. Building a professional network through my training endeavors put me in touch with a technology company that not only understood telemedicine but also had a means for connecting me with under-served, rural populations in my state of licensure. Fortunately, I was able to main-tain a part-time position with my employer (community mental health center), which allowed me to function in a role that I enjoyed as well as grow as a profes-sional. Working part time for the mental health center also provided financial secu-rity and stability as building a telemental health practice is not an overnight endeavor.

As a wife and mother of three school-aged children, working from a home office allowed me to have control over my schedule and the ability to dedicate down time (i.e., appointment cancelations) to practice-related or home-related tasks and duties at my discretion. Being able to more efficiently manage my time during the day has improved and increased the time available to my family in general. Changing out the laundry and grocery shopping are tasks that no longer have to be completed prior to or at the end of my work day. Independent practice allowed me to strike a much needed balance between my family and professional roles.

Independent telemental health practice has proven to be more financially lucra-tive than employment as a psychologist in rural Kansas. Keeping in mind that employment opportunities for licensed psychologists in rural areas are limited and wages are not competitive, the ability to bill for Medicare reimbursement has increased my annual income. After 2 years in independent practice working 3 days per week, I have replaced the annual income I was earning as a community mental health center employee. Telemental health service delivery at skilled nursing facili-ties minimizes clinical downtime and waste and allows for improved efficiency in regard to clinical productivity (i.e., patients are not scheduled "on the hour"; once a session is completed, the next patient can be seen relatively quickly). Establishing working relationships with the staff and other care providing professionals also provides for a consistent and reliable referral source to maintain a productive caseload.

Endeavoring to establish and build an independent telepractice has contributed to several opportunities that were not possible in my work as an employee of a com-munity mental health center. Through my independent practice, I am able to provide clinical supervision to mental health professionals seeking licensure (however, I do this in person rather than televideo). Additionally, medical facilities (e.g., rural hos-pitals and clinics) have become aware of the telemental health services that I pro-vide at skilled nursing facilities, and I have been approached with opportunities to grow my independent practice by collaborating and partnering with rural hospitals to provide outpatient telemental health treatment.

Telemental health provides benefits to rural communities and patients as well. Mental health resources are few in rural areas, and patients who reside in skilled nursing facilities may face more limits in access to care (e.g., travel may be limited by physical condition, providers may be 1–2 h away, appointments may be limited in frequency). Telemental health services also support facilities that are responding to federal mandates to reduce the overprescription of psychotropic medications in skilled nursing settings. Telemental health services provide residents of skilled nursing facilities with therapy and behavioral supports to manage psychiatric symptoms and improve quality of life, especially as psychotropic medications are reduced or discontinued from their treatment regimen. For severely depressed or anxious patients, telemental health interventions can increase motivation and follow through with physical and occupational therapies resulting in shorter rehabilitative stays. Additionally, therapeutic supports can improve medical care as many residents who suffer from psychiatric illness are more likely to report and disclose medical problems in psychotherapy than upon medical evaluation or through interactions with nursing staff. Another important benefit of telemental health services in skilled nursing facilities is the reduction in inpatient psychiatric admissions due to mental health crisis. Telemental health allows for residents and staff of skilled nursing facilities to connect with a provider and develop crisis interventions plans that are manageable within the facility.

Despite the rewards and benefits of providing telemental health treatment, there are challenges and difficulties associated with providing these services. To my dismay, the start-up time was not as short as I would have liked. I was advised that building my independent telepractice could take anywhere between 3 and 6 months. Yet I was sure that with dedication and follow through, my practice would build and grow at a quicker rate. In an ideal world, an independent practice can launch and be profitable, if all aspects fall in line perfectly. In reality, the start-up time may take even longer than 6 months. Therefore, it is important for professionals to develop a basic business plan and identify the essential elements to get started. Mental health professionals who are already in independent practice are likely to have a smoother transition into telemental health provision. The most significant time delays that I encountered were with establishing my business as an entity and navigating the enrollment process with Medicare, Medicaid, and other third-party payors. Despite my enthusiasm, the red tape associated with these entities did not yield to my aspirations or goals.

Currently, Medicare and Medicaid are good reimbursement sources for telemental health treatment for licensed psychologists and licensed clinical social workers, and many states also mandate third-party payors to reimburse telemental health services at the same rate as in-person services. However, relying primarily on Medicare and Medicaid as sources of reimbursement can be tenuous. Factors such as sustainable growth rate, sequestration, and revalidation can change reimbursement rates and delay or stop reimbursement for services. Any mental health provider relying Medicare and Medicaid as primary sources of reimbursement needs to be aware of the legislation that affects these programs, upcoming trends in reimbursement, and billing issues related to the population that is served.

In regard to day-to-day operations, telemental health practice can be interrupted or brought to a halt without warning for various reasons. Not only do I provide services to a rural area, but I also live in a rural area. In my location, there is currently only one Internet service provider that can sustain the bandwidth and Internet speed required to meet Medicare standards for telemental health connection. If there is an

Internet outage or problem in my area, there are no available backup systems to provide services to patients who are scheduled. Power outages have the same effect, of course. In skilled nursing facilities, unexpected state inspections or audits can interfere with the available space and personnel needed to coordinate treatment. Another risk to maintaining caseloads in rural skilled nursing facilities is staff turnover. If a director of nursing who is invested in and supportive of telemental treatment leaves a facility and is replaced with someone who does not see the value in telemental health service, the program can falter. Stakeholder investment is essential, and stakeholders can change rather quickly and without notice. Additionally, some facilities may need extra support and staff training in regard to how to effectively support a telemental health program and the need to maintain patient privacy during therapy sessions.

Providing telemental health services to residents of skilled nursing facilities comes with a unique set of challenges. Providing appropriate and comprehensive informed consent for telemental health treatment is complex in general, and this process can be more complicated when patients present with physical ailments, hearing impairments, communication limitations (often due to having a stroke or brain injury), and minimal experience using technology. Another frustration is that some patients are not appropriate for telemental health interventions for these same reasons. When the aim and goal of a telemental health program is to treat those with limited access to services, it can be quite discouraging to inform a patient that he or she is not a candidate for services.

Evidence Base

To date, there is limited research demonstrating the effectiveness of telemental health treatment in skilled nursing facilities and with the geriatric population (Grady et al., 2011) in general. Most available studies focus primarily on psychiatry services rather than psychotherapy. In their review of telemental health literature and research, Hilty et al. (2013) determined that telemental health is effective and increases access to mental health treatment. The authors found that most nursing home studies focused on the treatment of depression and dementia. Other studies have demonstrated the cost-effectiveness, treatment effectiveness, and patient and family satisfaction of telepsychiatry in rural nursing home settings (Holden & Dew, 2008; Rabinowitz et al., 2010; Weiner, Rossetti, & Harrah, 2011).

Although the finite number of published telepsychiatry studies point to the utility and cost-effectiveness of telemental health interventions, further research specific to psychotherapy needs to be conducted. More than 80 % of the 1.5 million nursing home residents in the United States suffer from psychiatric disorders including depression, anxiety, delirium, dementia, psychosis, and sleep disorders (Sheeran, Dealy, & Tabinowitz, 2013). The number of elderly patients in nursing homes is expected to increase as the baby boomer generation ages. The expected increase of geriatric patients with mental health disorders coupled with the Centers for Medicare and Medicaid Services initiative to reduce the use of antipsychotic medications in nursing homes points to the importance of increasing access to psychotherapy in skilled nursing facility and nursing home settings. However, research relevant to psychotherapy applications of telemental health is significantly lacking for this population.

In addition to identifying effective treatment protocols for geriatric patients with mental health disorders, research is also needed to address how other prevalent factors in this population may affect treatment efficacy. Sensory deficits, chronic pain, dementia, and psychosis may interfere with a geriatric patient's ability to participate in and benefit from psychotherapy delivered through technological means. Special attention should be paid to monitor size, audio quality, and video resolution as elderly populations may be less likely to adapt to interference or poor quality in telemental health delivery.

References

Grady, B., Myers, K. M., Nelson, E. L., Belz, N., Bennett, L., Carnahan, L., ... Voyles, D. (2011). American Telemedicine Association Telemental Health Standards and Guidelines Working Group: Evidence-based practice for telemental health. *Telemedicine Journal and e-Health, 17*, 131–148.

Hilty, D. M., Ferrer, D. C., Parish, M. B., Johnston, B., Callahan, E. J., & Yellowlees, P. M. (2013). The effectiveness of telemental health: A 2013 review. *Telemedicine Journal and e-Health, 19*(6), 444–454.

Holden, D., & Dew, E. (2008). Telemedicine in a rural gero-psychiatric inpatient unit: Comparison of perception/satisfaction to onsite psychiatric care. *Telemedicine Journal and e-Health, 14*, 381–384.

Rabinowitz, T., Murphy, K., Amour, J. L., Ricci, M. A., Caputo, M. P., & Newhouse, P. A. (2010). Benefits of a telepsychiatry consultation service for rural nursing home residents. *Telemedicine Journal and e-Health, 16*, 34–40.

Sheeran, T., Dealy, J., & Tabinowitz, T. (2013). 10—Geriatric telemental health. In K. Myers & C. L. Turvey (Eds.), *Telemental health* (pp. 171–195). Oxford: Elsevier.

Weiner, M., Rossetti, H., & Harrah, K. (2011). Videoconference diagnosis and management of Choctaw Indian dementia patients. *Alzheimers and Dementia, 7*, 562–566.

Chapter 9
Telepsychiatry Takes Teamwork

James R. Varrell and Olivia C. Boyce

"Coming together is a beginning. Keeping together is progress. Working together is success."

– Henry Ford

It's my 50th birthday, and I'm in a treatment team meeting with my peers at a Delaware-based community mental health center. "In" is a relative term, as I am 150 miles away from my team members, sitting in my home office and participating through a video screen in the center's conference room. We can see and hear each other just fine though and we are used to connecting this way. The distance may be a deterrent for some, but for me its commonplace. The Delaware team and I have worked together for several years now and have developed a great rapport. So much so, that on this particular day, the focus of the end of the meeting turns to me. From beyond the frame of the screen walks a nurse carrying a lit birthday cake. The room erupts in a chorus of "Happy Birthday." I smile as they place the cake in front of the screen, but my expression changes as the song ends and the "go ahead and blow out the candles" ribbing begins. They proceed to blow out the candles themselves and cut slices of chocolate cake as I look on with a mix of jealousy, flattery, and annoyance. They laugh as I get a knock on my office door, and I am hand delivered my very own cupcake. Sweet!

Now, I like to share this story with people not because I want to remind them of my age, but because it demonstrates that—with telepsychiatry—you can have your cake and eat it too. You can have the flexible lifestyle of telepsychiatry and still be

J.R. Varrell, M.D. • O.C. Boyce (✉)
InSight Telepsychiatry, 765 East Route 70, Building 100A, Marlton, NJ 08053, USA
e-mail: oboyce@in-sight.net

© Springer International Publishing Switzerland 2017
M.M. Maheu et al. (eds.), *Career Paths in Telemental Health*,
DOI 10.1007/978-3-319-23736-7_9

a part of a team. Providers worry that they may feel isolated if they transition to a virtual practice, and naysayers worry that telepsychiatry removes accountability and team approaches to care. Neither must be the case.

Psychiatry relies on collaboration. Teamwork is essential. If I am doing medication management, the consumer also needs therapy and other support. We all must communicate, whether we are in the same location or not. As a telepsychiatrist serving community mental health centers, I rely on in-person providers to be my on-site senses.

In this chapter, I am going to discuss how to create and maintain an effective team approach to care even when working remotely. This chapter will discuss how we build successful relationships between remote and in-person providers, how one should properly practice telepsychiatry through technology, and how to pick a telepsychiatry post that is the right fit.

My Telepsychiatry Story

My Telepsychiatry Career Path

As someone who has been doing telepsychiatry for over 17 years, I consider myself a bit of a dinosaur in the industry. When I started doing telepsychiatry evaluations for a rural New Jersey hospital in 1998, almost no one had heard of the concept. I couldn't have dreamed of the extent to which telepsychiatry would eventually consume my practice. Today, I have worked in almost all settings and with all populations you can think of via telepsychiatry and have the pleasure of leading a large clinical team of other telepsychiatrists. I love what I do because the opportunity with this medium of care is endless and I am constantly enthused by the ever-evolving development of the telepsychiatry industry.

My Telepsychiatry Training

Because I was an early adopter of telepsychiatry, I didn't have the luxury of any formal "training," mentors, or courses on telepsychiatry. I learned by doing and adapted my style through trial and error. Today, many of the providers who join my team are just as green as I was in my early telepsychiatry encounters. My associate medical directors, operational staff, and I do what we can to train, prepare, and mentor new providers for this form of care so that they can practice comfortably, appropriately, and effectively from the beginning. We use the best practice standards from national organizations like the American Telemedicine Association, lessons learned from our own work in the trenches, and a variety of mock encounters to help our providers get up to speed. Still, I am hopeful for a day when our next generation of behavioral health providers is trained to practice in this medium of care during school.

Why I Love Telepsychiatry

Each day I practice telepsychiatry, I feel fulfilled because I know I am able to help consumers, many of whom may not had access to care before live healthier lives. I also get joy from being involved with an ever-growing, pioneering field of practice. All that sappy stuff aside though, another big pull of telepsychiatry for me is the variety of practice it offers. Truth be told, I get bored easily, but since I am licensed in 25 different states and am often called on to fill coverage in the different states my company works, literally no day of practicing telepsychiatry is the same for me. I love the ability to see all different types of consumers in all different types of settings, and while most providers won't have that variety of practice to the same extent that I do, everyone will have the ability to work with new and different populations beyond those in their immediate physical area. Variety is the spice of life!

What I Find Challenging About Telepsychiatry

Working remotely can be extremely challenging, especially when you are a social person like me. This is one of the many reasons why I find it so important to build relationships with the on-site providers with whom I work. I also make it a point to work in breaks and reasons to get out of the house to socialize regularly.

My Take on Technology

I have always been a bit of a technophobe. When I started practicing telepsychiatry, I was extremely nervous about what I would need to know and do to make the technology work, but ultimately I learned that, as long as I was able to learn how to adapt my clinical practice and collaborate with on-site providers and support staff when needed, the technology should not be intimidating. Once everything is set up properly, the technology requirements for telepsychiatry are really plug and chug. Plus, technology is becoming ever more reliable, user-friendly, and ubiquitous as the days go on. I always remind my telepsychiatry peers that a clinician's focus should be on the care, not the medium.

Recommendations for New Telepsychiatrists

Picking a Partnership: With telepsychiatry, you have the luxury of working with different populations and communities than if you were only offering in-person services. Plus, you don't have to waste your time in the car! Even though you won't be working there in-person, it is still important that you are a good cultural fit for the organization. The goal should be to build a long-term working relationship, so consider how the organization's values, personality expectations, and modes of operations mesh with your own.

Questions to ask during the vetting process include:

- What model of telepsychiatry are they hoping to use?
- How will a telepsychiatrist fit into the regular workflow?
- Will a telepsychiatrist be primarily offering consultation or doing direct consumer treatment?
- Are they looking for a telepsychiatrist to write prescriptions?
- Do they want a telepsychiatrist to maintain primary "ownership" of his or her consumers?
- What support services are available to the remote provider?
- What support and resources are available to the consumer?
- How would success be defined?

These are the types of questions that are vital to work out early. Quality care requires consistent, long-term providers, so the onus is on you to develop a sustainable relationship before introducing consumers into the equation.

Communicating: It is vital that you learn how to communicate with your team when you are working remotely. The hardest part of making this adaption for me is that it often takes planning in order to connect. You don't have water cooler talk. You can't catch the therapist in the hall to ask a quick question. It takes additional effort and a shift of routine, but communicating through other channels is not impossible. Nearly anything can be done through phone, chat, email, or televideo. I recommend asking about and testing the best communication mechanisms during the orientation period so that the preferred communication channels are already comfortable before consumers come into place. Psychiatrists are social people so this medium may initially feel strange, but with time and effort, you will see that you are able to form remote relationships. These relationships are important for good consumer care, for the on-site staff's satisfaction with you, and for your own personal fulfillment, so if I could give anyone one piece of advice, building strong relationships would be it. Remember that you can't be successful without the help of the team.

Setting Up: When it comes to telepsychiatry, the technology is mostly plug and chug, but you do have to get familiar with it, just as you have to be familiar with how to communicate through technology. One of the first things to do is prepare your office space for optimal televideo session. Here is my set of tips for new telepsychiatrists:

Room Setup

- Conduct your encounters in a clean, organized space.
- Pay attention to what is visible within the parameters of your video image. An office backdrop setting with solid, neutral-colored walls are best when possible.

Sound

- Use a noise machine or ambient noise soundtrack to ensure privacy and help minimize interruptions outside your door. Utilize wall coverings and other simple sound-proofing measures to help to absorb noise and ensure top-quality sound.
- Know where your microphone is. Do not shuffle papers or tap near the microphone.
- Have a plan for reducing distracting background sounds: dogs barking, kids coming home from school, overhead pagers, doorbells ringing, construction, etc. are all possibilities when working from a home office, even when practicing behind closed doors.

Camera

- Sit between 2 and 3 ft from the camera.
- Mount your camera on a secure, flat surface at eye level.
- Check how you and your room look from the consumer's perspective before an appointment starts by using the "self-view" feature.

Lighting

- Make sure the entirety of the room and your face are well-lit with no shadows or black space in the shot.
- Pay attention to where your light sources are within the room. Is the lamp behind you giving you a halo? Could covering and uncovering the light as you talk with your hands be a distraction?
- Pull window shades down during the day to normalize the lighting if necessary. Do not have windows behind you.

Awareness

- Conduct sessions behind closed doors.

– Do not have other people or pets in your space during an appointment.
– Be aware of other people in the consumer's space and your own.

Presentation

– Be aware of the patterns on your clothing. Striped shirts are often distracting on camera.
– You may feel more comfortable in the privacy of your own home, but remember that your language, demeanor, and look can all affect your consumer's experience. Always present yourself in a professional manner.
– Be well groomed and wear professional attire at all times during an appointment. If you wouldn't wear it to an in-person appointment, then it is not appropriate for a televideo session.

By proactively setting up your space to account for these things, you will be able to focus your sessions on care, not the technological connection.

Communicating Via Televideo: In addition to setting up your room, it is also important to adjust your treatment style to project well via televideo. Here are some aspects to consider:

Eye Contact: Eye contact is very important during a televideo session. When you are talking, you should make a point to look into the camera, which can seem a little unnatural at first. While you will inevitably have to look down to take notes or type, be aware that that can potentially can look like your eyes are closing. Be cognizant of how you are perceived by the consumer.

Gestures: You want to be careful with your use of gestures via televideo; they can be an excellent way to express your points, but can also be distracting especially if you are gesturing outside of the frame of the camera. Ask others to critique how your gesturing improves or detracts from the experience before you begin working with consumers.

Introductions: It's important to know who else is in the room when doing a televideo session, so I recommend starting each session with introductions and potentially moving the camera around to see people who may not initially be visible within the frame of the shot. When meeting family members or other providers who may be in the room, thank them for their involvement and discuss everyone's important role in the care team.

Flow of Interview: Once you get going, the flow of your interview should not be too different from an in-person interview. Sessions should always start with consent, introductions of all of those who are in the room, and an introduction to what telepsychiatry is if the person is new to it. I will often ask if they have used Skype or FaceTime to talk with their friends or family and equate or televideo communications to that. Most people are quickly comfortable. I like to let the person know that I am working from New Jersey and we sometimes chat about the shore to break the ice.

Regulations: Additionally, it is vitally important that you understand the rules and regulations for this form of care in both your physical location and the physical location of your consumer.

Telemedicine legislation is ever-changing, so I hesitate to write anything for fear of it being outdated the moment it is published, but the biggest areas you should be well versed on include the following:

Licensure. Medical licensure is one of the biggest headaches for telepsychiatry providers. Current regulation and best practice requires a provider to be licensed in the state where their consumer is physically located.

Reimbursement. Private payer, Medicare, and Medicaid reimbursement legislation is slowly changing to allow for reimbursement for telepsychiatry. You should understand the reimbursement climate in your states so that you can be sure billing works. Do not assume that telemedicine reimbursement is guaranteed.

Physician-patient relationship. Many states have varying definitions on what is required in order for a legitimate "physician-patient relationship" to be established. This often turns into gray areas around whether or not an in-person appointment is necessary to deliver care.

E-prescribing. Telepsychiatry with a legitimate patient-provider relationship is sometimes unfairly confused with Internet prescribing via questionable online pharmacies. Thus, it is important to understand the policies of each state's medical and pharmaceutical boards before establishing a prescribing relationship.

Health Insurance Portability and Accountability Act (HIPAA). HIPAA compliance and patient health information security issues are important for making sure that the platform you are using is appropriate and safe for you and your consumers. This applies to the video technology you are using as well as how you are exchanging information other than via video. HIPAA compliance is about more than just data encryption.

Orientation: In addition to doing the preliminary research with the organization to make sure you will be a solid partnership, it is important to go through a full orientation with the organization just as if you were an on-site provider. You should be able to do this entirely via video, but it always helps if an on-site visit is possible. Topics for this orientation may include understanding emergency protocols, staff structure, formularies, normal length of sessions, documentation expectations, and more. I also recommend spending time meeting your team and getting to know how you will be working with each of them once the program launches.

Community Context: Additionally, during orientation, it is important to also get a feel for the larger community where your site is located. You should know the available community resources and know the normal referral agencies and organizations. You should also understand some of the cultural influences of the area you are serving. I find this useful for facilitating relationships with both consumers and staff members. Some providers even like to read the local news and check the local weather to know what is going on in their locations. Context matters.

Working with Your Team During a Session: The on-site staff is vitally important for the collection and reporting of vitals and other indicators like smell, mobility, and hygiene. You should get into a routine of how and when this type of important information will be relayed to you by the on-site staff. This collaboration can be as simple as a short discussion between appointments or sharing details within an EHR.

The on-site staff will also be your lifeline for introducing new consumers to this delivery model and for being there in case there are any technological or clinical road bumps. While on-site staff generally doesn't need to stay in the room during routine telepsychiatry sessions, you must know how to contact them so that they can step in as needed.

On-site staff members may also step in to help you order necessary lab work, or they can also send consumers' home with literature or information. I generally coordinate with the on-site staff to keep a folder of all of the handouts I could use organized within the televideo room. Then it is easy to ask the on-site staff to pull out the appropriate ones when they are in the room before or after an appointment. On-site providers can also help you to conduct diagnostic testing by either distributing hard copies then faxing, emailing, or loading them into a EHR to share them with you. Online diagnostic testing is also an option. Regardless of the medium, there are solutions for translating all of the normal things you do in person to a virtual practice. Even if you are working with consumers directly in their homes, it is important to create a mechanism for communicating and sharing information with a consumer's in-person providers.

Prescribing: As a psychiatrist, the obvious difference in what I do versus many of my telebehavioral health peers is prescribing medication. Prescribing and offering medication management via telepsychiatry is possible, and it is one of the biggest appeals of telepsychiatry given that 96% of counties in the US have a shortage of psychiatric prescribers. Prescribing is an area that needs to always be done appropriately, but given the dynamic nature of this industry, it is often difficult to find definitive guidelines for what exactly is appropriate. These are some of the standards I follow:

1. Always review records from a physician's physical exam.
2. When possible, consult with a physician who has an ongoing in-person relationship.
3. Have an on-site facilitator available to relay other physical findings, including vitals.
4. Supervise the use of the drug with regular medication management.
5. Adhere to all applicable standards of care and all applicable statutory and regulatory requirements.

Controlled Substances: The next question I often get is regarding controlled substances, another particularly sensitive area, but important particularly in my work as a child and adolescent psychiatrist. It is vital that you know the options for properly prescribing medication remotely in both yours and your consumer's physical location. These standards regularly change so make sure you are up to date. For prescribing, you may need to collaborate with in-person providers. You may need to check statewide databases. Even then writing prescriptions remotely may not always be permissible or advisable. For some states, it is necessary to consult with a primary care doctor or on-site prescribers for the actual medication.

Formularies: In regards to medication, it is also important to make sure you are adhering to the formularies at the sites and communities you are serving. It does no good to prescribe a prescription for a drug that is unavailable or prohibitively expensive, and you will quickly be dismissed as an outsider on the provider team if you are not well versed in the available formularies.

Careers Options in Telepsychiatry

Employment Model: Personally, I am a proponent of the employed model of telepsychiatry for a number of reasons. For one, it lends itself to more consistent, long-term relationships. This is important for consistency of care for the consumers we serve. For an organization, the employment model makes sense because it means fewer costly staffing transitions. For telepsychiatrists, the employment model lends itself to feeling supported and connected by a larger team. It also offers the opportunity for supervision, consultation, and mentorship opportunities with the team of employed providers. The employer takes care of headaches like malpractice coverage, IT support, billing and reimbursement, coverage for leave, training costs, licensure, and credentialing. This allows the provider to focus on clinical care. Additionally, employed models offer more accountability for all parties.

Independent Contractor: The independent contractor model gives providers increased flexibility, the ability to "moonlight" from almost anywhere, and the potential for a higher hourly rate. In order to pursue this model, you likely must find consumers through an organization or by yourself. For some people, the challenge and independence of maintaining your own practice is appealing; for others, it means a potential lack of stable work, additional stress, and the need to provide and maintain your own technology. There is a fairly low start-up cost because there are several online HIPAA-compliant platforms out there that allow you to transition from a brick and mortar practice to an online one. With marketing yourself online, you have the opportunity to potentially expand the reach of your practice to new consumers outside of your geographic location. You typically must supply your own insurance and can't expect standard employment benefits. There is also an argument that this model may result in less engagement with team members and peers. It can also be more difficult, though not impossible to collaborate if you are perceived as an outsider or temporary solution. I do know of some providers who band together in virtual practices and offer referrals and share consumers and expertise that way so it is possible. Still, for some, the ability to work independently is the ultimate win, so go forth entrepreneurs!

Conclusions

As behavioral health providers, we are dedicated to the same goal—improving people's lives through high-quality care. This is accomplished with a team that collaborates and communicates. As behavioral health providers, we know that the aim should be for a consistent care team, regardless of the medium or model. That team may be nontraditional, for example, a remote provider joining an on-site team or a consumer seeing their regular provider from home between on-site appointments. Other possibilities are that a remote provider could "follow" consumers to multiple sites throughout the community. Regardless, takeaways are that with technology we have the tools to connect consumers with behavioral health services like never before. We also have the ability to connect with peer providers to serve individuals, and to do one without the other would be remiss. Telepsychiatry takes teamwork. Working together is success.

Additional Reading

Cash, C. D. (2011). Telepsychiatry and risk management. *Innovations in Clinical Neuroscience, 8*(9), 26 (prescribing, this sentence only).

Chapman, M., & Janca, A. (2011). Bridging the distance between Urban and Rural psychiatry. *Current Psychiatry Reports, 13*(3), 174–177.

Cresswell, K. M., Bates, D. W., & Sheikh, A. (2013). Ten key considerations for the successful implementation and adoption of large-scale health information technology. *Journal of the American Medical Informatics Association, 20*(e1), e9–e13.

Doarn, C. R., Shore, J., Ferguson, S., Jordan, P. J., Saiki, S., & Poropatich, R. K. (2012). Challenges, solutions, and best practices in telemental health service delivery across the Pacific Rim—A summary. *Telemedicine Journal and e-Health, 18*(8), 654–660.

Nelson, D., Hewell, V., Roberts, L., Kersey, E., & Avey, J. (2012). Telebehavioral health delivery of clinical supervision trainings in rural Alaska: An emerging best practices model for rural practitioners. *Journal of Rural Mental Health, 36*(2), 10–15.

Smalley, K. B., Warren, J. C., & Rainer, J. (Eds.). (2012). *Rural mental health: Issues, policies, and best practices*. New York, NY: Springer.

Yellowlees, P., Shore, J., & Roberts, L. (2010). Practice guidelines for videoconferencing-based telemental health—October 2009. *Telemedicine Journal and e-Health, 16*(10), 1074–1089.

Chapter 10
Personal Health Records, Patient Portals, and Mental Healthcare

Carolyn Turvey

*"Ultimately, patient centered medicine is about sharing
information. It is also about respect and empathy."*

Maggie Mahar

Patricia was an older woman in the advanced stages of heart failure who was also depressed. She was embarrassed about being depressed, seeing it as a sign of weakness or failure. As her depression deepened, her cardiologist recommended she speak with a psychiatrist about how she was feeling. She avoided this at first, but eventually met with a clinician affiliated with her cardiology clinic. She told the psychiatrist that she thought her feelings of depression were normal given her illness and that all she had to do was "pull herself up by her bootstraps" to feel better. She did not see how "just talking about it" would help and she wondered what her psychiatrist was thinking about her.

At Patricia's medical center, patients could enroll on the patient portal that was tethered to the center's electronic medical record. Patricia had enrolled because access to her medical record was very helpful in managing her heart failure. She could double-check on her medication list and look up laboratory values. She was surprised to see that she could also view her notes from her visits with her psychiatrist. When she read them, she was relieved to see that there was no indication that the doctor thought she was "crazy" or weak. She was struck by how the doctor simply listed her symptoms and how she was coping and what things she and he were working on to help her feel better. The notes also helped her to remember some of the things they had discussed.

C. Turvey, Ph.D. (✉)
Department of Psychiatry, University of Iowa, Iowa City, IA 52245, USA
e-mail: Turvey@uiowa.edu

© Springer International Publishing Switzerland 2017
M.M. Maheu et al. (eds.), *Career Paths in Telemental Health*,
DOI 10.1007/978-3-319-23736-7_10

Patricia started to review her notes after each meeting with her psychiatrist. It helped her to come to understand her depression the way her doctor did, as an illness that could be treated, but also required some behavioral management on her part. Instead of feeling embarrassed when she read the notes, she felt empowered and encouraged. She started to engage in the behaviors she and her provider discussed and she stopped blaming herself for being depressed. Though she continued to have some bad days, her mood improved overall and she was able to reengage in enjoyable activities, even though she remained impaired from her heart failure.

Background and Training

Why Is a Clinical Psychologist Studying Personal Health Records and Patient Portals?

I am a clinical psychologist who retrained in psychiatric epidemiology. I have an interest in health service research, bringing effective treatments to patients who otherwise would not receive treatment. This underlies my ongoing interest in telemedicine and eHealth. I am going to discuss my recent focus on personal health records and patient portals which are not typically considered a part of mainstream telemedicine. However, these technologies are evolving as I am writing this piece and I foresee that patient health records and electronic portals will be the central technology for any truly patient-centered care.

I became interested in patient portals, and telemedicine in general, when I started conducting psychotherapy with homebound elders. Going into this work, my main focus was developing a therapy to help the elderly cope with functional impairment. As my patients were homebound, I started developing ways to conduct psychotherapy using communication technologies. Though coping with functional impairment was certainly a major concern for these homebound elders, another issue also emerged frequently. These patients had complex medical problems with multiple providers, yet their experience was that no single provider managed their comprehensive medical history. Moreover, communication between providers was poor—leading to both minor and major medical errors. Often patients reported feeling as fragmented as their care. "What doctor in charge of my health?" exclaimed one frustrated patient. "Why am I the institutional memory for the care this hospital provides me?" exclaimed another.

Even though I was not looking for lack of integration and coordination of care as a problem, it hit me over the head in the course of working with patients with complex chronic illness. Early on, I decided that part of the problem is that medical records reside where patients receive care and not with the patients themselves. Others had the same observation and started to develop personal health records. These would be electronic repositories managed by the patient or trusted caregivers which integrate health information from multiple providers. Personal health records can also include patient-generated data, such as daily blood pressure monitoring, history of taking over-the-counter medications, or exercise logs. The early models for personal health records were that patients could manage all their health information in either a PC-based or online program. This concept met a major barrier early on because developing such a record required that patients self-enter all the data. Most patients were not willing to do this (Tang, Ash, Bates, Overhage, & Sands, 2006). For some with complex medical histories, it would require Herculean effort. Some companies stated where they offer to collect patient's medical records and sort and enter the information into a comprehensive history. Though this offers one solution, many patients cannot afford such a service at current prices.

In tandem with the development of personal health records, the use of patient portals began to grow with the expanding adoption of electronic health records in larger medical centers. Patient portals give patients online electronic access to their medical record embedded within, and populated by, the specific institutions' electronic health record. Most often, patients cannot manipulate the data within their portal and they cannot add to, or annotate, the content accessed through this portal. However, patient portals do routinely provide secure messaging features where patients can "e-mail securely" their providers with nonurgent questions. They also often allow online prescription refill which is a highly valued feature. Patient portals addressed the issue of patients having to enter all their medical information—now this information is populated automatically by the electronic health record. However, until now, patients could not really do anything with this information or data.

Recently, patient portals can provide patients the ability to download and transmit their personal health information from a provider's electronic record. Moreover, more recent versions of this function generate a health summary file that is in standardized XML format. Therefore, the standardized electronic health summary from one provider can be integrated with those of other providers to form a comprehensive health history. Finally, the medical record can be truly patient centered and not provider centered!

The time span from when I first realized medical records needed to be patient centered rather than provider centered to the development of standardized, easily integrated electronic health summaries was about 10 years and occurred far more quickly than I ever expected. Though at the time of writing this chapter, many patients have yet to make use of this function, it is being promoted widely through the Office of the National Coordinator for Health Information Technology and major healthcare stakeholders such as the Department of Veterans Affairs and United Healthcare (HealthIT.gov, 2013; HealthIT.gov, n.d.; HealthIT.gov, 2013).

The Department of Health and Human Services developed the Blue Button Campaign (HealthIT.gov, 2013). The Blue Button is a registered trademark that is indicated by a round blue circle on the landing pages of patient portals with the words "Blue Button-Download my Data" underneath (Turvey et al., 2014). This symbol is the same across applications and is an indicator to patients that their portal allows them to download their data and do with it as they see fit. Patient self-management of their health information is also being promoted through the Office of the National Coordinator's Meaningful Use Criteria Stage 2 which states patients should be able to view, download, and transmit their health information (CMS.gov, 2013).

Do You Have to Get Special Technical Training to Explore the Impact of Personal Health Records and Patient Portals in Mental Healthcare?

The answer to this question depends on exactly what you want to do in exploring patient portals but most people do not need special training. I do not have special training in informatics, and, in all honesty, I am not even that technically minded. I am *most definitely not a digital* native. Nonetheless, I am heading a large multisite study examining how to train patients to use their portals to improve care coordination. My interest in this topic stems from my training in clinical psychology where I learned to listen empathically to patients. When I listened to my patients with complex comorbid chronic illnesses, they stated loud and clear that they needed a comprehensive integrated health history to guide and coordinate their ongoing healthcare. I continue to work on developing psychotherapy, but I could not ignore this other health information issue as it was clearly one of the most pressing problems for my patients.

Though I do not have or, in my opinion, need training in health informatics, I most certainly need to collaborate with people who have these technical skills. I collaborate with a computer programmer who specializes in "interoperability" which is the ability to have electronic health records from different vendors (e.g., Epic, Cerner) speaking the same language. He translates computer programming for me; I translate patient usability and comfort with integrating health records for him. Most of the difficult barriers to access to care, or to health information, require multidisciplinary collaboration.

Pros and Cons

Are There Concerns Specific to Mental Health Regarding Patient Portals and Personal Health Records?

Mental health practitioners have been some of the most vocal *against* allowing patients access to their medical records (Delbanco et al., 2010, 2012). As is often the case in mental health, both providers and others argue that information pertaining to mental healthcare must have additional safeguards to protect confidentiality and privacy due to the sensitive nature of the material discussed. I agree that the application and implementation of patient portals regarding mental healthcare must be taken very seriously. However, I disagree with most of the arguments made to somehow treat mental healthcare health information different from that of the rest of the medical record.

First, as special as the field of mental healthcare is, we are not the only professionals who hear highly sensitive material from our patients. Gynecologists, infectious disease specialists, or digestive disease specialties dealing with the downstream effects of extensive drug abuse all hear highly sensitive material from their patients or see evidence of sensitive health information in patients' physical presentation. Can we really argue this is more or less sensitive than information heard in the mental health consultation room?

Second, many mental health providers state they cannot be as candid in their notes now that patients can review the notes so easily. Irrespective of patient portals, patients have always had the right to review their medical records. Of course, having online access means far more patients will do so—but the right was always there and clinicians should always compose notes with that possibility in mind.

This second concern does raise one issue where I must admit, I do condone under certain circumstances, limiting patient access to all the information in their medical record. Though I think patients should have online access to their medical record, I believe there should be some venue within the electronic health record to allow for confidential provider-to-provider communication. I do not think this venue should be limited to mental health only. As stated, all medical professionals have access to patients' highly sensitive information. However, this privilege to document information in a medical record without patient review should be used very sparingly and not a part of the regular medical documentation practice.

Since studying patient portals and personal health records, I have made it a habit to ask clinicians if they have had any bad experiences with patients reading their records. One clinician did convey an instance that I believe meets the criteria above of warranting protected provider-to-provider communication that is not available to the patient. This clinician was working with a 13-year-old who, unbeknownst to the patient, was adopted. There it was, in just about every clinic note written for the patient—this person was adopted. The problem was the parents never told the patient he was adopted. As a 13-year-old, he has a right to a patient portal and electronic access to his medical record. Adoption is certainly an important piece of medical information as it bears directly on family history—a standard assessment in all initial diagnostic interviews. However, should a patient really learn that he was adopted from his patient portal? Does the health provider have the right to demand the parents reveal this information so the medical record information will not be one to break the news? I believe the answer is "no" in both instances, and this provides a good example of general clinical information, not specific to mental health, that may be best shared confidentially between providers.

In my ongoing questioning of clinicians about whether or not they have had bad experiences when patients read their medical record, there was one colleague who was threatened by a patient after reading his mental health note. This colleague was one of my beloved mentors within my medical center so I found it ironic that he, of all people, would experience what so many mental health clinicians fear—a patient will read their mental health note, become angry, and turn to violence. Fortunately, this situation de-escalated quickly and my beloved colleague remains unharmed. I recognize that the fears of mental health clinicians may, at some point, be realized in specific instances. However, I do not think such patient retaliation will occur as often as many clinicians expect. Since January 2013, the Department of Veterans Affairs has released all medical notes to all veterans without incident (Nazi, Turvey, Klein, Hogan, & Woods, 2014). Major medical centers across the country have done the same without incident. With so little evidence supporting that mental health patients "cannot handle the truth," can we really justify making access to their health information more cumbersome than that of patients in internal medicine or pediatrics? Obviously, I think not.

What Is the Future of Patient Portals, Personal Health Records, and Mental Healthcare?

In a word, I would say the future is "bright." A key focus of my work is integrating technologies so they talk to one another and are available to patients on different platforms. I see the personal health record as "home based" for all technologies involved in patient-centered medical care. It can be where the patient accesses his or her medical record, refills medications, and looks up potential drug-drug interactions for a new medication. Recently, medical centers are developing ways to embed videoconferencing technologies within the patient portal, so they can serve as the way to communicate with providers for a brief consultation or a complete mental health session. I love simplicity and efficiency, and I believe the ongoing development of potential functions stemming from personal health records will make them the main portal for delivering healthcare to patients. They will also serve to integrate health information and health services in a way that optimizes coordination of care. My interest in patient portals stemmed from the frustration I hear from patients about their fragmented care. Developing technologies that talk to each other, are interoperable, and are centered on the patient, not the care provider, is the best way to reduce this fragmentation so patients can feel their healthcare is based on a whole human with his or her fully integrated health story.

Another way personal health records are being harnessed is as a platform to house tools used in combination with mental healthcare. For example, if a cognitive behavioral therapist uses self-monitoring sheets, these forms can be housed on the patient portal for easy access and storage. Patients monitoring their behavior can also store these sheets in their record. Some personal health records provide tools to allow patients to easily graph their monitoring outcomes. They also facilitate ways of sharing these sheets electronically with their mental health provider. Currently, major technology firms are developing electronic monitors, such as Fitbit, to synchronize with patient portals or personal health records. Therefore, data such as activity level could be stored along with a patient's other health information.

Although these new developments are exciting, it is easy to imagine how we are quickly entering a "too-much-information age." How will patients and providers integrate electronic health record data from multiple medical providers with patient-generated data and a comprehensive health history? In a short period of time, patients went from having little and difficult access to their health information to having an unwieldy amount of information to manage and understand. The vendors and healthcare systems who listen best to what patients want to know and how best to present this information will succeed in what is becoming an increasingly competitive market.

References

2013. Retrieved from https://www.cms.gov/Regulations-and-Guidance/Legislation/EHRIncentive Programs/2016ProgramRequirements.html

Delbanco, T., Walker, J., Bell, S. K., Darer, J. D., Elmore, J. G., Farag, N, ... Leveille, S. G. (2012). Inviting patients to read their doctors' notes: A quasi-experimental study and a look ahead. *Annals of Internal Medicine, 157*(7), 461–470.

Delbanco, T., Walker, J., Darer, J. D., Elmore, J. G., Feldman, H. J., Leveille, S. G., ... Weber, V. D. (2010). Open notes: Doctors and patients signing on. *Annals of Internal Medicine, 153*(2), 121–125.

Increased patient participation with health IT. Retrieved April 23, 2013, from http://www.healthit. gov/providers-professionals/patient-participation

Nazi, K. M., Turvey, C. L., Klein, D. M., Hogan, T. P., & Woods, S. S. (2014). VA OpenNotes: Exploring the experiences of early patient adopters with access to clinical notes. *Journal of the American Medical Informatics Association, 22*(2), 380–389.

Putting the I in HealthIT: Who is Pledging It? (n.d.). Retrieved from https://www.healthit.gov/ patients-families/pledge-info

Tang, P. C., Ash, J. S., Bates, D. W., Overhage, J. M., & Sands, D. Z. (2006). Personal health records: Definitions, benefits, and strategies for overcoming barriers to adoption. *Journal of the American Medical Informatics Association, 13*(2), 121–126. PMID: 16357345; PMCID: 1447551.

Turvey, C., Klein, D., Fix, G., Hogan, T. P., Woods, S., Simon, S. R., ... Nazi, K. (2014). Blue Button use by patients to access and share health record information using the Department of Veterans Affairs' online patient portal. *Journal of the American Medical Informatics Association, 21*(4), 657–663. PMID: 24740865; PMCID:4078285.

Why would I want to use the blue button. Retrieved July 4, 2013, from http://www.healthit.gov/ bluebutton

Chapter 11
Work with Behavioral Health Technology

Jay H. Shore

"The only good is a hard hike"- James Shore, 1940–2013

"If you want to go fast go alone, if you want to go far go with others"- African Proverb/Dr. Francis McVeigh

Two quotes capture my career experience in the field of telemental health. The first is from my father (James Shore 1940–2013) who loved to hike and stresses to me the concept that the easy/quick work especially in the field of technology has often already been done when you begin a project. In order to be successful, one needs to have the expectation that there will be challenges and hard work ahead to be successful. The second quote comes from an old African proverb and is in some ways self-explanatory and is a favorite saying of a Department of Defense (DOD) mentor Dr. Francis McVeigh. It reminds me that everything I do has been part of a team which is especially true for work with Behavioral Health Technology. This contrasts with the classic academic model of CV building where disproportional credit often goes to the first author, lead investigator, or project lead.

My career path has led me to my current two key career roles that although have very different day-to-day activities and emphases, both are rooted in a commonality of leveraging technology to increase access to mental healthcare for underserved populations. I work part time for the Department of Veterans Affairs' Office of Rural Health's Veterans Rural Health Resource Center Western Region working with a team focused on improving care for rural Native veterans. An important part of this work involves a series of telemental health clinics that provide ongoing care to rural Native veterans struggling with posttraumatic stress disorder. I also work

J. H. Shore, MD, MPH (✉)
Department of Psychiatry, School of Medicine, Aurora, CO, USA

Community and Behavioral Health, Colorado School of Public Health, Aurora, CO, USA
e-mail: jay.shore@ucdenver.edu

© Springer International Publishing Switzerland 2017
M.M. Maheu et al. (eds.), *Career Paths in Telemental Health*,
DOI 10.1007/978-3-319-23736-7_11

123

part time for Colorado Access, a nonprofit organization that provides healthcare coverage largely to Medicare and Medicaid populations in rural Eastern Colorado. There I am Chief Medical Officer of Colorado Access subsidiary companies, AccessCare Technologies and AccessCare Services, created to leverage telemedicine to increase the access and quality of services for rural Colorado communities.

One of the stimulating aspects of my work is that I don't often have a "typical week" but I am always confronted with a wide and interesting range of situations, challenges, and work environments. A typical week may find me in the VA providing care via videoconferencing to an American Indian combat veteran living on or near a rural reservation in the Northern Plains. In this setting, I need to not only attend to the clinical concerns at hand and support the patient through the larger VA system, but I also have to coordinate care in that veteran's community as well as attend to cultural issues that may arise during the course of the clinical treatment. For example, for some older Native Veterans who follow traditional practices of their tribes, direct eye contact is not considered polite. Working with these patients, I have to attend to the level of eye contact that I am making as well as understand possible meanings of eye contact the patient is making. For example, is less eye contact intended as an act of courtesy an artifact of the videoconferencing system or an indication that a patient is upset or feeling down? During that same day, I may also be working with a team of people to support VA medical centers outside my region in developing their own series of clinics for rural Native veterans by providing input on administrative, clinical, and cultural issues that arise in these types of clinics.

My work with Colorado Access is an administrative and programmatic development capacity. There, I am often working to help implement telemental health clinics across and between different healthcare systems. These clinics involve both innovative clinical models such as providing psychiatric consults into primary care through virtual means (email, videoconferencing, phone) and attempting to create telemental health services with sustainable business models with long-term viability.

Regardless of the setting and organization, the work I am involved in always involves a strong evaluation component to help inform us about whether innovative clinical and administrative models that we are working on are meeting their goals of increasing care for the target population. The products of evaluation (papers, manuscripts, reports, presentation) are used to further refine and support these services. I have been very lucky to arrive at the stage where the programmatic and evaluation works are synergistic and help to feed into each other while contributing to building the scientific evidence base from which I work.

Training

As I look back on my training and career experience, it seems to me that it all naturally built to my current roles. At the time and even now, I certainly do not have a specific training goals but instead seek training and guidance for the work with which I am engaged. The two themes that emerge for me on my career development is, firstly, I have always had wonderful mentors either through luck, through circumstances, or by directly seeking them out. Secondly, I have recognized and taken advantage of significant career opportunities that have arisen.

I was lucky to have initial exposure to work with native peoples through my father's lifelong work as a cross-cultural psychiatrist and his early career with the Indian Health Service. This led me to connecting early with one of my key and primary career mentors, Dr. Spero Manso. A college degree in anthropology and pursuit of a Fulbright Fellowship (opportunity + mentorship) lead me to a year of work with the Australian Aboriginals prior to medical school training at Tulane. Interest in work with indigenous peoples continued there and stimulated my pursuit of a Masters in Public Health and a fourth year medical school rotation working with the Carib Indians in the Amazon Basin. I specifically pursued my residency in psychiatry hoping to graduate and join the University of Colorado's Centers for American Indian and Alaska Native Health (CAIANH), where Dr. Manson was director. A critical meeting occurred in my third year of residency when Dr. Manson sat me down to discuss different areas of opportunities to pursue research and programmatic work. CAIANH at the time was looking at the relatively "new" (1999–2000) and growing field of videoconferencing to reduce staff travel needed to collaborate with over a 100 different tribal partners and communities. Dr. Manson saw the use of videoconferencing and technologies as an important upcoming tool that could be leveraged to address the access and quality of healthcare disparities in this population. I was intrigued as well by telepsychiatry (live interactive videoconferencing) and could imagine the possibilities of working and reaching out to patients in need over vast distances.

This led, under CAIANH and Dr. Manson's mentorship, to the development of a specific project in this area, utilizing the existing community relationships and research infrastructure built by CAIANH. We created a project, identified funding sources, and managed to obtain an extramural National Institutes of Health (NIH) fellowship focused on a study to examine the reliability of telepsychiatry for assessment of rural Native veterans. I also began to work on a collaborative project between CAIANH, the Denver VA, and the Rosebud Sioux Tribe to develop and implement a telepsychiatry clinic in rural South Dakota for Rosebud Sioux Veterans. I was the clinician and lead administrator for the clinic which rapidly included the Hot Springs VA system and Rosebud Indian Health Service (IHS). It was there I began to work with teams of VA, University, and tribal employees that would teach, guide, and collaborate with me on this clinic model.

The initial success of the Rosebud clinic led to two further very important opportunities. I was approached by a former attending and future career mentor Dr. Herbert Nagamoto at the Denver VA to develop a series of telepsychiatry clinics at the Denver VA to train psychiatric residents in telepsychiatry while providing services to rural Colorado veterans. In a parallel fashion, Mr. Buck Richardson and Mr. James Floyd with regional VA entity (VISN 19) asked me to join them in duplicating the Rosebud Model within the VA system. This led to a partnership and collaboration for over a decade focused on expanding telemental health services for rural

Native veterans. We began working with a wide array of VA teams and staff as well as tribal partners to create a series of telemental health clinics out of Denver that currently serve 14 tribes through eight clinic sites in Montana and Wyoming.

The clinics caught the attention of Dr. Byron Bair who in 2008 was putting together the Veterans Rural Health Resource Center Western Region (VRHRC-WR) with his deputy director Ms. Nancy Dailey. This resource center was part of the new VA's Office of Rural Health. Dr. Bair invited me to join their team. The VRHRC-WR brought further focus, resources, and support for the clinics as well as an expanding focus on other programs, areas, and technologies that could improve care for rural Native veterans. Although not all my current work within the VA is telehealth focused, the different project and components (outreach, clinical programs, deepening understanding of barriers) all complement each other.

In my role with the University, I continued my NIH research as well as working on small telehealth pilot clinics in rural Colorado and Alaska. Several of these were time limited and ended with the pilot for lack of sustainable business models we had failed to create. One service to Alaska has remained however for over the past 8 years where I have functioned as the psychiatrist a couple hours a month for a 6-month residential alcohol treatment center for Alaska Natives.

Early in my career I joined the American Telemedicine Association (ATA) and committed to get involved deeply in this organization through presentations and attendance at the annual meeting and work with various ATA committees. The ATA was a very rich source of colleagues, collaborators, and national mentors in the field of telemental health. This network provided guidance and support of my work as well as allowing me to share my experience in telemental health and help my colleagues. Eventually, I ended up in ATA leadership roles which include serving on its Board of Directors and as Chair of the ATA's Special Interest Group in Telemental Health.

In 2005–2006, my NIH research funding was drawing to a close (the large portion of my University funding), and I had yet to identify the next steps and sources of funding. My roles in the ATA brought me to the attention of a Department of Defense organization Telemedicine and Advanced Technology Research Center (TATRC). TATRC is a US Army organization based out of Fort Detrick, Maryland, and bills itself unofficially as the "light cavalry" of Army Medical Research seeking out technologies with potential to enhance care and treatment of our military populations. TATRC's leaders at that time, Colonels Karl Friedl and Ronald Poropatich, sought me out at an ATA meeting to gauge my interest in serving as a part-time subject matter expert to help manage TATRC's growing behavioral health portfolio.

I spent the next 6 years working part-time with TATRC working across a wide spectrum of technology projects in behavioral health. This included project creation, management, and review for the Department of Defense. In this role I was exposed to a much broader array of technology applications (mobile apps, virtual reality, social networks) being applied in mental health. This helped to grow my knowledge on technology in medicine beyond videoconferencing as well as inform the interface of newer technologies with videoconferencing. TATRC which involved a lot of research management for the DOD gave me a better appreciation of the tension between research and implementation in the field of technology.

As US involvement in the wars in Iraq and Afghanistan began to decrease and shift, so did TATRC's mission and scope. At this time I began having discussion with Dr. Marshall Thomas, the director of the University of Colorado's Depression Center who was also the CEO of Colorado Access, a Medicare and Medicaid healthcare plan, and administrator of over 900,000 lives under coverage serving large parts of rural Colorado. Dr. Thomas was looking to develop telemental health on a more enterprise level for the Colorado region. These discussions led me to transitioning out of TATRC to assume a dual part-time role as the Director of Telemedicine for the Depression Center and Chief Medical Officer for two subsidiary Colorado Access companies (AccessCare Services and AccessCare Technologies) to help support enterprise development of telehealth in Colorado. The cumulative experiences throughout my career in telehealth and technologies helped prepare me to take on these roles which I currently am engaged.

As I reflect on my career pathway, I have had a diverse array of experience but they all have enough commonalities with a focus on technology that the disparate work often informs each other. I have benefited as well from cross-pollination, where problems, solutions, and lessons learned from one work environment can be adapted and applied to another. At each stage, I have had key mentors and colleagues that have mentored, guided, and advised me as I have taken on new experiences. This is the gracious group of people I have sought out in my work environments based on mutuality and specific expertise in technology, cultural, or behavioral health issues. I do not consider myself a "techy," but I generally know the fundamentals of each of the technology I work in. I feel that learning about technology for any given project or work environment is the most straightforward, while understanding process, politics, and how to be successful working across environments and teams has been the most challenging.

Another important theme that has emerged for me is that I have also selected technology based on programmatic needs. That is, for me, technology that I use or work with is for a specific need, directed at the goal of increasing the access and quality of mental healthcare for the populations with which I work. I consider myself generally agnostic about a specific technology, company, or product as long as it meets the overarching mission and goals.

During all stages of my career, I have been very fortunate (see references for examples of key work) to be able to evaluate and examine the technologies and programs that I work with and produce chapters, manuscripts, and guidelines. This has been extremely rewarding to be part of the creation of the evidence base that contributes to guiding the work in the field. Several of the evaluation projects or conceptual manuscripts that I have become involved arouse out of a clear need identified during my clinical experiences. Often careers in health and technology means one at times is working on the cutting edge of innovations in healthcare. It is critical for the field to document and evaluate one's efforts which can contribute to important data for providers and funders about specific technologies. For example, in the mid-2000s, I and two national mentors I met through the ATA were getting multiple queries on how to use telepsychiatry in emergency situations. As a group we had both programmatic data and individual clinical experience managing safety issues. This led to the production of an article whose intent was to proffer initial advice to the field in this area.

The positive aspects of my career path have been a varied career that is never boring. I feel constantly challenged and I am learning something new every day about people, technology, health, and systems. I have enjoyed working with different people from a diverse array of backgrounds, systems, and cultures which has often included frequent travel throughout the United States. I also take deep satisfaction in the work I am engaged in makes a difference to individual patients as well as the healthcare systems that are treating them. The mix of clinical work, research, administration, and program building provides a wonderful variety.

One of the challenges and downsides of this career path is that working across multiple systems creates loss of efficiency in terms of time. This is especially true of administrative processes such as training, traveling, and credentialing. Attempting to appropriately balancing the work load between systems while still remaining on task with individual projects and making oneself available is often a tightrope act. Learning patience with myself and multiple systems has helped better manage these pressures. Another challenge, which I think we all face in the healthcare field, is the length of time it takes to implement new services and ideas and see their impact. Finally, although traveling for work can be exciting, it can take a toll both physically and emotionally. For those with families, work travel can put an extra burden on loved ones. Decreasing my travel was one of the factors that led to change my work from DOD to Colorado Access.

Despite the challenges at times, I am grateful to be on my current career pathway and love my work. For me, the organic blend of my roles and the use of technology to help patient populations have been a winnable combination.

References

Morland, L. A., Greene, C. J., Rosen, C. S., Foy, D., Reilly, P., Shore, J., ... Frueh, B. C. (2010). Telemedicine for anger management therapy in a rural population of combat veterans with posttraumatic stress disorder: A randomized noninferiority trial. *Journal of Clinical Psychiatry, 71*(7), 855–863.

Shore, J. (2013). Telepsychiatry: Videoconferencing in the delivery of psychiatric care. *American Journal of Psychiatry, 170*(30), 256–262.

Shore, J. H., Aldag, M., McVeigh, F., Hoover, R., Cuilla, R., & Fisher, A. (2014) Review of mobile health technology for military mental health. *Military Medicine, 179*(8), 865–878.

Shore, J.H., Brooks, E., Savin, D., Orton, H., Grigsby, J., & Manson, S.M. (2008). Acceptability of telepsychiatry in American Indian veterans. *Telemedicine and e-Health, 14*(5), 461–466.

Shore, J. H., Hilty, D. M., & Yellowlees, P. (2007). Emergency guidelines for telepsychiatry. *General Hospital Psychiatry, 29*, 199–206.

Shore, J., Kaufmann, L. J., Brooks, E., Bair, B., Dailey, N., Richardson, B., ... Manson, S. (2012). Review of American Indian veteran telemental health. *Telemedicine and e-Health, 18*(2), 87–94.

Shore, J. H., Mishkind, M. C., Bernard, J., Doarn, C. R., Bell, I. Jr., Bhatla, R., … Vo, A. A. (2014). Lexicon of assessment and outcome measures for telemental health. *Telemedicine and e-Health, 20*(3), 282–292.

Shore, J. H., Savin, D., Orton, H., Beals, J., & Manson, S. (2007). Diagnostic reliability of telepsychiatry in American Indian veterans. *American Journal of Psychiatry, 164*, 115–118.

Turvey, C., Coleman, M., Dennison, O., Drude, K., Goldenson, M., Hirsch, P., … Bernard, J. (2013). Practice guidelines for video-based online mental health services. *Telemedicine and e-Health, 19*(9), 722–730.

Yellowlees, P., Shore, J., & Roberts, L. (2010). Practice guidelines for videoconferencing-based telemental health. *Telemedicine and e-Health, 16*(10), 1074–1089.

Chapter 12
The Accidental Telepsychologist: Creating Opportunities in a Burgeoning Field

Sara Smucker Barnwell

"The best way to predict the future is to invent it."

Steve Jobs

Narrative Vignette

Practitioners wanting to provide ethical, accessible evidence-based care facilitated by technology may necessarily be forced to expand their competencies beyond their training and, at times, comfort. A provider delivering care to a pregnant client with post-traumatic stress disorder sought a mechanism to continue delivering care after his client gave birth prematurely. Although pediatric providers determined that the child was in good health, the infant was hospitalized for observation and care in a hospital some distance away from the provider's office. The mother was understandably distressed after a long and extremely medically complex birth experience and reported significant exacerbation of premorbid PTSD symptoms. For practical reasons, neither the provider nor the patient could travel to the other's location. The provider wanted to support his client during this difficult time, but had myriad questions regarding whether it was appropriate to meet at a distance, whether meeting in this way was consistent with his evidence-based approach to therapy, what technologies he could use to deliver care to his client, and what his liability would be for delivering care at a distance. The provider sought to balance time-sensitive responsiveness to his client's needs with thoughtful, competent implementation of a plan for distance therapy.

S.S. Barnwell, Ph.D. (✉)
Department of Psychiatry & Behavioral Sciences, University of Washington,
Box 356560, Room BB1644, 1959 NE Pacific Street, Seattle, WA 98195-6560, USA
e-mail: sara@doctorsmucker.com

© Springer International Publishing Switzerland 2017
M.M. Maheu et al. (eds.), *Career Paths in Telemental Health*,
DOI 10.1007/978-3-319-23736-7_12

The provider sought consultation with a telehealth practitioner. A thorough discussion regarding the provider's goals, comfort with technology, and concerns resulted in the collaborative creation of a plan to serve the client via videoconferencing. The provider documented his plan, including the consultation, the choice of HIPAA compatible software, his risk vs. benefit analysis for the use of videoconferencing, and his understanding of hospital policy and the manner in which he would serve his client within his licensure jurisdiction. He created a brief emergency plan and informed consent for the use of videoconferencing and obtained his client's signatures. He discussed the risks and benefits of this approach with his client before initiating care. He contacted his client's insurer and obtained approval to receive reimbursement for these meetings. In this way, he was able to deliver client-centered care in a way that was ethical and appropriate. The availability of a consultative resource was central to his ability to be simultaneously cautiously thoughtful and responsive to client needs.

Training

I have enjoyed a career in telehealth that has engaged a diversity of roles—from technical support to director of a multisite federal telehealth program. There is a common theme that ties these experiences together—a pragmatic approach to making more evidence-based care available to serve our clients where they are. Each experience has been tremendously valuable in granting insight into the complex and nuanced regulatory and technological systems that underlie and enable technology-facilitated behavioral healthcare. Roles in corporations building businesses have been as compelling and instructive as more formal, classically academic training opportunities. To imply that my training has been linear and consistently driven toward a specific professional outcome would misrepresent a more exploratory path. It has been the pursuit of a passion, an empirical question, or an emerging area that guided my personal development. My narrative does not describe a commonly traveled path in telehealth, but offers insight into how one person operationalizes interests into results in the diverse field of telehealth.

At its core, my professional passion resides in the ethical democratization of telehealth technologies in behavioral healthcare. This passion takes many forms and includes activities like expanding access to evidence-based behavioral healthcare through direct telehealth services, creating training opportunities for clinicians seeking guidance in this seemingly inaccessible area of practice, and advancing the discourse that will shape how these technologies are adopted broadly. Because my interests reside in the practical application of a nascent care modality, much of my training occurred "on the fringe"—in small companies, in emerging areas of practice, or by the generous allowances of employers and mentors who permitted me to "try something new." The chronological overview of my most formative training opportunities offered below is not a path for others to follow, but rather demonstrates that telehealth offers the opportunity to create new paths and benefits from diversity of experience and interests. I encourage anyone interested in a career in telehealth to be creative and proactive in crafting the experience she seeks.

My journey began with exposure to diverse research methods and topics of study as an undergraduate at Wellesley College. I was a volunteer and then paid undergraduate research assistant with the college psychology department and its affiliated research centers. As a research assistant at the Center for Research on Women in 1997, I supported grant-funded research examining women's adoption of technology in educational environments. Unsurprisingly, women with greater openness to adopting new technologies (e.g., a personal computer, word processing, Internet use) enjoyed more positive educational outcomes (e.g., superior grades in school, on time graduation). These experiences introduced me to the world of behavioral health research and required me to be thoughtful regarding my own attitudes toward technology. I grew up in a Mennonite community in rural Ohio that modestly imbued me with themes of wariness regarding the costs of technological advancement to interpersonal relationships and community. I did not have an innate interest in technology, so the notion that technology could enhance these connections was novel and challenging.

These early research experiences fostered an interest in the intersection of human development and advancing technologies, and lead me to seek related experiences in the technology sector of private industry. In the late 1990s, there existed many Internet start-ups, but few in the behavioral health space. I joined a small Internet start-up company dedicated to connecting healthcare providers and patients online. This work introduced me to the complex legal requirements governing doctor-patient interactions online, the necessity of preserving patient/provider relationships in technology-facilitated environments, the value of patient- and provider-friendly technology interfaces, and providers' wariness regarding the legal and relationship risks that technology introduces. This experience was invaluable in highlighting the implementation complexities that arise when you innovate healthcare.

I entered a master's program at Harvard Graduate School of Education in 2000, hoping to further explore themes of behavioral health, adult development, and technology. Coursework with luminaries such as Carol Gilligan and Robert Kegan offered singularly inspirational training and drove me to investigate themes of technophobia among women in behavioral health. Harvard University also offered coursework in advanced statistical analysis, a tool that granted entrée into data analysis necessary for evidence-based research central to my later work. I took these skills to my doctoral training at the University of Southern California's clinical psychology program where I deployed them to leverage online assessment environments. My doctoral dissertation compared online and in-person assessment of drug and alcohol use, finding little statistically relevant difference between the two modalities.

In 2007, I sought real-world experience to learn how online assessment techniques were being implemented. I was compelled by the potential for online research methods to advance the reach of assessment measures in behavioral health, so I worked with several companies dedicated to online assessment tools for behavioral health providers and telephone- and online-based smoking cessation interventions. From this experience I gained perspective into the tremendous impact potential for telehealth technologies in behavioral health. The empirical literature in telehealth was small but burgeoning. As a clinical psychologist, I was eager to become involved in the work to bridge the gaps between research and practice. I ultimately found this nexus as a psychologist at the Veteran's Affairs Administration (VA) where I took a role as Director of Telemental Health programming.

My role in the VA system offered access to unparalleled telehealth training, collaboration, and practical opportunities. At Seattle VA, I found the ideal environment in which to combine thematic interests in behavioral health interventions and technology-enabled care access. As a federal entity, the VA enjoys licensure mobility in which practitioners may be licensed in one jurisdiction and incumbent on successful credentialing and privileging across care sites, practice in another. The VA offers formal training and certification on topics such as clinical video teleconferencing, managing emergencies remotely, the business aspects of telehealth implementation, and other critical implementation elements. With a rural client population geographically disconnected from an urban provider population, the VA has compelling service needs that require it to develop creative solutions. It also forces the VA to offer a myriad of clinical training opportunities to ensure that its provider programs operate in compliance. It is for these reasons that the VA has consistently provided telehealth thought leadership and professional training and attracted behavioral health providers with an interest in telehealth. The Seattle VA, like many others, maintains a formal relationship with local academic research. Seattle VA's longstanding relationship of academic collaboration and shared interest in telehealth with the University of Washington facilitated connections to academic telehealth projects. As a result of my work, I accepted an appointment as assistant professor in the Department of Psychiatry and Behavioral Sciences. I strongly encourage anyone seeking a career in telehealth to consider training, working, or volunteering in the VA or Department of Defense healthcare systems to gain access to training and clinical opportunities unavailable in other environments.

In 2009, the Seattle VA provided me the opportunity and staffing to create a small videoconferencing-based clinical program. Responding to the varied clinical demands of rural primary care clinics, the Seattle VA Telemental Health program sought to deliver evidence-based care into small clinics and Veteran residences. From 2009 to 2014, this small program grew from a single-site program with two providers delivering to a diverse program of 17 psychologists, psychiatrists, social workers, and nurses delivering care to 11 hospital sites and countless Veteran residences. Overseeing VA Puget Sound Health Care System Telemental Health Program at Seattle VA, I had the distinct pleasure to lead a team of behavioral providers who employed emerging technologies to serve clients who historically had limited access to care. Like many clinicians in large-scale federal institutions such as the VA and Department of Defense (and private practice alike), we used telephone, videoconferencing, mobile applications, online psychoeducation, and other telehealth modalities to increase care access to clients in rural or underserved communities, as well as clients with medical challenges that prohibit travel to outpatient environments. Perhaps more importantly, the opportunity to help build this program granted access to the end-to-end process of ideation to implementation—staff recruitment, training, clinical service delivery, policy creation, and technical infrastructure requirements. The adage "the devil is in the details" was salient, and the varied experiences offered through creating new programming offered a thorough education in the practical aspects of telehealth programming. I wanted to find a way to share this information with my colleagues.

I collaborated with Seattle VA training leadership to create ways of communicating the lessons learned through the creation of the Seattle VA Telemental Health team. This included a postdoctoral fellowship in psychology for Telehealth and Rural Outreach, telehealth rotation options for predoctoral interns, and training programs for VA Puget Sound mental health clinicians interested in telehealth. I collaborated with local and VA leadership to create new policy to help guide ethical telehealth provisions for Veterans. These experiences offered insight into how care is delivered at scale, what policy initiatives we need to drive and why, and how to transmit the lessons we learned.

From 2010 to 2013, I was honored to serve as a member of the APA, ASPPB, and The Trust Joint Task Force in telepsychology, a group charged with drafting national guidelines for the practice of telepsychology. The impact that this experience had on my current thinking about telehealth cannot be overstated. Exposure to the considerations of this community of policy makers, practitioners, and regulators offered me vastly greater insight into the challenges facing telehealth. I volunteered my time to consult with my state psychology board members interested in telehealth and gave lectures on telehealth in my professional community's regulatory and policy-making bodies. Exposure to this regulatory and policy making facilitated opportunities to volunteer with organizations committed to the advancement of telehealth (e.g., consultation with my own and other state boards, requests to participate in speaking engagements and discussion panels) that continued to challenge and grow my own thinking. Above all, experiences in policy creation and regulation bridged important gaps in my thinking between the practical and theoretical, federal and private practice environments, and even traditional psychological services and private industry.

In 2014, I began a small business, Telehealth Training Solutions, LLC. Like my career thus far, the work is diverse. I offer telehealth clinical services and collegial consultation in two local private practice groups interested in increasing their telehealth presence in our licensure jurisdiction. I deliver workshops and trainings to clinicians interested in technology-enabled behavioral health, publish articles related to telehealth, and consult with individuals and organizations regarding telehealth. I maintain a connection to the VA's telehealth service team, as well as the University of Washington Department of Psychiatry and Behavioral Sciences as a clinical professor.

In light of the emerging noninferiority literature for technologically facilitated behavioral intervention (see Morland et al., 2014), significant numbers of clinicians, companies, and regulators are increasingly interested in telehealth. Clients seek care aligned with the convenience and busy lifestyles of the clients they serve. Yet behavioral health providers are infrequently also technologists, and graduate training rarely expressly addresses issues of technology. The marketplace for telehealth technologies that enables behavioral healthcare is diverse and poorly articulated in terms of the demands placed on healthcare providers (e.g., HIPAA, HITECH compliance). As a result, practitioners often necessarily must step outside of their scope of knowledge and expertise to deliver telehealth interventions. Absent in a consultation community, many practitioners simply elect to abstain from incorporating technology into their practice out of concern for ethical and legal violation. Answers for difficult questions do not yet exist. However, the process of collaboration in search of the answer creates a foundation for the future. Because of this, my small business is meeting an identified need of the community and performing well in its first year of operation.

Pros and Cons

The diversity of my work is a tremendous positive inasmuch as it facilitates a holistic perspective as clinician, consultant to private practitioners and industry, and contributor to policy in telehealth. Understanding the telehealth landscape broadly is a poignant benefit of and to the clinical work I deliver. A grasp of the practical, clinical, and policy concerns central to telehealth allows me to deliver care and consult with other care providers confidently. Reaching across geographic, socioeconomic, health-related, and other barriers to care access provides me with a rich, diverse, and engaging clinical case load. The knowledge that I am reaching clients who might not otherwise receive care resonates with my own values and increases my satisfaction in my work.

Additionally, it is an exciting time to be involved in policy creation for telehealth. The canon is not yet established. There is great opportunity to support the ethical growth of the telehealth medium. Consultation provides opportunities to make connections with innovators in our own time, as well as exciting research and policy work that will shape our profession. For early career individuals such as myself, I believe that the telehealth field offers a uniquely compelling opportunity to be impactful in a growing space that may not consistently exist in other, more established practice areas.

Practically, as the mother of a young child and early career psychologist, the flexibility that this work affords has been central to attaining a work-life balance that feels sustainable without sacrificing a forward trajectory of professional development and advancement. Delivering videoconferencing care typically involves fewer barriers (e.g., shared professional office space, long commute hours, work hours that do not align with child care hours). Consulting and policy work can typically occur on a flexible schedule when delivered by a deadline. A specialty niche that is in growing demand allows for greater professional opportunities and flexibility to craft a work schedule that accommodates values and goals outside of professional life.

The diversity of my work that strengthens my perspective also provides its greatest challenge. Keeping abreast of changing clinical standards, policy, law, and research in the broad and diverse telehealth space can prove daunting. A substantial investment of unpaid hours will be required to approach the wealth of information associated with competence. In my own career, volunteer opportunities have frequently provided the richest and most personally valuable discourse. Thus, pursuing what is interesting may not consistently prove lucrative.

Videoconferencing and other distance therapies bring the perception of greater risk, despite a small literature to the contrary (see Luxton, Sirotin, & Mishkind, 2010). Technology necessarily outpaces regulation, and it is difficult to know the best, risk managed path—or to advise others on the best path. What videoconferencing software is the safest and most compatible with HIPAA? Which email vendor uses the most robust encryption? How comprehensive must a remote emergency management plan be? Will a mobile carrier provide a Business Associate's Agreement if I elect to text message with clients? Consider the challenges of interjurisdictional practice, and the manner in which the introduction of mobile devices, email, and videoconferencing may result in contact outside our jurisdiction without explicit knowledge. In a practice environment that often lacks explicit regulation governing telehealth, an increased burden of risk can fall on the individual practitioner to select a path that is most compliant with the guidance available.

Even when risk is well managed, the prevalence of negative attitudes toward technology and its advocates is substantial in healthcare. It is often my task to convince understandably wary administrators, clinicians, and/or policy makers that ethical telehealth is possible and that the very work "telehealth" is an anachronistic approach toward the inevitable integration of technology into psychological services.

Evidence Base

The evidence base in clinical telehealth is expanding at a tremendously rapid pace. Seminal papers began to explore themes of noninferiority of clinical outcomes (see Backhaus et al., 2012; Gros, Yoder, Tuerk, Lozano, & Acierno, 2011; Morland, Hynes, Mackintosh, Resick, & Chard, 2011) for interventions delivered over videoconferencing. Other key works begin to deliver evidence regarding the safety of clinically unsupervised clinical environments (see Luxton, O'Brien, McCann, & Mishkind, 2012; Luxton et al., 2010) or even the manner in which technology may critically advance our thinking about clinical safety (Luxton, June, & Kinn, 2011). Maintaining awareness of the empirical base for clinical telehealth is central to providing ethical care to clients, communicating telehealth's value to clinicians and administrators, and informing sound policy to protect the public.

Our profession offers increasing guidance based in the empirical evidence— from aspirational professional guidelines (see APA/ASPPB/Trust guidelines) to practical "how to" white papers (see American Telemedicine Association guidelines). Awareness of these guidelines in addition to federal (e.g., HIPAA, HITECH) and state guidelines (see Ohio Psychological Association guidelines) helps providers remain within current best risk management practices.

References

American Psychological Association. (2013). Guidelines for the practice of telepsychology. Retrieved from http://www.apa.org/practice/guidelines/telepsychology.aspx

American Telemedicine Association. (2013). *Practice guidelines for videoconferencing-based online mental health services.* Retrieved from http://www.americantelemed.org/practice/standards/ata-standardsguidelines

Backhaus, A., Agha, Z., Maglione, M., Repp, A., Ross, B., Zuest, D., ... Thorp, S. (2012). Videoconferencing psychotherapy: A systematic review. *Psychological Services, 9*(2), 111–131. http://dx.doi.org/10.1037/a0027924

Gros, D. F., Yoder, M., Tuerk, P. W., Lozano, B. E., & Acierno, R. (2011). Exposure therapy for PTSD delivered to veterans via telehealth: Predictors of treatment completion and outcome and comparison to treatment delivered in person. *Behavior Therapy, 42*, 276–283. doi:10.1016/j.beth.2010.07.005.

Luxton, D. D., June, J. D., & Kinn, J. T. (2011). Technology-based suicide prevention: Current applications and future directions. *Telemedicine Journal and e-Health, 17*, 50–54. doi:10.1089/tmj.2010.0091.

Luxton, D. D., O'Brien, K., McCann, R. A., & Mishkind, M. C. (2012). Home-based telemental healthcare safety planning: What you need to know. *Telemedicine Journal and e-Health, 18*, 629–633. doi:10.1089/tmj.2012.0004.

Luxton, D. D., Sirotin, A. P., & Mishkind, M. C. (2010). Safety of Telemental healthcare delivered to clinically unsupervised settings: A systematic review. *Telemedicine Journal and e-Health, 16*, 705–711. doi:10.1089/tmj.2009.0179.

Morland, L. A., Hynes, A. K., Mackintosh, M. A., Resick, P. A., & Chard, K. M. (2011). Group cognitive processing therapy delivered to veterans via telehealth: A pilot cohort. *Journal of Traumatic Stress, 24*(4), 465–469. doi:10.1002/jts.20661.

Morland, L.A., Mackintosh, M.A., Greene, C.J., Rosen, C.S., Chard, K.M., Resick, P., & Frueh, B.C. (2014). Cognitive processing therapy for posttraumatic stress disorder delivered to rural veterans via telemental health: a randomized noninferiority clinical trial. *Journal of Clinical Psychiatry, 75*(5), 470–476. doi:10.4088/JCP.13m08842.

Ohio Psychological Association. (2010). *Telepsychology guidelines.* Retrieved from http://www.ohpsych.org/psychologists/files/2011/06/OPATelepsychologyGuidelines41710.pdf

Chapter 13
Treating Emotional Consequences of Sexual Assault and Domestic Violence via Telehealth

Sarah Steinmetz and Matt J. Gray

> *"Nobody can go back and start a new beginning, but anyone can start today and make a new ending."*
>
> ~*Maria Robinson*

Mary was a 35-year-old mother who lived with her husband and two young children in a small rural town. Though Mary had been married to her husband for 7 years, she had become increasingly unhappy in her relationship as her husband's controlling behavior and violent outbursts progressively worsened. Mary had contemplated leaving her husband at several points throughout their marriage, but after each abusive incident, her husband's behavior would improve for a short period of time during which she would agree to stay. Mary didn't want her children to grow up in a single-parent home, and she questioned her ability to adequately raise her children without her husband's support. Despite these doubts, Mary ultimately decided to leave her husband after a particularly violent incident in which her husband repeatedly hit her in front of her children. Mary moved out with her children and sought help from a local nonprofit community agency which offers free and confidential services to victims of domestic violence and sexual assault. The agency helped Mary file a restraining order against her husband and provided her with legal advocacy services throughout the custody battle in her divorce proceedings. Although Mary felt confident that she had made the right decision for her family, she often felt guilty for leaving her husband and sometimes considered reconciling with him given his promises to change. Mary also began experiencing severe anxiety. She had difficulty sleeping, was regularly experiencing flashbacks to the times her

S. Steinmetz, M.S. • M.J. Gray, Ph.D. (✉)
Psychology Department, University of Wyoming, Laramie, WY, USA
e-mail: ssteinme@uwyo.edu; Gray@uwyo.edu

© Springer International Publishing Switzerland 2017
M.M. Maheu et al. (eds.), *Career Paths in Telemental Health*,
DOI 10.1007/978-3-319-23736-7_13

139

husband had hit her, and avoided any thoughts or conversations that reminded her of the abuse. The domestic violence shelter, recognizing Mary's experiences as potential symptoms of post-traumatic stress disorder (PTSD), referred her to the University of Wyoming's psychology clinic to receive trauma-focused, videoconferencing-based therapy. At the first session of therapy, Mary connected to her therapist via a videoconferencing unit from the domestic violence agency. Mary's therapist confirmed that Mary met criteria for PTSD through a diagnostic interview. After a few sessions together that were devoted to information gathering and rapport building, they decided to move forward with a tailored therapy plan drawn from the treatment manuals for prolonged exposure (PE; Foa, Hembree, & Rothbaum, 2007) and cognitive processing therapy (CPT; Resick & Schnicke, 1993). Mary was seen for seven, 60–90 min weekly sessions. She and her therapist utilized both in-session dialog and between-session written exercises to identify and combat her maladaptive cognitions relating to her abuse, and the therapist used exposure exercises to facilitate Mary's engagement with memories that she had been avoiding. Additionally, motivational interviewing (MI; Miller & Rollnick, 2013) techniques were supplemented to facilitate her decision making in regard to leaving her relationship. Assessment measures were administered every four sessions and indicated that Mary's PTSD symptoms were steadily improving over time. Indeed, Mary herself reported that she was no longer experiencing flashbacks, was sleeping well, and felt better able to discuss difficult topics about her abusive relationship when necessary. Further, she reported more confidence in her ability to manage her distress and make effective decisions for herself and her children.

Sexual assault and domestic violence are quite prevalent within the general population and can have significant implications for an individual's mental health. Results from the National Violence Against Women Survey indicate that approximately 52 % of women report a history of assaultive violence at some point in their lives (Tjaden & Thoennes, 1998). Prevalence reports for intimate partner violence have been estimated at 25 % (Tjaden & Thoennes, 2000), and information regarding the frequency of sexual assault is more difficult to determine, as most instances go unreported (Rennison, 2002). Regardless, assaultive violence is clearly a significant societal concern with an unfortunately high rate of occurrence.

A common consequence of domestic violence and sexual assault is post-traumatic stress disorder (PTSD; Breslau et al., 1998; Kessler, Sonnega, Bromet, Hughes, & Nelson, 1995; Resnick, Kilpatrick, Dansky, Saunders, & Best, 1993). As outlined in the *Diagnostic and Statistical Manual of Mental Disorders* (DSM-V; American Psychiatric Association, 2013), PTSD is the collection of persistent symptoms of re-experiencing (e.g., intrusive recollections or nightmares of the event), avoidance (e.g., avoidance of thoughts, feelings, or conversations associated with the trauma), negative cognitions or mood (e.g., inability to recall aspects of the traumatic event or distorted self-blame), and alterations in arousal and reactivity (e.g., exaggerated startle response, hypervigilance) following exposure to a traumatic event.

There are a number of secondary psychological difficulties that often emanate from assaultive violence aside from or in addition to PTSD. For instance, high rates of comorbidity between PTSD and depression have been documented among intimate partner violence (43 %; Stein & Kennedy, 2001) and interpersonal assault (52 %; Taft, Resick, Watkins, & Panuzio, 2009) populations. Further, as a consequence of pervasive avoidance behaviors to trauma-related cues and reminders, individuals with PTSD often abuse substances and may withdraw socially, thereby increasing the likelihood of developing substance dependence disorders and secondary depression (Kilpatrick, Acierno, Resnick, Saunders, & Best, 1997).

Fortunately, a number of empirically supported treatments (ESTs) exist to alleviate PTSD and associated forms of psychological distress following assaultive violence. Division 12 of the American Psychological Association has classified PE and CPT as having "strong research support" among a list of ESTs, and the International Society of Traumatic Stress Studies designated both therapies as best practice interventions (Foa, Keane, Friedman, & Cohen, 2009). Further, these therapies are becoming widely disseminated among large healthcare systems due to their effectiveness among populations coping from trauma. For example, the US Department of Veterans Affairs has endorsed and widely disseminated both therapies throughout their hospital systems, and the Substance Abuse and Mental Health Services Association recommended PE as its treatment of choice for clinicians providing services across the USA (Nemeroff et al., 2006).

Despite the increasing dissemination of these effective, evidence-based interventions for post-traumatic distress, rural providers and trauma victims are often unable to access and benefit from them. Though it is a common misconception that rural environments are free from high rates of violent crime, research suggests that the prevalence rates of interpersonal violence, such as sexual assault and domestic violence, are comparable in rural context (Scarpa, 2003). Rural populations experience considerable difficulty accessing services for a number of reasons. Logistical barriers, such as geographic obstacles and transportation difficulties, as well as individual and social factors (i.e., poverty, high rates of unemployment, poor health, and reduced social and health services) have been cited as possible reasons for disparate access to psychological services (Jameson, Chambless, & Blank, 2009; Wagenfeld, 2003).

One current means of connecting rural trauma survivors with specialized care is via secure, encrypted, videoconferencing-based technology. Videoconferencing is an innovative technological medium that allows individuals to communicate securely, with access to both visual and auditory information, through a computer monitor or video screen in real time. Accordingly, videoconference technology provides a suitable proxy for traditional in-person service delivery—especially in very rural areas where services would otherwise be unavailable altogether.

The Wyoming Trauma Telehealth Treatment Clinic (WTTTC) is one example of a clinical service that uses videoconference technology to provide individual therapy to clients in rural areas. The WTTTC is a university-based mental healthcare clinic that has established partnership with three rural domestic violence/rape crisis in remote areas. The distal crisis centers are nonprofit organizations that provide prevention and awareness education to the public regarding assaultive violence and immediate and practical support (e.g., temporary housing, food, clothing, and monetary assistance) to survivors of sexual assault and domestic violence. However, none of these centers have mental health professionals on staff. Thus, the WTTTC addresses this void by providing free, empirically based psychotherapy services by therapists who have had extensive training in trauma intervention theory and techniques.

Training Required

In terms of educational training required of treatment providers, a graduate degree corresponding to state credentialing criteria for entry-level practice should be considered a bare minimum for treating this population via telehealth. In most states, this translates to a PhD or PsyD in Clinical or Counseling Psychology for licensed psychologists and a master's degree in Social Work or Counseling Education for social workers and licensed professional counselors. Though these degrees and their corresponding licenses are necessary entry requirements for such practice, they would arguably be insufficient in the absence of specialized, trauma-focused training. Ideally, providers—regardless of discipline or professional degree—would seek intensive (e.g., multiday workshop) training in empirically supported trauma treatments such as prolonged exposure (Foa et al., 2007) or cognitive processing therapy (Resick & Schnicke, 1993) and would seek out ongoing supervision or consultation with experienced providers of these treatments. For work with individuals currently in abusive relationships who are actively contemplating leaving the relationship, we would recommend training and experience with motivational interviewing (Miller & Rollnick, 2013).

The WTTTC clinic utilizes secure, encrypted videoconferencing technology to provide psychotherapy and assessment services. However, little technology training is required for the therapists, clients, or staff at the distal domestic violence/rape crisis centers. The clinic would be neither viable nor successful if substantive training was required or if the interface was not very intuitive and user friendly. The WTTTC and each of the distal sites are equipped with Polycom VSX3000 videoconferencing units. These units are approximately the size of a flat panel computer monitor and are easily accommodated on any desktop. They strike a nice balance between excellent video and audio quality and affordability as each unit costs approximately $3000. The only additional requirements that distal sites had to adhere to were the availability of a high-speed Internet connection and the availability of a small, private room that could be used by clients for sessions.

It is helpful to have informational technology (IT) support at the proximal end—preferably provided by an individual with some familiarity with videoconferencing technology. In terms of training and experience required by the local technology support professional, a specific degree (e.g., computer science)—though perhaps helpful—is not essential. Rather, it would be necessary for such a person to have formal training and expertise in networking and prior experience working with various videoconferencing technologies. With respect to establishing an initial connection and occasional troubleshooting, the distal sites do not need to identify a technology support person with extensive videoconferencing experience. The local Internet service provider technician can typically confer with the primary site technical consultant to resolve any issues with connectivity that may arise—even without prior videoconferencing support experience. The distal sites were able to work with our IT consultant to establish connections in approximately an hour or two per site.

Technical difficulties, although rare, are a realistic possibility when providing services electronically. Accordingly, a backup plan for service provision should be discussed with the client to avoid interruption with service delivery. For instance, therapists from the WTTTC inform their clients that if the videoconferencing connection fails during session and cannot be corrected promptly, the session will be conducted over the telephone. Accordingly, clients and therapists should know how to contact one another via telephone during session in the event of a technology failure.

There are also some important ethical and therapeutic concerns to consider when attempting to deliver services via videoconferencing. Of paramount importance is client safety. In some instances, clients, particularly those who are victims of assaultive violence, may be so severely distressed that they are at risk for self-harm. Because of the preeminence of this particular safety concern and unclear ability to manage such crises distally, acutely suicidal or homicidal individuals are not eligible for telehealth services through our clinic. Rather, emergency resources in the community are the appropriate referral until this emergent need is adequately addressed given that it would be ethically difficult to manage acutely suicidal individuals from afar. The WTTTC can and does routinely provide follow-up services after such an acute crisis remits however. Lastly, despite the fact that a number of clients have been successfully treated with videoconferencing and have reported high satisfaction, some clients may find this method of service delivery unappealing, which can contribute to higher rates of attrition. Thus, it is beneficial for clinicians to inquire about and discuss with their client any concerns regarding this method of service delivery.

Pros and Cons of Clinical Setting

The WTTTC utilizes a university-based training clinic to meet the needs of rural domestic violence and sexual assault survivors, which results in a symbiotic relationship that benefits both doctoral student trainees and assault survivors alike. Given that the WTTTC is housed in the University of Wyoming Psychology Department Clinic, all cases are staffed by master's level therapists working toward a doctoral degree in Clinical Psychology and are supervised by licensed doctoral-level clinical psychologists. This arrangement allows student therapists to receive extensive training in trauma intervention theory and techniques while also providing them with the opportunity to gain experience delivering these treatments to a population of assault survivors not normally available in a university setting. This increased access to clinical populations is especially important because the WTTTC is located in a small, rural university town itself. Thus, student therapists working at WTTTC cannot only gain access to a larger clinical population but can do so conveniently at the university without having to travel great distances to see their clients.

WTTTC's utilization of a university-based training clinic benefits rural clients as well. Given that rural communities have greater difficulty securing qualified mental health professionals (Jameson, Chambless, & Blank, 2009), most rural residents with a psychiatric diagnosis fail to receive any mental health treatment. In fact, research shows that rural individuals seeking mental health services are typically seen by their primary care physician rather than a mental health specialist (Martin, Kupersmidt, & Harter, 1996). Thus, the WTTTC allows increased access to mental healthcare for rural clients and provides these services free of charge.

Further, with respect to rural crisis centers providing access to mental healthcare, these agencies have historically provided referrals to general counseling centers in the community, which typically do not specialize in evidence-based trauma interventions. Rural providers report significant obstacles to procuring specialized training in trauma treatment (i.e., geographical barriers, insufficient time to learn ESTs, lack of access to relevant information resources, and prohibitive expense of training), despite holding generally favorable attitudes toward ESTs for trauma (Richardson, Frueh, Grubaugh, Egede, & Elhai, 2009). Although generic supportive counseling can be helpful for victims, interventions focusing specifically on trauma-related distress have been shown to promote optimal post-traumatic symptom reductions (e.g., Nemeroff et al., 2006). Thus, not only does the WTTTC provide free mental health services for rural clients, but this care is a specialized, evidence-based therapy for trauma that is typically nonexistent in their hometowns.

Lastly, stigma associated with seeking mental health services and concerns about anonymity and confidentiality when receiving psychological services are more pronounced in rural settings (Hoyt, Conger, Valde, & Weihs, 1997; Rost, Smith, & Taylor, 1993). In very small communities, individuals are often reluctant to seek mental health services even when they are available due to the perceived stigma or embarrassment that may result from being seen by others upon entering or exiting a mental health clinic. Therapy through the WTTTC is provided in the domestic violence/rape crisis centers themselves, which provides the added benefit of confidentiality given that these facilities are not typically associated with receiving mental health services. Further, allowing the crisis center staff to assist with facilitating the initial contact between clients and therapists often increases client's receptivity to and comfort with psychotherapy.

Evidence Base for Interventions Described

As mentioned previously, one of the primary benefits the WTTTC has to offer rural assault survivors is its utilization of evidence-based, trauma-focused therapy. A more detailed examination of the research reveals a substantial amount of evidence for the trauma treatments themselves and provides preliminary support for the feasibility and efficacy of delivering these therapies to underserved domestic violence and sexual assault populations via videoconferencing.

PE (Foa et al., 2007), a cognitive-behavioral treatment, is one of three treatments frequently provided by the WTTTC and has proven to be one of the most effective interventions for PTSD (Foa & Meadows, 1997; Nemeroff et al., 2006; Rothbaum & Schwartz, 2002). The primary objective of PE is to facilitate the gradual confrontation of typically-avoided memories, images, objects, and situations associated with the traumatic experience through exposure exercises. Typically, imaginal exposure to the traumatic event begins by recounting the event in session, and the client is asked to listen to their traumatic memory for homework. Hierarchical in-vivo exposure is also part of the therapy and consists of gradually confronting safe trauma reminders such as objects or locations. A meta-analytic review of 13 randomized controlled trials demonstrated that PE is a highly efficacious treatment for trauma when compared to control groups (Powers, Halpern, Ferenschak, Gillihan, & Foa, 2010). Large effects were found for measures examining PTSD (Hedges's $g = 1.08$) and overall distress (Hedges's $g = 0.77$) at posttreatment assessment. Further, improvement appeared to remain fairly robust over time with follow-up assessment (ranging from 1 to 12 months) effect sizes ranging from large (PTSD Hedges's $g = 0.68$) to medium (overall distress Hedges's $g = 0.68$).

Additionally, CPT (Resick & Schnicke, 1993), a cognitive-behavioral treatment originally designed for rape populations, has received strong empirical support and is also recognized as a highly effective treatment for PTSD (Resick, Nishith, Weaver, Astin, & Feuer, 2002; Resick & Schnicke, 1992). The goal of CPT is to target and modify distorted beliefs and cognitions about the meaning and implications of the traumatic event through in-session dialog and between-session written exercises. CPT also contains an exposure component like PE, through writing about the event; however, the primary focus of therapy is to modify maladaptive beliefs pertaining to the meaning of the event. A study conducted by Iverson et al. (2011) shows that CPT not only improved PTSD and depression in a sample of women exposed to intimate partner violence, but that symptom reduction in turn actually decreased the likelihood of future victimization as well. Medium effects were found at a 6-month follow-up assessment for measures examining PTSD ($pr^2 = 0.07$) and depression ($pr^2 = 0.07$).

Finally, motivational interviewing (MI; Miller & Rollnick, 2013) can be useful when attempting to facilitate behavior change during treatment, such as when a client is reluctant to engage in treatment, has co-occurring substance dependence issues, or is experiencing ambivalence about terminating an abusive relationship (Motivational Interviewing Intimate Partner Violence Workgroup, 2010; Murphy & Maiuro, 2009). However, it should be noted that at this point in time, no research to date has examined the effectiveness of MI when working with populations coping with domestic violence and sexual assault issues.

Preliminary evidence gathered from the WTTTC suggests that utilizing telehealth technologies to deliver trauma-focused therapies (i.e., therapy based on the manuals of PE or CPT) to clients in remote areas can be a feasible and effective way to treat emotional and psychological consequences of sexual assault and domestic violence. Participants included in the investigation were women (aged 19–52) who received a full course of trauma-focused therapy (defined as six or more sessions) at the WTTTC and completed pretreatment and posttreatment inventories measuring PTSD, depression, and satisfaction with services. Since WTTTC's inception, dozens of clients have been referred. However, it should be noted that many clients generally presenting at crisis centers are unable to commit to an extended course of therapy by virtue of relocation, unyielding work schedules, etc. Thus, many clients seen through the WTTTC present for supportive 1–2 session consultations to help through immediate crises and were consequently not included in the study. Their inability to commit to extended therapeutic services was known at the time of initial contact, so these individuals were not considered therapy clients for study inclusion purposes.

Participants received individual sessions of trauma-focused, evidence-based therapy based on the treatment manuals for PE (Foa et al., 2007) or CPT (Resick & Schnicke, 1993). Additionally, in instances where there were additional concerns regarding separation from an abusive partner, MI (Miller & Rollnick, 2013) techniques were supplemented to facilitate decision making regarding relationship termination. Treatment components were applied flexibly, depending on the needs of the client, and sessions took place weekly, lasting 60–90 min depending on the specific treatment being implemented. Assessment measures (The Post-traumatic Stress Disorder Checklist [PCL; Weathers, Litz, Huska, & Keane, 1994]; the Center for Epidemiological Studies Depression Scale [CES-D; Radloff, 1977], and an 11-item Wyoming Telehealth Trauma Clinic Client Satisfaction Scale) were administered every four sessions.

Participants were all female, primarily identified as Caucasian (86.7%), and had a mean age of 30.20 (standard deviation [SD]=9.25). The majority of participants reported being either single (46.7%) or married (46.7%), and one individual indicated she was divorced. Eighty percent were referred for distress emanating from a domestically violent, and 20% were referred for distress related to a sexual assault experience. Participants reported high levels of PTSD (PCL M=50.07; SD=17.77; Weathers et al., 1994) and depression symptoms (CES-D M=27.47; SD=14.12; Radloff, 1977) at the beginning of treatment. The mean number of videoconferencing sessions received was 13.33 (SD=13.89).

Participants demonstrated a clinically meaningful decrease in PTSD symptoms over the course of treatment (posttreatment PCL M=32.20; SD=12.68; Monson et al., 2008). Using Cohen's d (Cohen, 2007) to calculate treatment effect size, participants exhibited large reductions on PTSD symptoms ($d=1.17$). On the CES-D, participants' posttreatment score was 13.07 (SD=9.07), also indicating a large reduction in depressive symptoms ($d=1.24$). Additionally, clients' reports of satisfaction with the provision of psychological services via videoconferencing on the satisfaction survey revealed very high levels of satisfaction (M=52.93, SD=2.43 on a 55 point scale). These findings provide encouraging, preliminary support for the utility of videoconferencing-based therapy to effectively meet the needs of rural survivors of sexual assault and domestic violence. The large effect sizes (i.e., 1.17–1.24) for symptom improvement found in the WTTTC investigation are comparable to effect sizes (i.e., 0.62–1.91 for PE and CPT) documented for the cognitive-behavioral interventions found in the *Practice Guidelines from the International Society for Traumatic Stress Studies* for PTSD (Rothbaum, Meadows, Resick, & Foy, 2000).

These data, while preliminary, have valuable implications for practicing psychologists serving clients in rural areas. Most notably, they suggest that clinicians should consider the possibility of utilizing videoconferencing technology to meet the mental health needs of rural communities thereby assisting such populations in overcoming the numerous logistical barriers to accessing evidence-based psychological services. It was previously unclear whether quality of services would be compromised when delivering treatment via distance technology because of stigma associated with seeking services, or because of clients' perceptions that the therapist is distant or the therapy less personal than traditional in-person sessions. However, the results of this investigation suggest that such concerns, though understandable, are inaccurate. Rather, evidence indicates that treatment provided via videoconferencing is capable of achieving comparable gains that accrue during traditional in-person services. And, because many rural areas offer no psychological services at all, the ability to mitigate any degree of symptoms of emotional distress through videoconferencing technology is a valuable improvement to the standard level of care.

In conclusion, in light of modern technological advances, it is no longer acceptable for rural populations to remain underserved and deprived of optimal healthcare services. With the advent of high-quality distal technologies such as secure and encrypted videoconferencing, it is now possible to overcome many of the barriers that keep rural clients disconnected from the necessary mental health services needed. The WTTTC is just one example of how bridging this longstanding divide can successfully result in rural clients receiving effective, specialized therapy treatments. Hopefully, these encouraging preliminary outcomes are an indication that an increasing multitude of telehealth services are becoming available to distal communities further helping to alleviate the mental healthcare disparities that result from rurality.

Acknowledgment The authors would like to thank the Verizon Foundation for their generous support of and funding for the Wyoming Telehealth Trauma Treatment Clinic.

References

American Psychiatric Association. (2013). *Diagnostic and statistical manual of mental disorders* (5th ed.). Arlington, VA: American Psychiatric Publishing.

Breslau, N., Kessler, R. C., Chilcoat, H. D., Schultz, L. R., Davis, G. C., & Andreski, P. (1998). Trauma and posttraumatic stress disorder in the community: The Detroit Area Survey of Trauma. *Archives of General Psychiatry, 55*, 626–632. doi:10.1001/archpsyc.55.7.626.

Cohen, J. (2007). *Statistical power analysis for the behavioral science* (2nd ed.). Hillsdale, NJ: Erlbaum.

Foa, E., Hembree, E., & Rothbaum, B. (2007). *Prolonged exposure therapy for PTSD: Emotional processing of traumatic experiences therapist guide.* New York, NY: Oxford University Press.

Foa, E. B., Keane, T. M., Friedman, M. J., & Cohen, J. A. (Eds.). (2009). *Effective treatments for PTSD* (2nd ed.). New York, NY: Guilford.

Foa, E. B., & Meadows, E. A. (1997). Psychosocial treatments for posttraumatic stress disorder: A critical review. *Annual Review of Psychology, 48,* 449–480. doi:10.1146/annurev. psych.48.1.449.

Hoyt, D. R., Conger, R. D., Valde, J. G., & Weihs, K. (1997). Psychological distress and help seeking in rural America. *American Journal of Community Psychology, 25,* 449–470. doi:10.102 3/A:1024655521619.

Iverson, K. M., Gradus, J. L., Resick, P. A., Suvak, M. K., Smith, K. F., & Monson, C. M. (2011). Cognitive-behavioral therapy for PTSD and depression symptoms reduces risk for future intimate partner violence among interpersonal trauma survivors. *Journal of Consulting and Clinical Psychology, 79,* 193–202. doi:10.1037/a0022512.

Jameson, J., Chambless, D., & Blank, M. (2009). Empirically supported treatments in rural community mental health centers: A preliminary report on current utilization and attitudes toward adoption. *Community Mental Health Journal, 45,* 463–467. doi:10.1007/s10597-009-9230-7.

Kessler, R., Sonnega, A., Bromet, E., Hughes, M., & Nelson, C. (1995). Posttraumatic stress disorder in the National Comorbidity survey. *Archives of General Psychiatry, 52,* 1048–1060. doi:10.1001/archpsyc.1995.03950240066012.

Kilpatrick, D., Acierno, R., Resnick, H., Saunders, B., & Best, C. (1997). A 2-year longitudinal analysis of the relationships between violent assault and substance abuse in women. *Journal of Clinical and Consulting Psychology, 65,* 834–847. doi: http://dx.doi.org/10.1037/0022-006X.65.5.834.

Martin, S. L., Kupersmidt, J. B., & Harter, K. S. M. (1996). Children of farm laborers: Utilization of services for mental health problems. *Community Mental Health Journal, 32,* 327–340. doi:10.1007/BF02249451.

Miller, W. R., & Rollnick, S. (2013). *Motivational interviewing: Helping people change* (3rd ed.). New York, NY: Guilford Press.

Monson, C. M., Gradus, J. L., Young-Xu, Y., Schnurr, P. P., Price, J. L., & Schumm, J. A. (2008). Change in posttraumatic stress disorder symptoms: Do clinicians and patients agree? *Psychological Assessment, 20,* 131–138. doi:10.1037/1040-3590.20.2.131.

Motivational Interviewing Intimate Partner Violence Workgroup. (2010). *Partner Abuse, 1,* 92–103. doi:10.1891/1946-6560.1.1.92.

Murphy, C. M., & Maiuro, R. D. (2009). *Motivational interviewing and stages of change in intimate partner violence.* New York, NY: Springer.

Nemeroff, C. B., Bremner, D., Foa, E. B., Mayberg, H. S., North, C. S., & Stein, M. B. (2006). Posttraumatic stress disorder: A state-of-the-science review. *Journal of Psychiatric Research, 40,* 1–21. doi:10.1016/j.jpsychires.2005.07.005.

Powers, M., Halpern, J. M., Ferenschak, M. P., Gillihan, S. J., & Foa, E. B. (2010). A meta-analytic review of prolonged exposure for posttraumatic stress disorder. *Clinical Psychology Review, 30,* 635–664. doi: http://dx.doi.org/10.1016/j.cpr.2010.04.007.

Radloff, L. S. (1977). The CES-D Scale: A self-report depression scale for research in the general population. *Applied Psychology Measurement, 1,* 385–401. doi:10.1177/014662167700100306.

Rennison, C. M. (2002). *Rape and sexual assault: Reporting to police and medical attention, 1992–2000.* Washington, DC: Bureau of Justice Statistics, U.S. Department of Justice.

Resick, P. A., Nishith, P., Weaver, T. L., Astin, M. C., & Feuer, C. A. (2002). A comparison of cognitive processing therapy with prolonged exposure and a waiting condition for the treatment of chronic posttraumatic stress disorder in female rape victims. *Journal of Consulting and Clinical Psychology, 70,* 867–879. doi:10.1037/0022-006X.70.4.867.

Resick, P. A., & Schnicke, M. K. (1992). Cognitive processing therapy for sexual assault victims. *Journal of Consulting and Clinical Psychology, 60,* 748–756. doi:10.1037/0022-006X.60.5.748.

Resick, P. A., & Schnicke, M. K. (1993). *Cognitive processing therapy for rape victims: A treatment manual*. Newbury Park, CA: Sage.

Resnick, H. S., Kilpatrick, D. G., Dansky, B. S., Saunders, B. E., & Best, C. L. (1993). Prevalence of civilian trauma and posttraumatic stress disorder in a representative national sample of women. *Journal of Consulting and Clinical Psychology, 61*, 984–991. doi:10.1037/0022-006X.61.6.984.

Richardson, L. K., Frueh, B. C., Grubaugh, A. L., Egede, L., & Elhai, J. D. (2009). Current directions in videoconferencing tele-mental health research. *Clinical Psychology Science and Practice, 16*, 323–338. doi:10.1111/j.1468-2850.2009.01170.x.

Rost, K., Smith, G. R., & Taylor, J. L. (1993). Rural-urban differences in stigma and the use of care for depressive disorders. *Journal of Rural Health, 9*, 59–62. doi:10.1111/j.1748-0361.1993.tb00495.x.

Rothbaum, B. O., Meadows, E. A., Resick, P., & Foy, D. W. (2000). Cognitive-behavioral therapy. In E. B. Foa, T. M. Keane, & M. J. Friedman (Eds.), *Effective treatments for PTSD* (pp. 60–83). New York, NY: Guilford Press.

Rothbaum, B. O., & Schwartz, A. C. (2002). Exposure therapy for posttraumatic stress disorder. *American Journal of Psychotherapy, 56*, 59–75. PMid:11977784.

Scarpa, A. (2003). Community violence exposure in young adults. *Trauma, Violence, and Abuse, 4*, 210–227. doi:10.1177/1524838003004003002.

Stein, M. B., & Kennedy, C. (2001). Major depressive and posttraumatic stress disorder comorbidity in female victims of intimate partner violence. *Journal of Affective Disorders, 66*, 133–138. doi:10.1016/S0165-0327(00)00301-3.

Taft, C. T., Resick, P. A., Watkins, L. E., & Panuzio, J. (2009). An investigation of posttraumatic stress disorder and depressive symptomatology among female victims of interpersonal trauma. *Journal of Family Violence, 24*, 407–415. doi:10.1007/s10896-009-9243-6.

Tjaden, P., & Thoennes, N. (1998). *Prevalence, incidence, and consequences of violence against women: Findings from the National Violence Against Women Survey (No. NCJ 172837)*. Washington, DC: U.S. Department of Justice, Office of Justice Programs.

Tjaden, P., & Thoennes, N. (2000). *Extent, nature, and consequences of intimate partner violence: Findings from the National Violence Against Women Survey (No. NCJ 181867)*. Washington, DC: U.S. Department of Justice, Office of Justice Programs.

Wagenfeld, M. O. (2003). A snapshot of rural and frontier America. In B. H. Stamm (Ed.), *Rural behavioral health care: An interdisciplinary guide* (pp. 33–40). Washington, DC: American Psychological Association.

Weathers, F. W., Litz, B. T., Huska, J. A., & Keane, T. M. (1994). *PTSD checklist—Civilian version*. Boston, MA: National Center for PTSD, Behavioral Science Division.

Chapter 14
Engaging and Supporting Children and Families: Technology-Enhanced Services Research

Deborah J. Jones

In full disclosure, I certainly could not have predicted during my own training that today I would be a college professor, let alone one for whom technology would be an essential part of my research. My belief that I would go to college was there as long as I can remember. My parents instilled it in me. My grandparents reinforced it. I believed it. Although such a firm belief may be expected in families with a history of college graduates, neither my parents, nor my aunt or uncle, nor my grandparents or great-grandparents had gone to college. I would be the first. Yet, what I had in family support and my own drive and motivation, I lacked in any sort of understanding of what happened once one earned admission to college—very basic things, such as majors and career options, were actually quite overwhelming to me, a part of a world that seemed abstract and even elusive. Perhaps as a way to deal with the ambiguity, I focused on what I could control—I focused on working hard and doing well, which felt concrete and objective and, in turn, anxiety reducing. This problem-focused approach led to a major in psychology with a concentration of credits in chemistry, a combination of credits that could be viewed as happenstance, rather than a master plan. As such, happenstance led to more angst than answers, particularly as college graduation approached. I admittedly had no clearer understanding of what I was supposed to do next as a "college graduate" or why.

In her wisdom, my mother suggested entering a master's program in psychology, with the hope that I could perhaps use that time to more clearly learn and understand my options in a field that I enjoyed. After this conversation, I quickly put my application materials together and was lucky enough to be admitted to the Counseling Psychology Program at Loyola College in Maryland (now Loyola University). Although I could not have known it at the time, two of my professors at Loyola had just earned their Ph.D.s from the University of Georgia and were, lucky for me,

D.J. Jones, Ph.D. (✉)
Department of Psychology & Neuroscience, University of North Carolina at Chapel Hill, Chapel Hill, NC 27599, USA
e-mail: djjones@email.unc.edu

© Springer International Publishing Switzerland 2017
M.M. Maheu et al. (eds.), *Career Paths in Telemental Health*,
DOI 10.1007/978-3-319-23736-7_14

151

eager and motivated to mentor. I am not quite sure what led them to realize that I could use and even desperately needed their guidance, as I honestly do not remember talking with them in depth about my background or confusion. Yet, they soon took me under their wings, quite literally, and got me involved in their research, gave me examples of what it meant to be an academic psychologist, and advised me on applying to doctoral programs in clinical psychology.

I too was lucky to be admitted to the University of Georgia where I worked with two professors, one who studied services for families from the marital perspective and the other from the parent–child perspective. My training was cognitive behavioral, data driven, and evidence based, although before the time when the tension regarding manuals percolated. That said, I was solidly trained in the importance of case conceptualization, the interrelationship of case conceptualization and the treatment plan, and the need for revisions to both as treatment progressed or, alternatively, failed to progress. Consistent with my training, I enjoyed family-based approaches and was particularly drawn to treating children with externalizing problems. During my training, I had done behavioral parent training (BPT) in clinic-based settings for early onset disruptive behavior disorders (DBDs). I had also worked in a multimodal day treatment program for youth with disruptive and antisocial behaviors, as well as an inpatient child and adolescent treatment program where youth often had dual internalizing and externalizing disorders. Finally, I had worked in an inner-city school mental health system with youth who had been or were at-risk for suspension for delinquent behaviors. In each of these cases, we were offering the standard of care for youth and their families; however, I came to realize that the treatments we know will work often fail to serve the children and families who may need it most (see Gardner et al., 2009 for a review).

In considering how to improve this seemingly unacceptable and frustrating state of the field, was an interest in or consideration of the potential role of technology as an innovative or even remotely practical service-delivery vehicle the first idea that came to mind? The answer is a resounding "no." Rather, a request for grant applications using technology to reach underserved groups led to a conversation in my kitchen with a visiting friend regarding mobile phones and, in turn, a grant application. Research clearly demonstrates that low-income families are more likely to have a child with an early onset disruptive behavior disorder, yet, less likely than other socioedemographic groups to engage in treatment (see Dekovic et al., 2011; Jones et al., 2013; Lundahl, Risser, & Lovejoy, 2006; Piquero, Farrington, Welsh, Tremblay, & Jennings, 2009, for reviews). Statistics were available at the time to show that if low-income families were going to purchase technology, it was going to be a mobile phone and, more recently, a smartphone (Jones et al., 2010, 2013). They are handheld, portable, and relatively cost effective, providing underserved families access in ways that would otherwise not be possible with more traditional technologies. Yet, what I did not fully realize at the time of the original application is that my colleagues and I were actually proposing using smartphone functionality that was not yet available. I now realize the positive reframe on what was truly a naïve approach is that this is what those who are much more innovative than me call "thinking outside the box." As luck would have it, technology evolves and by the time we were funded, smartphones included all of the features that I had proposed and lots of other functionality to consider as well.

Technology as a Service-Delivery Tool: A Promising Pilot and Evidence Base

For our ongoing services research, smartphones continue to make sense for the population we are focused on serving low-income families of children with early onset DBDs. If our low-income families are going to have a technology, it is a mobile phone and many of them do have smartphones. In turn, it is our goal to capitalize on a device that is already in the hands or soon to be in the hands of our target consumers. As Steve Jobs (2005) so eloquently said in his Stanford University Commencement Address, "Technology is nothing. What's important is that you have a faith in people, that they're basically good and smart, and if you give them tools, they'll do wonderful things with them." Our pilot data suggests a promise for smartphones in particular to serve as one tool that we believe has the capacity to allow low-income families to remain engaged in services between sessions and amidst acute and chronic stressors that are such a pervasive challenge in their lives (Jones et al., 2014).

Families who participated in our pilot randomized control trial (RCT) were low income (defined using federal poverty level guidelines, including both income and number of people living in the home; US DHHS, 2014), with participating caregivers, on average, 37 years old, predominately female (87%), and the majority (80%) working at least part time. Clinical interview and caregiver-report data were used to determine whether children met criteria for clinically significant disruptive behaviors, an eligibility criterion for the study. Approximately half (53%) of our child clients were boys, with an average age of 5.67 years (range = 3–8 years old).

All interested and eligible families received the standard, two-phase "Helping the Noncompliant Child" (HNC; McMahon & Forehand, 2003) program, one of five evidence-based behavioral parent training (BPT) programs with common core theory and treatment techniques that evolved from the work of Constance Hanf at the University of Oregon (Jones et al., 2013; Reitman & McMahon, 2012). HNC in particular involves weekly clinic-based sessions including the therapist, caregiver, and child, as well as a weekly brief (15–20 min) midweek call between sessions to review and coach skill practice and progress at home (McMahon & Forehand, 2003). In HNC, caregiver–child dyads start in Phase I, "differential attention," in which "child's game" (i.e., child-directed play) is used as a context for teaching the caregiver to (a) increase the frequency and range of positive attention; (b) eliminate instructions, questions, and criticisms; and (c) ignore minor inappropriate behavior. Caregivers are instructed to practice child's game for at least 15 min per day and told that coparents (e.g., another biological parent, caregiver, or caretaker who cannot participate in treatment) also should practice. Caregivers progress to Phase II when the mastery criteria, determined via therapist coding of parent–child interactions in each session, for Phase I skills are met (McMahon & Forehand, 2003).

In Phase II of HNC (McMahon & Forehand, 2003), "compliance training," caregivers are taught the difference between unclear and clear instructions, to give the "clear instruction" sequence, and to use a nonphysical consequence, "time-out," for occasions of noncompliance and other inappropriate behavior that cannot be ignored (e.g., aggression, oppositionality). Phase II skills are taught within the context of "parent's game" (i.e., parent-directed activities, such as a cleanup task), although caregivers are instructed to continue to practice "child's game" at home to maintain mastery of Phase I skills. Program completion is based on caregivers meeting mastery criteria for all Phase I and II skills, which require an average of 8–12 sessions (McMahon & Forehand, 2003).

Our technology-enhanced HNC (TE-HNC; Jones et al., 2010, 2014) program was developed in the context of prior health services research, as well as research on BPT in particular, which suggests that some level of therapist involvement is likely necessary for the most distressed and disadvantaged families (e.g., Webster-Stratton, 1990, 1992; Webster-Stratton, Kolpacoff, & Hollinsworth, 1988; also see Mohr, Cujpers, & Lehman, 2011; Tate & Zabinski, 2004, for reviews). Accordingly, families randomized to TE-HNC received the standard clinic-based HNC program, as well as smartphone components that were developed to enhance, rather than replace, clinic-based, therapist-guided services, by engaging and supporting families between sessions and in the context of high levels of acute and chronic stressors more likely experienced by low-income families in particular (see Conger & Donnellan, 2007, for a review). Our smartphone enhancements were developed via an interdisciplinary partnership including (a) researchers with expertise in BPT with underserved families, (b) a clinician advisory panel (20 % male, 20 % ethnic minority) that included therapists who practice at least one Hanf-model BPT program, (c) an industry partner with experience developing sustainable technological applications, and (d) health economists with expertise in health-care efficiency, efficacy, and value.

In addition to the standard HNC weekly sessions, TE-HNC caregivers stayed in contact with the therapist and program between sessions using five proof-of-concept smartphone enhancements. Building upon the recommendations of our technology partner, we utilized relatively low-cost and available technologies to establish and test each of the functionalities we posited would be helpful to families, with the idea that if the pilot data supported the use of the technology, we would invest our time and resources in developing an integrated version of the functionalities in the next stage of research. First, caregivers accessed a series of daily surveys through their smartphone. Surveys were designed using widely available survey technology and simply delivered to the caregiver via the smartphone. Surveys were intended to be brief (approximately 3 min to complete) and are tailored to the particular skill the caregiver and child are working on (e.g., rewards) and the assigned home practice (e.g., child's game). In addition, each week, caregivers received a skills video, which was housed on the smartphone, for each of the new HNC skills that they were learning in session. The skills videos were also produced to be brief (3–5 min) and included psychoeducation and modeling of skills caregiver–child actor pairs, as well as reminders regarding the important role of using the skills outside of session and sharing the video with other coparents and caregivers who may be involved in the care of the child. Third, caregivers video recorded one home practice per week using the video camera function on the smartphone. Families shared the video of the home practice with the therapist at the start of the session, and then the therapist provided tailored and feedback, including both positive (e.g., "You did a great job using rewards in response to your child's ok behaviors you want to see or see more, including using his 'inside voice' during play") and constructive (e.g., "Don't forget, use your ignoring skill, no look, no talk, no touch, when he starts slamming the toys on the table, since that is a 'not ok' behavior you want to see less"). Fourth, TE-HNC families also had the standard midweek call like all HNC families; however, the TE-HNC midweek call was a video call, using the video call feature on the smartphone, which allowed the face-to-face connection and support. Finally, therapists sent tailored text message reminders to caregivers regarding skill and home practice and the dates and times of the next midweek call and session.

Consistent with our hypotheses, relative to HNC, TE-HNC yielded (1) increased (range $d=0.63$ to $d=2.59$) engagement (i.e., weekly session attendance, midweek call participation) and skill generalization (i.e., home practice), (2) boosted behavioral outcomes [Eyberg Child Behavior Inventory (ECBI) Intensity Subscale $d=0.99$; ECBI Problem Subscale $d=0.54$; Eyberg & Pincus, 1999]; (3) lower implementation costs ($491 for HNC vs. $478 for TE-HNC) resulting from fewer sessions/family ($M=8$ TE-HNC; $M=10$ HNC); and (4) increased consumer satisfaction ($d=1.48$).

Building upon these promising preliminary findings, we are currently conducting a fully powered RCT with a larger sample ($N=102$ projected), upgraded technology (i.e., an iOS application), and additional posttreatment follow-ups (3 and 4 months). The smartphone enhancements in this current project are essentially an integration of the smartphone components we tested in the pilot into an iOS application, which includes both a client-side (i.e., a smartphone application that bundles the daily surveys, skills videos, and video call) and a server-side or administrative interface through which the therapists can now communicate directly with their respective clients. The HIPPA-compliant server-side, administrative interface identifies each family by a numerical code and allows therapists to indicate which skill the family is on in the HNC program, as well as the day and time of the next appointments (midweek call, session). Then, the interface automatically "pushes" the relevant daily survey, skills video, and reminders to the family through the application on the client's phone throughout the week between sessions. The responses to the daily survey and the weekly video recording of home practice are automatically uploaded to the therapist via the administrative interface and server side of the application, so that the therapist can review the family's practice and progress and provide tailored feedback and the next midweek call or session.

As such, the new design and integrated technology will allow us to determine whether we observe statistically significant patterns favoring TE-HNC relative to HNC, the mechanisms that account for these differences, and whether TE-HNC leads to greater maintenance (or less deterioration) in new skills and improved outcomes once clinic-based treatment concludes. We recently completed Year 1 of this

4-year project, so we have some time before outcome data will be available. However, we are pleased to continue to have the opportunity to offer evidence-based treatment to all of the low-income families we serve along the way.

Clinical Case Vignette: Michael and Lola

Consistent with increasingly conservative parameters by many research ethics boards regarding what constitutes "identifiable data," including demographic data like age and race, we chose to provide an exemplar, rather than actual, family in our pilot RCT. Michael is a 26-year-old Latino single father who at the time of enrollment resided in a one-bedroom apartment with his 4-year-old daughter, Lola. Michael immigrated to the United States from Central America as a child and recently became a US citizen. Both Michael and Lola speak primarily English, including in the home. Michael reported that he was never married to Lola's mother, who is Caucasian and has not been in the family's life since Lola's birth. Michael's mother, Gustavina, who resides approximately 10 min away from Michael and Lola, does assist with childrearing, including serving as the primary caregiver for Lola when Michael's work schedule includes long hours or back-to-back shifts. Michael started community college; however, he had to drop out due to financial and child care challenges. He currently works several part-time jobs, including as an aide in a nursing home.

Michael reports that Lola has always been a "restless" and "difficult-to-manage" child; however, her problem behaviors have reportedly continued to worsen as she approaches school age. The primary concerns that Michael expressed during the phone screen and baseline assessment were Lola's increasing levels of noncompliance (e.g., temper tantrums at home and in public), oppositionality (e.g., sticking out her tongue out at adults when disobeying), and aggression (e.g., biting and scratching cousins and other children), which reportedly occur at home and preschool. Michael reported seeing advertisements for the project on the local bus, as well as at the Laundromat; however, he decided to call after Lola bit another child in the elevator of their apartment building. Based on the clinical interview, Lola met criteria for oppositional defiant disorder. Given that the family also met other study criteria, including low-income status, Michael and Lola were scheduled for their first appointment with their therapist, Margarita, at which point they were randomly assigned to the TE-HNC Program.

Michael and Lola met weekly (1 h sessions) for 8 weeks with Margarita. During Phase I, when Michael was learning the *attends, rewards, and ignoring* skills, he reported feeling awkward initially. He reportedly felt increasingly motivated to practice the skills throughout the day; however, once he realized how much Lola enjoyed the sustained positive attention for her "ok" behaviors or behaviors he wanted to see more (e.g., doing things the first time she was told, keeping her hands to herself), he reported relaxing and enjoying the new skills and their more positive time together. Michael reported that he was particularly appreciative of a new repertoire of *rewards* options, as he previously resorted to "bribing her" with sweets, which he felt uncomfortable using. Once the family moved onto Phase II, Michael reportedly appreciated the *clear instruction* sequence and the *time-out* skill, as it reportedly allowed him to feel more calm and in control in spite of his frustration with Lola's noncompliance.

With regard to the technology-enhanced aspects of the TE-HNC program in particular, Michael most appreciated the *skills videos* series, which he watched at least once weekly on his own and with his mother. He indicated that the *skills videos* allowed him to share what he was learning in session with his mother so that they could be consistent in their use of the skills in managing Lola's behavior. Michael did not complete the *daily surveys* daily as proscribed; however, he did complete a survey at least once per week, which allowed Margarita to better understand how skill practice and progress was going at home. Primarily the challenge for the family was finding a time for *child's game*, the proscribed 15-min context for the daily home practice of skills, given Michael's busy schedule and shift work. Discussion of his responses to the *daily surveys*, however, allowed Margarita to problem solve with Michael regarding his schedule and to come up the best days (Monday, Wednesday, Friday, and weekends) and time (after dinner) for a briefer (10 min) practice when he most consistently had a flexible window of time with Lola. Michael's *video recording of home practice* revealed some opportunity for more creativity in the choice of toys that they were using for the *child's game* activity. That is, Michael was having some difficulty finding opportunities to use *attends and rewards* when Lola was coloring or flipping through picture books. A review of the toys and activities that the family had in the home with Margarita, however, revealed more appropriate, interactive options for *child's game*, including a doll house, blocks, and several puzzles, which Michael reported made home practice more enjoyable for both him and Lola. Finally, Michael used the *midweek video call* component of the technology far more creatively than the research team or Margarita envisioned. That is, during a *midweek video call* regarding the challenges of using *time-out*, the standard consequence for noncompliance or other disruptive behavior (i.e., oppositionality, aggression) in BPT programs, Michael took the initiative to walk Margarita around the apartment using the two-way camera that is the vehicle for the face-to-face video call in order to get assistance with selecting the most optimal *time-out* spot. *Time-out* is a particularly difficult skill for many families to navigate, given the nuances essential to successfully implementing the skill, as well as the space constraints of many homes. Space constraints are particularly important to consider in our research with low-income families like Michael who rarely, if ever, have a spare chair or a corner completely free of reinforcing stimuli for attention-seeking children. In turn, the *midweek video call* provided Margarita a virtual "window" into Michael and Lola's home that would otherwise not be possible in standard, clinic-based service-delivery models. Our clients' innovative use of the technology and the opportunity to learn from them is certainly one advantage of the work that we are doing. There are, of course, other advantages, as well as disadvantages, which will be discussed briefly in the next section.

Advantages and Disadvantages of Technology-Enhanced Services Research

In my experience, technology-enhanced services research has both pros and cons, as does any other focus of research (see Jones, 2014, for a review). I will start with the advantages. First, by definition of conducting technology-enhanced services research, we have the capacity to provide free, state-of-the-field, evidence-based services to families who may not otherwise have access. Given that everyone in our research receives the standard-of-care clinic-based treatment, we know that whether they are assigned to the technology-enhanced group or not, we have an opportunity to be helpful. The key question is not whether children's disruptive behavior will improve; rather, does the technology enhance the opportunities for caregivers to learn and practice and be supported in using the skills between sessions, potentially, bolstering the probability that they will continue to be motivated to come to the clinic for services and, in turn, continue to have the opportunity to benefit from treatment.

The second advantage really stems from the first. That is, my staff, graduate students, and undergraduate research assistants have the opportunity to be involved in hands-on, services research with underserved families. They are involved in all stages of the project from grant writing to data collection and analyses to presentations at conferences and manuscript writing and submission. As such, they not only learn how to set up their own technology-enhanced services work, if that is what they choose to do some day, but they also experience the value added when you are conducting research that makes a difference every single day, regardless of the study outcomes.

There are also, of course, challenges. In my experience, as well as the experiences I have heard from many others around the country doing this work, a primary one, if not the primary one, seems to be that the infrastructure in university research settings may not be progressing as quickly as technology or our research questions and hypotheses. Ideally, university research settings would have an infrastructure that supports technology-enhanced services research from the ground up, including development and maintenance of the technology (e.g., iOS application developers who collaborate with researcher) and tailored research support (e.g., HIPAA compliant server space reserved for research projects) of the application.

Yet, in reality we typically end up turning to industry, where the goals (i.e., finish the product, invoice for payment) may be very different than how we conceptualize our goals in service-based research. For example, we needed to develop and support an open iOS application and had a very specific and limited grant budget to support those activities. When the company underestimated the amount of time it would take and exhausted our remaining funds to build one, albeit very important, facet of the application (i.e., HIPPA upload of home practice videos from client-side of application to therapist server side of application), this meant that we had to forego building other features of the application. Of course, this is not ideal in terms of our research questions and hypotheses, which were formulated with the original scope of work in mind.

Given these challenges, we are working closely with our university officials to improve and strengthen the infrastructure for technology-enhanced services research internally so that we do not have to turn to industry, as well as to improve collaboration with industry partners so that both group's goals are met. Related to this point, there is certainly a niche market for technologists and small businesses to partner with researchers and academics in order to undertake collaborative services research, a vision supported by the small business technology transfer (STTR) and small business innovation research (SBIR) grants at the National Institute of Health. These mechanisms set aside funds specifically for these collaborations, award the grant funding to the small business, and encourage research collaboration by requiring the small business to partner with academic researchers. Such mechanisms will certainly go far to increase the likelihood of collaborative, rather than competing, goals between industry and science and, ultimately, improve our service-delivery options for our consumers.

Summary

In summary, my research aims to capitalize on technology to enhance the reach and impact of evidence-based treatment, particularly to those families who may otherwise have more difficulty engaging and benefitting from treatment. Our current work with low-income families suggests that promise of smartphone technology to increase the connection and support between the therapist and families of children with early onset DBDs to cost effectively enhance treatment outcome. As we continue the follow-up on this pilot work, we stay up to date of innovations in technology that may allow us new avenues for improving the reach and impact of services. Of note, while we work with underserved families, we do not have any hypotheses regarding how the impact of our technology would be different with families in other sociodemographic groups; rather, we simply posit that smartphones are an ideal delivery vehicle for low-incomes families in particular who are more likely to have smartphones than any other technology (i.e., higher income families also own smartphones, as well as many other devices, which may simply increase the flexibility in the range of potential delivery vehicles for services research). That is, in the words of Steve Jobs (2005), we believe that if given the tools, in this case more support and connection between sessions via a smartphone application, low-income families can and will benefit from treatment and our data to date suggest immense promise in this approach.

Acknowledgments   Funding for this work is provided by NIMH R34MH082956 (ClinicalTrials. gov Identifier: NCT01367847) and R01MH100377 (ClinicalTrials.gov Identifier: NCT02191956). This work would not be possible without: Dr. Melissa Napolitano, George Washington University, a friend and colleague whose question "Have you thought about mobile phones" in my kitchen during a visit inspired this line of research; Joel Sherrill, Program Chief, Child and Adolescent Psychosocial Intervention Program, for his formative and ongoing guidance on this line of research; our clinician advisory panel, which included April Harris-Britt, Ph.D., AHB Psychological

Associates; Kathryn J. Smith, MSW, Center for Child and Family Health; Jennifer Youngstrom, Ph.D., UNC Child and Family Clinic; Sarah Stearns, Ph.D., Dartmouth-Hitchcock Psychiatry Associates; and Timothy Verduin, Ph.D. NYU Child Study Center, for their review and input on all aspects of the TE-HNC program; our collaborators, including Rex Forehand, Ph.D., University of Vermont; Olga Khavjou and Amanda Honeycutt, PhD, Research Triangle International; and Greg Newey (Research Technology Solutions) and Sean Doherty (CrossComm Inc). Finally, we would like to thank project staff (Patrick Turner and Mary Jacobs), therapists (Margaret Anton, MA, Michelle Gonzalez, MA, Laura Khaeler, PhD, and Jessica Solis, MA), and the families who participated in this project for their time and contributions.

References

Conger, R. D., & Donnellan, M. B. (2007). An interactionist perspective on the socioeconomic context of human development. *Annual Review of Psychology, 58*, 175–199.

Dekovic, M., Slagt, M. I., Asscher, J. J., Boendermaker, L., Eichelsheim, V. I., & Prinzie, P. (2011). Effects of early prevention programs on adult criminal offending: A meta-analysis. *Clinical Psychology Review, 31*, 532–544.

Eyberg, S. M., & Pincus, D. (1999). *Eyberg Child Behavior Inventory & Sutter-Eyberg Student Behavior Inventory—Revised: Professional manual.* Odessa, FL: Psychological Assessment Resources.

Gardner, F., Connell, A., Trentacosta, C. J., Shaw, D. S., Dishion, T. J., & Wilson, M. N. (2009). Moderators of outcome in a brief family-centered intervention for preventing early problem behavior. *Journal of Consulting and Clinical Psychology, 77*, 543–553.

Jobs, S. (2005). *Stanford Commencement Address* (June 12, 2005). http://news.stanford.edu/news/2005/june15/jobs-061505.html

Jones, D. J. (2014). Future directions in the design, development, and investigation of technology as a service delivery vehicle. *Journal of Clinical Child and Adolescent Psychology, 43*, 128–142.

Jones, D.J., Forehand, R., McKee, L., Kincaid, C., & Cuellar, J. (2010). Behavioral Parent Training: Is there an 'app' for that? the Behavior Therapist, 33, 72–77. PMCID: PMC3244113; NIHMSID: NIHMS192670.

Jones, D.J., Forehand, R., Cuellar, J., Kincaid, C., Parent, J., Fenton, N., & Goodrum, N. (2013). Harnessing innovative technologies to advance children's mental health: Behavioral parent training as an example. *Clinical Psychology Review, 33*, 241–252.

Jones, D.J., Forehand, R., Cuellar, J., Parent, J., Honeycutt, A., Khavjou, O., ... Newey, G. (2014). Technology-enhanced program for child disruptive behavior disorders: Development and pilot randomized control trial. *Journal of Clinical Child and Adolescent Psychology, 43*, 88–101.

Lundahl, B., Risser, H. J., & Lovejoy, C. (2006). A meta-analysis of parent training: Moderators and follow-up effects. *Clinical Psychology Review, 26*, 86–104.

McMahon, R. J., & Forehand, R. L. (2003). *Helping the noncompliant child: Family-based treatment for oppositional behavior.* New York, NY: Guilford.

Mohr, D. C., Cujpers, P., & Lehman, K. (2011). Supportive account-ability: A model for providing human support to enhance adherence to eHealth interventions. *Journal of Medical Internet Research, 13*, e30.

Piquero, A. R., Farrington, D. P., Welsh, B. C., Tremblay, R., & Jennings, W. G. (2009). Effects of early family=parent training programs on antisocial behavior and delinquency. *Journal of Experimental Criminology, 5*, 83–120.

Reitman, D., & McMahon, R. J. (2012). Constance "Connie" Hanf (1917–2002): The mentor and the model. *Cognitive and Behavioral Practice, 20*, 106–116.

Tate, D. F., & Zabinski, M. F. (2004). Computer and internet applications for psychological treatment: Update for clinicians. *Journal of Clinical Psychology, 60*, 209–220.

U.S. Department of Health and Human Services (2014). Health and Human Services Department. https://aspe.hhs.gov/2014-poverty-guidelines#guidelines.

Webster-Stratton, C. (1990). Long-term follow-up of families with young conduct problem children: From preschool to grade school. *Journal of Clinical Child Psychology, 19*, 144–149.

Webster-Stratton, C. (1992). Individually administered videotape parent training: "Who benefits?". *Cognitive Therapy and Research, 16*, 31–35.

Webster-Stratton, C., Kolpacoff, M., & Hollinsworth, T. (1988). Self-administered videotape therapy for families with conduct-problem children: Comparison with two cost-effective treatments and a control group. *Journal of Consulting and Clinical Psychology, 56*, 558–566.

Chapter 15
The Application of Technology to an Academic Clinical Practice and Career: Evidence-Based Medicine, Telepsychiatry, and Distance Education

Donald M. Hilty

> We need approaches to the solutions that aren't just arithmetic and additive, but are in some sense logarithmic. This will require us to reach across historic boundaries and unlock the potential of collaboration across the usual disciplines.
> Jeffrey S. Flier, MD – Dean of the Faculty of Medicine, Harvard's First Forum on Health Care Innovation, July, 2013...
> Contextual Imperatives of the Forum were:
> 1. Making Value The Central Objective
> 2. Promoting Novel Approaches to Process Improvement
> 3. Making Consumerism Really Work
> 4. Decentralizing Approaches to Problem Solving
> 5. Integrating New Approaches Into Established Organizations
>
> To keep up with increasingly complex needs of patients - particularly those without access to health care – and the skills needed for the physician of the future, we need innovation by technology and models of service delivery to logarithmically or exponentially help. Underlying foundations for these initiatives are starting with patients'/learners' needs, interdisciplinary learning, joint decision-making, incremental growth, managing change and academic/institutional competency.
>
> Don Hilty, MD

D.M. Hilty, M.D. (✉)
Keck School of Medicine, Psychiatry and Chief and Program Director, Psychiatry Addiction Medicine, Kaweah Delta Medical Center, 400 West Mineral King, Visalia, CA 93291, USA
e-mail: donh032612@gmail.com

© Springer International Publishing Switzerland 2017
M.M. Maheu et al. (eds.), *Career Paths in Telemental Health*,
DOI 10.1007/978-3-319-23736-7_15

Narrative: Use of a Day in the Professional Life of a Clinical Psychiatrist, Telepsychiatric Health Services Researcher, and Medical Educator

Overview/Background. My day is a combination of service (patients, trainees, and faculty), learning/reflection, academic health center practice in psychiatry, and evaluation/research/scholarship. I started as a clinician, then developed a health services mood researcher using telemedicine for the rural underserved. My interest in learning and teaching styles led me to work as a master educator (teaching, curriculum development, and evaluation) in psychiatry, rural health, and other fields of medicine. As these changes occurred, my use of technology consolidated into three distinct areas: (1) searching evidence bases for clinical care, (2) provision of psychiatry by video and other modalities, and (3) distance education with multiple sites, interactive learning, and skill-building methods.

Evidence-Based Clinical Practice. I entered medical school, and the facsimile appeared, the PC became more popular, and the electronic health record (EHR) was in early development (used one in 1991 as an intern at California Pacific Medical Center, which was one of ten pilot EHR facilities in the USA). In just 20 years, practice is more complex, interesting, and potentially more sound—technology facilitates a great deal of this. First, resources (books, articles, breaking news) are available on line, and they are more synthetic in quality or capacity; experts synthesize by data and pattern analysis, and you can see more of the landscape in front of you by surfing. Second, as a learner who develops skills best through patients and cases, I have realized that technology supports me better. How? The EHR organizes, collates, and runs reports; the databases with drug interactions do more than I can (plus I don't have to recall all of that minutia); and finally, I get news on updates automatically by search engines. The review of my work—for quality improvement, mainly—is also easier for most of the same reasons.

Telepsychiatry. My faculty career at UC Davis started in 1995 and expanded from clinical to clinical research to technology and education. I simply followed my passion. I had seen low bandwidth connections in the 1980s and early 1990s, but UC Davis had a network with 128 K and 40 potential sites. I could connect with rural clinics, whose primary care providers wanted assistance in learning to manage depression (or in difficult cases, me managing for them). UC Davis had some pilot work in other areas of medicine, and I launched services in 1996, got contracts starting in 1998, and then got grants from then on. I partnered with loosely arranged telemedicine sites and developed clinical research with ten clinics/grant, usually on depression treatment by primary care doctors from 1 to 4 hours from Sacramento. Telemedicine's evolution has taken off, too, with advances in hardware/software (HD systems, cameras, and bandwidth to 384–1024K), wireless systems/remote monitoring, and asynchronous (previous) models.

Key steps in this process were alignment of patient needs with granting agencies, collaboration with others, and decision-making on how to get the "most" out of what we were doing in terms of efficiency and impact. Funding from the California

Endowment, Federal Communication Commission, Rural Utilities Office, AHRQ, UC Davis, and other grantors made this possible. My mentors helped, too: Thomas S. Nesbitt, MD, family medicine; Dale M. Hilty, PhD, counseling and Jungian psychology; and Robert E. Hales, MD, MBA. I moved from depression care by psychiatrists (additive), to distributing that knowledge and skills to primary care doctors (logarithmic), and then to augmenting rural network grants using my academic skills (adding grant writing skills was logarithmic to their work). Synchronous video was successful, but not all could make that happen, so we explored more accessible modes (e.g., telephone) and asynchronous work (e-mail and store-and-forward telepsychiatry)—combining models proved even more logarithmic as it overcomes cost, time schedules, time, and other barriers.

Medical and Distance Education. I began work in medical education, most formally, through building the 5-year MD/MPH UC Davis Rural Program in Medical Education (Rural-PRIME). In addition to regular medical education and contextualized rural curricula, Dr. Nesbitt and I thought technology was a key piece. It would help them with day-to-day clinical skills (as it did for me above); it would connect them with consultants who provided care to patients and teaching to them while at sites, and role-modeling that rural practice did not have to be so isolating. I thought we could go further and asked the question, "Why not connect the students at 4–5 different sites using a bridge for interactive teaching?" We reformatted five of the Education Building conference rooms ($20,000/room), and I choreographed the learning for interactive seminars during the family medicine, pediatrics, OB/GYN, and psychiatry clerkships. It took a significant effort to change the learning culture—the school's parties had more traditional models of learning, but the new generation of learners, though, gravitated to distance learning and use of technology! (Bowe et al., 2003; Simonton 1999) Change involved work with faculty educators in a non-phobic, incremental way for more smooth integration of their trainees. When I moved to USC in Los Angeles, the context is different, but it has still plenty of the same dimensions—underserved patients, poor/difficult access (comparatively difficult transportation problems), and medical student and psychiatric residency sites in a circle with a 1–2 h radius from USC Medical Center. We again need a logarithmic education plan rather than a piecemeal, additive plan.

Background and Training

Background. I was born in rural Ohio and lived in a town of 6000 people until 5, then West Central Ohio (1 h from Columbus) in a town of <1000 people. My father was a funeral director, and this may be related to themes of education, health, and helping others. I began tutoring in first grade. As the youngest of five kids, I was mentored a bit and avoided siblings' mistakes. I met a fantastic science teacher in biological sciences in high school: this led to interest in science, state science fair projects, and picking a biological science college major at a state university in Ohio. I later became more interested in health sciences and endocrinology and joined the pre-med club. I was a tutor and study skills instructor in a learning center. Technology came easier to me than most. My college roommate was a computer science major (i.e., geek), but I did not understand most of that. I traveled to Tours, France, for a semester to study French—I began to see how others valued, lived, and decided things differently based on culture.

Training: Initial Phase of Clinical Skills, Attitudes, and Confidence. Medical school at University of Cincinnati was chosen based on skills acquisition and decision-making education that I judged superior to other schools in the Midwest—I was not disappointed. This unbeknownst to me turned out to be a logarithmic step—skills for a lifetime of learning more than getting the best knowledge (90 % which is obsolete already). I thought family medicine might be for me (additive…that is all I knew), but decision-making/analysis of data and procedures led me to internal medicine and the med-psych interface. Classmates carried me through the knowledge morass of years 1–2—all the details of learning—and I did vice versa for the clinical skills including patient care in years 3–4. I would have been happy as a cardiologist or a medical psychiatrist—I chose psychiatry. Perhaps later, my interest in procedures transformed into use of computers and technology. Residency training landed me in metropolitan San Francisco, in the heart of the HIV epidemic. My teaching and leadership developed, along with a passion for helping those with medical disorders (e.g., cancer, AIDS) and mood problems (i.e., depression, bipolar disorder).

Training: Advanced Phase of Health Services Research, Education, and Technology. I became a clinical researcher by sitting on human subjects committees, taking courses on epidemiology/research design/grant writing and working on others' projects. There were no mentors in telepsychiatry, so I adapted by finding health service and psychiatric researchers to help—they all thought this telepsychiatry "would never work…" but never told me until later! I joined the Association for Academic Psychiatry which helped me tremendously with teaching and career development. I also took courses annually on teaching skills and applied my health services research skills to educational evaluation—I have some proficiency after nearly 20 years and on-the-job training through Rural-PRIME (Srinivasan et al., 2011). A sabbatical with expert medical educators at University of California San Francisco (UCSF) (Patricia O'Sullivan EdD and David Irby PhD) also developed my skills. Reflections on this path: it takes tremendous drive to learn on the job rather than getting coursework/degree in a training program; however, if you do it, it is particularly meaningful as you work on the job by applying the knowledge and skills directly to it. My next step is an executive MBA as the principles and content of that training are harder to learn on the fly.

Perspectives on the Pros and Cons of Using Technology in My Career

There are many positives in using technology—for patients, families, trainees, systems of care, communities, academic centers, and myself. First, technology makes a difference in *availing care and making it better or more complete.* Telemedicine may be used to add care or consultation at a distance (e.g., a telepsychiatric consultation to primary care, a therapist for cognitive behavioral therapy), provide more specialized care (e.g., a child and adolescent psychiatrist), or complement other care (i.e., filling in "holes" in services). Second, for education and training, primary care providers learn about mental health or how to prescribe and when trainees are included; they see a variety of patients (see additional systems of care). They ask a lot of questions and inspire us to do better, too. Third, these examples usually involve or accentuate interdisciplinary teamwork with different ideas, skills, and knowledge. Finally, telemedicine offers opportunities for learning about technology and different types of practice.

The negatives or hardship in adapting technology to patient care may have more to do with overall life experience than medicine specifically. One obstacle is now largely overcome—that is, the lack of mentors or general familiarity with technology—particularly for the younger generations. Another obstacle is resistance to change, stigma, and cynicism. This usually manifests as belief that innovation (telemedicine, distance education) will not work, it is not real science or good practice, and it is too far afield. I got questions like "Why bother?" or "That is odd not to see someone in person...you cannot really connect with the patient." I still kept my vision and these experiences inspired me. At times, I did such a lot of innovation related to medicine, technology, education, and research that it was hard and folks did not understand; while it is a leap to make an analogy related to eventual Nobel Prize winners, about 20 % of their seminal papers were rejected by multiple journals. Finally, costs and availability of technology are now not an impediment—patience over time is needed.

What Does It Take to Innovate or to Be an Innovator?

There is a literature on this in many fields, with healthcare innovation highlighted above (Dyer et al., 2011). Narratives and stories may reveal some key ingredients. Quotes from others in my life are the equivalent of an informal 360 evaluation of my path and may trigger ideas for others. My wife says, "Don is brilliant...few know how far this spans. [But] he drives me crazy when he first explains an idea...he looks at all the views and learns from ones that are opposites. He says that technology doesn't work a lot of the time, but he keeps going and it then does?" Family recalls, "He seemed to do everything well [growing up]. There was little to do in a town of 1000 people so he created his own games." Brother and mentor Dale reports "We talk for hours sometimes on ideas and mistakes...we are very critical, but we always step back to assess our part in things."(Scriven and Paul 1987) The kids say, "He knows a lot of technology, but sometimes makes the dumbest mistakes...maybe he does not know that much?" My bosses—like those of innovators tire of the innovation, saying "No...no...no [we cannot do that, either]." "He is never satisfied with the status quo." "He pushes [others] too hard on changing technology." Colleagues and friends report, "His ideas and emails...are beyond cryptic." "Sometimes I don't follow what he is saying [either]." "He is the Bob Dylan of telepsychiatry." "Don has had to make changes—significant ones to communicate better and spread interest in technology...but don't underestimate him...he gets it done." (Mann et al., 2009)

Evidence Base

The foundation or evidence bases for most of this work are consultation-liaison psychiatry, telemedicine, health services research, and healthcare disparities. One key concept is care or service that is effective and translatable to many, rather than "just" judged as efficacious in rigorously controlled situations. Effectiveness implies that telemental health works. Ideally, effectiveness should be considered for the patient, provider, program, community, and society. In telemedicine and telemental health, few authors have explicitly addressed effectiveness; however, research appears to be changing this (Hilty et al., 2013). The underlying premise of being "effective" is the assurance that the chosen technology is specific to the objective of the service being offered. Randomized controlled trials (RCT) (e.g., for depression in adult disease management and telepsychiatric consultation vs. usual care over 12 months) are effective and are the gold standard, but are hard to duplicate.

Secondly, care by technology has to be as good as or better than traditional care, which is usually shown by comparison and non-inferiority studies (Fortney et al., 2013; Hilty et al., 2013). Some have noted that with some populations (i.e., children and adolescents), telepsychiatry may be better than in-person services because of the novelty of the interaction, direction of the technology, the psychological and physical distance, and the authenticity of the family interaction. Reports have shown reduced length of hospitalization, better medication adherence, symptom reduction of disorders, and effective therapy such as using evidence-based treatments for PTSD.

In addition, models became of interest early based on psychiatric consultation to hospital and primary care settings, as more than one model could meet the need for patients and primary care providers (Hilty et al., 2013). Collaborative care by Katon et al. upgraded traditional consultation models, and it involved co-provision of medication for primary care patients by the psychiatrist and primary care provider (Fortney et al., 2013; Katon et al., 1997). This model is expensive in terms of provider time, education initiatives required, and getting the specialist where he or she is most needed. A phone and e-mail physician-to-provider consultation system for adults and children with developmental disabilities, using a 24-h warm line, made distribution easier but was limited by the providers not knowing the consultant. Telepsychiatry (synchronous telepsychiatry; STP) over time builds trust and disseminates expertise more efficiently (Yellowlees et al., 2010b). For example, an integrated program of mental health screening, therapy on site, and telepsychiatric consultation (phone, e-mail, or video), with continuing medical education (CME) and training on screening questionnaires, provided missing services in a rural health network. Tele-collaborative care has recently been shown to work and a current study compares asynchronous telepsychiatry (ATP) to STP (Yellowlees et al. 2010a).

Finally, innovation by technology should not be done in isolation (i.e., avoid silos)—the best of education, teamwork or interdisciplinary work, and business should be applied to make it work (Langan-Fox et al., 2000). We return to the opening above: value, novelty, innovation, and satisfaction for the many customers involved are fundamental.

References

Bowe, C. M., Lahey, L., Kegan, R., & Armstrong, E. (2003). Questioning the "big assumptions". Part II: Recognizing organizational contradictions that impede institutional change. *Medical Education, 37*(8), 723–733. Key point: Innovation, use of technology occurs in a complex context of health, community, academia and business (e.g. management of change).

Dyer, J. H., Gergerson, H. B., & Christensen, C. M. (2011). *The inventor's DNA*. Boston, MA: Harvard Business Review Press. Key point: This gives cases and a historical context of invention and innovation.

Fortney, J. C., Pyne, J. M., Mouden, S. P., et al. (2013). Practice-based versus telemedicine-based collaborative care for depression in rural federally qualified health centers: A pragmatic randomized comparative effectiveness trial. *American Journal of Psychiatry, 4*(170), 414–425. doi:10.1176/appi.ajp.2012.12050696. Key point: Telepsychiatry consultation to primary care is as good as or better than usual care.

Hilty, D. M., Ferrer, D., Parish, M. B., Johnston, B., Callahan, E. J., & Yellowless, P. M. (2013). The effectiveness of telemental health: A 2013 review. *Telemedicine Journal and e-Health, 19*(6), 444–454. Key point: This is the best review of the evidence base on telemental health.

Katon, W., Von Korff, M., Lin, E., et al. (1997). Collaborative management to achieve depression treatment guidelines. *The Journal of Clinical Psychiatry, 58*(Suppl 1), 20–24. Key point: Distribute limited resource (specialty expertise) by teaching primary care providers how to provide mental health services (logarithmic).

Kolb, D. (1984). *Experiential learning: Experience as the source of learning and development*. Englewood Cliffs, NJ: Prentice-Hall. Key point: Experience at the level of the learner (assessed before introducing teaching), simplicity and supervised learning helps us perform better and reduces resistance to change.

Langan-Fox, J., Code, S., & Langfield-Smith, K. (2000). Team mental models: Techniques, methods, and analytic approaches. *Human Factors, 42*(2), 242–271. Key point: Teamwork is better than work alone; more minds are better than one. In telemedicine, clinical, technical, administrative, and leadership collaboration is essential.

Mann, K., Gordon, J., & MacLeod, A. (2009). Reflection and reflective practice in health professions education: A systematic review. *Advances in Health Science Education and Theory Practice, 4*, 595–621. Key point: Reflection is essential to career, personal and obstacle analysis and growth.

Scriven, M., & Paul, R. (1987). *Critical thinking as defined by the national Council for Excellence in Critical Thinking*. Presented at the 8th Annual International Conference on Critical Thinking and Education Reform, Rohnert Park, CA. Key point: This is the best, long-term definition of critical thinking, which is required for innovation and success.

Simonton, D. K. (1999). *Origins of genius*. London, UK: Oxford University Press. Key point: Great inventors incubate dilemmas, remain patient, and eventually find insightful solutions.

Srinivasan, M., Li, S. T., Meyers, F. J., Pratt, D. D., Collins, J. B., Braddock, C, ... Hilty, D. M. (2011). Teaching as a competency for medical educators: competencies for medical educators. *Academic Medicine, 86*(10), 1211–1220. Key point: Teleconsultants have to be great clinicians and educators, too.

Yellowlees, P. M., Odor, A., Burke, M. M., et al. (2010a). A feasibility study of asynchronous telepsychiatry for psychiatric consultations. *Psychiatric Services, 61*(8), 838–840. Key point: This is the first pivotal validation of store-and-forward telepsychiatry.

Yellowlees, P. M., Shore, J., & Roberts, L. (2010b). Practice guidelines for videoconferencing-based telemental health, American Telemedicine Association. *Telemedicine Journal and e-Health, 16*, 1074–1089. Key point: Best telepsychiatry guidelines available in the field.

Chapter 16
Enhancing Mindfulness-Based Cognitive Therapy with a Virtual Mindfulness Coach

Eva Hudlicka

The first rule is to keep an untroubled spirit. The second is to look things in the face and know them for what they are. Marcus Aurelius

Vignette

Introduction and Background

Mindfulness meditation practice has recently received much attention in mental health and represents a core element of a number of treatment approaches, including Mindfulness-Based Cognitive Therapy (MBCT) (Williams, Russell, & Russell, 2008), Dialectical Behavior Therapy (DBT) (Chapman, 2006), Mindfulness-Based Relapse Prevention (MBRP) (Bowen, Chawla, & Marlatt, 2010), and Acceptance Commitment Therapy (ACT) (Hayes, 2004).

Mindfulness is best described as a state of awareness characterized by "full attention to, and awareness of, the internal and external experience of the present moment" (Chambers, Lo, & Allen, 2008) and a nonjudgmental attitude toward whatever thoughts, images, feelings, or sensations enter awareness. A typical mindfulness practice session includes both concentration meditation and mindfulness meditation. Concentration practice involves a focus on a single stimulus, typically the breath, and as the mind wanders the meditator gently guides his/her attention to the breath. This practice often results in relaxation and the lowering of the sympathetic nervous system activity. Mindfulness practice involves paying attention to

E. Hudlicka, Ph.D., L.I.C.S.W. (✉)
Psychometrix Associates, Therapy 21st & School of Computer Science, University of Massachusetts-Amherst, Amherst, MA 01003-9264, USA
e-mail: hudlicka@cs.umass.edu

© Springer International Publishing Switzerland 2017
M.M. Maheu et al. (eds.), *Career Paths in Telemental Health*,
DOI 10.1007/978-3-319-23736-7_16

whatever enters awareness, accepting its presence in a nonjudgmental manner, letting it go, and awaiting with curiosity whatever may enter awareness in the next moment.

The Marcus Aurelius quote above captures both of these aspects of mindfulness practice. The concentration practice is relaxing, calming the mind, and contributing to an "untroubled spirit." The mindfulness practice helps us "look things in the face and know them for what they are," by clearly seeing, and accepting, the reality of the present moment. As evidence accumulates regarding the benefits of mindfulness, more and more people are seeking mindfulness training and coaching, and increasing numbers of therapists are incorporating mindfulness into their practice.

Although many training programs are available, these are often costly or unavailable in a particular geographic area, making access difficult. This chapter describes a novel way of providing mindfulness training and coaching, via a virtual synthetic character: the Virtual Mindfulness Coach. The vignette below presents a scenario describing how the virtual coach can be used by a therapist to enhance treatment.

Vignette: Using the Virtual Mindfulness Coach When a Face-to-Face Meeting with a Client Is Not Possible

A Face-to-Face Meeting Is Not Possible

Consider the following scenarios.

Yet another snowstorm has **brought** transportation to a standstill and your client Janina, a highly anxious middle-aged woman, called to cancel her appointment. She sounded very disappointed, especially as you had just begun to discuss introducing her to mindfulness meditation in the previous session. She was excited to begin to learn how to meditate and very hopeful that this will finally begin to address her long-standing anxiety issues. Janina has struggled with motivation to continue treatment, due to previous failures of therapy to provide relief from her anxiety. She has a history of dropping out of treatment when disappointed. Her distress during the phone conversation was palpable and you are concerned that her motivation will wane again and that she may terminate treatment.

Richard, a 45-year-old unemployed man, has had another panic attack last week. His symptoms have reached a level of intensity where he has been unable to leave his house to attend therapy. Unfortunately, due to your schedule and the location of his home, you are unable to do a home visit. Richard desperately wants to speak with you and continue the mindfulness training you initiated recently, but his symptoms make it impossible for him to come to his regular session in the office.

Your 6-year-old daughter Jennifer just came down with a bad cold last night. Your regular babysitter is out of town and your spouse is busy with a conference all week. You have no choice but to cancel your therapy sessions for the day. You are feeling very guilty for not being able to be there for your clients, especially since several of them are going through a crisis.

A 'Virtual Mindfulness Coach' Provides Mindfulness Training and Coaching

In the past, these situations would have created gaps in care as your clients would have had to wait for the next session. Now, however, there is another solution. You have recently introduced the *Virtual Mindfulness Coach* into your mindfulness-based cognitive therapy practice (MBCT). The coach is a virtual character, an embodied conversational agent, that provides interactive, customized mindfulness training and coaching to your clients between sessions. Clients can access the coach on multiple devices: tablets, smart phones, laptops and desktops. No specialized hardware or communication media are necessary. Following an initial download from the internet (and occasional updates), the Virtual Mindfulness Coach is available on the clients' devices and does not require internet connectivity, unless the client wishes the clinician to actively participate in a training or coaching session.

The coach offers a 4-week training program in mindfulness meditation, followed by customized, interactive coaching (Hudlicka, 2013). The training period provides the information necessary to begin a mindfulness practice, includes didactic material and guided meditations, and provides ample opportunities for questions. The material is provided in four lessons, with one lesson introduced each week. Following the 4-week training period, the coach provides ongoing support to help your clients establish a regular practice. This involves addressing particular common problems that novice meditators typically experience (e.g., restlessness, boredom, sleepiness), as well as keeping track of client-specific preferences or problems and targeting the coaching assistance accordingly.

The coach interacts with your clients in natural language and displays facial expressions that convey appropriate emotions, to enhance your clients' engagement—empathy and concern when their practice is not going well, and joy when they report success. The coach character's appearance can be modified to match your clients' individual preferences for ethnicity and demographics. (Your elderly client might prefer a younger-looking female coach, whereas your young adult client may prefer a middle-aged male coach, who reminds her of one of her college professors.) The coach's style of interaction can also be customized to your client's preferences. (A young adult will likely prefer a less formal style of conversation, whereas a middle-aged client will probably feel more comfortable with a more formal style.)

The Virtual Mindfulness Coach Meets the Required Privacy Requirements

Following an initial downloading of the virtual mindfulness coach software and content, over a secure connection, all subsequent interaction with the virtual coach is conducted locally, on the client's device. All HIPAA privacy requirements are therefore maintained. If the client prefers to be connected with the therapist during a training or coaching session, this can be accomplished via established secure communication channels. The client also has the option to share some of their dialogue with the coach with you and thereby provide you with additional information to support treatment. Since this information is encrypted, transmission of this information over secure connections is possible and meets established privacy requirements.

The Virtual Mindfulness Coach Gets to Know the Client

Much as you have come to know your clients over time, the Virtual Mindfulness Coach also learns about your clients, as they interact with the coach during the initial 4-week training period, and the subsequent coaching. For example, the coach knows that your anxious client struggles with restlessness during meditation sessions, so she/he frequently checks in about this client's anxiety level and makes specific suggestions on how to address feelings of restlessness. The coach also keeps track of what has worked for particular clients in the past and what was not so helpful, so she/he can customize the advice she/he offers. Furthermore, with the client's consent, you can interact with the coach directly, to provide additional information about the client that will enhance the coach's "affective user model" of the client and enable the coach to provide more individualized, customized training and coaching, to increase effectiveness.

Therapist Can Join Client-Coach Sessions, If Requested by the Client

While some clients may prefer to work with the coach on their own, others may prefer to have you involved in the interaction, at various points during the training and coaching. Your involvement can take several forms, depending on your client's preferences and your availability. It may be as simple as speaking with your client during a mindfulness training or coaching session, providing additional support, clarifying some content, offering additional suggestions, or answering a specific question. This can be done by via any HIPAA-compliant communication medium, either audio-only or including video, to enhance engagement and the sense of presence.

Alternatively, you may join the training or coaching session in a manner that allows you to see all of the interaction that is taking place with the Virtual Mindfulness Coach and augment the interaction as necessary, to ensure that the client's needs are met. For example, if the client asks a particular question and you feel that the coach's answer is not complete, you can provide additional information, customized to the client's needs, based on your knowledge of his/her background.

Client-Coach Interaction Can Be an Additional Source of Information About the Client's Progress and Needs

Another level of interaction is possible if your client wishes to share with you more details about the interactions she/he has with the coach. This enables you to have access not only to the actual dialogue that your client conducts with the virtual coach, but also to the information the virtual coach gathers about your client, to support customized interaction: the "affective user model" of the client.

Access to this information enables you to not only track your client's progress and identify any gaps in knowledge or hindrances to practicing mindfulness, which you can then address directly, but also to become aware of any acute issues your client may be facing, which may require your attention or intervention. For example, your client may reveal to the virtual coach that she/he is feeling increasingly anxious or depressed, or that she has recently resumed some undesirable behavior (e.g., smoking, substance use). With the client's permission, alerts can be set in the coach that allow you to be notified of these developments. This in turn enables you to provide the appropriate interventions in a timely manner. It is important to note that any of this information sharing must be allowed by the client and can be terminated by the client at any point.

Positive Outcomes

Use of the Virtual Mindfulness Coach, in conjunction with face-to-face therapy, has a number of potential positive outcomes. First, the coach provides additional training material and delivers customized training anywhere and anytime, between sessions, and when you are not available. The ability to customize the training materials to each client's needs increases engagement and the likelihood that the training program will be successful.

Second, the coaching component of the Virtual Mindfulness Coach provides the support necessary to help clients establish a regular mindfulness practice. Many students of mindfulness fail to establish a regular practice and thus fail to obtain the benefits of mindfulness, which require frequent and regular practice. The coaching segment provided by the virtual coach addresses this problem directly, by providing individualized suggestions about how to overcome specific and typical problems encountered by novice meditators (e.g., restlessness, boredom) and by providing practical advice regarding the establishing of a regular practice (e.g., set up a dedicated place in the house, a regular time, etc.). Preliminary data suggest that the coach is effective in helping clients establish a regular practice (Hudlicka, 2013).

Finally, by providing additional, accessible, and customized training and coaching, use of the coach has the potential to improve treatment outcomes of therapeutic approaches that directly incorporate mindfulness practice (e.g., MBCT, DBT, ACT).

In conclusion, with the Virtual Mindfulness Coach available as an adjunct to your face-to-face practice, you feel less concerned about your clients missing a session. The coach helps your clients stay on track with their practice, so they can get the full benefit of a mindfulness-based therapy. In addition, if your client agrees to share with you his/her communication with the coach, the additional information you may obtain from these interactions may help you provide better care, by quickly becoming aware of the client's problems and emerging needs. The virtual coach may also help the client feel more connected to you in-between sessions, and this may reduce the need for between session contacts, or even require fewer sessions as the treatment progresses.

Training Required for Psychotherapist

Use of the virtual coach as a component of therapy requires, at a minimum, a license to practice psychotherapy, as well as personal experience with mindfulness. Ideally, the clinician also has a regular practice of mindfulness, as that will enhance his/her ability to guide their clients in establishing a regular practice. In cases where mindfulness is a component of another therapeutic protocol, such as MBCT or DBT, familiarity and training in the specific approach is also necessary. Beyond this, the only other general requirement is an openness and interest in the use of advanced technologies (artificial intelligence, affective computing, virtual agents) and their use in clinical practice.

The clinician must also be familiar with the functionality and capabilities of the Virtual Mindfulness Coach; that is, with the course content and the coach's adaptation and coaching strategies, as well as with the structure and use of the affective user model that the coach generates as it interacts with the clients. This knowledge will allow the clinician to make the best use of the coach's functionality and enable him/her to answer any questions the clients may have, as well as to troubleshoot in situations where the limits of the coach's capabilities are reached; e.g., when the coach does not understand some natural language input. Gaining this basic level of familiarity with the coach requires 1 or 2 days of training and an additional 1 or 2 days of practice.

For clinicians who may be more interested in the actual underlying technology, there is also the additional possibility to work with the coach designers and developers to enhance the content and the coach's adaptive strategies.

Last but not least, the clinician must be familiar with any organization-, state-, and license-specific privacy requirements for the use of telemental health technologies and technologies in general. As these rules and requirements are still evolving, as are the associated technologies, keeping up to date with emerging guidelines and requirements is essential.

In terms of a more personal story: my own path to clinical practice and telemental health is not typical. My PhD is in computer science, more specifically, in the area of artificial intelligence (AI). Within AI, my interest in cognitive modeling led to a job in the Department of Cognitive Sciences and Systems at BBN Labs, where I gradually transitioned from artificial intelligence research to cognitive modeling. Our cognitive modeling research focused on models of stress on decision making, and it was during this time that I began to recognize the strong influence of emotion on decision making and on cognition in general. I also became interested in psychotherapy and intrigued by the possibility of developing computational models of emotions and exploring their usefulness in understanding the mechanisms of psychotherapeutic action.

While still at BBN, I decided to pursue my interest in psychotherapy more formally. The shortest path to obtain the necessary training to practice psychotherapy was via an MSW, and I obtained my MSW part time, while continuing my research in cognitive modeling at BBN, and gradually becoming increasingly interested in emotion modeling. I very much enjoyed the clinical work, and my plan was to have a dual career practicing psychotherapy and continuing to work in cognitive/affective modeling. I saw then, and continue to see, much synergy between these two areas. During my second year internship in clinical work, I was fortunate to have a clinical supervisor who shared my vision of the usefulness and promise of combining computational modeling and psychotherapy.

After finishing my MSW, I began actively pursuing funding for emotion modeling and founded my own company, Psychometrix Associates, to focus on this research area. My work at Psychometrix focused primarily on the development of computational models of affective biases on decision making, to help identify the underlying mechanisms mediating these effects. Understanding these processes has direct implications for psychotherapy, as it would enable more detailed assessment and individualized treatment plans. An example of this type of modeling work is described in Hudlicka (2008b). I also began to pursue more applied research in this area, in the form of affect-adaptive interaction and affective user modeling (Hudlicka & McNeese, 2002). During this time, the field of affective and social computing was growing rapidly, and affective virtual characters and social robots began to emerge, with a variety of applications in mental health (Hudlicka, 2005; Hudlicka et al., 2008, 2009) (see also discussion in section "Effectiveness of Virtual Character-Mediated Training and Coaching in Mental Healthcare" below). My interest in applying affect-adaptive interaction in mental health technologies led to the development of the Virtual Mindfulness Coach described in this chapter.

Affective and social computing technologies are increasingly being applied in mental health, and their potential for enhancing assessment and service delivery is just beginning to be recognized (Hudlicka, 2008a; 2016). The use of these technologies is particularly relevant for telemental health. It is important to understand that these synthetic agents are not intended to replace human therapists or face-to-face therapy; it will be a long time before synthetic agents have the linguistic, conceptual, and empathic capabilities of human therapists. Many researchers express well-founded doubts whether this could ever happen. However, the intent is not to replace human therapists, but rather to enhance treatment by supporting homework exercises and by providing problem-solving assistance, psycho-education, and direct support for behavior change, as an adjunct to face-to-face therapy.

Pros of the Employment Position

This is an exciting time to be engaged in clinical work! Increasing emphasis on evidence-based treatments, emerging research from affective and cognitive science and neuroscience, and the increasing availability of advanced technologies such as affective and social computing are all contributing to the creation of customized, accessible, and innovative treatment approaches in mental healthcare. The Virtual Mindfulness Coach described in this chapter is just one example of these technologies. The ultimate objective is of course to provide more effective and efficient services to clients, by improving access to, and effectiveness of, evidence-based treatments. At the same time, a great deal of personal satisfaction can also be derived from the use and exploration of these technologies.

Opportunities exist not only for the enhancement of individual treatment, but also for research that systematically explores the effectiveness of technology-enhanced treatment and contributes to the further development of mental healthcare technologies. Opportunities exist for productive collaborations among researchers and practitioners from multiple disciplines, including clinicians, affective science researchers, and computer scientists. Such collaborations hold the promise of identifying an increasing number of areas where technology can enhance treatment and improve outcomes. These include applications of the virtual coaching technologies across a variety of contexts that involve training and behavior change coaching, as well as supportive, psycho-education, and problem-solving interventions. Examples of other promising technologies include serious games to support skill acquisition and a variety of cognitive-behavioral treatments and social robots to provide social skill training for children on the autism spectrum.

Cons of the Employment Position

Clearly, use of technologies such as the Virtual Mindfulness Coach requires a positive attitude toward these types of advanced technologies and an understanding of their potential to enhance clinical practice. For clinicians who do not have this mind-set, the use of these technologies may feel sterile or even frustrating.

Assuming a generally positive attitude to advanced clinical technologies, there is no downside to integrating these technologies into one's practice. Of course, ongoing monitoring is necessary to ensure that the clients are benefiting from the use of these technologies. It is assumed that technologies such as the Virtual Mindfulness Coach would only be used with the clients' explicit permission and their desire for, and benefit from, their use.

Ideally, feedback would be possible to the designers and developers, so that modifications can be made to better meet clients' needs, to incorporate emerging findings about the treatment protocols involved, and to take advantage of continued advances in technologies. In the case of the virtual coach, these would be virtual agent technologies, affective user modeling, natural language understanding, speech understanding, and affective computing: all of these used to enhance the coach's interaction capabilities and effectiveness. A possible drawback of using the virtual coach could occur in situations where there was inadequate coordination with the designers and developers of these technologies, which would hinder necessary modifications and updates.

Beyond this, the only possible problems with the use of these types of technologies are regulatory and reimbursement issues. The rapid advances in technologies supporting behavioral health treatment represent a challenge to the regulatory bodies in mental health. Rules for the appropriate use of these technologies are emerging, and new guidelines are being formulated by both regulatory agencies (e.g., state licensing boards) and by professional organizations (e.g., APA, American Telemedicine Association). These trends are likely to continue for some time, as the regulatory agencies and professional organizations catch up to the rapid technological developments and advancements, and as empirical data regarding the efficacy and appropriate use of these technologies become available. The potential downside of this state of affairs for the practitioner is a degree of uncertainty regarding rules and guidelines for the use of these technologies and the associated necessity to keep up with emerging changes.

Related to the above is the issue of reimbursement. As is the case with regulatory agencies and professional organizations, insurance companies are also grappling with the best ways to integrate advanced technologies into mental health treatments and establish guidelines for reimbursements. This degree of uncertainty requires the clinician to both stay abreast of emerging reimbursement rules, but also to engage in advocacy to ensure that emerging technologies are available to clients, and that clinicians using these technologies are appropriately reimbursed for their efforts.

Evidence-Based Interventions

Virtual coaches represent advanced technologies that have only recently begun to be explored in psychotherapy. Extensive empirical evaluations will be necessary to determine when and how these technologies are most usefully integrated into practice, to enhance clients' therapeutic experience and treatment outcomes, as well as to improve access to evidence-based treatment methods.

While extensive empirical studies have yet to be conducted with virtual therapeutic agents, evidence from three related areas suggests that virtual character-enhanced treatments, and virtual character-mediated training and coaching, represent promising areas in technology-enhanced and telemental health practice. Below I discuss evidence from these related areas: (1) demonstrated efficacy and benefits of psychotherapeutic approaches that incorporate mindfulness as an integral component of treatment (e.g., DBT, MBCT, MBRP); (2) demonstrated benefits of a regular practice of mindfulness on mental and physical health, cognitive and executive functions, and a general sense of well-being; and (3) increasing evidence regarding the effectiveness of virtual character-mediated training and coaching in mental health settings.

Benefits of Therapeutic Approaches Incorporating Mindfulness

Above I listed several therapeutic approaches that incorporate and/or emphasize mindfulness. Due to the relatively recent emergence of mindfulness as an adjunct to therapy, fewer evaluation studies exist than for more established treatment methods (e.g., exposure therapies for anxiety disorders). Nevertheless, emerging evidence from clinical studies, and from meta-analyses of existing data, suggests that mindfulness-based treatments are effective and that the mindfulness component of these treatments enhances outcomes.

A recent meta-analysis of 6 RCTs of Mindfulness-Based Cognitive Therapy (MBCT) (total $N = 593$) (Piet & Hougaard, 2011) concluded that MBCT was effective in preventing a relapse of depression in patients with recurrent major depressive disorder in cases of three or more episodes of depression. Preliminary evaluations suggest that MBCT may also be effective for active depression, anxiety disorders, and bipolar disorder (Sipe & Eisendrath, 2012). A number of studies have shown the effectiveness of another therapeutic approach that emphasizes mindfulness: Dialectical Behavior Therapy (DBT) (Chapman, 2006). Finally, Acceptance and Commitment Therapy (ACT) has also recently undergone formal evaluation studies. While the data are still preliminary, and some of the reported studies have methodological limitations, nevertheless a recent meta-analysis of ACT treatment provides evidence of medium to large effect sizes (Hayes et al., 2006; Powers et al., 2009), and the APA now classifies ACT as an empirically supported treatment with moderately strong empirical support (Gaudiano, 2011).

Benefits of Mindfulness

Regular practice of mindfulness meditation is associated with a number of health benefits. Evidence from existing studies indicates that mindfulness practice enhances health-related quality of life, affecting both physical and psychological symptoms (Lazar, 2005; Reibel, Greeson, Brainard, & Rosenzweig, 2001). Benefits of mindfulness meditation have been demonstrated in stress reduction (Shapiro, Schwartz, & Bonner, 1998), pain reduction (Kabat-Zinn, 1990), enhanced immune responses (Davidson et al., 2003), reduction of symptoms in anxiety disorders (Evans et al., 2008), prevention of relapse in major depression (Teasdale et al., 2000), improvement in a subjective sense of well-being (Brown & Ryan, 2003), and improvements in cognitive functions (Chambers et al., 2008).

Effectiveness of Virtual Character-Mediated Training and Coaching in Mental Healthcare

Virtual coaches use the emerging technologies of *embodied conversational agents* (ECA's) (Cassell, Sullivan, Prevost, & Churchill, 2000) and *relational pedagogical agents* (Bickmore, 2003). ECAs are animated virtual characters, displayed on a computer or a mobile device screen. ECAs play the roles of teachers, mentors, advisors, social companions, and, increasingly, of virtual coaches (Clarebout, Elen, Johnson, & Shaw, 2002; Hayes-Roth, Amano, Saker, & Sephton, 2004; Johnson, Rickel, & Lester, 2000; Prendinger & Ishizuka, 2004; Rickel et al., 2002). The use of ECAs requires minimal or no training, due to their capability to engage in natural interaction with humans through dialogue and nonverbal expression. The latter includes facial expressions, gaze, and gestures, which together help control conversation flow and augment the ECA's visual and behavioral realism. *Relational pedagogical agents* represent a subset of ECAs, designed both to train a particular subject or skill and to develop the type of a longer-term relationship with the user that helps facilitate coaching (Bickmore, Gruber, & Picard, 2005). The use of ECAs and relational pedagogical agents has recently begun to be explored in healthcare settings, where these virtual entities act as coaches, trainers, and counselors.

References

Bickmore, T. (2003). *Relational agents: Effecting change through human-computer relationships* (Ph.D. thesis, media arts & sciences, MIT, Cambridge, MA).

Bickmore, T., Gruber, A., & Picard, R. (2005). Establishing alliance in automated health behavior change interventions. *Patient Education and Counseling, 59*, 21–30.

Bowen, S., Chawla, N., & Marlat, A. (2010). *Mindfulness-Based Relapse Prevention for Addictive* Behaviors: A Clinician's Guide. New York: The Guilford Press.

Brown, K. W., & Ryan, R. M. (2003). The benefits of being present: Mindfulness and its role in psychological well-being. *Journal of Personality and Social Psychology, 84*, 822–848.

Cassell, J., Sullivan, J., Prevost, S., & Churchill, E. (2000). *Embodied conversational agents.* Cambridge, MA: MIT Press.

Chambers, R., Lo, B. C. Y., & Allen, N. B. (2008). The impact of intensive mindfulness training on attentional control, cognitive style, and affect. *Cognitive Therapy Research, 32*, 303–322.

Chapman, A. (2006). Dialectical behavior therapy. *Psychiatry, 3*(9), 62–68.

Clarebout, G., Elen, J., Johnson, W. L., & Shaw, E. (2002). Animated pedagogical agents: An opportunity to be grasped? *Journal of Educational Multimedia and Hypermedia, 11*, 267–286.

Davidson, R. J., Kabat-Zinn, J., Schumacher, J., Rosenkranz, M., Muller, D., Santorelli, S. F., ... Sheridan, J. F. (2003). Alterations in brain and immune function produced by mindfulness meditation. *Psychosomatic Medicine, 65*, 564–570.

Evans, S., Ferrando, S., Findler, M., Stowell, C., Smart, C., & Haglin, D. (2008). Mindfulness-based cognitive therapy for generalized anxiety disorder. *Journal of Anxiety Disorders, 22*, 716–721.

Gaudiano, B. (2011). Evaluating acceptance and commitment therapy: An analysis of a recent critique. *The International Journal of Behavioral Consultation and Therapy, 7*(1), 55–67.

Hayes, S. C. (2004). Acceptance and commitment therapy, relational frame theory, and the third wave of behavioral and cognitive therapies. *Behavior Therapy, 35*, 639–665.

Hayes-Roth, B., Amano, K., Saker, R., & Sephton, T. (2004). Training brief intervention with a virtual coach and virtual patients. *Annual Review of CyberTherapy and Telemedicine, 2*, 85–96.

Hayes, S.C., Luoma, J.B., Bond, F.W., Masuda, A. & Lillis, J. (2006). Acceptance and commitment therapy: model, processes and outcomes. Behaviour Research and Therapy, 44 (1), 1–25.

Hudlicka, E. (2005). A Computational Model of Emotion and Personality: Applications to Psychotherapy Research and Practice. In Proceedings of the 10th Annual Cyber Therapy 2005 Conference: A Decade of Virtual Reality, Basel, Switzerland.

Hudlicka, E. (2008a). What are we modeling when we model emotion? In *Proceedings of the AAAI Spring Symposium on "Emotion, Personality and Social Behavior", TR SS-08-04* (pp. 52–59). Menlo Park, CA: AAAI Press.

Hudlicka, E. (2008b). Modeling the mechanisms of emotion effects on cognition. In *Proceedings of the AAAI Fall Symposium on "Biologically Inspired Cognitive Architectures", TR FS-08-04* (pp. 82–86). Menlo Park, CA: AAAI Press.

Hudlicka, E. (2013). Virtual training and coaching of health behavior: Example from mindfulness meditation training. *Patient Education and Counseling, 92*(2), 160–166.

Hudlicka, E. (2016). Virtual companions, coaches, and therapeutic games in psychotherapy. *Artificial Intelligence in Mental Healthcare.* In D. D. Luxton (Ed.) Elsevier.

Hudlicka, E., Lisetti, C., Hodge, D., Paiva, A., Rizzo, A., & Wagner, E. (2008). Artificial agents for psychotherapy. In *Proceedings of the AAAI Spring Symposium on "Emotion, Personality and Social Behavior", TR SS-08-04* (pp. 60–64). Menlo Park, CA: AAAI.

Hudlicka, E., & McNeese, M. (2002). User's affective & belief state: Assessment and GUI adaptation (with M. McNeese). *International Journal of User Modeling and User Adapted Interaction, 12*(1), 1–47.

Hudlicka, E., Payr, S., Ventura, R., Becker-Asano, C., Fischer, K., Leite, I., ... von Scheve, C. (2009). *Social interaction with robots and agents: Where do we stand, where do we go?* Proceedings of the 3rd International Conference on Affective Computing and Intelligent Interaction, Amsterdam, NL, September.

Johnson, W. L., Rickel, J. W., & Lester, J. C. (2000). Animated pedagogical agents: Face-to-face interaction in interactive learning environments. *International Journal of Artificial Intelligence in Education, 11,* 47–78.

Kabat-Zinn, J. (1990). *Full catastrophe living: Using the wisdom of your body and mind to face stress, pain, and illness.* New York, NY: Delta.

Lazar, S. (2005). Mindfulness research. In C. K. Germer, R. D. Siegel, & P. R. Fulton (Eds.), *Mindfulness and psychotherapy.* New York, NY: The Guildford Press.

Piet, J., & Hougaard, E. (2011). The effect of mindfulness-based cognitive therapy for prevention of relapse in recurrent major depressive disorder: A systematic review and meta-analysis. *Clinical Psychology Review, 31*(6), 1032–1040.

Powers, M.B., Zum Vorde Sive Vording, M.B., V.S. & Emmelkamp. P.M.G. (2009). Acceptance and Commitment Therapy: A Meta-Analytic Review. Psychotherapy and Psychosomatics, 78, 73–80.

Prendinger, H., & Ishizuka, M. (2004). *Life-Like characters.* New-York, NY: Springer.

Reibel, D. K., Greeson, J. M., Brainard, G. C., & Rosenzweig, S. (2001). Mindfulness based stress reduction and health-related quality of life in a heterogeneous patient population. *General Hospital Psychiatry, 23,* 183–192.

Rickel, J., Marsella, S., Gratch, J., Hill, R., Traum, D., & Swartout, W. (2002). Toward a new generation of virtual humans for interactive experiences. *IEEE Intelligent Systems,* 32–38

Shapiro, S. L., Schwartz, G. E., & Bonner, G. (1998). Effects of mindfulness-based stress reduction on medical and premedical students. *Journal of Behavioral Medicine, 21,* 581–599.

Sipe, W.E. & Eisendrath, S.J. (2012). Mindfulness-based cognitive therapy: theory and practice. Canadian Journal of Psychiatry, 57 (2), 63–69.

Teasdale, J. D., Segal, Z. V., Williams, J. M. G., Ridgeway, V. A., Soulsby, J. M., & Lau, M. A. (2000). Prevention of relapse/recurrence in Major Depression by Mindfulness-Based Cognitive Therapy. *Journal of Consulting and Clinical Psychology, 68,* 615–622.

Williams, J. M. G., Russell, I., & Russell, D. (2008). Mindfulness-based cognitive therapy. *Journal of Consulting and Clinical Psychology, 76*(3), 524–529.

Chapter 17
Getting Better: How a Client Satisfaction Survey Can Enhance Both Your Marketing and Treatment Outcomes

Keely Kolmes

> *"What can I do to effectively market my practice in the digital age? Online consumer sites on which clients vent about poor services or rave about their favorite psychotherapist are a frightening new challenge for clinicians. I wish I had an effective, easy, and ethical way to provide a representative sample of what my patients think about the quality of my services."*

Vignette

A clinician is sitting in-session with a long-term client. The client seems uncomfortable today, seeming to be distracted by something. As the clinician presses the client, noticing the change in her client's manner, the client confesses that he looked online for the psychotherapist's office information to refer a friend, and he discovered that the psychotherapist has a couple of negative reviews on Yelp. The psychotherapist is surprised. She didn't know she had a page on Yelp. She does her best to explore with the patient what it was like for him to find the reviews and how it affected him. She asks him if it made him feel differently about their work, and he notes that the reviewers seemed "fake" and that they had not reviewed other services and had just made accounts to slam the psychotherapist. But he also notes that he felt a protective pull to also create a fake account to write supportive words about the clinician. The psychotherapist explores this pull to protect and lets the client know that she appreciates his care but that this act is unnecessary. She thanks the client for bringing this uncomfortable topic up and exploring with her how it made him feel.

K. Kolmes, Psy.D. (✉)
200 Montgomery St. Suite 400, San Francisco, CA 94104, USA
e-mail: drkkolmes@gmail.com

© Springer International Publishing Switzerland 2017
M.M. Maheu et al. (eds.), *Career Paths in Telemental Health*,
DOI 10.1007/978-3-319-23736-7_17

183

But she is also rattled after the session. When she rushes to Yelp later, to see what is there, she is even more distressed. These are terrible reviews. How will they affect her practice? Will people fear coming in to see her? Will current patients leave therapy? What can she do?

Training

As a long-term user of the Internet and online communities since 1993, I have become accustomed to navigating digital culture. From the early years of AOL, CompuServe, and eWorld, I spent time in online chat rooms and made friends whom I still speak with today. In the mid- to late 1990s, I explored online FirstClass bbs's where I served as a moderator on multiple forums in which we regularly met locally to socialize offline. Later, I ventured onto sites such as Friendster, Tribe, Orkut, etc. and eventually Twitter and Facebook where online sharing began to allow people to host content on their own pages. I have visited all of these Internet spaces and had temporary online "homes" on them.

I was self-employed as a computer consultant from 1993 to 1996. I started my graduate training in clinical psychology in 1996. As my professional identity as a psychologist developed, I became an active member of several online professional communities for psychologists. In 2008, I started expanding my personal social media life to a more professional one. I created a website and began blogging actively about the integration of our APA ethics code with our online activities to answer questions that were developing in my mind and to answer the questions that my colleagues were asking me. I also created a LinkedIn, Twitter, and Facebook account for my practice.

My blog postings on digital ethics developed into online and live CE courses. Since 2010, I've provided over 60 trainings from 2 to 6 h. Some of these have been in Australia and Canada, using online technology. I also began to develop a consultation practice which covers both digital ethical dilemmas and technical support to psychotherapists who need help adjusting their privacy settings and understanding how to manage the technical aspects of various social media platforms (e.g., managing their address books, knowing how to retract invitations sent to connect as a contact, understanding how to hide the visibility of their connections, questions about online endorsements, etc.).

In 2009, I created my @drkkolmes Twitter account, and for the better part of a year, my account was listed among twitter's top 50 health Tweeters, along with Dr. Andrew Weil, the Red Cross, and the CBC. Within my first 2 years on Twitter, I amassed over 87,000 followers.

In 2010, I began to see the need for an informed consent document that would address many of the clinical and ethical dilemmas that I was blogging about and consulting on with other practitioners. I began to write my Private Practice Social Media Policy which I blogged about and invited commentary on via Twitter and my blog. I finalized it in the spring of 2010 and used social media to share and disseminate my document, giving it a Creative Commons license allowing people to adapt it for their own practices but disallowing commercial use of my policy. My Social Media Policy has been internationally cited, taught, and adapted across health disciplines. I have received emails of thanks from massage therapists in London who are using it, as well as doctors in New Zealand and Australia. It has been gratifying to watch it spread, and my best estimate is that tens of thousands of clinicians have adopted it for their own practices.

I was the Digital Director of APA Division 42, Psychologists in Independent Practice from 2011 to 2012. During that time, I helped revise their new website, and I created and managed their Flickr, Twitter, LinkedIn, Facebook, and YouTube accounts. I also moderated the 1000+ member LISTSERV of clinicians and developed their LISTSERV moderation team, which still continues as a team, rather than having one moderator. I currently serve on the California Psychological Association's Ethics Committee and continue to consult, speak, and teach on Digital Ethics. I have recently been elected as California Psychological Association's state representative at APA's Council of Representatives (beginning in 2015). I have also been elected as the 2015 Member at Large for APA Division 42, Psychologists in Independent Practice. I am a member of the 2014 Leadership Institute for Women Psychologists. Lastly, I will be serving on the Cabinet of 2015 APA President, Barry Anton, representing independent practitioners and technology and ethics issues.

Since 2010, I have also been doing research on clients' and psychotherapists' discoveries, both accidental and intentional, of online information about one another and how these encounters influence the clinical relationship. I have also completed research on revenge porn and cyber harassment that happens on the Internet. One of my research papers has been published in *Professional Psychology: Research and Practice*, and another was an invited paper on the Future of Social Media in Professional Psychology, in the same journal.

During my research, I discovered that one important source of online overlap for psychotherapy patients and their providers is when clients post reviews of their therapist on sites such as Yelp, Healthgrades, Yahoo or Google Business, or Angie's List. Sometimes this affects other clients who find positive, negative, or neutral information about their own psychotherapist. These reviews often negatively affect the psychotherapists, who may feel discomfort over a negative review or worry that their colleagues will think they have solicited the review (which would violate our ethical standard against soliciting testimonials from current patients or others who are subject to undue influence). But these reviews are also serving as a new online currency for happy or disgruntled patients. Some give a positive review as a therapeutic "gift," to their clinician. Others use these reviews to punish a provider who has disappointed them. But unlike licensing boards, while these reviews may turn clients away, they do not actually lead to any formal sanctions against a provider who is acting in ways that are damaging or unethical. There are also some providers, such as those who perform custody evaluations, who may be more likely to generate negative reviews since the nature of their work is to provide an evaluation that can leave many of those who came to see them unhappy with the outcome.

In my study of 332 psychotherapy clients, 25 % had seen an online review of their psychotherapist (Kolmes & Taube, 2011). Of that group, 20 % indicated that the review influenced their feelings about their treatment. Some clients also felt compelled to protect a psychotherapist they liked who had received negative reviews. This is introducing a new clinical dilemma in which patients who do not know one another may be drawn into a public flame war (a hostile and insulting public interaction between internet users). This is an unusual and new circumstance for those who are used to the work of psychotherapy being private.

Some clinicians have tried to respond to negative online reviews by having colleagues and mentors post positive reviews of their services. But this can also be problematic. While not specifically prohibited by our ethics code, it can be hard to decline a colleague's request for an online review intended to remedy a negative one. And it can also place our colleagues in the same precarious place as our clients, described above, in which our colleagues now must "duke it out" online with our upset client who is fighting to have the last word.

Miller, Duncan, Brown, Sparks, and Claud (2003) have discussed the value of making outcome evaluations a routine part of therapeutic services. Their Outcome Rating Scale (ORS) is becoming a widely used instrument for clinicians who are invested in measuring and understanding treatment outcomes.

As a consultant to clinicians encountering ethical and clinical dilemmas on the Internet, one of my most common emerging consultation themes is clinicians who have received a negative online review from a disturbed client who uses various online forums to rant about the practitioner. Since such forums pull for extreme positive or negative reactions and since clinicians are effectively gagged from replying, due to confidentiality, our profession is in need of alternate ways to respond to such reviews. Some clinicians have requested that I start support groups for those of them who struggle with the shame and helplessness of not being able to respond to reviews. It should be noted that the few court cases in which clinicians have attempted to sue clients for defamation have ruled against the doctors, deciding that online reviews are opinions, and, as such, are protected speech. I do not necessarily disagree with this ruling, but I have believed there is a solution that is missing.

To deal with this evolving dilemma, and because I strongly believe in consumers' rights to express their feelings about the services they access and to find out more about a providers strengths and weaknesses, I did an anonymous online survey to ask consumers of psychotherapy services what dimensions would be most important to them when looking at online reviews of psychotherapists on the Internet. I asked questions to find out what is missing from the major review sites and what they, as patients, would most want to know from previous patients of the provider. I got 145 responses to my survey questions.

Getting Better is the outcome of using these responses to develop a better measure of client satisfaction. It includes some aspects of outcome measures by asking whether the therapy goals were met, but it takes the questionnaire a step further by asking about additional themes such as the patient's sense that their psychotherapist liked them, what treatment issues they hoped to resolve, how many sessions they attended, and whether the clinician demonstrated cultural competence on a variety of dimensions (if this was something the patient sought).

This product adheres to professional ethics in that it is only given to terminated patients, no testimonials are solicited (or shared), there are plenty of opt-out opportunities, and only aggregate data is provided, so patient identity is completely masked from any viewer.

In fact, the questions asked do not include name, age, sex, or any of the 18 protected health information (PHI) identifiers that must be handled with special care as defined by HIPAA. It also helps clinicians to understand what their strengths are as well as their areas for growth, encouraging us all to get better, while also helping patients find a clinician who can help them get better. This product is currently available for individual and group practices, as well as clinics, and I am discussing partnerships with state psychology associations in regard to offering it as a membership benefit.

Pros

My career has allowed me to have an international presence and to collaborate with clinicians worldwide in training, education, writing, and thinking about ethical dilemmas from a multidisciplinary and international perspective. For example, Australian therapists and counselors have different ethical requirements than those in the USA, and it is intellectually stimulating to discuss and review the differences and help them to consider appropriate approaches to Internet challenges in the twenty-first century that are applicable to the laws and ethics of their country. Ethics codes in the USA for different types of mental health professionals vary. I have been able to earn money speaking via webinar or traveling to groups of people who found me through LISTSERVs, Twitter, or my LinkedIn presence. My ability to earn passive income outside of my psychotherapy office by selling products on my own site is a boon. I've also been able to parlay my Internet accessibility into paid consultation time with clinicians nationally and internationally on ethical issues related to online culture, thanks to my online store.

Cons

Being so visible and available on the Internet can lead to the challenge of an unmanageable inbox and a lot of individuals seeking "quick questions" or hoping to have conversations with me about technology, ethics, or sexual issues. As I've grown more visible, this has taken up a lot of time. I can no longer be as generous with my email responses and have had to implement a fee, at least for colleagues, for what is actually consultation. While this may be seen as a pro, it also reduces some of the pleasure of just being able to connect and chat with people online which once felt easier when I had more time. But the volume of such requests became unmanage-able after a couple of years. Of course, emails from people in pain who are seeking resources from me have also increased, and often it is from people in places where I do not know of the available resources. I hear about quite difficult situations in which I am unable to help much from such a distance (such as when people from other countries are hoping to obtain telemental health services from me or find a transgender affirming and competent clinician). This leaves me often in the position of trying to find resources and referrals in other territories that are unfamiliar to me, and sometimes I will come up empty-handed. This is incredibly frustrating to me and the people seeking services.

References

Kolmes, K., & Taube, D.O. (2011) *Summary of client-therapist encounters on the web: The client experience*. Retrieved June 2012, from http://drkkolmes.com/research/-client survey
Miller, S. D., Duncan, B. L., Brown, J., Sparks, J. A., & Claud, D. A. (2003). The outcome rating scale: A preliminary study of the reliability, validity, and feasibility of a brief visual analog measure. *Journal of Brief Therapy, 2*(2), 91–100.

Chapter 18
How a Decade of Telemedicine Has Reshaped a Career

Robert N. Cuyler

> *"Gee, Doc, all my other shrinks told me not to talk to the television, now you say I can."*

Vignette

With that comment, 2 weeks into a first project providing behavioral health services via telemedicine, I felt like we were on the right track. Twelve years ago, as chief operating officer and clinical director of Heritage Health Services, it was my role to recruit and manage psychiatrists who could provide diagnostic, treatment, and medication management services to a network of rural community hospital-based intensive outpatient programs for seniors with behavioral health problems, primarily depression and anxiety. The planning stages of the telemedicine project faced considerable skepticism from client hospitals and their medical staff. Could a doctor effectively assess a new patient, oversee a treatment plan, and manage medications from a distance? Would our patients, rural senior citizens, accept seeing a doctor over videoconference, adapt to a new technology, as well as overcome their frequent struggles with fear and stigma related to a mental health diagnosis?

Our early client was a little different, however, having struggled with schizophrenic symptoms for years and now experiencing a significant increase in auditory hallucinations. He readily engaged in the initial interview with Dr. Don Hauser, a longtime colleague and eager pioneering participant in this telemedicine trial. Accompanied by the clinic nurse, who had explained the telemedicine process and

R.N. Cuyler, Ph.D. (✉)
Clinical Psychology Consultants Ltd, LLP, 5959 West Loop South, Ste 600,
Bellaire, TX 77401, USA
e-mail: cuyler@sbcglobal.net

© Springer International Publishing Switzerland 2017
M.M. Maheu et al. (eds.), *Career Paths in Telemental Health*,
DOI 10.1007/978-3-319-23736-7_18

obtained consent, the patient readily engaged with Dr. Hauser concerning his history and current symptoms. He experienced no apparent confusion, mistrust, or distortion of the remote consultation despite his active psychotic symptoms. Tens of thousands of successful patient visits later, the viability of tele-behavioral health in this setting is secure.

A thread that runs throughout my career is an interest in improving access to care through innovative delivery models. My involvement with partial hospitalization and intensive outpatient programs came to involve developing and managing programs, advocacy work on insurance parity legislation, and board membership and presidency of the Association for Ambulatory Behavioral Healthcare. Consulting activity in the area led to an invitation by a client to join a start-up health-care company specializing in delivering behavioral health services in rural community hospitals. The challenges of finding well-trained psychiatrists able and willing to travel to remote locations for patient care led to my involvement in telemedicine.

A dozen years ago, several important trends began to converge. Medicare had recently revised their telemedicine reimbursement regulations to cover a number of core behavioral health services when delivered to beneficiaries in a rural health-care location. Internet bandwidth was increasingly available in rural communities, with affordable business-class options supplementing the very expensive internet infrastructure that typically characterized earlier grant-based telemedicine projects. Similarly, business-grade videoconference cameras became available at price points for projects like mine that had no grant dollars and required a sustainable business model from the start.

Although far from complete, the evidence base for the effectiveness of behavioral telemedicine is robust and consistent. Across a variety of populations and settings, behavioral health services delivered by interactive videoconference can be considered to deliver equivalent diagnostic accuracy and treatment outcomes when compared to traditional "face-to-face" settings (Grady et al., 2011). A recent overview of the field of telemedicine by the Agency for Healthcare Research and Quality concludes "The best evidence for telemedicine, especially live interactive office/hospital-based telemedicine, is in the psychiatry and neurology specialties, where verbal interaction is a key assessment component (Locatis & Ackerman, 2013)."

Since audio/video connectivity can be achieved across a wide variety of platforms, it is critical that practitioners choose systems that offer the quality, reliability, security, and privacy protection necessary to provide services in organized health-care settings (Yellowlees, Shore, Roberts, & American Telemedicine Association, 2010) and in the emerging field of online behavioral health services (Fishkind, Cuyler, Shiekh, & Snodgress, 2012; Turvey et al., 2013). The ease by which connectivity can be established now is staggering when the cost and complexity of telemedicine deployment only a decade ago are recalled by telehealth veterans. However, I am frequently troubled by conversations with mental health professionals who are using free, consumer-grade platforms to conduct patient care, sometimes across state lines, without sufficient consideration of professional standards, privacy regulations, review of best practices, or the readily available outcome literature.

As I assist new practitioners and organizations with telemedicine design and implementation, a group of organizing principles emerges from my experience.

Identify the Problems That Need Solving

In our case, several fundamental issues positioned telemedicine as a solution. The foremost was that our growing company needed a pool of capable, flexible, and team-oriented psychiatrists to staff the intensive outpatient programs. Finding such doctors meeting these criteria and willing to drive several hours each way to reach our rural community hospital clinics was becoming an increasing challenge. As the company began to grow to multiple states in the Southwest, our client hospitals often were increasingly distant from medical director candidates. Continued growth and viability of the company depended on a psychiatric workforce that was urban, well compensated, and busy. Telemedicine quickly became the vehicle for engaging doctors who were interested in providing care via technology and in using their scarce professional time efficiently by eliminating the need to travel.

Research All Mission-Critical Requirements

Behavioral health telemedicine is complex, involving technology, state and federal laws, professional licensure standards, and coordination of care at the practitioner and patient sides. From my background of professional association work, I was very familiar navigating complex regulations in order to learn the essentials neces-sary to put effective, compliant procedures in place. New to telemedicine technolo-gies, I quickly identified and worked with technology vendors who could supply and support the telemedicine equipment. Meanwhile, I learned as much as I could on the essentials of videoconference configuration, encryption, and troubleshoot-ing. Next, I researched all applicable laws and professional standards dealing with telehealth, including informed consent, prescribing standards, and hospital staff credentialing policies.

Get the Support and Endorsement of All Critical Stakeholders

In addition to ensuring that the project met all necessary standards, building credibil-ity and engaging the buy-in of the many stakeholders involved in the telemedicine project was essential to getting initial approval and continuing support. Since tele-medicine projects typically involve at least two health-care organizations and their management teams, it is essential that the leaders on all sides are fully briefed on the project and are willing to extend the administrative support and resources necessary to get the project launched and sustained. Expecting support from the IT or medical records departments of a distant telemedicine site to provide necessary services without the explicit direction of their management team can court disaster.

Develop a Detailed Project Plan

With tasks related to recruitment, credentialing, technology purchase/installation/configuration, medical record management, and staff support, a detailed project plan with tasks, time frames, and accountability is essential to map out all the steps necessary for implementation. Some steps are accomplished in parallel and others in sequence. As our business depended on a large set of requirements that had to be met before a start, a single loose end could delay a clinic launch, which immediately impacted our revenues and margin and potentially affected credibility, reputation, and the good will necessary for ongoing collaboration.

Test and Train

Behavioral health telemedicine involves two essential features, technology and clinical delivery, which require technology testing, personnel orientation, training, and competency testing. In many ways, establishing a video connection between a practitioner and patient has become one of the easiest parts of behavioral telemedicine. Nevertheless, establishing a health-care-grade connection requires good bandwidth, configuration of equipment that takes into account firewalls, router settings, encryption processes for privacy protection, and repeated testing of call quality and stability. However, a technologically sound connection is only the starting place. Establishing a sound climate for patient care is the next step for good telehealth delivery. Microphone placement, camera angle, furnishings, and lighting all affect the patient-care environment and should be modified to create an environment that most closely replicates for the patient the experience of being in the same room as the practitioner. Educating the patient prior to a first visit on process, expectations, and the role of a telepresenter (if applicable) improves comfort level and satisfaction. The practitioner should be thoroughly trained on operation of the telemedicine equipment. Optimally, the equipment allows the practitioner to control the distant camera, allowing for close up or wide-angle views as clinically appropriate.

In most facility-based telemedicine settings, a telepresenter is involved at the patient-care site, and their training on camera operation, troubleshooting, access to tech support, patient education, and coordination of care is essential for efficient and effective care. Those coordination tasks include management of medical records, prescriptions, treatment plan development and updates, and referral/discharge planning.

Modify Job Descriptions and Expectations

Involvement in behavioral telemedicine will certainly involve new roles and expectations for key staff. Consistent with the need for training described above, job descriptions must be altered to reflect the new staff duties that support telemedicine. Layering of new job responsibilities informally on existing duties may create confusion, conflict, and resentment. The formal modification of a job description on the other hand establishes clear expectations for key staff and emphasizes that telemedicine has become an established new way of doing business.

Establish Benchmarks and Measure Key Performance Indicators

Measurement of key outcomes supports both the business case and clinical impact of behavioral telemedicine. Such benchmarking can be critical for internal decision support when technology costs, support costs, and revenue growth can determine the viability and sustainability of a telemedicine initiative. Measurement of patient outcomes, patient satisfaction, and practitioner satisfaction is crucial in establishing organizational best practices. These same measures are often crucial in demonstrating value to existing customers and in supporting business development for new opportunities. For our project, we conducted research demonstrating equivalent outcomes for in-person and telemedicine delivery of psychiatric services. Presentation of the outcome research at the American Telemedicine Association bolstered external credibility and enhanced business development efforts.

Training Needed

Trained as a clinical psychologist in the pre-digital era, I had no exposure in training to technology. Largely self-taught in the use of computers, I found the transition to videoconference technology reasonably easy to manage, with the assistance of telemedicine vendors and tech support experts who briefed me on the essentials of IP addresses, routers, ports, bandwidth, and encryption. My research and clinical diagnostic backgrounds also assisted greatly in learning to problem-solve and debug balky telemedicine systems. Similarly, with no background in business in graduate school, I took my on-the-job training managing budgets and personnel in hospital leadership roles, assisted by key executive education courses in business, finance, and negotiation skills at Rice University's Jones School of Business. However, the most important opportunities for continued learning involved my mentors, partners, and colleagues in our start-up business, which operated and grew for 10 years before a sale to a larger behavioral health management company.

Since leaving the company that acquired Heritage, I've had a variety of activities related to telemedicine, including a 1-year stint as interim CEO of JSA Health, an emergency telepsychiatry company. In that role, I negotiated and oversaw clinical applications of telemedicine including crisis stabilization settings, hospital emergency departments, community mental health centers, psychiatric hospitals, and university student health services. Current consulting activities include organizational strategic planning for telehealth and assisting health-care organizations with under-performing telemedicine programs.

A particular interest in human factors in behavioral telehealth has led to opportunities in practitioner and telepresenter training and competency testing. Deep involvement in the complexity of project planning and implementation resulted in a collaboration and coauthorship of a book on telemedicine implementation with organization re-engineering guru, Dr. Dutch Holland (Cuyler & Holland, 2012). Resuming direct patient care in the last several years, I have provided a portion of my psychotherapy practice via telemedicine, over secure laptop-based systems. Most of that work has been with health-care professionals seeking therapy who live in distant communities. Client choice for engaging me for distance therapy typically has involved the shortage of psychotherapists in the home community as well as the desire to avoid the limitations to privacy inherent in the small circle of health-care professionals available in their home communities.

Pros and Cons of a Telehealth Career

My involvement in behavioral telemedicine has been an energizing and fulfilling part of continuing career development. Being involved on the frontiers of telemedicine implementation and practice in the private sector, I've benefitted greatly from the many groundbreaking behavioral telemedicine projects that established the technical standards and evidence base of the field. The empirical base supports the delivery of most mental health services at a distance, with an expectation of equivalent outcomes and satisfaction compared to "face-to-face" care. The delivery of behavioral health care via telehealth remains a work in progress, although rapidly evolving. A patchwork of Medicare, Medicaid, and state insurance regulations continue to inhibit widespread adoption of behavioral telehealth. Exceptions are in settings in which clients can be treated in rural setting, covered by a proven payer such as Medicare or Medicaid. Delivery of services in particular settings such as crisis stabilization programs and hospital emergency departments hold great promise (Fishkind & Cuyler, 2013), due to the daunting logistical challenges of providing specialty care in person in settings where practitioners are not regularly available.

Conclusions

Given the growing intertwining of digital media into all aspects of life, it is expectable that technology-assisted behavioral health services will continue to emerge at a rapid pace. Some models will follow the conventional video-enabled, face-to-face model and to a significant extent replicate familiar ways of providing care. New frontiers include asynchronous connectivity, computer-delivered therapies, and virtual reality simulations. Technological advances and consumer preferences will, in all likelihood, proceed well in advance of the regulatory environment and professional standards. Telemedicine will likely play a large role in new models of service delivery, with shifts toward integrated care and pay-for-performance models and beyond traditional fee-for-service models. On the other hand, a variety of online therapy models may enable individual and small group practitioners to expand the reaches of practice to increase access and convenience for clients. No single business model has yet emerged for behavioral telemedicine that combines financial viability/sustainability and evidence-based best practices.

For the behavioral health professional, multiple careers may become the new norm as the health-care system transforms. The importance of choice, flexibility, and ease of connectivity to consumers will certainly influence the ways that practitioners deliver care. Technological savvy, business acumen, and a thorough understanding of regulatory and reimbursement issues will help prepare tomorrow's practitioners for the future. The ability to incorporate the accumulated wisdom and evidence base of behavioral health into evolving and innovative delivery models will characterize the best of the new practitioner.

Chapter 19
Work Smarter, Not Harder: Expanding the Treatment Capacity of a University Counseling Center Using Therapist-Assisted Online Treatment for Anxiety

Brian M. Shaw, Geoff Lee, and Sherry Benton

> *"We do not reject our traditions, but we are willing to adapt to changing circumstances, when change we must. We are willing to suffer the discomfort of change in order to achieve a better future."*
>
> *Barbara Jordan*

Dr. Michaels and Jocelyn Vignette

Upon arriving at work, Dr. Michaels opens her appointment schedule to plan for the day. She has six therapist-assisted online (TAO) clients to meet with, scheduled at 20-min intervals over the next 2 h. In preparation for her appointments, Dr. M logs into the secure TAO clinician portal using a web browser, where she views a list of her active clients. Selecting Jocelyn's record, she views the modules J completed, tracks the frequency with which J has logged into system, monitors her completed homework, and views a graph depicting J's symptom levels across her 4 weeks enrolled in the TAO program. Dr. M sees that her client has been progressing well through the program and has completed the most recent learning module on mindfulness as well as the assigned logs for the week. She makes a note to highlight J's improvement by sharing the graph of her progress during their session.

Seeing that it is time for their weekly check-in appointment, Dr. M clicks on the video conferencing tool within the TAO portal. Dr. M begins the session by briefly checking-in with the client and setting the agenda for their 15-min appointment. When asked about any questions or concerns she had completing the module, J reports that she found practicing mindfulness challenging, stating that she

B.M. Shaw, PhD (✉) • G. Lee, PhD • S. Benton, PhD
University of Florida, Gainesville, FL, USA
e-mail: brian.shaw@ufl.edu

© Springer International Publishing Switzerland 2017
M.M. Maheu et al. (eds.), *Career Paths in Telemental Health*,
DOI 10.1007/978-3-319-23736-7_19

struggled to stay present and keep her mind from wandering. Dr. M normalizes her experience, encouraging J by emphasizing the role of practice and by providing a few tips that J might use when she finds her mind wandering. J mentions that she is continuing to use the TAO mobile app for monitoring her anxiety, tracking her use of relaxation exercises, and challenging unhelpful thoughts. J also notes that the personalized text reminders have reminded her to complete treatment activities and helped her to stay on track in the program.

Next, Dr. M introduces the module for the next week, titled "Coping with Worry", and explains the exposure log, a log introduced in the next module. Noting that there are only a few minutes remaining in the appointment, Dr. M checks in with J on any remaining questions and confirms their appointment time for the next week. Dr. M and J then say goodbye, log out, and end the video conferencing session.

Following the appointment, Dr. M completes a clinical note for the appointment utilizing a short template form designed to be completed in 2–3 min. The contents of the note include an indication that J completed the assigned module, a note about J's symptom improvements, and a confirmation of the date and time of the next appointment.

This concludes Dr. M's TAO session with J and she proceeds to prepare for her next client.

Introduction

As employees of a large university counseling center in the USA, a continual challenge has been meeting the growing student demand for services with limited resources, a challenge reflective of the majority of university counseling centers in the USA. With limited budgets for hiring additional staff members, commonly used strategies for addressing this problem have included increasing counselor caseloads, decreasing session frequency, setting sessions limits, limiting the scope of services, establishing wait-lists, and referring students to community mental health resources. Unfortunately, such approaches can result in less than optimal outcomes for students seeking help. As such, we were interested in exploring ways to respond to an increase in demand for services with less of a compromise to our existing services. Supply and demand problems are not unique to university counseling centers: the Veteran's Administration, community mental health centers, many rural communities, and employee assistance programs struggle with meeting the demand for effective mental health treatment.

An additional concern for us were the changing characteristics of the student population we serve. Students today are more technology oriented and frequently obtain information and communicate extensively online. Thus, unsurprisingly, many students have expressed an interest in and preference for web-based mental health resources and services. Web-based resources and services provide more convenient access and are less limited by the constraints of traditional counseling services. Moreover, our center was asked to provide services for students of our university's growing online degree programs, the majority of whom were not located near our campus and would be unable to present for traditional face-to-face counseling. We were interested in exploring ways that we might offer services that would be more accommodating to the changing preferences and needs of our students and reduce barriers that might prevent students from obtaining services.

Based on these concerns of meeting increasing demand and accommodating changing student preferences and needs, our counseling center explored ways to leverage technology in service of our students. While our skills with technology varied among us, from basic technology skills to previous experience developing software applications, we shared a common openness to trying new things and to venturing away from the "beaten path" of traditional counseling center services. The solution we developed is called therapist-assisted online (TAO) which utilizes a combination of web-based resources with brief weekly video conference sessions with a counselor. Based on our experiences and initial outcomes with clients using TAO this past year, we anticipate similar programs will become more commonplace as a component of mental health treatment services in a variety of contexts and will present new job opportunities for mental health professionals.

About TAO

TAO was designed to help college students overcome common college mental health concerns, delivering treatment in a way that is consistent with student usage patterns of online mental health resources. The TAO program currently offers a 7-week anxiety treatment program with plans to expand to other mental health concerns in the future. We chose anxiety because it is the most common presenting problem in college counseling, with 45% of our students presenting with this concern.

To enroll in TAO, a student completes initial paperwork and attends a screening session with a clinician to ensure that the student is a "good fit" for the program.

The main criterion for enrolling in the program is that the student's primary presenting concern fits the focus of the TAO program, which is currently anxiety. We also screen for coexisting substance abuse problems and for suicidality, as these factors may necessitate a referral to a treatment model that more directly addresses these issues and can more closely monitor associated risks. Other considerations include assessing the students' comfort level with technology and confirming their access to a computer or mobile device with video conferencing capability. Due to licensure laws, TAO clients must also live within the state where we practice. As part of the enrollment process, we require students to provide personal contacts the counselor can utilize in the event of an emergency.

Once enrolled in the program, clients log into to a secure web-portal each week to complete interactive learning modules. Examples of weekly module topics include: understanding anxiety, relaxation and anxiety reduction, examining and changing thinking patterns, mindfulness, and maintaining a healthy lifestyle. Clients complete treatment homework either through the website or using the TAO mobile app. Clients also receive personalized text messages that provide daily contact (enhancing treatment continuity), offer support and encouragement (supporting motivation), and remind them to complete treatment homework (compliance).

Therapists have access to a clinician portal for monitoring their clients. Through the portal, clinicians can review the modules and activities clients have completed. Clinicians can also review the results of weekly assessments clients complete in order to track treatment progress and monitor for symptoms that might necessitate an escalation of care.

A defining component of TAO is a weekly 10–15 min HIPAA compliant video conferencing session. These sessions are designed to be structured and brief and provide support and encouragement to clients as they proceed through the program. These sessions also provide an opportunity for the counselor to gain additional information on client progress and address any potential obstacles the client may encounter while completing the program. The end goal of TAO is to provide an effective and convenient treatment modality for clients with less direct contact time required of therapists.

Research Support for TAO

Research has long supported that the counseling relationship is a key component of change in traditional counseling services. Research into online treatments has produced similar findings, indicating that the therapeutic alliance appears to be an important therapeutic change factor in improvements to client well-being and symptom reduction for therapist-assisted treatments (Pugh, Hadjistavropoulos, Klein, & Austin, 2014). Compared to online self-help, therapist involvement improves client engagement in treatment, translating into increased treatment compliance, increased completion rates, and ultimately better outcomes for clients (Andersson & Cuijpers, 2009; Berger et al., 2011; Spek et al., 2007). The therapeutic relationship is maintained in TAO through weekly video conferencing sessions between the counselor and client. Despite having significantly shorter interaction times than traditional counseling services (10-15 min compared to 50 min), studies have found clients participating in similar programs report high treatment satisfaction and strong therapeutic alliances, comparable to those found in traditional counseling (Andrews, Cuijpers, Craske, McEvoy, & Titov, 2010; Preschel, Maercker, & Wagner, 2011).

When adopting any new treatment approach, it is important for counselors to consider the theoretical base used. TAO incorporates multiple evidence-based theoretical perspectives, with an emphasis on cognitive behavioral therapy (CBT). As a thoroughly researched approach, CBT has been shown to be highly effective in the treatment of a variety of mental health concerns (Butler, Chapman, Forman, & Beck, 2006). CBT is easily adaptable for online use based on its structured approach, which incorporates psychoeducational content with directed tasks and promotes clients taking an active role in the treatment process (Muresan, Montgomery, & David, 2012). Research has supported the efficacy of CBT-based treatments delivered online, indicating clients enjoy and respond well to this form of treatment, in some instances preferring it to other forms of treatment (Andersson, 2009; Andersson & Cuijpers, 2009; Andrews et al., 2010; Proudfoot et al., 2003; Spek et al., 2007). Arecent meta-analysis of 22 randomized controlled trials of therapist-assisted online CBT programs similar to TAO (Andrews et al., 2010) found these treatments resulted in superior outcomes compared to controls, demonstrated large effect sizes and comparable completion rates to face-to-face therapy, low rates of relapse, and treatment gains remaining 1-year after treatment completion.

TAO Pilot Study

To specifically assess the efficacy of the TAO program, our center completed a 12-month pilot study with college students who were seeking treatment for anxiety. Our study compared TAO against our traditional individual and group services by assessing outcomes using a pre- and post-test assessment comparison. The primary assessment instrument used for our study was the behavioral health measure-20 (BHM-20; Kopta & Lowry, 2002). The BHM-20 was developed to assess symptoms and treatment outcomes in the college student population. Preliminary results suggested TAO clients experienced significantly greater symptom reduction and life functioning improvement compared to clients receiving face-to face treatment at the conclusion of the 7-week treatment. Consistent with recent research, clients using TAO also reported high levels of satisfaction with the treatment and client completion rates were comparable to face-to-face counseling. We are planning additional controlled studies in the future to further assess the efficacy of the TAO program and to guide future development and refinements.

Training Requirements

Between us, we have a variety of background experiences in mental health. Two of us are licensed psychologists, while the other is a licensed mental health counselor. We have a range of 5–25 years of experience working in mental health, with most of our experience in university counseling centers. We believe all TAO counselors should have a master's or doctorate degree in a mental health discipline and obtain state licensure to practice mental health.

We also have obtained and recommend specific training in distance counseling that emphasizes the knowledge and skills needed to competently adapt face-to-face counseling skills to services delivered via video conferencing. Quality training in distance counseling provides information and guidance about legal and ethical issues related to the provision of online services, such as how to manage confidentiality and respond to crisis situations. Prior to our involvement in the TAO program, none of us had experience in providing distance counseling services.

Depending on one's theoretical orientation, training may also be needed in the theories utilized by the program, including CBT. Our experience varied from having general knowledge to extensive training and practice with CBT. For counselors with little knowledge of CBT, training can be helpful to better understand the approach of interventions in TAO and to be better able to provide guidance to clients when needed. CBT training can also help counselors to be more focused and directive in online sessions. For example, setting the agenda, a technique emphasized in CBT, is important for counselors to use in order to maintain the boundaries of a 10–15 min weekly check-in.

Lastly, counselors will need training in using the specific technologies of the TAO program. For example, counselors will need to learn how to access online modules, retrieve assessment results, and participate in video conferencing sessions. In our experience, we have found demonstrations of the software provided in combination with supportive resources (such as a consultation group) will quickly allow counselors to become proficient in using the technology.

Advantages and Disadvantages of Working as a TAO Counselor

Despite our comfort level with exploring new technology solutions, we also brought some initial reservations about how technology would affect the counseling process and whether it would shape the nature of our work in an undesirable way. Having now worked with our solution for the past year, we have identified a number of advantages and disadvantages that therapists considering working with TAO or similar solutions should consider.

An advantage of TAO counseling is greater efficiency of the counselors' time, made possible by shorter sessions with clients and more streamlined paperwork. We comfortably see two to three clients an hour with substantially less time required in indirect service activities including documentation. Also, TAO counseling sessions typically require less emotional investment from counselors as clients are more self-directed in their treatment and there is less in-depth exploration of issues with the client in counseling sessions. This difference may help promote better counselor self-care and help prevent counselor burnout.

For counselors working in an agency setting, TAO counselors may have greater flexibility in their work schedule. Our center currently allows TAO counselors more flexible work hours and the ability to work from home. For counselors in private practice, TAO counseling services may create opportunities for additional income, based on seeing more clients each hour. Across both contexts, we expect distance counseling to become the standard rather than the exception in mental health services. Thus, mental health professionals with the knowledge, skills, and experience in this area will have a clear advantage in a changing job market with greater job security in the future.

A disadvantage of working as a TAO counselor is counselors may find it challenging to adjust to a new therapeutic role. Factors to consider include accepting the absence of the in-person interaction, adjusting to shorter session times, serving in more of a consultant role, adopting a more directive style, and providing a more manualized treatment. Clinicians that enjoy working as a generalist or prefer depth-oriented work may find TAO to be less fulfilling than more traditional work. In our experience, we have found having a caseload that includes both traditional and TAO clients addresses this concern. Additional disadvantages are that there are presently a limited number of opportunities to use TAO and TAO-like programs and existing interventions only cover a subset of presenting client concerns. Also, insurance companies have been slow to include emerging web-based interventions in their covered services, thus counselors may face difficulty getting reimbursed for TAO sessions for clients using insurance.

Conclusion

Like most mental health professionals, we did not envision our counseling work would transform from 50 min face-to-face sessions to 15 min check-ins via video conferencing. Yet at the heart of our motivation to work in the helping profession was a desire to assist people make changes that improve their quality of life and we believed technology-based solutions had the potential to aid this goal. Having now experienced firsthand working with clients in TAO, we are more convinced of the future expansion of TAO and similar intervention programs in the mental health field and believe this model offers an exciting opportunity for counselors.

References

Andersson, G. (2009). Using the Internet to provide cognitive behaviour therapy. *Behaviour Research and Therapy, 47*, 175–180.

Andersson, G., & Cuijpers, P. (2009). Internet-based and other computerized psychological treatments for adult depression: A meta-analysis. *Cognitive Behaviour Therapy, 38*, 196–205.

Andrews, G., Cuijpers, P., Craske, M. G., McEvoy, P., & Titov, N. (2010). Computer therapy for the anxiety and depressive disorders is effective, acceptable and practical health care: A meta-analysis. *PLoS One, 5*(10), e13196. doi:10.1371/journal.pone.0013196.

Berger, T., Caspar, F., Richardson, R., Kneubühler, B., Sutter, D., & Andersson, G. (2011). Internet-based treatment of social phobia: A randomized controlled trial comparing unguided with two types of guided self-help. *Behaviour Research and Therapy, 49*, 158–169.

Butler, A. C., Chapman, J. E., Forman, E. M., & Beck, A. T. (2006). The empirical status of cognitive-behavioral therapy: A review of meta-analyses. *Clinical Psychology Review, 26*(1), 17–31.

Kopta, S. M., & Lowry, J. L. (2002). Psychometric evaluation of the Behavioral Health Questionnaire-20: A brief instrument for assessing global mental health and the three phases of psychotherapy outcome. *Psychotherapy Research, 12*, 413–426.

Muresan, V., Montgomery, G. H., & David, D. (2012). Emotional outcomes and mechanisms of change in online cognitive-behavioral interventions: A quantitative meta-analysis of clinical controlled studies. *Journal of Technology in Human Services, 30*(1), 1–13.

Preschel, B., Maercker, A., & Wagner, B. (2011). The working alliance in a randomized controlled trial comparing online with face-to-face cognitive-behavioral therapy for depression. *BMC Psychiatry, 11*(1), 189.

Proudfoot, J., Goldberg, D., Mann, A., Everitt, B., Marks, I., & Gray, J. A. (2003). Computerized, interactive, multimedia cognitive behaviour therapy for anxiety and depression in general practice. *Psychological Medicine, 33*, 217–227.

Pugh, N. E., Hadjistavropoulos, H. D., Klein, B., & Austin, D. W. (2014). A case study illustrating therapist-assisted Internet cognitive behavior therapy for depression. *Cognitive and Behavioral Practice, 21*, 64–77.

Spek, V., Cuijpers, P., Nyklíček, I., Riper, H., Keyzer, J., & Pop, V. (2007). Internet-based cognitive behaviour therapy for symptoms of depression and anxiety: A meta-analysis. *Psychological Medicine, 37*, 319–328.

Chapter 20
Improving Veterans' Access to Trauma Services Through Clinical Video Telehealth (CVT)

Wayne Roffer

> *You may not control all the events that happen to you, but you can decide not to be reduced by them.*
>
> Maya Angelou

As the Iraq and Afghanistan conflicts wind down, the Department of Veterans Affairs (VA) has seen a large increase in the number of veterans seeking care. The VA has over 150 regional medical centers, 300 vet centers, and 800 community-based outpatient clinics (CBOCs) serving veterans who reside further away from the main hospital. Many of these community centers, though, lack specialty care programs, thus creating a barrier to those who live in more rural areas, are in school, or trying to find employment. The VA has been offering clinical video telehealth (CVT) as a way to provide veterans with improved access to care, especially to specialty programs, for whom such care would be difficult, if not impossible. This could not be truer then for those 10–20 % of Iraq and Afghanistan veterans who struggle with post-traumatic stress disorder (Litz & Schlenger, 2009) and who need to access the PTSD clinical teams (PCT) and other specialty trauma recovery programs. Clinical video telehealth brings certain key advantages to remote care, including convenience and security. Clinical video telehealth has afforded the VA the opportunity to reach veterans who otherwise would struggle to access care. For CBOCs without specialty trauma programs, veterans no longer have to travel to the large medical hospitals, rather can visit their local CBOC where a provider will "see" them remotely. For veterans who cannot access the CBOC, providers can bring specialty care directly to veterans in their home. A number of studies have demonstrated the efficacy and safety of delivering evidence-based psychotherapy for PTSD via CVT, including such care into veterans' homes.

W. Roffer, Psy.D. (✉)
Department of Veterans Affairs, 1700 S. Lincoln Ave, Lebanon, PA 17042, USA
e-mail: drwayneroffer@gmail.com

© Springer International Publishing Switzerland 2017
M.M. Maheu et al. (eds.), *Career Paths in Telemental Health*,
DOI 10.1007/978-3-319-23736-7_20

"Kevin," a 22-year-old, recently discharged Iraq/Afghanistan veteran, has been struggling at work and school since returning home. His marriage has begun to suffer as isolation, depression, and alcohol use has increased. After failing two classes, an outburst at work that may cost him his job, and a DUI, Kevin sought help from his local VA medical center, an hour and half from where he lives. Kevin was referred to the PTSD Clinical Team (PCT) at the medical center where, after an in-depth evaluation, he was diagnosed with post-traumatic stress disorder and alcohol use disorder. Due to the complexity involved in treating co-occurring PTSD and substance use disorders (SUD), Kevin was referred to the facility's PTSD/SUD specialist. After discussing treatment options, Kevin opted for an evidence-based psychotherapy (EBP) called cognitive processing therapy (CPT). However, Kevin was concerned about having to travel an hour and half each way every week for 12 weeks (the length of treatment). While the closest community-based outpatient clinic (CBOC) was only 35 min away, there was no access to specialty trauma services at this location. As a result, traveling to the medical facility appeared to be his only option. Fortunately, the PTSD/SUD specialist was able to offer another option: telemental health via clinical video telehealth (CVT). This could bring the CPT sessions directly to Kevin in his home at a mutually convenient day and time. Using his own computer, webcam, and Internet connection, along with free software provided to Kevin by the VA (to secure the call), Kevin was able to "see" his provider weekly from the convenience of his home. Without having to worry about money/ transportation issues, childcare, scheduling with work/school, or even the weather, Kevin's adherence to treatment was perfect. At the predetermined date/time, he would call in to his provider from his computer and participate in a live, one-to-one therapy session. Both provider and Kevin made use of the webcams to check for completion of homework, and the provider utilized secure messaging as a way to send Kevin handouts to complete for the following week. After 12 sessions, Kevin's social and occupational functioning improved significantly and was abstinent from alcohol for 8 weeks.

The above scenario is not based on any one individual with whom I have worked, rather reflects a recurring theme observed regarding recently returning veterans from the Iraq/Afghanistan conflict: young, striving to succeed at work/school, and trying to start or support a family. The latter two issues can at times struggle to materialize because of emotional and behavioral health problems—unfortunate consequences of war. Depression, anxiety, PTSD, and substance use are a growing problem seen in these veterans, especially those who have seen combat. The barriers they face in starting their lives anew inhibit many from seeking services they so desperately need.

Despite 150 regional medical centers, 300 vet centers, and 800 community-based outpatient clinics (CBOCs), many veterans struggle to access necessary care. Some of the reasons are geographical in nature, that is, veterans who live in rural, remote areas making access to such care difficult. Local vet centers and CBOCs, though, may not offer specialty programs, such as trauma behavioral health, optometry, or audiology. Lastly, the nature of the emotional or behavioral health concern may make leaving the home or traveling to a medical center or clinic difficult. For these reasons, the VA has been increasing its ability to offer specialty programs to veterans who otherwise would not be able to receive such care.

Since the 1960s, the VA has been pioneering telemental health. What first started out as remote connections between VA and private hospitals has grown into a national VA network of specialty care providers, capable of delivering services to veterans across hundreds of miles. Originally known as video telehealth, or VTel, telemental health has evolved into a more sophisticated program known as clinical video telehealth (CVT).

While the Department of Veterans Affairs occasionally posts telemental health/CVT job openings (as I write this chapter, a search for "CVT psychologist" yielded two results nationally), providers do not need to apply for one of these positions to provide telemental health services. As the PTSD/SUD specialist for the Lebanon VA Medical Center in Lebanon, PA, my job description mentioned nothing about CVT. It wasn't until during the course of my work that the need to provide such services surfaced. In fact, many of my colleagues who provide CVT where not hired specifically for that purpose. I arrived at the VA in March 2010 looking to further my personal and professional growth. Within the first 2 years of employment, I had already received specialty training in Cognitive Processing Therapy (CPT) and Prolonged Exposure Therapy (PE)—the "gold standards" of treatment for PTSD. While CVT was available throughout the VA, I hadn't yet encountered a situation where it was needed in my day-to-day activities.

While the main medical facility where I work handles the bulk of behavioral health care, we have an extensive CBOC network. As the only PTSD/SUD specialist for the facility, I am expected to deliver specialty PTSD/SUD care to those veterans unable to make it to the main medical center. To travel to the various CBOCs would be time consuming and lessen my overall availability for patient time. Eventually, I kept receiving more and more referrals from veterans who could not come to the main medical center for various reasons. House arrest for drug charges, financial instability and lack of transportation, and their behavioral health conditions themselves created significant barriers to specialty care. CBOCs were out of reach for some of them, and for those who lived within a reasonable distance, specialty behavioral trauma care was not available. With my strong computer background and interest in almost all things "techy" I began to look toward CVT as a possible solution.

While I piloted a remote CVT specialty trauma group for our trauma program, the best response we received from veterans was with a new pilot program the VA began to roll out, called CVT to Home. This program is a system for delivering telehealth services, including telemental health, to veterans right into their homes. The caveat for our region, though, was that veterans had to use their own computer, webcam, and Internet. Fortunately, this has not been a significant problem in my experience. The VA would provide the software free of charge, along with support staff to troubleshoot when necessary. A new clinic was started with excellent results. While my clinic at the time was fixed to one day a week, there were various times available. For the most part, this worked well and I saw a number of veterans remotely over the course of a year. Eventually, demand and changes in veterans' needs forced this clinic to evolve further. Currently, my CVT to home clinic is available 5 days a week during normal business hours.

Preparing for telemental health within the Department of Veterans Affairs is not that much different from other institutions, as well as the private practice. Clinical video telehealth requires professional and technical training. Telemental health in the VA can be delivered by providers from a variety of mental health professions, including psychiatry, psychology, social work, nursing, and vocational and addiction rehabilitation. Likewise, most treatment modalities can be utilized, including individual, group, medication management, family, couples, and psychological testing. What you can provide via CVT is based on your profession and what you have been trained in. As mentioned earlier, a number of interventions available to me I received training in while employed by the VA.

The Department of Veterans Affairs maintains a very high standard when it comes to professional training. Psychologists, for example, must hold (or be license eligible for) an unrestricted license to practice. In most cases, they must have attended an American Psychological Association (APA)-approved doctoral and internship program. Other disciplines may have similar educational requirements. An advantage in working for the VA, though, is the license does not have to be in the same state as where you reside/work. When I moved to Pennsylvania to work for the VA, I kept my license in Connecticut until such time I was able to transfer my license to Pennsylvania (Pennsylvania's psychology license was cheaper and I wanted to have the option for adjunct private work). Whether you obtain/change your license to the state in which you are going to work for the VA depends on a number of factors, including cost of licensure and CE requirements (another potential cost). While inter-state licensure is a "hot button topic" when it comes to telemental health, it is much less an issue in the VA. As long as you are practicing while on federal property (i.e., a VA facility), any state license will allow you to see patients at any VA, VA-run facility, or patient home from any VA or VA-run facility.

In addition to modalities of treatment, various interventions can be utilized with telemental health in the VA, including cognitive-behavioral, existential, humanistic, even psychodynamic. The VA, though, stresses evidence-based treatments, of which most are grounded in cognitive, behavioral, and cognitive-behavioral theories. It is noted that many of the treatments advanced by the VA for in-person therapy, and that can apply to telemental health, are evidenced based, including CPT, PE, acceptance commitment therapy for depression (ACT-D), CBT for depression (CBT-D), and interpersonal therapy for depression (IPT). While providers may have prior training in these interventions, the VA has a standardized training protocol for these interventions, developed and research specifically for use with veterans. The VA provides excellent opportunities for training in one or more of these interventions, depending on your position and need. In the case of CPT and PE, for example, each one I attended consisted of 2.5 days of in-person training, followed by a 6-month consultation consisting of at least two cases followed closely by an expert within the VA on that particular intervention.

Technical training, though, is another issue. While most individuals know how to turn on and off a computer, telemental health is more than looking into a camera and talking to your patient. There are many nuances involved with telemental health, including room staging/set-up, dealing with equipment failures, handling emergencies, and even learning not to shout at the screen! The VA offers an in-house online training program to prepare providers for CVT. Providers must first complete a two-part online training in the learning management system, an online education-training program for VA employees. These modules offer an introduction to clinical video telehealth and managing emergencies. After successful completion of these modules, providers then complete a CVT skills assessment. Historically, this was done live with a "teacher" but has since been moved online. The skills assessment "tests" your knowledge of the online training modules and ensures you know the basics of operating the equipment. For those new to the equipment, consultation with providers already rehearsed in CVT is a good idea, as is consulting with the facility's local Telehealth Council (membership of individuals overseeing the implementation of CVT in the facility) and/or the Facility Telehealth Coordinator (FTC). After successful completion of the training requirements, you are awarded a certificate of training that is kept on file.

There are a number of advantages for pursuing telemental health within the VA. Some mentioned earlier, training and licensure flexibility, are strong drawing points. Salary is another one. Political arguments aside, the pay within the federal system is fair compared to private sector counterparts. Salary depends on a number of factors, including grade level (e.g., GS12 vs. GS13), prior experience/number of years within the VA (called "steps"), and locality pay (some parts of the country pay more due to cost of living and other adjustments). In general, the average base salary for a GS13 level psychologist (typical level for frontline psychology providers) is $80,000–$110,000. The actual amount will again depend on the part of the country where you work, prior experience, and number of years in the federal system. A board of peers determines the actual starting amount.

Other advantages of telemental health in the VA include access to advance and latest equipment and technology at no cost to you, strong infrastructure, and available support staff, including IT, telehealth technicians, national support desk, and crisis intervention resources. Additionally, facility developed emergency plans have already been created reducing the anxiety often associated with developing such plans. HIPPA and privacy/security are highly valued and as such, security within the VA system is one less thing an individual has to worry about.

Advantages to patients are also abundant. VA telemental health programs provide increased access to geographically remote areas and to areas where recruitment and retention of services, especially specialty areas, have been difficult. CVT brings increased access to specialty services and higher level of care that otherwise could not be obtained by some patients. Telemental health provides a significant degree of convenience in the form of reduced travel costs to patients (as well as providers who would otherwise have to travel between the medical facility and CBOC or between two CBOCs). Reduced travel time and ability to access care directly from home provides a degree of flexibility in scheduling not available with in-person treatment. The VA makes such scheduling easy with an online scheduling package that automatically reminds veterans of their next telemental health appointment across multiple days prior to their session, as well as providing information on downloading and accessing the software if and when necessary. One of the greatest advantages seen with telemental health in the VA is improved adherence to treatment. Studies and experience have demonstrated a reduction in no-show rates for patients involved in telemental health services. The ability to better access care and remain committed to treatment has led to a reduction in psychiatric hospitalization utilization (Godleski, Darkins, & Peters, 2012).

Disadvantages are generally the same as found in other institutions. Technical training is limited to a degree. On-site learning comprises a large part of training, along with consultation with peers and others knowledgeable in the area of CVT. Bandwidth is limited at times, which can affect audio and video quality. You may have to rely on a remote technician, nurse, etc. to provide additional clinical information despite never having met or worked with them before. In striving to provide the best experience for veterans and providers, high quality (i.e., expensive) equipment is often sought. To that end, though, contracts are limited to one or two suppliers so choice of equipment is generally outside of your control. As with many institutions, budget issues may arise and such equipment may not be easily obtained or readily available all the time. And as always, technical problems may not always be able to be resolved "on the fly." While the VA has a national telehealth helpdesk, they are not able to communicate with patients directly. Problems that arise on the patient end have to be relayed through you or a local telehealth technician, with the reply relayed back to the patient the same way. As a result, solutions may not come quickly, resulting in the need for a back-up plan, such as telephone contact or rescheduled in-person session.

Most "generic" forms of psychotherapy can be utilized through CVT. More recently, the VA (and outside third party researchers) has been examining the administration of those "gold standards" of treatment for PTSD delivered via CVT. The studies have evaluated both CPT and PE and have routinely found that not only is the administration of these interventions via CVT safe, but also effective (Morland, Hynes, Mackintosh, Resick, & Chard, 2011; Thorp, Fidler, Moreno, Floto, & Agha, 2012; Tuerk, Yoder, Ruggiero, Gros, & Acierno, 2010).

In summary, the Department of Veterans Affairs has one of, if not the, largest telemental health networks and infrastructure in the country. The advantages in working for the VA go beyond "benefits" to include excellent opportunities for training in telemental health and evidence-based psychotherapies. There is a steady stream of referrals for behavioral health care, as well as a number of different opportunities to delivering such care to veterans. Working with veterans has been one of the most rewarding experiences of my personal and professional career.

References

Godleski, L., Darkins, A., & Peters, J. (2012). Outcomes of 98,609 U.S. Department of Veterans Affairs patients enrolled in telemental health services, 2006-2010. *Psychiatric Services, 63*(4), 383–385. doi:10.1176/appi.ps.201100206.

Litz, B. T., & Schlenger, W. E. (2009). PTSD in service members and new veterans of Iraq and Afghanistan wars: A bibliography and critique. *PTSD Research Quarterly, 20*(1), Winter 2009.

Morland, L. A., Hynes, A. K., Mackintosh, M., Resick, P., & Chard, K. (2011). Group cognitive processing therapy delivered to veterans via telehealth: A pilot cohort. *Journal of Traumatic Stress, 24*, 465–469. doi:10.1002/jts.20661.

Thorp, S. R., Fidler, J., Moreno, L., Floto, E., & Agha, Z. (2012). Lessons learned from studies of psychotherapy for posttraumatic stress disorder via video teleconferencing. *Psychological Services, 9*(2), 197–199. doi:10.1037/a0027057.

Tuerk, P. W., Yoder, M., Ruggiero, K. J., Gros, D. F., & Acierno, R. (2010). A pilot study of pro-longed exposure therapy for posttraumatic stress disorder delivered via telehealth technology. *Journal of Traumatic Stress, 23*(1), 116–123. doi:10.1002/jts.20494.

Chapter 21
Telemedicine in Genetic Counseling

Susan Landgren

"There is an urgent need for public education in genetics. That might seem an odd statement in view of its extensive coverage in the media. No doubt, the information storm will continue, and much of what is published is of high quality, but, more than anything, the public needs fair assessments of what genetics can and cannot do." (Steve Jones, 2000, Genetics in Medicine: Real Promises, Unreal Expectations – One Scientist's Advice to Policymakers in the United Kingdom and the United States, Milbank Reports, Milbank Memorial Fund, New York, ISBN 1-887748-36-9)

Professor Steve Jones, University College London, Fellow of the Royal Society

Heredity plays a crucial role in health. Both our genes and the environment influence virtually every aspect of our growth and development. Knowledge about the role of heredity is increasing at an extraordinary pace as our understanding of genetics advances. Yet, genetics is a relatively new branch of biology. In 1866, an amateur botanist named Gregor Mendel described patterns of heredity in pea plants. While he worked carefully to develop hypotheses about inheritance and test those hypotheses, he was not at all focused on human inheritance. He was interested in the development of hybrids in plants.[1] It was not until the middle of the twentieth century that the patterns of inheritance (now called Mendelian genetics) that Mendel identified were understood to apply to most organisms that reproduce sexually.

---

[1] A translation of Mendel's paper on hybridization in peas is available at http://www.mendelweb.org/Mendel.html, accessed January, 2014

S. Landgren, M.S. (✉)
Billings Clinic, 801 North 29th Street, Billings, MT 59107, USA
e-mail: slandgren@billingsclinic.org

© Springer International Publishing Switzerland 2017   213
M.M. Maheu et al. (eds.), *Career Paths in Telemental Health*,
DOI 10.1007/978-3-319-23736-7_21

The mid-twentieth century was a time of extraordinary progress in understanding how characteristics are passed from one generation to the next. The role of a chemical called deoxyribonucleic acid (DNA) as the "text" coding for the inherited characteristics was established by an experiment published in 1944 by Oswald Avery, Colin MacLeod, and Maclyn McCarty. By 1952, Alfred Hershey and Martha Chase demonstrated that DNA was the genetic material of virtually all organisms. In the mid-1970s, a gene (one of the "sentences" of text) coding for an inherited trait was sequenced (broken down into "words" and "letters"). In the late 1980s, the molecular and biochemical basis for a human disease (cystic fibrosis) was fully understood. Consequently, genetics in medicine is a relatively new field. Yet by 2003, the sequence of almost all the nucleotides (the "letters" that make up the "text" coding for human hereditary patterns) had been documented. In this relatively new field of medicine, our knowledge is changing at an extraordinarily rapid pace.

Rapid changes in our knowledge of genetics make genetic counseling a particularly exciting profession. By March of 2013, scientists had identified more than 1,800 disease genes through the Human Genome Project. In a new initiative, the Cancer Genome Atlas, scientists are focusing on identifying and understanding genetic abnormalities seen in major cancers. The US Department of Health and Human Services believes that because of "a deeper understanding of disease at the genomic level, we will see a whole new generation of targeted interventions, many of which will be drugs that are much more effective and cause fewer side effects than those available today."[2]

Providing medical genetic services generally requires a team including physicians, cytogeneticists, laboratory technicians, and genetic counselors. Since virtually every aspect of the human form and physiology is affected by genetic information passed from parent to child, it is not surprising that physicians and counselors who work in genetics often specialize even further. Genetic subspecialties include prenatal diagnosis, pediatric genetics, and the genetics of cancers.

Genetic counselors have training in the biology and biochemistry of genetics and the psychology of counseling at the master's or doctoral level, although there are currently no Ph.D. programs in genetic counseling. In 2004, there were 32 accredited graduate programs[3] training genetic counselors in 22 states (Table 21.1) as well as in 3 provinces in Canada (Table 21.2). Exposure to telemedicine during this training is limited. Occasionally, during a clinical round, a genetic counseling student might observe a session through a telemedicine network. Otherwise, telemedicine in genetic counseling requires on-the-job training by colleagues or mentors.

Genetic counselors help patients understand and adjust to the psychological, biological, and familial implications of hereditary conditions. Patients who come to see a genetic counselor may have a hereditary condition themselves or may be concerned because someone in their family has the condition. Couples with an affected

---

[2] US Department of Health and Human Services, National Institutes of Health, 2013, Human Genome Project, NIH On-line Factsheet, accessed October, 2013

[3] Accreditation of genetic counseling programs is provided by the Accreditation Council for Genetic Counseling (ACGC).

Table 21.1 ACGC-accredited programs for training genetic counselors in the United States

State	Program	State	Program
Alabama	University of Alabama at Birmingham	Minnesota	University of Minnesota
Arkansas	University of Arkansas Medical Sciences	New York	Long Island University-C.W. Post
			Mount Sinai School of Medicine
			Sarah Lawrence College
California	University of California, Irvine	North Carolina	University of North Carolina at Greensboro
	California State University, Stanislaus		
	Stanford University		
Colorado	University of Colorado Denver	Ohio	Case Western Reserve University
			Ohio State University
			University of Cincinnati College of Medicine
District of Columbia	Howard University	Oklahoma	University of Oklahoma Health Sciences Center
Georgia	Emory University School of Medicine	Pennsylvania	Arcadia University
			University of Pittsburgh
Illinois	Northwestern University Medical School	South Carolina	University of South Carolina
Indiana	Indiana University Medical Center	Texas	University of Texas Graduate School of Biomedical Sciences at Houston
Maryland	Johns Hopkins University/ National Human Genome Research Institute	Utah	University of Utah
	University of Maryland School of Medicine		
Massachusetts	Boston University School of Medicine	Virginia	Virginia Commonwealth University
	Brandeis University		
Michigan	University of Michigan	Wisconsin	University of Wisconsin-Madison
	Wayne State University		

Source: After the Accreditation Council for Genetic Counseling, 2013, Accredited Programs, http://gceducation.org/Pages/Accredited-Programs.aspx, accessed December, 2014

Table 21.2 ACGC-
accredited programs for
training genetic counselors
in Canada

Province	University and program
British Columbia	University of British Columbia
Ontario	University of Toronto
Quebec	McGill University

Source: After the ACGC, 2013, Accredited Programs,
http://gceducation.org/Pages/Accredited-Programs.
aspx, accessed December, 2014

child who are contemplating another pregnancy and older couples who are planning a pregnancy can consult with a genetic counselor to assess potential risks. Most patients are referred to a counselor by a physician, although self-referrals are becoming common.[4] Genetic counseling is often completed in one or two sessions.

Since there is so much known about genetics and so many different approaches to explaining that information, the genetic counselor needs to adjust the approach of each counseling session to address the needs of the patient. In some sessions, the genetic counselor is advised in advanced about the condition of concern (through review of medical records or pre-appointment interview when a patient schedules an appointment). However, many counseling sessions take place when the diagnosis is not yet known.

It is not unusual for a number of other family members to join the patient in the counseling session. This is useful to the patient's family because other members of the family may be at risk for the condition being discussed. It is also useful to the patient and counselor because family members often provide psychological and emotional support for the patient. Furthermore, it is useful to the counselor because other family members may have important knowledge about the patient's family medical history.

Genetic counseling sessions begin with introductions, so the counselor knows the relationship of everyone attending the session. The counselor first reviews the reason for the session with the patient. This is followed by a brief description of the nature of heredity and the interaction of genetic and environmental factors. The counselor then discusses the family history of the patient. During this process, the counselor documents information about the patient's siblings, parents, grandparents, aunts, uncles, and cousins. Depending on what is revealed in this part of the counseling dialogue, the session then turns to medical and/or familial concerns. Throughout the session, the counselor questions the patient to verify that the patient has understood what has been covered. If genetic testing is an option, the counselor describes the process, costs, and implications of having knowledge of one's genes. If testing is not an option, the counselor explains why. Support groups are identified and the patient is provided contact information as well as information about other resources.

---

[4] See, for example, Deborah Kotz, The Boston Globe, 2013, Increase in breast cancer gene screening: the Angelina Jolie effect, http://www.boston.com/lifestyle/health/blogs/daily-dose/2013/12/03/increase-breast-cancer-gene-screening-the-angelina-jolie-effect/2HsXjeZh6MdTE5B8T3nGMI/blog.html, accessed January, 2014

While the number of genetic counselors is increasing, there are still limits on patient access to genetic counseling services. Geographically, the United States is huge (at 3.5 million square miles, only Russia and China have larger land areas than the United States). Many patients live far from the nearest counselor. Patients in rural areas might need to drive hundreds of miles to meet with a counselor face to face. Fortunately, technology has made it possible to offer genetic counseling through telemedicine networks. These telegenetics sessions are similar to face-to-face sessions. One such counseling session is described briefly below:

Maude is a 52 year old widow who lives in Williston, North Dakota. During routine breast self-examination she finds a suspicious lump in her left breast. She is frightened because her younger sister died of breast cancer just two years earlier, so she immediately makes an appointment to see her primary care physician. Her primary care physician refers her to the Leonard P. Nelson Cancer Center where a biopsy is scheduled. The treating oncologist suggests that Maude also schedule an appointment with a genetic counselor. The nearest counselor is 317 miles away in Billings, Montana.[5] Rather than drive to Billings, Maude's oncologist arranges for a telegenetics counseling session. The session is like a video-telephone call, but is run on secure telemedicine systems including facilities in the Billings Clinic and the Mercy Medical Center in Williston. During the session, Maude and her counselor discuss the history of cancer in Maude's family. Maude is surprised to learn that it isn't just the history of breast cancer that matters. There are a number of cancer syndromes that involve cancers that originate in other parts of the body and also affect the probability of a breast cancer having a hereditary origin. Based on Maude's family history, there are a number of tests that could be run to determine if Maude has genes that could affect her cancer risks and medical management. The counselor discusses the nature of heredity and the benefits and limitations with testing. After Maude has absorbed all this new information and consulted with the counselor again by telephone, she decides to be tested for the BRCA1 and BRCA2 genes. Eventually, Maude's oncologist uses the results of that testing in recommending a particular surgical option to remove the cancerous lump in Maude's breast and choosing appropriate post-operative treatments for Maude.

In 2013, there were 3260 certified genetic counselors (CGCs) in the United States and 235 in Canada. Some were "grandfathered" under rules that allowed their genetic training to have been obtained through a variety of sources. Newer CGCs must have a master's degree in genetic counseling from an Accreditation Council for Genetic Counseling (ACGC)-accredited program. CGCs must also have accumulated experience counseling patients about genetics and have passed the certification examination offered by the American Board of Genetic Counselors (ABGC). There are no CGCs in the Territory of Guam, the Commonwealth of the Northern Mariana Islands, the Commonwealth of Puerto Rico, and the US Virgin Islands, although there are six in the District of Columbia. Based on the US Census statistics, there were approximately 95,000 residents in the United States for each certified genetic counselor. Based on Canadian population statistics, there were approximately 148,000 residents in Canada for each certified genetic counselor. However, there are no CGCs in

---

[5] There are also counselors in Fargo, North Dakota, 393 miles away and Great Falls Montana, 416 miles away.

Table 21.3 The ten states
with the largest number of
ABGC-certified genetic
counselors

State	Number of certified genetic counselors
California	500
New York	261
Pennsylvania	196
Massachusetts	171
Texas	146
Maryland	136
North Carolina	131
Ohio	129
Illinois	123
New Jersey	112

Source: After the ABGC, 2013, Find Counselor, https://
abgcmember.goamp.com/Net/ABGCWcm/Find_
Counselor/ABGCWcm/PublicDir.aspx?hkey=0ad511c0-
d9e9-4714-bd4b-0d73a59ee175, accessed December, 2013

Labrador, New Brunswick, and Prince Edward Island provinces nor in the Northwest, Yukon, and Nunavut territories (Tables 21.3 and 21.4).

Furthermore, because of the population distribution throughout the United States, many states have very few genetic counselors on a per capita basis. Alabama, Arizona, Arkansas, Florida, Kansas, Nevada, Oklahoma, Tennessee, and Wyoming all have less than one certified genetic counselors for every 200,000 residents. Louisiana, Mississippi, and West Virginia have only about one counselor for every million residents.[6] The limited number of genetic counselors in these states provides many opportunities for counselors to offer telegenetics services.[7]

The rewards and challenges for genetic counselors who participate in telecounseling are similar to those for genetic counselors who are not part of a telemedicine network. In 2012, full-time certified genetic counselors earned between $35,000 and $260,000 per years, with an average salary of about $70,000 to $75,000.[8] The extremes of low and high salaries are outliers not representative of the profession as a whole. On average, genetic counselors in administrative and teaching positions earn more than those in purely clinical roles. Those with further advances degrees (either a Ph.D. or an M.D.) earn more than those with only a master's degree. Board-certified counselors generally earn more than those who are not certified, with a notable exception being genetic counselors whose practices began prior to the orga-

---

[6] After the ABGC, 2013, Find Counselor, https://abgcmember.goamp.com/Net/ABGCWcm/Find_
Counselor/ABGCWcm/PublicDir.aspx?hkey=0ad511c0-d9e9-4714-bd4b-0d73a59ee175,
accessed December, 2013, and the US Department of Commerce. US Census Bureau, 2011, 2010
Census values by state.

[7] Interestingly, the District of Columbia has almost five certified genetic counselors for every
100,000 residents. Delaware, Maryland, Massachusetts, and Utah all have more than one certified
genetic counselor for every 50,000 residents.

[8] National Society of Genetic Counselors 2013; 2012 Professional Status Survey: Salary and
Benefits

Table 21.4 The ten states with the smallest number of ABGC-certified genetic counselors

State	Number of certified genetic counselors
West Virginia	1
Wyoming	2
Alaska	4
Mississippi	4
North Dakota	5
Louisiana	6
Montana	6
South Dakota	6
Vermont	6
Idaho	11

Source: After the ABGC, 2013, Find Counselor, https://abgcmember.goamp.com/Net/ABGCWcm/Find_Counselor/ABGCWcm/PublicDir.aspx?hkey=0ad511c0-d9e9-4714-bd4b-0d73a59ee175, accessed December, 2013

nization of a certifying process. Generally those with more experience earn more than recent graduates or recently certified counselors.

Most genetic counselors are classified as "exempt" employees.[9] Consequently, many counselors spend more than 40 h per week fulfilling their responsibilities at work. This is one consequence of being treated as a professional. However, because most employers recognize the professional status of their genetic counselors, they also receive some important professional benefits. Many employers provide budgets for purchase of books, travel to professional meetings, continuing medical education studies, and occasionally sabbaticals. Sabbaticals are more likely to be offered in educational positions or to counselors who have a Ph.D. or an M.D.

One of the marked disadvantages of clinical genetic counseling positions is that many genetic counselors provide services primarily to patients whose prognoses are poor. Another large cohort of patients seeking genetic counseling services includes parents dealing with the possibility or fact that the prognosis for their child or children is not good. These patterns introduce substantial elements of emotion into the job. Not only is a clinical genetic counselor an educator, the counselor must also provide brief psychological counseling and support for patients. In many sessions, tears are shed as the counselor supports a patient making a heart-rending decision.

Clinical genetic counselors need to feel comfortable with dealing with the emotions associated with difficult medical situations. They need to cope with the challenges of birth defects, other childhood hereditary conditions, pregnancy losses, and cancers in patients of all ages. For those with the strength and empathy to address these issues and provide support to affected patients, the most significant benefits for the counselor are the reactions from the patients they counsel. Almost all the

---

[9] Employees classified as exempt are not entitled to overtime pay as guaranteed by the Fair Labor Standards Act (FLSA). If an employee is classified as exempt, their employer is not required to pay them overtime pay.

patients counseled learned about genetics in school. The abstract lessons of the classroom become a reality as they are helped to understand how an inherited trait is affecting them and their family. With this knowledge comes an extraordinary strength and the counselor can easily understand the role the counseling has played in helping the patient gain that strength.

Telegenetics counseling sessions are similar to face-to-face sessions. The telegenetics sessions are video-telephone call. Technicians at the sending and receiving locations handle the technical aspects of the telegenetics session. The sessions begin with introductions. The counselor then discusses the nature of heredity and evaluates the patient's knowledge of the subject. The counselor then asks the patient about family medical issues to develop a history of the family, which is documented in a pedigree. Using information from the referring physician and the family medical history, the counselor assesses the risk the patient faces for a particular hereditary condition. The counselor presents options for genetic testing and discusses the implications of knowing if the patient has or is a carrier of particular genetic information. Finally, the telegenetics session focuses on medical and familial issues.

Inasmuch as genetics is a relatively new field, genetic counseling is a relatively new healthcare profession, and telemedicine is a relatively new technology; the literature on telegenetics is limited. A review of the literature was published in 2012.[10] In 2000, Gray et al. describe a pilot program for telegenetics in Wales in a letter to the editor of the *Journal of Telemedicine and Telecare*. This is the first telegenetics counseling reported in the United Kingdom and the first this author has seen documented anywhere.[11] This outreach effort supported patients more than 175 miles away from the practitioner's location. Gray and his colleagues conclude that telegenetics is "an innovative and potentially cost-effective means" of providing genetic services to distant locations. Pilot programs in Maine[12] and an unnamed location in the United States more than 100 miles from the nearest genetic counselor[13] are described in 2005 and 2006, respectively, in peer reviewed articles. The results of these pilot efforts show a high level of patient satisfaction when video conferencing is used to conduct pediatric and prenatal genetic counseling. These pilot efforts support the idea that telecounseling is an appropriate way to provide genetic counseling services to populations with limited access to genetic services.

Additional studies have shown that telecounseling provides a high level of satisfaction for both the genetic counselor and the patient. One possible exception to this

[10] Hilgart, J. S., J.A. Hayward, B. Coles and R. Iredale, 2012, Telegenetics: a Systematic Review of Telemedicine in Genetics Services, *Genetics in Medicine* 14: 765–776

[11] Gray, J., K. Brain, R. Iredale, J. Alderman, E. France and H. Hughes, 2000, A Pilot Study of Telegenetics—Letter to the Editor, *Journal of Telemedicine and Telecare*, 6: 245–247

[12] Lea, D. H., J.L. Johnson, S. Ellingwood, W. Allan, A. Patel and R. Smith, 2005, Telegenetics in Maine: Successful Clinical and Educational Service Delivery Model Developed from a 3-year Pilot Project, Genetics in Medicine 7: 21–27

[13] Abrams, D.J, and M.R. Geier, 2006, A Comparison of Patient Satisfaction with Telehealth and On-Site Consultations: A Pilot Study for Prenatal Genetic Counseling, Journal of Genetic Counseling 15: 199–205

pattern is satisfaction with the psychosocial aspects of the counseling.[14] This may reflect difficulty reading emotions from facial expressions and body language based on images on a screen. As telecounseling on genetic issues expands, it may be useful to assure that the patient is accompanied in the session by a local practitioner (e.g., nurse or social worker) or by a close family member or friend. Some of these issues might also be addressed by expanding the technology. If the patient is recorded with two cameras, one focused just on the face and the other showing the whole body, and the counselor sees both images on a split screen, it may be easier to read more subtle indicators of distress.

Early telegenetics sessions in Billings occasionally included a full team of providers with the patient at one location and a team of specialists at another. While this provided extraordinarily positive results in difficult cases, the large amount of healthcare resources used (four or more physicians in sessions often lasting close to an hour) prevented this telecounseling model from being widely used. Telecounseling for clinical genetic care will not replace face-to-face genetic counseling sessions. It does however have the enormous advantage of providing essential genetic counseling services to distant locations without requiring the counselor or the patient to travel.

Conclusions and Summary

Field Guide to Technology Careers in Mental Health. Both environmental factors and heredity play roles in virtually every aspect of human health. This chapter introduces the complexity of our knowledge concerning hereditary conditions. Hereditary conditions most commonly addressed include those affecting the outcomes of pregnancy and treatment for cancers as well as those impacting childhood development.

The treatment of genetic conditions is generally provided by a team of medical practitioners. The team often includes genetic counselors. Genetic counselors, who have graduate training in genetics and psychology, are educated to provide patients

---

[14]Stalker, H.J., R. Wilson, H. McCune, J. Gonzalez, M. Moffett and R.T. Zori, 2006, Telegentic medicine: Improved Access to Services in an Underserved Area, *Journal of Telemedicine and Telecare* 12:182-185; Shah, N.N., L.D. Fleisher, H.H. Andersson, B.B. Butler, B.H. Thompson, J. Benkendorf, A. Keehn, D. Flannery, D.C. Alverson, S. Au, L. Robin, J. Puente, J. Ridenour and M.S. Watson, 2009, Impediments and Solutions to Telegenetics Practice: Meeting Report, http://www.nccrcg.org/docs/NCC/Telegenetics/ACMGTelegeneticspolicyMeetingReportFINAL.pdf, accessed January, 2014; Zilliacus, E.M., B. Meiser, E.A. Lobb, J. Kirk, L. Warwick and K. Tucker, 2010, Women's Experience of Telehealth Cancer Genetic Counseling, *Journal of Genetic Counseling* 19: 463–472; Zilliacus, E.M., B. Meiser, E.A. Lobb, P.J Kelly, K. Barlow-Stewart, J.A. Kirk, and K.M. Tucker, 2011, Are Videoconferenced Consultations as Effective as Face-to-face Consultations for Hereditary Breast and Ovarian Cancer Genetic Counseling?, *Genetics in Medicine* 13: 933–941; McDonald, E., A. Lamb, B. Grillo, L. Lucas and S. Miesfeldt, 2013, Acceptability of Telemedicine and Other Cancer Genetic Counseling Models of Service Delivery in Geographically Remote Settings, *Journal of Genetic Counseling*, ePublished ahead of print release

with a basic understanding of genetics and to support the patient in making medical decisions.

Genetic counseling involves evaluation of the medical histories of the patient and their relatives to assess the risk of disease occurrence or recurrence. The counselor educates the patient about inheritance, genetic testing, and disease management and prevention. The counselor reviews resources about the condition and ongoing research. The genetic counselor then provides support to the patient as choices are made about treatment.

Telegenetics provides genetic counseling services to patients who live far from the nearest genetic counseling practice. The session is like a video-telephone call, but is run on secure telemedicine systems. Because of the relatively small number of genetic counselors and their uneven distribution throughout North America, telegenetics is becoming more common. There are currently few genetic counselors whose practices are primarily via telegenetics (most of those are associated with testing companies). However, as we learn more about genetics and understand the increasingly important role of genetics across all disciplines in medicine, this pattern is likely to change.

References

Abrams, D. J., & Geier, M. R. (2006). A comparison of patient satisfaction with telehealth and on-site consultations: A pilot study for prenatal genetic counseling. *Journal of Genetic Counseling, 15*, 199–205.

Gray, J., Brain, K., Iredale, R., Alderman, J., France, E., & Hughes, H. (2000). A pilot study of telegenetics—Letter to the editor. *Journal of Telemedicine and Telecare, 6*, 245–247.

Hilgart, J. S., Hayward, J. A., Coles, B., & Iredale, R. (2012). Telegenetics: A systematic review of telemedicine in genetics services. *Genetics in Medicine, 14*, 765–776.

Lea, D. H., Johnson, J. L., Ellingwood, S., Allan, W., Patel, A., & Smith, R. (2005). Telegenetics in Maine: Successful clinical and educational service delivery model developed from a 3-year pilot project. *Genetics in Medicine, 7*, 21–27.

McDonald, E., Lamb, A., Grillo, B., Lucas, L., & Miesfeldt, S. (2013). Acceptability of telemedicine and other cancer genetic counseling models of service delivery in geographically remote settings. *Journal of Genetic Counseling, 23*(2), 221–228.

Shah, N. N., Fleisher, L. D., Andersson, H. H., Butler, B. B., Thompson, B. H., Benkendorf, J., ... Watson, M. S. (2009). Impediments and solutions to telegenetics practice: Meeting report. Retrieved January 2014, from http://www.nccrcg.org/docs/NCC/Telegenetics/ACMGTelegeneticspolicyMeetingReportFINAL.pdf

Stalker, H. J., Wilson, R., McCune, H., Gonzalez, J., Moffett, M., & Zori, R. T. (2006). Telegentic medicine: Improved access to services in an underserved area. *Journal of Telemedicine and Telecare, 12*, 182–185.

Zilliacus, E. M., Meiser, B., Lobb, E. A., Kirk, J., Warwick, L., & Tucker, K. (2010). Women's experience of telehealth cancer genetic counseling. *Journal of Genetic Counseling, 19*, 463–472.

Zilliacus, E. M., Meiser, B., Lobb, E. A., Kelly, P. J., Barlow-Stewart, K., Kirk, J. A., & Tucker, K. M. (2011). Are videoconferenced consultations as effective as face-to-face consultations for hereditary breast and ovarian cancer genetic counseling?, *Genetics in Medicine, 13*, 933–941.

Chapter 22
Clinician to Trainer to Technologist and Consultant: The Wild and Wonderful Path eLearning and mHealth

Many minds are better than one.

Ecclesiastes, 4:9, in Myles Coverdale's Bible, 1535:

Marlene Maheu

Vignette

Claire sipped a warm cup of tea while waiting for her next patient. When her patient arrived 25 min late, she settled her new iPad into her lap and browsed over to the TeleMental Health Institute's (TMHI) Online Training Center. She "logged" in to the same page she left yesterday. Claire's profile tells her that she's completed three of the four courses needed for her Certificate in TeleMental Health. She smiled to herself. One more course to go.

Claire plans to move to Florida to get away from the increasingly difficult New York winters. Her best friend and former office mate recently moved to Cocoa Beach. She helped Claire find the 1800 square foot, beachside condo of her dreams. Claire will have a direct ocean view from her living and bedroom windows. Her down payment was transferred to the escrow officer last week, and she will take possession of her new home next month.

Claire will be retiring after 40 years of full-time practice and will be slowly migrating her to Cocoa Beach. She plans to keep some of her patients with her for as long as needed and continue visiting New York regularly for family visits. She'll rent another colleague's office and have in-person sessions with those patients who

M. Maheu, Ph.D. (✉)
5173 Waring Rd., San Diego, CA 92120, USA
e-mail: mmaheu@telehealth.org

© Springer International Publishing Switzerland 2017
M.M. Maheu et al. (eds.), *Career Paths in Telemental Health*,
DOI 10.1007/978-3-319-23736-7_22

will most assuredly want to see her when she regularly returns to her New York neighborhood, too.

Not only will her telepractice give her patients the continuity of care they need, but she will be able to maintain a steady source of supplemental income that she'll be needing. Her retirement plan will cover the basics, but she knows she'll want the financial freedom to buy a few luxuries, including the extravagance of furnishing her new condo with "beachy" furniture. Besides, she loves being a clinician and isn't ready to be completely retired yet—not yet.

Claire decided to undergo a 39 h certification program at TMHI so as to have the peace of mind she prefers when faced with mandatory compliance to legal, regulatory, and ethical requirements. Many of the concepts in the TMHI training seemed vaguely familiar to Claire from graduate school, but before her training, she was at a loss to know which ones apply to her situation and what they would mean in terms of the technologies she is choosing to use. Learning about these foundational issues is exactly what she had hoped to find in the training. Looking for clear instructions, protocols and one-to-one consultation, she discovered much more than she had anticipated.

Claire found TMHI's roadmap and easy-to-understand checklists to be exactly what she needed to get started. The many different "vignettes" illustrated practical solutions for her as she faced decisions at multiple turns. She also knew that TMHI would keep her updated with changes in legal, regulatory, ethical, and practical as they occur in the rapidly changing world of technology.

As a clinician, Claire appreciated the many features of the TMHI eLearning environment that allowed her to read for a while and then bookmark her page for easy access later if a late client suddenly appeared. She enjoyed watching several recent webinars that were recorded when she couldn't attend the live event. She appreciated being able to scan through slides for those webinars quickly, to get right to the points she wanted to note in her written "migration plan" to Cocoa beach. When the time came for her to file her paperwork for continuing education hours with her licensing board, she simply printed her course completion certificates from her own computer and mailed them to her board. She especially enjoyed the monthly tele-consults where she could directly ask her questions of the TMHI faculty by telephone in a small group.

Claire has able to obtain the information she needed to learn which laws apply to her, develop her business plan, select the types of technologies she needs for her patient population, make reasonable financial projections to see if her efforts will be worthwhile, and begin gathering the needed documents for her transition. Following the TMHI "roadmap," she has begun to invite the patients who she considers appropriate for her remote telepractice, answer their questions, and complete the needed informed consent documents for everyone who has agreed to continue their work with her after the move to Florida.

From Graduate School to the Tech World

Born the youngest child of a blue collar, immigrant family with French as my first language, I approached undergraduate school with the secret terror of an imposter. Sure they'd discover me and ask me to leave; I quickly learned that my differences were valued. My newfound confidence was heightened by several years of Gestalt therapy with Erv and Miriam Polster, where I learned to trust my senses and develop what I later called a "spidey sense" that led to confidence about people, situations, and where things were going. My academic training led to a PhD in clinical psychology, with a dissertation-focused worksite smoking cessation programs and their delivery as accelerated by competition and cooperation. That process included the training of multiple colleagues to help deliver a structured, behavioral smoking cessation program to large groups of smokers. My early career then was spent in the development of programmed training. Unbeknownst to me at the time, that formative experience set the stage for what I am doing today via technology.

After completing my doctorate in 1985, my private practice had become the exclusive focus of my professional life. While my practice was booming, I suffered from orthopedic challenges that made it difficult to sit for hours at a time. After a careful review of my own goals, I realized that I craved something new and was ready for a change.

Upon hearing of the Internet in 1994, I was intrigued and attended a Learning Annex class about Internet opportunities in San Diego. The class was more than I had anticipated. Immediately after class, with my mind abuzz with possibilities, I marched up to the presenter. Within 5 min, we shook hands on an agreement that I would write a "Dear Abby" column for his online magazine. Although this was a volunteer effort in the face of an already hectic schedule, I was thrilled to take a leap of faith. I knew that I'd learn a lot about a whole new arena and was very enthusiastic about the opportunity.

Seeking direction from the American Psychological Association (APA) for ethical models of working in the Internet as a psychologist, I was informed that they didn't have anyone addressing this new phenomenon. Within days, I was invited to chair a subcommittee to explore ethical issues on the Internet. Before I knew it, more than 50 colleagues were writing articles and answering Q&A for my own magazine, located at, "SelfhelpMagazine.com." The project grew quickly, and I somehow managed to organize hundreds of clinicians and programmers who volunteered for this ethics project. The work took me to new vistas with learning, lecturing, and writing about online legal and ethical issues. My interest soon morphed to researching models for both self-help and direct care as interventions for the online populations who came to our SelfhelpMagazine website. I also became more involved at the APA level, working in a variety of groups related to telehealth and ethics.

Just 3 years later in 1997, a single presentation at the APA about legal and ethical considerations in behavioral telehealth led to seven book authoring offers. I didn't know exactly what was happening, but I knew that it had momentum, and I was enjoying the ride. Three book contracts soon followed, sparking years of collegial interaction and more intellectual stimulation than I could have ever dreamed. Consultation opportunities also began to appear. Startups were plentiful, and many needed ethical direction. After consulting with managed care companies, technology companies, universities, clinics, hospitals, small group, and individual practitioners, I recognized the opportunity to reach yet more colleagues through online professional education. Because I had retained the copyright to my early book writing, those early book manuscripts formed the architecture for the professional training organization formed in 2009, now known as the TeleMental Health Institute, Inc. (TMHI). We opened our doors in 2010 and the project is now housed at www. telehealth.org.

As a psychologist/entrepreneur, starting the Institute was not only a labor of love but also a big financial investment. A software had to be purchased, server fees had to be paid, and programmers needed to be hired. A management team needed to be put into place to assign and verify tasks. A corporate structure had to be developed, complete with legal consultation, accounting, and bookkeeping. The required time and energy slowly led me away from my private practice until I was only seeing a handful of patients a week. My new and exciting focus propelled me into a world of management, full-time professional speaking, writing, and consulting on legal, ethical, clinical, and practical issues related to technology for behavior change. Many mentors supported me along the way—and still do.

My early graduate school provost, Joanne Callan, PhD, taught me that publishing was the golden path to being respected as a clinician. Lili Freidland, PhD, understood my vision and invited me to be the chair of the first telehealth group ever formed at the American Psychological Association (APA). Barry Gordon, PhD, taught me how to conduct research according to the APA ethics code and worked with me for years to deliver a wide variety of convention programs at the California Psychological Association and the APA. Myron Pulier, MD taught me how to think, write and operate as a leader and consultant. Since then, dozens of other colleagues have worked with me to share both challenges and successes related to my work as it has culminated at TMHI.

Pros and Cons of Being a Psychologist/Entrepreneur

The Pros

When I look back on the 30 years since graduate school, my chosen professional path has deviated dramatically from where I began, but offers significant advantages over the professional life that I had imagined. At the top of my long list of "pros" to my chosen path is the joy of shaping a new breed of interdisciplinary behavioral health professional who now can reach people in unprecedented ways. With thousands of professionals who have trained at our institute from 39 countries, I have been able to surround myself with a rich variety of behavioral leaders. Amid these technology-minded colleagues, I enjoy the challenge and excitement of spearheading innovative approaches to how behavioral services can be delivered. Recipients of our work serve not only clients who want direct care but millions more who can now access self-help in a wide variety of formats online and with mobile devices. This blend of activities helps me have and share insights into where the profession is not only going, but needs to go. I've been able to help define telemental health and a variety of technologies for all clinical behavioral groups, including the development of guidelines and standards.

Probably the most rewarding of all the "pros" of being an entrepreneur in the arena of behavioral telehealth is the mentoring and collaboration with dozens of esteemed colleagues who have volunteered to help grow the Institute. While some of these colleagues come to us as "scholars" who obtain our coursework in exchange for working to help us grow, the TMHI work/study program has already involved more than 30 licensed colleagues from all disciplines, ranging from psychiatry, psychology, counseling, social work, behavior analysis, and speech pathology. They have each focused on some aspect of improving our content, reporting, and fixing processes such as gamification and other engagement strategies, promoting our courses and webinars online, creating new opportunities for us by introducing us to their circles of colleagues, and much more.

Several have continued on with us after their graduation to become faculty for our graduate school training program, business partners, TMHI speakers who travel to address best practices and consult with a variety of clinics, hospitals, and businesses that serve behavioral health. Other writing partners have spent countless hours helping brainstorm not only the content of our training but the ways in which we can best communicate our efforts to the world, online, in jointly written books and articles, popular media, interviews, and professional presentations that have spanned several countries. Not a week goes by without new collaboration, an exciting invitation, or expression of appreciation.

Second in line of "pros" for my work these days is the excitement of working with health IT companies' intent on improving how care is delivered. Offers for collaboration and consultation come from every continent. I now consult with international technology start-ups, large membership associations, universities, insurance companies, worldwide information technology (IT) companies, telephone companies, technology developers, conference planners, clinics, hospitals, owners of small group practices, and independent practitioners. The range of problems they face and services they are developing are inspirational, creative, and deeply satisfying. They bring an unpredictable element to my workday, making every day challenging, engaging, and, frankly, fascinating.

Working with a wide variety of existing groups seeking to establish a telemental health service for their existing medical or behavioral program is equally energizing. These include primary care medical offices (e.g., Federally Qualified Health Centers) or specialty medical groups (e.g., plastic surgery) seeking to grow their income streams by including a behavioral telehealth component for presurgical as well as postsurgical behavioral interventions. These groups bring a variety of fascinating questions about how to legally and ethically begin to develop licensed provider networks across state lines and national borders, as well as across behavioral health disciplines (e.g., psychiatrists, psychologists, social workers, counselors, marriage and family therapists).

Similarly, both community mental health services and smaller specialty agencies are realizing that they can allow their patient populations to receive timelier and even potentially better care when patient contacts are increased through videoconferencing or other technologies. To meet these growing requests of the TeleMental Health Institute, we have incorporated as both a for-profit and nonprofit entities and contracted to deliver team consultation in partnership with technology-focused behavioral colleagues with whom I have developed relationships throughout now more than two decades in the field.

Last but not least, we at the institute are very enthusiastic about the growing need for telemental health training at the graduate school level. Our coursework has been repackaged and our eLearning platform re-configured to accommodate graduate schools to offer our pre-packaged, series of two, 3-credit graduate courses. They are excited about the competitive edge such course offerings will give them in the marketplace when attracting graduate students. Their input as to how we can improve our courses to make their institutions more competitive in the graduate school marketplace has also been an eye-opener. When compared to the other three groups that we serve (information technology start-ups, medical and behavioral programs), the graduate school market is quite different. Timelines are longer, resistances are more entrenched, and budgets are tighter. However, bright innovators lurk in graduate school halls, and the students are increasingly insisting that their coursework be relevant to the world they inhabit. Working with them is personally inspiring and energizing.

At this point, the institute is receiving regular invitations from new initiatives that are seeking telemental health consultation, staffing, training, graduate education, and/or speaking. Advisory board invitations are a monthly occurrence. New companies are looking for visionary principals. Others want introductions to exceptional and reliable vendors for a wide variety of products and services. Funding agents contact us to ask if we know start-ups needing capital. Start-ups want to meet potential funding sources. In this mix, I find myself contracting with the best of the group to render service in a variety of ways. On a daily basis, the brightest, the most accomplished, and most professional of colleagues surround me. I also maintain a very small private practice, just because I love being a therapist. It grounds me in the realities of people's lives, their struggles and the breakthroughs possible with psychotherapy.

My work has also grown into the non-profit world with two organizations: the *Coalition for Technology in Behavioral Science* (CTiBS) and the Telehealth Institute (TI). CTiBS is an interprofessional group of behavioral specialists who work on specific initiatives such as 1. Developing competencies for technology-related areas such as telemental health; 2, Developing and administering credentials for identified competencies; 3. Publishing a journal, now established as the Journal for Technology in Behavioral Science (JTiBS); and 4. Collaborating with national associations to bring education and collaboration acorss behavioral disciplines. As the Founding President and CEO of CTiBS, I have enjoyed the collaboration of remarkable colleagues focused on assuring the quality of service being delivered to behavioral telepractice clients/patients

The "Cons"

While writing, training, and public speaking came naturally to me, running an online business requires a very different set of skills. When I started, I was unprepared for the challenges of running a small, online business. Hiring and managing programmers, understanding their language, evaluating and pricing software features, buying and dealing with hosting services, coping with technical failures, making decisions about hardware, and offering customer support required skills that were not initially in my repertoire. I was taken aback by malicious programming code (Trojans and viruses), hackings, disgruntled contractors, social media attacks, relentless monthly fees, equipment failures, and competitors sneaking in and violating my copyright—sometimes masquerading as "friends."

Learning how to write courses for an audience that predominantly learns by listening (as opposed to young people, who learn by reading), long hours, uncertainty in the marketplace, and skepticism about my subject matter from stodgy colleagues have all kept me up at night. The marketplace has matured along with me.

Staffing has been a continued problem. Early financial projections that didn't materialize, expensive attorneys, demanding accountants, sporadic bookkeepers, and unreliable technical staff didn't help. Begrudgingly, I developed very good hiring, contracting, and firing skills. Today, my engagements are more productive, interviews are shorter, and I know when to let someone go much earlier than before. Luckily, my forages into hiring have turned up some of the most competent and dedicated professionals to be found anywhere. Similarly, our Institute's offering of a work/study program has produced more than 30 "scholars," each of which have donated an average of 200 h to the help grow the Institute.

One of the more significant "cons" to my chosen path has been the prejudice I've experienced in some of the national professional associations. Not only is technology controversial, but being labeled an "entrepreneur" has been problematic, in that the mere fact that I am a business owner has branded me as "suspicious." As I recently stated at a board of directors meeting for one of these large associations in Washington DC, "It is time that professional associations stop demonizing all entrepreneurs. Technology companies are perched all around us, plucking our brightest to leave our professional ranks to join them by offering more lucrative and exciting opportunities. Why aren't the associations figuring out how to embrace us, rather than excluding us from decision-making positions within our associations? Don't we deserve to be judged individually, and not as a tainted group of shysters? Don't we all have to adhere to the association's same ethics code?.

In sum, my path started as a psychology student and has led to more creativity than I ever imagined. I cannot wait to get to work on Monday mornings. In fact, I wake up at 5 am to my home-based "office," where I allow myself to ease into the day by sipping tea as I route email to one staff member or another. My staff and I begin taking calls at 7 am. My workday is interrupted by a daily visit to the gym, meditation, and a walk with my dog. Being the executive director of the TeleMental Health Institute allows tremendous creative freedom, intellectual stimulation through collaboration, and a significant role in understanding and shaping the technological changes that are accelerating around us. The lack of business and technical training in my early professional development as well as ongoing prejudice against entrepreneurs at the professional associations has been a significant "cons" in my professional life. It is for this reason that I am such a staunch advocate of at least an introduction to business and technical training as well as telemental health training in our graduate schools. (Models such as Nick Cummings, PhD's of Behavioral Health program at Arizona State University are worthy of examination. In partnership with the Mayo Clinic, they are forging new ways of thinking about graduate training.)

Evidence-Base

1. The TeleMental Health Institute has complied more than 3500 primary references to substantiate the evidence for telemental health. More than 1000 of those references can be found at this searchable web address: www.telehealth.org/bibliography
2. In addition to that database, we have closely followed the theory and practice of eLearning environments with:

    (a) Conrad, R. (2011). Engaging the Online Learner: Activities and Resources for Creative Instruction. Jossey-Bass.
    (b) Haythronwaite, C. & Richard N.L. Andrews, Richard (2011). E-learning Theory and Practice. SAGE Publications.

3. Horton, W. (2011) e-Learning by Design. Pfeiffer.

Chapter 23
From Psychologist to EHR Developer

Susan Litton

> *"Follow your bliss . . . and don't be afraid. If you follow your bliss, doors will open for you that wouldn't have opened for anyone else."*
>
> ~Joseph Campbell

Vignette

Before PSYBooks was launched, my typical day vacillated between writing specifications for the app and then implementing them. Writing specs for an application is sort of fun. You have to try to think like a user — imagine them needing to do a certain task and then figure out the absolute best way they can accomplish it. For example, all PSYBooks users need to be able to enter sessions and payments. Sounds easy, right? But what if the therapist has more than one office and may see the same client at both? Your "add session" form has to be able to handle that. Or consider the situation where the client is a child and the person paying the bill is a parent. Maybe the parents are divorced and dad pays for some visits and mom pays for others. Each parent needs a statement at the end of the year telling how much they paid. How do you develop an "add payment" form to handle all of that—and especially when you're trying to make the program super-easy to use? The number of possible user scenarios is mind-boggling, and your job as the person writing the

---

For purposes of this chapter, the acronym "EHR," which is short for electronic health record, will be used synonymously with terms such as "EMR" (electronic medical record) and "practice management system."

S. Litton, Ph.D. (✉)
PSYBooks, LLC, 2944 Blackwood Rd., Decatur, GA 30033, USA
e-mail: susan@psybooks.com

© Springer International Publishing Switzerland 2017
M.M. Maheu et al. (eds.), *Career Paths in Telemental Health*,
DOI 10.1007/978-3-319-23736-7_23

specs is to try to imagine *all* of them and then write your specifications accordingly. Part of the fun for me has been that I never settle for "a" solution for a task. Instead, I keep working at it until I find "the" solution I feel will be the easiest and most intuitive for the user. If my first draft for a certain task requires ten clicks for the user to complete, I keep rolling it around in my brain until I can get it down to four or five. Trying to come up with the best possible user experience is almost like a game for me.

Once the specs are written, the other part of a typical prelaunch day involved implementation, e.g., things like writing code or designing graphics. I hired developers to do the heavy lifting since, although I know quite a bit about coding, I don't consider myself an expert. Basically, I wrote the specs and created all the graphics and then divided coding tasks between myself and the other developers. There were also business types of tasks I had to do from time to time, such as researching and implementing the necessary steps for procuring trademarks and merchant accounts and making sure the app was 100 % HIPAA/HITECH compliant. When you're the entrepreneur of a start-up, everything is up to you. You can hire people, but ultimately, you're the one responsible for keeping all the balls in the air and pushing everything forward.

Post-launch has been a bit more of a zoo. In addition to the tasks above (most of which are on-going), I now spend time supporting subscribers, developing advertising schemes, and trying to get more involved with the larger community of people involved with digital behavioral health. *All* of it has been fun, but truth be told, I'm still happiest when I'm at my computer actually writing code.

Training

Since I've always loved learning, my training in web design/development was a big part of my bliss. I began by dabbling. I signed up for IT-related workshops and then day-long events and conferences. After a couple of years, it became obvious that these bits and pieces were just whetting my appetite so I began researching university IT programs. I eventually discovered The Art Institute of Atlanta which had an entire degree program called, at that time, Web Design and Development. I started off as a nondegree student, squeezing in courses where I could between clients. (I continued my work as a clinical psychologist through all of this.) However, being a nondegree student just lasted for a few semesters. Since my Myers-Briggs type is INFJ, I'm a "finisher." And besides, I was having the time of my life, so why not go the whole nine yards?

For me, it's good that I did. As a degree student, I was required to complete a senior project, and it was that senior project that eventually became PSYBooks. However, some people can do big, splashy things on the Web and be mostly self-taught. That's one of the nice things about IT: a lot of information is available for free. If you're interested doing something with IT, don't let the amount of training I've had discourage you. My "bliss" involved going to school and getting a degree. Your training might look very different. Pay attention to those little niggling thoughts that poke at you and just keep following them. The training that's right for you will unfold.

Pros and Cons

As with everything, there are pros and cons to each of my professions. I've chosen a self-employed/entrepreneurial path for both my behavioral health and my IT careers. However, if that's not your cup of tea, both fields also have jobs with employment opportunities so don't feel you have to hang out your own shingle. I don't know that one field is inherently more lucrative or personally satisfying than the other, but there are some notable differences:

People contact. Although some therapists talk about private practice as being isolating, I actually find my IT work to be more so. With private practice, you at least see your clients throughout the day, and if you share office space with colleagues, you might bump into them from time to time, too. With IT work, it's mostly just you and your computer. Even if you're in an office building with other people, your actual work day is spent staring at a computer monitor.

Tangible signs of progress. On the other hand, it's much easier to see tangible signs of progress in the IT world. You can write some code, click the necessary buttons and sit back and watch it work. Or you can create a graphic and lean back to evaluate it, and — even if you're not crazy about it — you've got something tangible and observable to show for your efforts. This is very different from the therapist's world where progress can be difficult to observe or measure and it's not always even clear when you're finished.

Scheduling issues. Picture this: on a day when I'm not seeing clients and am working solely on PSYBooks, I don't even have to get out of my pajamas if I don't want to. It's just me and my computer, and the computer doesn't care. Also, being somewhat prone to insomnia, if I wake up at 3 am, I can work on PSYBooks. Alternatively, if I get tired and need a break mid-morning, I can take a nap. Neither your schedule nor your dress code can be that relaxed when you're seeing clients.

Evidence Base

Unfortunately, there is almost no research on the use of EHRs within the field of behavioral health. There are a few studies using EHRs in physical health settings, but much of this research is geared toward evaluating specific tools (usually patient portals) instead of EHRs in general. Also, there is currently very little data studying the relationship, if any, between the use of EHRs and quality of health care, long-term outcomes, or even provider efficiency (Emont, 2011). Additionally, there are problems with the existing research, especially when trying to apply it to mental health populations. An attempt will be made to show that (1) caution must be used in generalizing conclusions from research done with physical health EHRs to mental health EHRs; (2) more attention needs to be paid to the characteristics of EHRs when designing research studies; and (3) consideration should be given to whether it is appropriate to expect EHRs to demonstrate meaningful use when applied to patient outcomes.

Physical Health EHRs vs. Mental Health EHRs

EHRs designed for physical health tend to be very different from those designed specifically for mental health. One reason is that most physical health EHRs are meant to be used in hospital settings as well as doctors' offices. This is an important aspect of a physical health EHR because a patient's records can be accessed by any doctor associated with that healthcare system, both within the hospital and after the patient is released. However, mental health providers typically do not need their EHR to integrate into a specific hospital's recordkeeping system, and most are not designed this way.

Also, physical health applications must account for the fact that in these settings, patients are usually seen by a nurse and/or other mid-level practitioner(s) and then by one or more doctors. This may require the EHRs to have different "workflows" for each type of staff member. In contrast, in mental health settings, especially private practice, the therapist is often the only healthcare professional the patient sees for any particular appointment.

Finally, physical health practitioners must routinely document physical signs and symptoms such as height, weight, vitals, immunizations, lab results, etc. Since behavioral health providers do not generally collect this information, their EHRs don't have to have specific templates for it.

For these and other reasons, EHRs for physical health are typically more difficult and costly to develop and also have steeper learning curves than do mental health EHRs. Also, because of the additional complexity, physical health EHRs often require some degree of tailor-made programming and/or installation to make the application "fit" a particular healthcare organization. Estimates of the cost of purchasing and installing physical health EHRs have been reported to range from $15,000 to $70,000 per provider with monthly network and/or maintenance fees added on top of that (How much is this going to cost me? (2013)). Even when we only consider private practice, installing a physical health EHR can be costly. One physician network in north Texas estimated the implementation cost for an average of five physician practice as $162,000, with an additional $85,500 in maintenance expenses reported during the first year (Fleming, Culler, McCorkle, Becker, & Ballard, 2011). Because of these costs plus the sheer amount of data that is likely to accumulate in a physical health EHR, once such systems are installed, the doctors may well feel "stuck with it."

In contrast, web-based behavioral health EHRs usually do not have installation fees and typically cost less than $100.00 a month to maintain. Because they are less complex, behavioral health EHRs are usually reasonably easy to learn. Most users who are at least somewhat computer savvy can teach themselves to use the EHR if it has good documentation and a way to contact support staff if needed. Additionally, most online behavioral health EHRs don't require a contract. Because of this, mental health practitioners never feel stuck with their decision. If they don't like their current EHR, it's not that hard to change to a different one.

Another factor that makes it difficult to generalize findings from physical health EHRs to mental health EHRs is that physical health practitioners are being mandated and incentivized to use EHRs whereas for mental health practitioners, it's still a personal decision (Blumenthal & Tavenner, 2010). Since most research has been done in physical health settings, it is likely that providers in those studies have felt some degree of pressure to use the EHR. Often the doctors themselves had little if any input into which EHR was chosen for their facility, yet they are compelled to use it. On the other hand, a mental health practitioner is more likely to have had at least some input in choosing their EHR, and many will have had total control over this decision.

Characteristics of EHRs: No Two Are Alike Nor Do They Stay the Same

Even if we find a way to eliminate or at least mitigate differences between physical and behavioral EHRs, there are some characteristics of EHRs in general that make research challenging.

The first is that efforts to standardize EHRs are still very much in their infancy. Although we do have certification standards set forth in the establishment of the permanent certification for health information technology (2011), developers are not required to adhere to them and many don't, especially since the standards are difficult to achieve, a bit controversial, and continue to evolve. Furthermore, since EHR certification is linked with incentive payments — which excludes most mental health professionals — there's even less motivation for developers of behavioral health EHRs to apply for certification. From a developer's perspective, it simply doesn't make sense to invest hundreds of thousands of dollars to satisfy specifications that (1) aren't required, (2) are opposed by many, (3) may well change, and (4) may actually make your product worse instead of better. However, the lack of standardization is problematic in that it makes it impossible to compare results from a study using "Brand A" EHR to a similar study using "Brand B." For example, Brand A might only have a total of 10 tools or features whereas Brand B might have 400. Obviously these two studies would likely yield very different results.

A second factor that complicates EHR research is that good software developers — especially those with web-based applications — are more or less continually improving their products. This may include adding new features, refining existing ones, fixing bugs, or simply giving the product a fresh new look and feel. Web-based software tends to be updated on the fly, as opposed to desktop software where updates, if done at all, are typically released as a "patch" the user must download. This continual development is a good thing — something to be encouraged — but it adds yet another wrinkle for research. For example, say a study uses Brand C EHR and that, perhaps unbeknownst to anyone, the results of the study are at least partially skewed by deficiencies in the EHR. Not only have the results of this study been compromised by a confounding variable (i.e., problems in the software), but assuming the developers find and fix the issues, subsequent studies with the same EHR would likely produce very different results. To make matters worse, most bug fixes of this type are within the realm of "routine maintenance" for the developer, so they're not typically publicized. Also, if it's a "behind the scenes" bug, it's possible that users wouldn't notice it — either before or after the fix. Therefore, results of the two studies could end up with differences that would be almost impossible for the researchers to understand or explain.

A final thing to consider is a concept called "user-friendliness" or "usability." Nielsen (2012) lists five key components to usability:

1. *Learnability*: How easy is the software to learn?
2. *Efficiency*: Once you've learned it, how quickly can you perform necessary tasks?
3. *Memorability*: How likely are you to remember how to use the software when you haven't used it for a while?
4. *Errors*: How many errors do you make, how serious are they, and how easy is it to recover from them?
5. *Satisfaction*: Do you enjoy using the software?

Some software developers put a great deal of effort into usability whereas others do not. Obviously, studies using EHRs with high usability marks are likely to produce very different results from studies which use less user-friendly EHRs.

Conclusions

In summary, most mental health EHRs and their users are likely to be very different than their physical health counterparts. Furthermore, there are substantial issues in trying to compare studies that use different EHRs or even in making the assumption that one EHR will stay the same over time. Perhaps we are asking the wrong question. Instead of trying to determine how to do better evidence-based research with EHRs, perhaps we need to look at whether we should be doing this type of research in the first place. An EHR is basically just a set of tools and services for the health-care provider, replacing things like paper charts, accounting software, and filing cabinets. We don't typically ask whether our filing cabinets and accounting software improve the quality of healthcare we provide. We just accept them as tools that, hopefully, keep our lives a bit more organized and make our practice management tasks easier.

On the other hand, we can and *should* conduct research with behavioral health EHRs to address meaningful use criteria such as standardization, security, and efficiency. It also seems reasonable to ask how specific *tools* in an EHR might affect patient outcome. For example, it's easy to imagine that tools such as patient portals or video platforms might translate into better patient care. Even here, though, we need to make sure our studies accurately define the specific tool being used (i.e., not just assume that one video platform or patient portal is equal to another) and also that we ask the correct questions. For example, when evaluating patient portals, does the portal offer secure email which allows the healthcare provider and patient to interact? Does the patient have access to their records? If so, which ones? Can the patient make corrections and/or additions to their records? Is the portal user-friendly for both the provider and the patient? Similar sets of questions would need to be answered when evaluating video platforms. Also, our studies need to be clear that we're evaluating a specific tool not EHRs themselves. Not all EHRs have these tools, and conversely, there are some standalone tools of this sort that do not provide the other features of EHRs. In summary, research is warranted to make sure our behavioral health EHRs are secure, efficient and have some type of standardization for common tasks. However, trying to extend the definition of meaningful use to apply to patient outcomes may be trying to contort an EHR into something it's not and was never intended to be.

References

Blumenthal, D., & Tavenner, M. (2010). The "meaningful use" regulation for electronic health records. *The New England Journal of Medicine, 363*, 501–504.

Emont, S. (2011). *Measuring the impact of patient portals: What the literature tells us.* Retrieved October 2014, from http://www.chcf.org/publications/2011/05/measuring-impact-patient-portals

Establishment of the Permanent Certification for Health Information Technology; Final Rule. Fed. Reg. 76, 5 (January 7, 2011) Rules and Regulations 45 CFR pt. 170.

Fleming, N. S., Culler, S. D., McCorkle, R., Becker, E. R., & Ballard, D. J. (2011). *The financial and nonfinancial costs of implementing electronic health records in primary care practices.* Web Site Disclaimers Health Aff.

How much is this going to cost me? (2013) Retrieved Oct 2014, from http://www.healthit.gov/providers-professionals/faqs/how-much-going-cost-me

Nielsen, J. (2012). *Usability 101: Introduction to usability.* Retrieved Oct 2014, from http://www.nngroup.com/articles/usability-101-introduction-to-usability/

Chapter 24
A Psychologist and a Software Developer

Mark R. McMinn

> *Computers themselves, and software yet to be developed, will*
> *revolutionize the way we learn.*
>
> (Steve Jobs)

Vignette

Dr. Johnson, a psychologist, welcomes her patient into the office for a psychotherapy session. She then hands the patient an iPad to administer the Outcome Rating Scale (ORS; Miller, Duncan, Brown, Sparks, & Claud, 2003), a 4-item rapid assessment instrument designed to measure patient well-being on a session-by-session basis. After 60 s, the patient hands the iPad back to Dr. Johnson who then presses a button and shows the patient a graph illustrating how therapy is progressing. Near the end of the session, Dr. Johnson again hands the iPad to the patient to administer the 4-item Session Rating Scale (SRS; Duncan et al., 2003), a working alliance measure. They briefly discuss the psychotherapist-patient relationship.

Dr. Johnson uses this iOS application (app), called the Therapy Outcome Management System (TOMS), with each of her patients, as do many other psychologists and counselors around the world. Whenever she wants, she can download a summary of her treatment effectiveness with all the patients she sees. And each time she uses the TOMS, she has the option of uploading de-identified data from her session to a cloud-based server for purposes of ongoing psychotherapy research. The database now has ORS and SRS data from over 25,000 psychotherapy sessions conducted in various countries.

M.R. McMinn, Ph.D. (✉)
Graduate Department of Clinical Psychology, George Fox University,
414 N. Meridian St. # V104, Newberg, OR 97132, USA
e-mail: mmcminn@georgefox.edu

© Springer International Publishing Switzerland 2017
M.M. Maheu et al. (eds.), *Career Paths in Telemental Health*,
DOI 10.1007/978-3-319-23736-7_24

Training

Several years ago, one of my graduate students, Nicholas Wiarda, approached me with the idea for the TOMS. Nick isn't a software developer, but he is a natural networker and he has good ideas. He did all the background work, securing permission to use the ORS and SRS and helping design the interface, while I did the coding. We released the TOMS in 2012 and have enjoyed seeing this app benefit therapists and patients throughout the world. In addition, we now have de-identified outcome and alliance data from over 25,000 psychotherapy sessions and are starting to explore new frontiers in how psychotherapy research might be done with "big data."

But I'm getting ahead of myself. Let me back up and review the training path that brought me to this point in my career.

I left the family farm at age 18 to study at Lewis and Clark College in Portland, Oregon. Because I love science and mathematics, a chemistry major seemed the natural choice. At some point along the way, I took an introductory psychology class and decided to add a psychology major. As I approached graduation, I struggled knowing whether I wanted to pursue graduate work in psychology or chemistry and ultimately decided on psychology.

Back in those days, some liberal arts colleges were testing an idea where they allowed students to take a computer language instead of a foreign language. It probably wasn't a good idea, but it has worked out fairly well for me. As a senior having not yet met my foreign language requirement, I opted to enroll in a BASIC (Beginner's All-Purpose Symbolic Instruction Code) class, having no idea how much that class would alter my professional goals and direction.

After college, I headed off to Vanderbilt University to get a PhD in clinical psychology. My research was in weight management, and I remember using my nascent computer skills in writing SPSS commands. Each week I would come to our research meetings with an armful of printouts from the university's high-speed dot matrix printer. My peers, professors, and I would study each result with interest. I also completed a minor in biochemistry by taking classes at the Vanderbilt Medical School, which helped in my predoctoral National Institute of Mental Health (NIMH) grant titled "psychobiochemistry and learned helplessness in the obese." About the time I graduated with my PhD, I also bought my first personal computer — a $3000 machine that did only a small fraction of what my phone does now.

After an internship and residency in medical psychology, I began teaching at a small college, which I have done throughout my career — first at George Fox College for 9 years, then at Wheaton College in Illinois for 13 years, and now back at George Fox University for 9 years. During all these years, I have been involved in writing software. Mostly it has been a vocation, but occasionally I have published software also.

During my early years as an academic, I taught an ethics class. It always seemed strange to me that we teach ethics using case studies where we already know the outcome. For example, the Tarasoff case in California seems relatively clear once we know that a scorned lover kills the woman he loves after disclosing his intentions to his psychotherapist. But what if we didn't know the outcome? If a psychotherapist simply knew that a patient had uttered a threat, would it affect the ethics decision-making process? To address this, I wrote a simple ethics case simulator where students were presented with limited information. Once they made a decision, then they were given additional information. The choices they made affected the information they then received, using a simple decision-based tree model. The simulator was published, though it has now been out of print for many years. Back in those early days, I also published software to teach students how to avoid gender-specific language. Sometime later, a doctoral student and I developed a computer-based system to teach Rorschach scoring, which was published by Psychological Assessment Resources until it went out of print.

About 5 years ago, I began doing software development and consulting for the Austen Group, a business that provides consulting services for independent colleges. My work with the Austen Group involved both psychometrics and software development as we developed tools to help college administrators consider the effectiveness of their sports programs. My work with the Austen Group continues, though it has decreased since RuffaloCODY acquired them in 2013.

Now, back to the present time and the TOMS. When Nick approached me about the TOMS, he quickly convinced me that it would work best on a mobile device. Though I had written software for 30 years, I didn't know how to write for phones or tablets. Over Christmas break that year I started the journey of learning Objective-C which was then the primary language used to write iOS software (Apple has since introduced a simpler language called Swift). Fortunately, a Stanford University course on iOS development was available on iTunes University. I watched each lecture multiple times, stopping frequently to practice the skills I was learning. Then a computer science colleague at George Fox University was kind enough to let me sit in on his iOS development class, which further reinforced what I had learned in the iTunes University class. On a sabbatical the previous year, I had also taken community college courses in database management and XML programming, both of which have proven useful in mobile application (app) development.

Beyond coursework and reading many books, learning a new computer language requires trial and error, and the patience to persist. For the first year or two of iOS development, I felt stuck more often than not, but it's amazing how many resources are available online. I can just type my programming dilemma into Google and sit in astonishment as I review online discussions that help me figure out how to move forward (e.g., stackoverflow.com is a great resource for developers, as are the Apple videos produced each year at the Worldwide Developers Conference).

With time, I became quite comfortable with iOS and now have over a dozen apps on the iTunes Store and Mac Store. These include psychotherapy monitoring apps, such as the TOMS, and also a suite of competency assessment products to help the APA-accredited doctoral program at George Fox University keep track of competencies achieved by students. I hope to make this competency assessment software available to other doctoral programs in the years to come.

Pros and Cons

Some people recommend doing crossword puzzles to maintain cognitive flexibility as one gets older. I figure writing software is just as good. For those who love it, as I do, it's a great intellectual challenge. Writing good software is a fascinating blend of engineering, creativity, science, and art.

Also, software development allows me to flexibly structure data sets so that they can be analyzed. For example, all the de-identified TOMS data is stored in a cloud-based database on a session-by-session basis. Each therapist, client, and session has a unique identification number generated by a process known as MD5 hash. This number can never be unencrypted, thereby making the data secure and anonymous. But the session-by-session data storage format isn't that useful by itself.

For example, if a cognitive therapist in Australia sees a client today and administers the ORS with the TOMS, then that ORS score is immediately uploaded to the ORS file stored in the database (assuming the therapist has granted permission to upload scores). If the therapist then administers the SRS at the end of the session, it is uploaded to the SRS file in the database. This happens dozens or even hundreds of times every day. While it might be interesting to look at a stack of 25,000 ORS scores, it would be much more useful to see these scores in context. How many sessions has this client completed, and what ORS and SRS scores were recorded for previous sessions? This requires that the ORS and SRS files in the database be reorganized and merged to create a single SPSS file that would then allow for these analyses. How can these large files be reorganized and merged? The only way I know is to write custom software to make it happen. This is the sort of flexibility that knowing software development affords me.

Another benefit pertains to rapport with my doctoral students. Most of my students are between 20 and 35 years of age, and they know a great deal about mobile devices. They sometimes seem surprised when they find out that a guy in his late-50s also knows something about apps and app development. It seems to build credibility.

I have also enjoyed clinical benefits to writing software. I have written numerous test-scoring software programs for my own use, both to save the expense of commercially available products and to reduce the errors that inevitably come with hand scoring. These cannot be made available to others because of copyright laws, but as long as I purchase the hand-scoring materials and double- and triple-check the accuracy of my scoring software, I feel comfortable using my own test-scoring software as a clinician.

Regarding cons, at this point, I have not found a way to make independent software development profitable. Though I was paid well for my consulting work with the Austen Group, most of my software development has been speculative and independent. In today's software market, most apps are either free or they sell very few copies. Even the TOMS, which sells better than any other app I have written and at a fairly steep price for apps ($14.99), only generates $300 on a typical month after Apple retains their 30%. This modest monthly revenue is then split between Nick, me, and the person who holds the copyright on the ORS and SRS. It's no way to make a living. If you are a mental health professional who takes on software development, I suggest you keep your day job.

Relatedly, it is quite time-consuming, especially as you are learning. Because software development requires intense concentration, I often spend time late at night or early in the morning writing code. When I add up all the late nights and early mornings, I must admit to spending a lot of time on something that generates very little income. That said, it does awaken a creative energy in me that is quite invigorating and enlivening.

I should also mention the challenge that comes with the rapid rate of change in the software world. Each year Apple comes out with a new mobile operating system, which means that every app needs to be revisited and revised each year, whether or not it is selling well enough to justify my time. The alternative would be to simply remove the app from the iTunes Store. As a consumer, I appreciate the frequent updates to the iOS operating system. As a developer, I don't.

Finally, one needs to be cautious about software bugs, especially when the software is available to other professionals. Even one significant error in a software program could have substantial implications for mental health care providers and those they serve.

Evidence Base

Psychotherapy outcome and process research is a deeply established tradition in health service psychology, forming the basis for the interventions psychologists offer (Barlow, 2008; Norcross, 2011). Most often this takes the form of randomized clinical trials (efficacy studies) or large-scale post hoc consumer satisfaction data (effectiveness studies). Smartphones and tablets and their low-cost applications (apps) provide another opportunity for large-scale outcome and process research. Whereas most effectiveness data is collected weeks, months, or even years after the completion of psychotherapy, the TOMS allows for real-time data collection in a cost-effective way and from a worldwide sample. The TOMS database affords my doctoral students and me opportunity to explore this new frontier for psychotherapy research.

In a recent symposium at the 2014 APA annual convention, four doctoral students and I reported data collected through the TOMS app. Each of the studies demonstrated how big data could be used as a supplement to traditional psychotherapy outcome and process research, drawing on data from the large-scale TOMS database to address a particular research question. One student explored the relationship between diagnosis and working alliance. Another studied whether a poor working alliance in the first session dooms the eventual outcome of psychotherapy. A third student questioned whether working alliance could be predicted based on therapist characteristics. The fourth student tried to identify predictors of successful outcome in psychotherapy. While the limited scope of this chapter precludes exploring these findings in detail, each of these research questions illustrates how the TOMS app can be used to promote evidence-based practice among psychotherapists.

Another student I supervise is currently completing his doctoral dissertation using data from the TOMS database. He is asking six focused research questions that he will be able to address from the data. This dissertation fascinates me not only because of the six questions he is addressing, but because it illustrates emerging possibilities for how psychotherapy data may be collected in the future.

As the database grows in the years ahead, the potential for meaningful research will also grow. Just as big data is transforming business and education, so it may also bring benefit to understanding how and when psychotherapy works well, and when it does not.

References

Barlow, D. H. (Ed.). (2008). *Clinical handbook of psychological disorders*. New York, NY: Guilford.

Duncan, B. L., Miller, S. D., Sparks, J. A., Claud, D. A., Reynolds, L. R., Brown, J., & Johnson, L. D. (2003). The Session Rating Scale: Preliminary psychometric properties of a "working alliance" inventory. *Journal of Brief Therapy, 3*, 3–11.

Miller, S. D., Duncan, B. L., Brown, J., Sparks, J. A., & Claud, D. A. (2003). The Outcome Rating Scale: A preliminary study of the reliability, validity, and feasibility of a brief visual analog measure. *Journal of Brief Therapy, 2*, 91–100.

Norcross, J. C. (Ed.). (2011). *Psychotherapy relationships that work*. New York, NY: Oxford.

Chapter 25

Primary Care Psychology in a Military Treatment Facility: The Internal Behavioral Health Consultant (IBHC)

Gerald R. Quimby

> *"We learn more by looking for the answer to a question and not finding it than we do from learning the answer itself."* Lloyd Alexander

Relaxation for a Stressed Navy Spouse

It is 8:00 in the morning and the medical staff is gathering for the morning huddle. This is a brief meeting to get the staff on the same page for the day's activities. During the huddle, announcements are made, staffing issues are discussed, upcoming procedures are noted, patient care issues are discussed, and provider availabilities are announced. As an IBHC, I state my availability for appointments and bring up issues the clinic team may need to know. Most huddles are short, lasting about 10 min. Following the huddle, I meet with the physicians whose patients I saw the day before to brief them on patient progress and any issues of which they need to be aware. After these short physician briefs, I return to my office, check through my appointments for the day, and begin to review the notes of the day's upcoming patients.

At 8:20, one of the medical assistants walks into my office to inform me that she has booked a patient at 8:30. She tells me the patient is a 24-year-old married woman

The views expressed in this article are those of the author and do not necessarily reflect the official policy or position of the Department of the Navy, Department of Defense, nor the US Government.

G.R. Quimby, Psy.D., M.A., M.S. (✉)
Loyal Source Govt. Services, Inc., 36 Island Drive, Middletown, RI 02842, USA
e-mail: drgrquimby@gmail.com

with two young children who came to see Dr. Smyth because she was having trouble breathing and experiencing pressure on her chest. The medical assistant then tells me that the patient's labs and EKG were all negative and that her vitals were normal. She ends by saying, "Doc thought you should see her because she was anxious and crying during the whole exam and afraid she had a bad heart."

In the few minutes I have before I see her, I glance through the EMR (electronic medical record) to review her appointment history, medical issues, past and present medications, and recent labs; I found nothing remarkable. Mostly visits to the clinic associated with her two uncomplicated pregnancies and regular well-woman checks. Her labs were also unremarkable and she was not currently taking any prescription medications. Also of note, there was no recorded family history of heart disease, diabetes, hypertension, or high cholesterol. Given this information, my initial impression is that this is an otherwise healthy young woman. I go out to the waiting area and greet my patient and lead her back to my office.

Because she is a new patient to me, I begin our appointment by stating an introductory script which clearly describes who I am, what I do, what she can expect, and a notice about the limits of confidentiality (Navy Bureau of Medicine and Surgery, 2012; Rowan & Runyan, 2005). After she acknowledges understanding, I begin the assessment by telling the patient, "Dr. Smyth was concerned about your tearfulness during his exam and thought it would be a good idea if I were to talk to you. Is this your understanding of why you are here?" The patient nods and takes a tissue to her eyes as tears begin forming at the corner of her eyes.

She tells me that she and her husband have only been in Hawaii for a month after being transferred from Connecticut. She complained that her husband is already deployed again. He is on a submarine and will be underway for several months. She is unable to talk to him every day. "I feel like I'm chasing my tail all day long," she tells me. She goes on about her children, two boys ages 2 and 4 years old, who are constantly getting into things. She complains that she has problems with the plumbing in her home and the landlord does not seem to be in a hurry to fix it. In addition, she is frustrated that her friends and family are 5000 miles away and not always available when she needs to talk because of the time difference. She says that this is making her feel so alone here in Hawaii. She speaks for a few more minutes about all the aforementioned issues and ends with, "and I have a headache that won't go away."

I notice that as she speaks, she often strays off into several side stories providing background and detail of her issues. I refocus her by asking questions to investigate differential diagnoses and that also help me narrow down her myriad concerns into a more manageable conceptualization of her overarching problem(s) that we can tackle in our 30-min appointment. After 10 min, I summarize what she has told me and share what I have determined to be her primary problem.

"It sounds like you have quite a bit on your plate. I have a sense that you are feeling overwhelmed with having to be the only one to take care of everything around the home with no one else to turn to."

She nods enthusiastically and blurts out, "Yes! Yes! It's just too much to do by myself. I don't know what to do so I do nothing and then things get worse. I'm like so stressed."

"Exactly" I reply.

She continues, "And now on top of everything else I'm having problems breathing and my chest doesn't feel right, and Dr. Smyth can't find anything wrong and ..."

I interrupt to explain how stress adversely affects many systems in the body (Lovallo, 2005) and how autonomic arousal relates to her current situation and makes her feel the way she does (e.g., headache, fatigue, unable to concentrate). My goal here is to provide this patient with a basic education about how stress affects the body and then discuss with her some evidence-based methods to manage it (Hunter, Goodie, Oordt, & Dobmeyer, 2009). I normalize her experience by telling her that what she is experiencing is common among military wives (Easterling & Knox, 2010) and point out the good news: there are several things she can do to improve her ability to cope with her daily stressors. We discuss several options for her self-based stress management (e.g., a thought diary, reconnecting with family, keeping a video journal of her daily experiences to send to her husband or share when he returns, deep breathing to managing an immediately stressful situation, connecting with other military wives on base for support). After a brief discussion, she indicates that she would like to learn how to do deep breathing, because she sometimes gets so stressed in the moment that she feels like she is spinning out of control; she recognizes this is problematic for a mother of two young children! Together, we practice deep breathing in the appointment. Then, she practices individually to the point that she feels like she can properly do it on her own at home.

It is important to note that while I am talking with the patient, I am going online to retrieve handouts on anxiety, stress, stress management, and relaxation. As an IBHC, I have access to several online resources provided by the DoD which offer a collection of informational handouts covering a wide variety of behavioral health topics. I navigate to the section on stress management to download the appropriate handouts to print and give to the patient to take home and read. We briefly go over the handouts which help demystify the deep breathing process and help motivate her to trying them as our primary intervention in this appointment. I also recommend that she browse the App Store on her smartphone to search for relaxation and meditation apps that she likes and to use them daily. I give her a sheet which lists some that I have personally checked out and recommend. I caution her to choose apps from reputable sources and that I would like to see the one(s) she has selected during our next appointment.

I end the appointment by writing out a behavioral prescription for her:

1. Read the stress handouts and practice the recommendations given.
2. Practice the relaxation exercises daily.

I also encourage her to find other military wives to talk with. I point out that Easterling and Knox (2010) found this to be the most helpful stress reduction activity for military wives. We set a follow-up appointment with the plan to work on specific things she can do to manage her world while keeping her stress level under control. Her medical record was updated throughout the appointment so that her primary care treatment team can see what we are doing.

Later that day I follow up with Dr. Smyth, her primary care provider, and explain that I believe that she is experiencing acute stress due to several major life changes including dealing with the move to Hawaii, not being settled in before her husband was deployed, and feeling isolated from friends and family. All of this is compounded by the normal stress of motherhood. I explain that the treatment plan will be to utilize behavioral methods to reduce her anxiety, improve her physiological reaction to stress, and increase her local base of support. Dr. Smyth asks if I believe that she would benefit from medication. Although I am familiar with antianxiety medications, I am not a prescriber and medication management is outside my scope of expertise. However, as a behavioral health consultant, I tell him that I would prefer to give the behavioral methods a trial first given that evidence suggest these will improve the patient's symptoms and that the patient stated that she preferred to not take medications. Dr. Smyth agrees to the plan and heads off to see his next patient. I head back to my office just in time to dial into the monthly IBHC teleconference call.

Training Requirements

Pathways to the Position

The Internal Behavioral Health Consultant position is filled by a mental health professional. This is a fairly broad term which includes social workers, mental health counselors, marriage and family therapists, psychologists, psychiatric nurse practitioners, and psychiatrists. Currently the position tends to be filled by master's-level clinical social workers and doctoral-level psychologists (Rowan & Runyan, 2005). Licensed professional counselors (LPC and LMHC) and licensed marriage and family therapists (LMFT), although licensed for independent practice in many states, have only just recently been recognized by the Veteran's Administration and Department of Defense as independent practitioners, and it is not likely that they would be selected for a DoD IBHC position. Overall, health psychologists are best suited for this position due to their training in mental health and specialization in medical conditions.

Healthcare within the DoD is comprised of a heterogeneous workforce with a mix of active duty military, public health service, civilian government employees, and government contractors. Likewise, the IBHC position is filled by any one of the aforementioned types of government employment. It is also worth noting that although this chapter is written from the point of view of an IBHC in the Navy's program, the Army and Air Force (Wilson, 2004) have the same position under similar titles. While the Army, Navy, and Air Force each have their own name for the overall program, they generally use the title Internal Behavioral Health Consultant for the actual position. If you're wondering why I left out the Marine Corps and the Coast Guard, fear not. The Marines are cared for through the services of Naval Medicine, and the Coast Guard (of which I am a veteran) generally rely on whatever medical facility, military or civilian, is most accessible due to its small size and locations. At least one IBHC position can be found at all Military Treatment Facilities (MTF) that service at least 3000 adult enrollees (Department of Defense, 2013). This includes hospitals and branch clinics throughout the United States, with some locations overseas such as Guam and Spain as well.

Basic Education

An IBHC is required to hold the minimum of a master's degree in a behavioral health-related field of study from an accredited institution. The accreditation is a combination of the school's regional and professional accreditation such as the Southern Association of Colleges and Schools (SACS), American Psychological Association (APA), or National Association of Social Workers (NASW). The IBHC must be licensed at the highest level for independent practice. This means that as a provider, you can practice independently and without supervision.

Core Competencies

Preferred Training and Experience

There are many aspects of integrated behavioral health practice that set it apart from the typical mental health therapist practice, so simply meeting the basic educational requirements is no guarantee that you will be hired as an IBHC. First of all, you will be working in a medical setting with physicians, nurses, and medical assistants (Haas & deGruy, 2004). For those coming from a purely mental health setting or small practice, they may find the medical setting quite foreign. Having some experience working in a medical setting will make you more attractive to the services as you will have gained familiarity and hopefully comfort with the fast-paced environment and interacting with medical professionals.

As an IBHC, your work often requires some degree of knowledge of human physiology and systems. This is not typically taught in graduate schools for social and behavioral sciences, so having continuing professional education in areas outside your profession is generally a must. For example, I worked with a patient who was referred to me for anxiety after having several emergency room visits for heart palpitations and chest pain. The medical records indicated normal cardiac function and that the patient was quite healthy. While conducting the assessment, I found that along with the typical symptoms of anxiety (increased heart rate, heavy chest, short and rapid breaths, tension, perspiration) the patient described other symptoms that are not typical of anxiety (nausea, shaking hands, confusion, tingling, and hunger). Interestingly, the patient said that those feelings resolve after he eats something like an apple, something he neglected to disclose to his physician.

As one of my mentors like to put it, "Sometimes dogs can have tics AND fleas." In this particular case, the tics can be the anxiety and the fleas, hypoglycemia (low blood sugar). Upon further exploration of the patient's diet and exercise routines, it was found that his diet was high in carbohydrates. This high-carb diet was likely causing an insulin spike, ultimately leading to hypoglycemic attacks. Many times patients will tell the IBHC things that they do not talk to their primary care provider about. Therefore, it will be up to you to relay this information to the provider.

When describing patients, psychologists can be verbose and even overly "wordy." Physicians are not. I am convinced that the word "terse" came into being with modern medicine. One of the first things you will have to get used to is working within the framework of the "2-min drill." In essence, the IBHC has no more than 2 min to fully describe the patient, his or her condition, current and past treatments and effectiveness, prognosis, and recommendations. This is an exercise drilled into physicians from application to medical school through residency. Psychologists on the other hand are trained in writing incredibly effusive psychological assessments (that sometime resemble novellas) so the transition can be quite challenging for some.

Training Provided

The IBHC position was created in the primary care model and with the primary care environment in mind. This model sharply differs from the usual and customary therapeutic practice of the fifty-minute hour. Instead, the IBHC works within the framework of a 20–30-min appointment. Additionally, the focus is on short-term intervention with the goal of self-sustainment. This is typically accomplished in four visits or less. While not typical for most mental health providers, this is very much in the mold of medical encounters with primary care physicians.

This change in methodology requires the therapist to obtain specialized training in order to get into the rhythm of the patient encounter in medical model of care. This is so important that such training is required before an IBHC is permitted to see patients. When you are hired for the position, you will be required to attend the IBHC training which lasts 1 week. The training is comprised of a series of lectures and discussion to orient you to the history, principles, and future goals of the model. The majority of time is spent in intensive simulated patient care. This provides practice in working within the model and features many role-play scenarios of varying complexity that are designed to help the trainee gain some degree of confidence and comfort in working in this fast-paced model and with health-related presenting problems.

During the simulated patient care training, trainees alternate between fulfilling the role of the IBHC and the role of the patient. The trainees provide feedback to one another, and there are expert instructors who observe and evaluate trainee performance and offer helpful suggestions and recommendations to sharpen assessment and therapeutic skills. The overarching idea during this simulated patient care is that this patient will only see you once. You may not be able to resolve his or her problem, but what intervention could you give to improve this patient's functioning? As you can imagine, it is very fast-paced and anxiety provoking at first, but as you gain experience, you begin to feel more comfortable and settle into the new process.

All Things Considered

What to Expect

Having your profession identified with solely "mental illness" poses some obstacles in a medical setting. As a psychologist, I often find that I must first convince my patients that just because their primary care provider referred them to me it does not mean that mental illness is suspected. It is difficult for patients to understand why they are seeing a psychologist when they have hypertension, irritable bowel syndrome, or chronic pain. On the other hand, as an IBHC, you are not able to provide the kind of therapeutic services you may be accustomed to providing.

For example, where you may be used to the traditional eight to twelve 1-h sessions, the IBHC is working in 1–4 medical-style appointment of 20–30 min each using primarily cognitive and behaviorally based interventions (Hunter, Goodie, Oordt, & Dobmeyer, 2009). For patients who require more long-term treatment, the IBHC will refer patients to specialty services. The IBHC focuses on the psychological issues affecting the patient's immediate overall health, whereas the traditional therapy typically focuses on exploring the patient's more entrenched and deeply-rooted mental health problems.

Working as an IBHC is challenging, exciting, and at times, stressful. Working in a primary care environment, you never know when a new patient will walk in your door, so you have no idea of what conditions you will encounter on any given day. The day could be composed of routine cases or sprinkled with difficult and complex ones. You learn to expect the unexpected and expect to be exposed to new and novel presenting problems. Working in primary care truly is a growth experience where you find how much you know and how much you have yet to learn. This is the inspiration for the quote at the beginning of this chapter.

Technology

Depending on where you work, there will be varying levels of technology infrastructure. While some offices are using shiny new workstations, you may find yourself with outdated equipment and software that can make your job more challenging.

Computer security is a highly visible and a serious matter in healthcare, especially within the government sector. As such, things that we take for granted such as using a thumb drive or viewing video on YouTube® can be restricted and unusable. This can make your interventions more challenging as there are many outstanding resources available on YouTube that *could* be utilized in sessions, but restricted access to such media may make it impossible. Of course, the work-around is to have the patient view it at home. However, sometimes it is best if the IBHC is there to answer questions or clarify complex information.

Weighing the Good with the Bad

While this chapter describes the IBHC position within the DoD healthcare system, you should know that psychologists and clinical social workers are finding their way into more and more primary care settings around the country (DeLeon, Rossomando, & Smedley, 2004). There are different arrangements as well, such as being a direct employee of the hospital, clinic, or practice; contracting with a clinic; or being just an "on-call" consultant. As you can imagine, each arrangement has its own set of pros and cons. For example, the military likes to begin the day at "O-dark-thirty." If you like to sleep in, this could be a problem; if you're an early riser, not so much.

The IBHC working in primary care is successfully using existing technologies to augment treatment in ways that advance the clinician's knowledge base and skills but also giving patient's the tools they can use on their own. To accomplish this, the IBHC must be familiar with all the resources that they "prescribe" to their patients. Not only how to use them but also to note any potential for harm, loss of privacy and confidentiality, and misinformation. Working within a 20–30-min patient encounter, we are indeed fortunate to have these technologies that allow us to extend our reach and reinforce our interventions through the various tools we have at our disposal. The Internet, smartphone apps, secure video, email, and all the associated applications challenge us to find new and effective ways to promote and maintain good health. Knowing what is available and how to apply the technology can go a long way toward providing effective healthcare.

References

DeLeon, P. H., Rossomando, N. A., & Smedley, B. D. (2004). The future is primary care. In M. Heldring, R. G. Frank, S. H. McDaniel, & J. H. Bray (Eds.), *Primary care psychology* (pp. 317–325). Washington, DC: American Psychological Association.
Department of Defense. (2013). *Integration of Behavioral Health Personnel (BHP) Services Into Patient-Centered Medical Home (PCMH) primary care and other primary care service settings.* Department of Defense Instruction Number 6490.15.

Easterling, B., & Knox, D. (2010). Left behind: How military wives experience the deployment of their husbands. *Journal of Family Life*. Retrieved from http://www.journaloffamilylife.org/militarywives.html

Haas, L. J., & deGruy, F. V. (2004). Primary care, psychology, and primary care psychology. In L. J. Haas (Ed.), *Handbook of primary care psychology* (pp. 5–19). New York: Oxford University Press.

Hunter, C. L., Goodie, J. L., Oordt, M. S., & Dobmeyer, A. C. (2009). *Integrated behavioral health in primary care: Step-by-step guidance for assessment and intervention*. Washington, DC: American Psychological Association.

Lovallo, W. R. (2005). *Stress & Health. Biological and psychological interactions*. Thousand Oaks, CA: Sage.

Navy Bureau of Medicine and Surgery. (2012). *Behavioral Health Integration Program in the Medical Home Port: Practice standards manual*. Version 1. Washington, DC.

Rowan, A. B., & Runyan, C. N. (2005). A primer on the consultation model of primary care behavioral health integration. In L. C. James & R. A. Folen (Eds.), *The primary care consultant* (pp. 9–27). Washington, DC: American Psychological Association.

Wilson, P. G. (2004). The air force experience: Integrating behavioral health providers into primary care. In S. H. McDaniel, J. H. Bray, M. Heldring, & R. G. Frank (Eds.), *Primary care psychology* (pp. 169–185). Washington, DC: American Psychological Association.

Chapter 26
Promoting and Evaluating Evidence-Based Telepsychology Interventions: Lessons Learned from the University of Kentucky Telepsychology Lab

Robert J. Reese and Norah Chapman

> *"Injustice anywhere is a threat to justice everywhere."*
> *- Martin Luther King, Jr.*

Our paths to being introduced and ultimately excited about telepsychology are distinct and yet inextricably linked. We present our "telepsychology" stories separately to provide our unique and yet also shared perspectives on the promise of using technology to deliver psychological services. We will also share what we have learned along the way that has influenced our clinical understanding of providing services both using technology and in person. We will also present our perceptions influenced by our research findings conducted as part of the University of Kentucky Telepsychology Research Lab.

Robert J. Reese: I Needed a Job!

After receiving my master's degree in clinical psychology, I decided to work for a year to save money before applying to graduate programs to pursue my doctoral degree. A job opening at an employee assistance program (EAP) was not my first choice, but there were not many options in the city I lived so I jumped at the opportunity. The EAP provided brief, solution-focused counseling telephonically to employees across North America who worked for the companies served by the EAP. I was not wild about the position, mainly because the counseling services

R.J. Reese, Ph.D. (✉)
University of Kentucky, Lexington, KY, USA
e-mail: jeff.reese@uky.edu

N. Chapman
Spalding University, Louisville, KY, USA

© Springer International Publishing Switzerland 2017
M.M. Maheu et al. (eds.), *Career Paths in Telemental Health*,
DOI 10.1007/978-3-319-23736-7_26

provided at the EAP were telephonically based, but the pay was pretty good, and my good friend from my master's program was going to work there, too. We were not very optimistic about counseling on the telephone working, but we also needed a paycheck. We would joke that we were working for a "fast-food" service and would say things like, "Would you like fries with that reframe?"

Then we actually started providing services telephonically, and quite simply, we were blown away. I noticed several things—I will mention a few here. First, counseling over the phone and in person was similar in many ways. The basic counseling skills acquired from my training and in-person practicum experiences were easily transferable. We could not see each other but generally this felt like a nonissue. I learned to ask about what I could not see. Second was that it seemed that the counseling process was generally the same but, at times, seemed to be faster. Clients often seemed to get to the point quicker, leaving me wondering if it was the feeling of anonymity or that we were able to connect with people more quickly given that the time between requesting a session was shorter. Perhaps it was both things. Third, I quickly began to realize I was working with people who either did not have the financial resources for mental health counseling, typically have no insurance, or have insurance with inadequate mental health coverage or they were living in areas where there were few professional counselors. I was working with individuals who often had no other option for mental health services. My friend and I quickly came to view telephone counseling very, very differently! Not only were we helping people but we were helping those who often had few other professional options.

For example, I can remember conducting a couple counseling session with a truck driver on the road and his partner was back home. The telephone allowed for the convenience of meeting in different places and also allowed them to deal with their situation sooner rather than later. I learned two things from the series of sessions with this couple. First, they admitted not seeing one another, and the telephone made it easier to talk to each other without getting upset—more focus was placed on content of the message without being distracted by facial expressions. This process was important to recognize and something I have tried to emulate for in-person couple treatment by having partners turn their back to one another and communicate when intense emotions become counterproductive. Second was that technology offers an opportunity to offer services to those who would be less likely to see a mental health professional in person. Counseling on the telephone was perceived by the truck driver as an "easy way to try out this counseling stuff."

As I prepared for returning to graduate school in 1996, I went to the psychotherapy outcome literature to see the research on telepsychology services. I was shocked to find very few studies, and most of the studies I found were of marginal quality. I had found a dissertation idea, although telepsychology was not yet considered mainstream in psychology. My dissertation evaluated treatment effectiveness of the EAP where I worked compared to in-person study benchmarks. My results found what I expected—treatment outcomes and the therapeutic bond were equivalent across treatment formats (Reese, Conoley, & Brossart, 2002). Clients also indicated that they valued convenience more than anonymity, cost, or control of the session (e.g., could hang up), and the majority of clients who had received counseling in person and over the telephone preferred the telephone (Reese, Conoley, & Brossart, 2006). Although the study contributed to advancing telepsychology research, the lessons I learned from my experience contributed to more questions that continue to inform the direction of my career today.

Norah Chapman: I Wanted to Graduate!

I was introduced to the field of telepsychology by way of my dissertation chair and major advisor, Robert J. Reese (Jeff). While his telepsychology interest was intriguing to me from a research perspective from the beginning of my program, I was enamored with it after practicing in this area under his supervision. Similar to Jeff's process, I developed an unexpected affinity and appreciation for this work. I first became attracted to the convenience of telepsychology, but quickly connected to the meaningfulness of the work it afforded us to do.

In graduate school, efficiency can mean survival. I quickly identified that using technology to conduct psychological services meant I could practice from the convenience of our campus telemedicine department. I was able to participate in videoconference-based training on campus, simultaneously linked to professionals in India conducting similar work to our research team. All I had to do was walk down the street from my department to join, and I had fascinating multicultural exchanges and valuable clinical training.

From this initial exposure, I was eager to participate in Jeff's research team to develop and evaluate videoconferencing-based psychological services with underserved population. As one of the practitioners delivering the intervention, I was able to see firsthand how telepsychology had the potential to significantly improve accessibility for families with psychological needs. I will never forget the clients we served who made me look beyond my privilege of convenience and taught me a number of valuable lessons about the effectiveness of telepsychology. First, just as I had experienced on campus, I was able to hear that clients only had to make a short drive to a nearby agency to access the services we were providing, rather than driving over an hour to access them in person. Such convenience allowed for more equity, in that telepsychology seemed to be a viable way to support families' needs in a way that did not mean extensive travel time, cost, or time away from work. Second, the technology allowed us to conduct the program in approximately the same way as we would have done in person, such as show videos and conduct synchronous discussion. Third, conducting the project as a research study allowed us to extend the evidence base of services. It was our hope that extending the empirical support would help improve the likelihood that others would implement such programs in areas where accessibility to psychological services was low and establish its credibility for services to be covered by insurance.

Such lessons learned from our telepsychology lab were invaluable, particularly in the early stages of my training. The experiences I gain in both the research and practice of telepsychology did not just contribute to progress in my training, but it became significantly meaningful work that I am dedicated to continuing now as an early career psychologist.

Lessons Learned from the UK Telepsychology Research Lab

Group training. We have been involved in multiple research studies as part of our lab that have generally focused on service delivery formats that have less research attention, particularly the use of a group format. We completed a study focused on providing group parent training to help improve child behavior and parenting self-efficacy with families in rural areas (Reese, Slone, Soares, & Sprang, 2015). We provided the Group Triple P (Sanders, 1999), an evidence-based parent training program, using videoconference technology that was supplemented with individual telephone-based consultations. In general, we learned that providing psychoeducational services in a group format can work quite well. We also learned a number of lessons not only about the use of technology but also about a community engagement model in which to offer such services.

First, we learned that to have a successful intervention program with families in rural areas, we would need to recruit and also bridge a number of cultural factors to establish our credibility with referral sources. Doing so meant traveling to rural counties to meet such professionals in person, as well as learning how to "market" our program in a culturally sensitive way to successfully reach the population we hoped to target. For example, we learned that delivering the intervention in a school setting versus a counseling center or hospital would reduce barriers of stigma. Second, we learned through our research study that the Group Triple P worked about as well in person as it did through videoconferencing on child behavior and parenting self-efficacy (Reese et al., 2014). Such equity across conditions supports intervention effectiveness and, we hope, builds credibility for insurance reimbursement. In addition to the community engagement model of project development and equitable program outcomes across conditions, we noted several differences in the process by which services were delivered that warrant consideration for future research and practice. We describe each below.

Humor. Throughout the group intervention, we attempted to use humor to develop and maintain rapport with families. We noticed that our attempts to make brief jokes did not get the same response as they did in person. Not even a polite chuckle. Parents often just looked at the camera or smiled politely. As we processed this experience, we often wondered if the brief lag in transmission somehow made it difficult for the same effect to occur through the technology as it would in person. We wondered if such nuances in communication were not transmitted as effectively through technology and what, if any, altercations would need to be made to our communication style for such distinctions to be transmitted the way it was intended.

Group dynamics. Another process difference noted was related to managing group dynamics. As clinicians who ran multiple in-person groups prior to this study, we were well versed in knowing how to manage members who tended to monopolize the conversation. One of the clients in a group often shared her experience of feeling overwhelmed as the caregiver of her grandchildren. She tended to speak more than other parents about her experiences each week. At one point in the group discussion, I (NS) noticed this dynamic becoming a pattern and knew some intervention needed to occur to ensure other parents had the opportunity to share. When intervening with such group members in person, I typically politely interrupt the person to pause them for a moment to summarize and then check in with group members to see what they are thinking; however, when doing so over videoconferencing, the parent either continued to talk or other parents remained quiet. I, ultimately, had to learn to be more direct with facilitating group process effectively over videoconferencing.

Cultural differences. The final difference noted in the process was related to cultural considerations. For example, the Group Triple P (Sanders, 1999) program uses video demonstrations with Australian families who have heavy accents. Families in rural areas commented occasionally that the video demonstrations were difficult to understand. In fact, a few families were at times put off by the way in which the information was shared on screen. One mother reflected that those in the area we were serving did not speak that way, reflecting a cultural disconnect. Given that the demonstrations were being transmitted through videoconferencing, we wondered if the accent seemed more pronounced. It may be beneficial to ensure that materials used in evidence-based programs adapted for telepsychology be culturally consistent with those whom are being served.

Group telesupervision. Another opportunity for the use of technology is to provide psychotherapy supervision. A study completed in our lab had supervisees compare their in-person and videoconference group supervision experiences (Reese et al., 2009). Supervisees had half of their supervision sessions in each format for the academic semester. At the conclusion of the semester, they rated the supervisory working alliance and supervision satisfaction similarly across formats. Qualitatively, supervisees reported that the videoconference format promoted "getting down to business faster" and contributed to being more time efficient. Again, we found that technology did not negatively alter the processes of service delivery, which seems to fit our understanding of the broader telehealth literature. Specific to supervision, this has implications for training. Currently, the American Psychological Association Commission on Accreditation (2014) limits telesupervision to no more than 50 % of the clinical supervision provided for a practicum experience. Why 50 %? More research needs to be done in this area, but our research and experience have found these formats to yield similar supervisory outcomes. The finding of equivalence in comparison to in-person services seems to be the prevailing norm whether the focus is on adults, children, group therapy, telesupervision, or even different types of technology. Although videoconferencing is the only telepsychology format that is eligible for third-party reimbursement, telephonic-based psychotherapy outcomes have been found to be equivalent to those in person (e.g., Mohr et al., 2012).

Empathic accuracy and therapeutic alliance. Although there are several studies indicating the equivalence of treatment outcomes using telepsychology and in-person, we were curious if the processes were perceived as similar by clients given our experiences with some of the subtle differences noted earlier. We conducted a study

(Reese et al., 2014) that compared empathic accuracy and the therapeutic alliance with volunteer clients who were randomly assigned to a telephone, videoconference, or in-person-based counseling session. Briefly defined, empathic accuracy is the ability to correctly identify the emotion or thought expressed by another. We found that empathic accuracy and alliance ratings were similar across delivery formats. The finding that surprised us was that empathic accuracy predicted the therapeutic alliance in the telephone and videoconference formats but not in person. Specifically, it appears that empathic accuracy plays a more crucial role when counseling is delivered using technology. Perhaps the format change and/or the differences in available visual information result in more emphasis being placed on feeling understood by the therapist. A clinical implication may be that a therapist providing telepsychology services needs to take extra care to make empathic statements with clients.

Conclusions

Our clinical and research experiences with telepsychology have left us to conclude that using technology can be an effective medium for providing an array of psychological services for people who are geographically isolated and/or have difficulty accessing traditional services. Our experiences with individuals from eastern Kentucky and low socioeconomic backgrounds have been encouraging and, at times, inspiring. Specific to our experience, evidence-based group parenting interventions can be transported to technology-based service delivery formats and yield similar outcomes to in-person group parent training. Telepsychology also offers the promise to be a social justice application of applied psychology, allowing for services to be provided more easily to underserved populations.

We have also learned that the clinician should carefully consider how one's skills translate to different technology formats. The use of humor, communicating empathy, and perhaps several other dimensions seem to have subtle differences that are magnified when cultural and social contexts are considered. These subtleties need to be further fleshed out in future research and offer exciting opportunities for telepsychology researchers to address. Our hope is to continue contributing to research that will help promote the promise that telepsychology offers to enlarge psychology's positive impact on society.

References

American Psychological Association Commission on Accreditation. (2014). *Commission on accreditation implementing regulations.* Retrieved from http://www.apa.org/Ed./accreditation/about/policies/implementing-guidelines.pdf

Mohr, D. C., Ho, J., Duffecy, J., Reifler, D., Sokol, L., Burns, M. N., ... Siddique, J. (2012). Effect of telephone-administered vs face-to-face cognitive behavioral therapy on adherence to therapy and depression outcomes among primary care patients. *JAMA: Journal of the American Medical Association, 307,* 2278–2285. doi:10.1001/jama.2012.5588.

Reese, R. J., Conoley, C. W., & Brossart, D. F. (2002). Effectiveness of telephone counseling: A field based investigation. *Journal of Counseling Psychology, 49*, 233–242. doi:10.1037/0022-0167.49.2.233

Reese, R. J., Conoley, C. W., & Brossart, D. F. (2006). The attractiveness of telephone counseling: An empirical investigation of client perceptions. *Journal of Counseling and Development, 84*, 54–60. doi:10.1002/j.1556-6678.2006.tb00379.x

Reese, R. J., Aldarondo, F., Anderson, C. R., Lee, S., Miller, T. W., & Burton, D. (2009). Telehealth in clinical supervision: A comparison of supervision formats. *Journal of Telemedicine and Telecare, 15*, 356–361. doi:10.1258/jtt.2009.090401

Reese, R. J., Mecham, M. R., Vasilj, I., Simpson, N. B., Lengerich, A. J., Brown, H. M., & Cornett, H. L. (2014, August). *The effects of telepsychology format on the therapeutic alliance and empathic accuracy.* Poster presented at the annual meeting of the American Psychological Association Conference, Washington, DC.

Reese, R. J., Slone, N. C., Soares, N., & Sprang, R. (2015). Using telepsychology to provide a group parenting program: A preliminary evaluation of effectiveness. *Psychological Services, 12*, 274–282. doi:10.1037/ser0000018

Sanders, M. R. (1999). The Triple P Positive Parenting Program: Towards an empirically validated multilevel parenting and family support strategy for the prevention of behavior and emotional problems in children. *Clinical Child and Family Psychology Review, 2*, 71–90. Retrieved from http://www.springerlink.com/content/104849/?MUD=MP

Chapter 27
Virtual Reality Therapy for Treatment of Psychological Disorders

Max M. North and Sarah M. North

> *"The most important attribute of intelligence is kindness."*
>
> – Unknown

Vignette

Virtual Reality Therapy scenarios enable clients to face their deepest fears in a nonthreatening and controlled environment, becoming gradually desensitized. Such a cutting-edge VRT experiment and research is being conducted at the state-of-the-art Visualization & Simulation (VS) Research Center at Southern Polytechnic State University. The center's environment provides unique opportunities for researchers and students to conduct multidisciplinary and collaborative research. The highlight of the research conducted in prior Virtual Reality Laboratories and at the VS research center is the groundbreaking discovery that resulted from the first known controlled studies of virtual reality in the treatment of psychological disorders, pioneered by Dr. Max North and colleagues. Reports of these innovative research studies have been published in prestigious scientific journals and conference proceedings and are being followed by other scientists. These studies have not only attracted serious scientists to this area of research, they have resulted in numerous queries and coverage by several television networks, including CBS, radio stations, and newspapers, including the New York Times, London Times, U.S. News, and the Atlanta Journal Constitution. This research established a new paradigm that appears to be attracting serious scientists from the computer science, psychology, and medical fields.

M.M. North, Ph.D. (✉)
Visualization & Simulation Research Center, Southern Polytechnic State University,
Marietta, GA, USA
e-mail: dr.max.north@gmail.com

S.M. North, Ph.D.
Computer Science Department, College of Science and Mathematics, Kennesaw State
University, Kennesaw, GA, USA

© Springer International Publishing Switzerland 2017
M.M. Maheu et al. (eds.), *Career Paths in Telemental Health*,
DOI 10.1007/978-3-319-23736-7_27

A typical complete procedure of administrating VRT is as follows:

A screening process is conducted to ensure that the client has no serious physical or psychological conditions and is suffering from a fear of public speaking. The client, before each session, completes an ATPSQ (Attitude Toward Public Speaking Questionnaire). This measurement indicates where the client is improving and where the client is continuing to experience problems. During the treatment, the client is exposed to an audience of 0–40 people and the following situations:

1.	*Speaking in an empty auditorium*
2.	*Speaking in an auditorium with an audience*
3.	*Speaking to an audience in which members talked to each other and paid no attention to the speaker*
4.	*speaking to an audience whose members laughed at him*
5.	*Speaking to an audience in which members continuously asked the speaker to speak louder*

A modified version of the SUD (Subjective Units of Disturbance) scale is used every few minutes during exposure to the phobia in order to measure the anxiety level of the client. The client gives a numerical rating, on a 0 (no discomfort) to 10 (panic-level anxiety) scale, and a descriptive analysis of their anxiety for each situation. The document correlated with the client indicated level of anxiety.

Each treatment is usually conducted weekly for five sessions during a time that is most convenient for the client. During the first session, the client talks about his or herself and the issues related to public speaking. In every proceeding session, the client is given the option of reading aloud 11 irrational and counterproductive ideas taken from Ellis' Rational-Emotive Psychotherapy (note: The selection of Ellis' excerpts is completely arbitrary, the session can easily be modified by the therapist and replaced with almost any reading activity). Each session concludes with the client completing the modified Attitude Toward Public Speaking Questionnaire. Equipment for this particular experiment consists of a Pentium-based computer, a mounted microphone, and a head-mounted display with head-tracker (Virtual – I/O). The VRT software program used VREAM™ Virtual Reality Development Software Package and Libraries (VRCreator™) to create a virtual reality scene of a university's auditorium located on campus (see Fig. 27.1). The virtual auditorium seats 40 people, is 100 ft deep, 48 ft wide, and 55 ft high.

Training

Dr. Max North has pursued and achieved the following degrees to assist him in pioneering Virtual Reality Therapy theories and technology; and conducting research in this innovative field. However, similar to the required training for the standard therapy practice, a degree with license to practice therapy should be sufficient for conducting treatment using Virtual Reality Therapy.

Fig. 27.1 A client is receiving the Virtual Reality Therapy treatment

- Ph.D., Major: Counseling Psychology—Psychological Services, Concentration: Human-Computer Interaction {Virtual Environments, and Cognitive & Behavioral Sciences} Dissertation: "Effectiveness of Virtual Environment Desensitization in the Treatment of Agoraphobia in a College Student Population."
- M.S., Major: Computer Science, Concentration: Information Management Systems.

Advantages of VRT and Mild Concerns

The prominent advantages of VRT over traditional exposure therapy (In-vivo or Desensitization) are as follows:

- Increased safety of the virtual environment and control over the level and intensity of virtually generated stimuli.
- Efficiency and effectiveness of treatment compared to standard exposure therapy.
- Improved client confidentiality during the treatment sessions.
- Elimination of risks of any potential physical injury during the VRT treatment.
- Customization of VRT scenarios to fulfill the client's expectation and perception, leading to improved treatment success.
- Simplicity of repetitions of any specific virtual sceneries as well as adjusting of stimuli.
- Reduced treatment sessions and periods in each session due to the increased efficiency and effectiveness of generated stimuli.

- Lower treatment cost compared to other standard therapies, due to the use of virtual seniors.
- Attraction toward new modality of treatment: Some clients may consider using VRT technology because they may have a perception that the new VRT technology may work for them better than traditional treatments.

Mild concerns are mostly related to the implementation and adoption of VRT, but not to the treatment itself. The symptoms experienced during the VRT are mild and minimal, and include dry mouth, dizziness, increased heart rate, and nervousness. The following are a short list of possible concerns:

- Many practitioners may not be aware or possess required knowledge to adopt the innovative VRT technology and techniques.
- Practitioners may not be able to afford to acquire VRT hardware and software.
- There may not be affordable training courses for practitioners learning to use VRT in treatment.
- A small number of clients may not believe in or being comfortable to use the new technology.

Evidence Based Intervention

Virtual Reality Therapy (VRT) as described in this document.

Career Development and Beyond

Prelude

The intent of this section is to describe in detail my career development and how I chose to incorporate technology in my field as an educator and researcher; I hope to provide ideas and examples for mental/behavioral health professionals to encourage them to incorporate technology into their own works.

I was born into a family who encouraged me to study and seek knowledge. I liked to read a variety of books, especially books related to science, technology, psychology, philosophy, and self-improvement. From an early age, I was curious to know how and why people behave the way they behave. When I was introduced to computer programming, I became fascinated with being able to program them to perform specific instructions. Eventually, I was thinking and pursuing for a way to program or reprogram the human mind. And that is why Virtual Reality Therapy was a natural step for my discovery and research.

When in college, I took courses in computer and information sciences alongside courses in psychology. This pairing led to unique outlook. After obtaining my master's degree in computer science with a concentration in management information systems, I began to work as faculty in a university setting. I then earned my doctoral degree in Counseling Psychology/Psychological Services with a concentration in Cognitive and Behavior Sciences. My main focus was on using virtual reality technology to help the general public. My dissertation (the first known study of VRT) was in the use of VRT to treat psychological disorders. I graduated with a Ph. D. in 1995. Since then, I have seriously and successfully pursued VRT research and its applications. I have published over 80 peer-reviewed papers; in addition, I have written the first book in Virtual Reality Therapy (North et al. 1996 in this document), and I have provided many interviews to the media on what I hope will continue to be an essential tool for mental health professionals.

VRT Discovery and Innovative Research

In November 1992, while testing a virtual reality experiment using one of our co-researchers in a virtual reality scene, we discovered that she experienced emotional and physical symptoms that resembled the experiences of a person reacting to a phobia. VRT projects were conducted at Clark Atlanta University sponsored by several grants from Boeing Computer Services (Virtual Systems Department) and the U.S. Army Research Laboratory. Since then, I have conducted innovative research as a faculty member at Kennesaw State University and Southern Polytechnic State University. With funding from the U.S. Army Research Office, I have created state-of-the-art Visualization & Simulation Research Center that allows me and other scientists to continue VRT research activities.

Opportunities and Possible Challenges

Using technology in mental/behavioral health fields provides tremendous career opportunities for practitioners to extend their specialization skills, increase their marketability and ultimately gain competitive advantages. A short list of opportunities is as follows:

- Specialized career opportunity providing a higher marketability and competitive advantage.
- Improved efficiency and effectiveness of treatment, thus increasing financial income and resources.
- Increased career satisfaction through providing a better quality of treatment for the clients.

As mentioned earlier, possible challenges are mostly related to the implementation and adoption of VRT. The following are a short list of possible challenges:

- At the beginning, practitioners may need to dedicate additional time and effort to acquire VRT systems and the training needed to use these systems.
- There may be a need to modify the inventory of assessment and treatment process to be aligned with new VRT technology and techniques.
- A small number of clients may not believe in or be comfortable using the new technology.

Skills Acquired and/or Enhanced Using Technology in Mental/Health

In brief, the following group of skills were acquired or enhanced while I was pursing the use of technology for treatment of psychological disorders. These skills generally will improve the quality of care that practitioners are able to provide to clients, ultimately improving their effectiveness and their careers. The following table lists only a few of these skills:

- Perseverance and Diligence
- Problem-solving, Creativity, Resourcefulness, Critical thinking
- Research and Exploration, Data and Information collection, and Data analysis
- Collaboration and Networking
- Confidence and Professionalism

Conclusions and Recommendations

A brief conclusion of the self-review so far clearly shows that diverse education and experience in the fields of mental/behavioral health and technology may create the necessary condition for professionals to pursue and incorporate technology in their works. While it may not be possible for all professionals to discover new technology, techniques, or theories, any professional should be able to utilize what has already been discovered by others. All that is needed is to have a passion to learn and to be willing to have the patience to understand each unique technology, gradually incorporating it into one's career. As a popular advertisement expresses: "Just do it…"

Reference

North, M. M., North, S. M., & Coble, J. R. (1996). *Virtual Reality Therapy, an innovative paradigm.* Colorado Springs, CO: IPI Press. ISBN 1-880930-08-0.

Chapter 28
Matching Person and Technology

Marcia Scherer

> *When matching a person with the most appropriate technology*
> *for their use: You become an investigator, a detective. You find*
> *out what the different alternatives are within the constraints.*
>
> – From Living in the State of Stuck, 2005

Assistive technology devices are products that make up for lost or weak functions, such as wheelchairs and walkers for people with mobility difficulties, hearing aids and closed captioning for those with hearing loss, and a variety of computer software and hardware options to aid accessibility to access data and information.

The availability of skilled assistive technology professionals who understand the importance of a consumer-driven process and are able to provide appropriate and adequate services is key to an individual obtaining a quality assessment of needs and the most personally appropriate technologies for personal use (e.g., Scherer, 2005a, 2014). The importance of assistive technology services is underscored in various federal statutes, including the Americans with Disabilities Act, together with state policies. Nevertheless, many professionals who provide services to persons with disabilities are unaware of particular technologies, do not know how to obtain and fund them, and do not have an effective process for matching a person with the most suitable devices. Moreover, although many professionals realize they need to be more consumer-responsive, they lack the training needed to accomplish this.

The following is taken from an actual case report of a professional at a community rehabilitation agency where the Matching Person and Technology process was used to inform decisions about the most appropriate interventions for a particular consumer with cerebral palsy.

> *Tim and I started the Matching Person and Technology (MPT) process with his target activity already in mind. Due to the spasticity and tremors that he experiences in his hands and fingers from his cerebral palsy, he is unable to control his hands or fingers to manipulate the pages of books without ripping them. His long term goal is to take classes one day*

M. Scherer, Ph.D., M.P.H., F.A.C.R.M. (✉)
Institute for Matching Person & Technology, 486 Lake Road, Webster, NY 14580, USA
e-mail: IMPT97@aol.com

© Springer International Publishing Switzerland 2017
M.M. Maheu et al. (eds.), *Career Paths in Telemental Health*,
DOI 10.1007/978-3-319-23736-7_28

without fear that he will not be able to independently read the required books. He hopes to find a device that he can easily incorporate into his lifestyle.

We completed the Initial Worksheet for the Matching Person & Technology Model to help us focus in on the area that Tim wanted to target for assistive technology (AT) use. Next, Tim and I completed the consumer version of the History of Support Use which reviewed the devices that Tim had tried in the past for a variety of support needs, and revealed Tim's rather negative memories of trying to find devices that he would actually use, particularly communication devices. At our next meeting, Tim and I completed two forms: the Assistive Technology Device Predisposition Assessment (ATD PA)—Person and the Assistive Technology Device Predisposition Assessment (ATD PA)—Device. While completing these forms, the questions sparked conversation around topics that Tim and I had never discussed. I found out a lot about Tim's overall attitude toward trying AT and about his confidence levels. His incentives for using AT included his desire to read books at his leisure, to pursue his hobby of collecting coffee table books about history, to decrease his frustration levels, to increase his success at reading, to decrease his embarrassing moments like when he returns ripped books to the library, to overcome his fears of not being able to read required books for school so that he can pursue his career, and to be a happier person, overall. Some disincentives that came up during our conversations included his fears of not fitting in because of yet another large device to show off his disability, memories of bad experiences about devices that did not do what he thought that they would, and anxiety about not being able to use the device. Although I was surprised at the negativity that surfaced during a lot of our discussion, I still felt pretty confident that one of the electronic page turners was going to be a good match for him.

As I read through the ATD PA scoring analysis, many of the results caused me to question the success of an electronic page turner. Noteworthy is the fact that Tim saw a lot more limitations than capabilities in himself, had a negative general mood state, might be dissatisfied with his current well-being/quality of life, and did not seem to feel he had a strong natural support system. In addition, according to the results, he demonstrates low self-esteem and may have difficulty exploring undertaking new strategies or new directions at this time and may not be ready to accept a significant new challenge. I started to question my initial optimism about the use of an electronic page turner wondering if it might be too much of a device at this time. I shared the results with Tim who said that he wanted to go ahead with the search for a device and at the same time, give more thought to how he was feeling.

As Tim and I discussed all of the options, we talked more about his general feelings about himself and his future. He recognized a lot of his fears and said that when he had gotten his wheelchair and his communication device he felt a lot of the same feelings. He admitted that he had been feeling very anxious about the cost of the electronic devices, and the size of them; however, he was excited and did not want to hurt my feelings as I was so excited about the electronic devices. We had a good 'meeting of the minds', and I shared that the only reason we were doing this search was to find something that would work for him, and that while I appreciated his thoughtfulness, I would not be hurt at all if we switched gears. When I asked him if he thought it would be a good idea to speak with his psychologist about his present state of mind, and his high levels of frustration, he said that he thought that would be helpful. We followed up with a call to his psychologist who thought that starting with a simple, easy to use device would give Tim opportunity for success that would build his confidence levels. In concordance with the results of the ATD PA analysis, she felt that Tim should focus on improving his self-image and his overall well-being before introducing any major changes in his life.

The process from beginning to end was a learning one for me. I recognize that I got overzealous and immediately thought that I had found an easy solution with the electronic page turner. Finding out how depressed Tim really seems to be was unexpected for me and how much was brought out by the questions on the MPT helped me to see the whole picture. I learned that it is important to really listen to what is being said; to not jump to conclusions; and that I could easily be one of those people who help someone to get a device that they don't end up using. Unintentional, but devastating.

Training

My career has focused on assessing the psychosocial correlates of technology use and nonuse by persons with disabilities. The theoretical model that I developed from my National Science Foundation-sponsored dissertation research, *Matching Person and Technology (MPT)*, is described in a trilogy of books:

1. Scherer, M. J. (2012). *Assistive Technologies and Other Supports for People with Brain Impairment*. New York: Springer Publishing Co
2. Scherer, M. J. (2005a). *Living in the State of Stuck: How Assistive Technology Impacts the Lives of People with Disabilities, Fourth Edition*. Cambridge, MA: Brookline Books. (First Edition published in 1993; Second in 1996; Third in 2000)
3. Scherer, M. J. (2004). *Connecting to Learn: Educational and Assistive Technology for People with Disabilities*. Washington, DC: American Psychological Association (APA) Books

I am a rehabilitation psychologist who studied testing and assessment, research methods and statistics, and individual counseling skills. I am a fellow of the American Psychological Association in Rehabilitation Psychology; Evaluation, Measurement, and Statistics; and Applied Experimental and Engineering Psychology. I am also a Fellow of the Rehabilitation Engineering and Assistive Technology Society of North America (RESNA) and the American Congress of Rehabilitation Medicine.

After receiving my Ph.D. and Masters in Public Health degrees from the University of Rochester, I joined the faculty of the National Technical Institute for the Deaf/Rochester Institute of Technology (NTID/RIT) as Assistant Professor in Educational Research and Development and was promoted to Associate Professor in 1995. In 1989, I also became Senior Research Associate, International Center for Hearing and Speech Research (ICHSR), a joint program of Rochester Institute of Technology and the University of Rochester Medical Center. There my research focused on assessing assistive and educational technology use by students and older persons with significant hearing loss.

While maintaining my Sr. Research Associate position with ICHSR, I served as Director of Consumer Evaluations for the National Institute of Disability and Rehabilitation Research (NIDRR) and sponsored Rehabilitation Engineering Research Center on Technology Evaluation and Transfer (University at Buffalo) from 1996 to 1998. As Director of Consumer Evaluations, I was responsible for developing a consumer-driven assessment process to define the most desired product features in ten categories of assistive technology.

In 1997, I was appointed Associate Professor of Physical Medicine and Rehabilitation at the University of Rochester Medical Center (and then promoted to Professor in 2008). Also in 1997, I formed the Institute for Matching Person and Technology, Inc. to enhance the quality of life of technology users through research, assessment, training, and consultation. The focus is on supporting the match of individuals with the most appropriate assistive, educational, workplace, healthcare, and general technologies.

I have also served as Principal Investigator for two National Institute of Health research grants, one from the Centers for Disease Control and Prevention and one from NIDRR. I have also collaborated as a partner on several NIDRR-funded centers and projects, all related to better Matching Person and Technology.

The research I have conducted has benefited from my education in both psychology and epidemiology (emphasis within the Master in Public Health program which assesses risk, relative risk, screening protocols, etc.) and has indicated that the overarching factor associated with technology abandonment/discard is the failure to assess and consider user needs and preferences in device selection. Also, successful technology use requires adapting the technology to the person's capabilities and temperament, not vice versa. It is also important to adapt the person, family, co-workers, and others, to technology use. These issues can be addressed most appropriately in a comprehensive process that considers the person's ongoing needs and takes a long-term view of an individual's technology use and which is, first and foremost, consumer-directed, such as the method used in the *Matching Person and Technology (MPT) model and accompanying assessment instruments.*

Pros and Cons

Positives of the work I do include having colleagues and their students adopt the MPT Model and use the measures. This meant they absorbed my work and want to work with consumers in technology decision-making and selection. A challenge remains, however, with today's many fiscal and time constraints on providers and professionals who want to listen to the voice of the consumer, get to know the person, and work with that person on goal achievement, inclusion/participation, and life quality.

The biggest negative was going into a new and unstudied area and, thus, not having a number of mentors available. And this leads to another con—not having a direct benchmark for pricing, salary, etc. Current cons are overloading my schedule and trying to keep pace with the requests for giving invited presentations, collaboration, sharing information, providing article reprints, and so on. When you are in a new area, this will happen!

Evidence base

Many psychologists work with individuals with physical, sensory, or other disabilities or chronic health conditions. While support from technology can come from various telehealth and other technology applications, it may also involve adopting use of a product that becomes an integral part of that person's functioning, persona, and self-image. *Assistive technology devices (ATDs)* are specialized or everyday technologies used to support the functioning of a particular individual with a disability and include such familiar products as wheelchairs, walkers, communication devices, products to augment hearing and vision, and many more. In fact, there are about 40,000 different ATDs on the market today.

An assistive technology device (ATD) is what the person uses. How they obtain and maintain it falls under the purview of assistive technology services. The increased availability of assistive technology options has made the process of matching a person with the most appropriate device more complex because people's predisposition to, expectations for, and reactions to technologies and their features are highly individualized and personal. These predispositions, expectations, and reactions emerge from varying needs, abilities, preferences, and past experiences with and exposures to technologies. Predispositions to technology use also depend on adjustment to disability, subjective quality of life or sense of well-being, a person's outlook and goals for future functioning, expectations held by one's self and others, and financial and social support for technology use. In addition to the needs and preferences of the user, a good match of person and technology requires attention to aspects of the environments in which the technology will be used and the various functions and features of the technology. If the match is not a quality one from the standpoint of the consumer, the technology may not be used or will not be used optimally. Indeed, the overall nonuse or discard rate has been approximately 30 % for the past 30 years.

An assessment process exists which has been effective in organizing the influences impacting technology use: the Matching Person and Technology (MPT) Model and assessment instruments (Scherer, 2005b). It consists of instruments which have been validated for use by persons with disabilities ages 15 and up (a measure targeted to technology use by infants and children has also been developed: Matching Assistive Technology and Child has a version for K-12 special education students).

The development and validation of the Matching Person and Technology assessments followed the recommended steps of professionally approved standards as found in *Standards for Educational and Psychological Testing*: (a) concept definition and clarification, (b) draft of items and response scales, (c) pilot testing, and (d) determination of measure quality and usefulness (Scherer, 1995).

The MPT is used to identify the most appropriate technology for a person and indicates barriers that may exist to optimal technology use, areas to target for training for optimal use, and the type of additional support that may enhance use. After the person has received the most appropriate technology for his or her use, the MPT forms are administered at one or more times post AT acquisition to assess changes in perceived capabilities, quality of life/subjective well-being, and such psychosocial factors as self-esteem, mood, self-determination, and social participation and support.

Ongoing research on the validation of the instruments has shown their utility within and across specific populations of individuals with disabilities. The MPT Model has been confirmed by several other assistive technology researchers and authors (e.g., Cook & Polgar, 2002; Lasker & Bedrosian, 2001; Wielandt, Mckenna, Tooth, & Strong, 2006). MPT results have been used clinically and incorporated into AT funding requests and justification reports as well as program evaluations. The MPT Model and assessments have been translated into six languages and have been the focus of eight doctoral dissertations. Both the book *Living in the State of Stuck* and the *Matching Person & Technology (MPT) Model Manual and accompany assessment instruments* are used in many academic courses for rehabilitation and allied health professionals and included as a reference text for the Credentialing Examination in Assistive Technology sponsored by the Rehabilitation Engineering and Assistive Technology Society of North America (RESNA). The Assistive Technology in Occupational Therapy self-paced clinical course sponsored by the American Occupational Therapy Association advocates the MPT assessment, "Assistive Technology Device Predisposition Assessment." Of the 59 programs studied in Europe, Canada, and the USA by the European Union-sponsored project, Empowering Users Through Assistive Technology (EUSTAT), the Institute for Matching Person and Technology was selected as one of the top seven "outstanding programs."

Validation studies conducted by independent investigators of the psychometric properties of the MPT assessments are summarized in Scherer and Sax (2010). Finally, the *Matching Person & Technology (MPT) Model Manual and accompanying assessment instruments* are reviewed in Buros Publications, Tests in Print V and Mental Measurements Yearbook (Buros Institute, University of Nebraska, Accession # 14092065). The validity assessment "Assistive Technology Device Predisposition Assessment" is also available on the *Rehabilitation Measures Database:* http://www.rehabmeasures.org

References

Cook, A. M., & Polgar, J. M. (2014). *Mosby; assistive technologies: Principles and practice* (4th ed.). St Louis, MO: Mosby.

Lasker, J. P., & Bedrosian, J. L. (2001). Promoting acceptance of augmentative and alternative communication by adults with acquired communication disorders. *Augmentative & Alternative Communication, 17*(3), 141–153.

Scherer, M. J. (1995). A model of rehabilitation assessment. In L. C. Cushman & M. J. Scherer (Eds.), *Psychological assessment in medical rehabilitation* (pp. 3–23). Washington, DC: APA Books.

Scherer, M. J. (2004). *Connecting to learn: Educational and assistive technology for people with disabilities.* Washington, DC: American Psychological Association (APA) Books.

Scherer, M. J. (2005a). *Living in the State of Stuck: How assistive technology impacts the lives of people with disabilities* (4th ed.). Cambridge, MA: Brookline Books (First Edition published in 1993; Second in 1996; Third in 2000).

Scherer, M. J. (2005b). *The Matching Person & Technology (MPT) model manual and assessments* (5th ed.). Webster, NY: The Institute for Matching Person & Technology, Inc. [CD-ROM].

Scherer, M. J. (2012). *Assistive technologies and other supports for people with brain impairment.* New York, NY: Springer.

Scherer, M. J. (2014). From people-centered to person-centered services, and back again. *Disability and Rehabilitation: Assistive Technology, 9*(1), 1–2.

Scherer, M. J., & Sax, C. (2010). Measures of assistive technology predisposition and use. In E. Mpofu & T. Oakland (Eds.), *Rehabilitation and health assessment: Applying ICF guidelines* (pp. 229–254). New York, NY: Springer.

Wielandt, T., Mckenna, K., Tooth, L., & Strong, J. (2006). Factors that predict the post-discharge use of recommended assistive technology (AT). *Disability and Rehabilitation: Assistive Technology, 1*(1–2), 29–40.

Chapter 29
Integrating Behavioral Health into Rural Primary Care Clinics Utilizing a TeleMental Health Model

Dawn Sampson and Mindy Mueller

> *"Go confidently in the direction of your dreams! Live the life you've imagined."*
>
> Thoreau

Scenario

Sitting down at your computer, in your own home, you log-in to your secure internet-based videoconferencing system to begin your work day. The day starts by talking with the rural health clinic staff regarding the patients that will be seen that day and consulting and coordinating with other providers regarding the individual patients and the integrated care being delivered. Some of the patients are new referrals to you and will require consent forms to be reviewed and signed and assessments conducted, while others are patients returning for follow-up care and treatment. Throughout the day clinic staff will assist you by checking in patients, reviewing insurance eligibility, scheduling, faxing documents to be signed and reviewed and on occasion, contacting and staying with patients when additional providers and community resources are needed - if a patient is assessed and found to be at risk of harming self or others. The patients referred to you are known to the clinic and are referred by their primary care providers to address mental health issues. Among the patients you will see today is a 17 year old boy, struggling with anxiety. His father was referred to you last year by his primary care provider and psychiatrist (a contracted specialist utilizing video-conferencing technology at the clinic). At the time, his father was struggling with anxiety and an alcohol and drug addiction. During treatment, you consulted as needed with both the psychiatrist and family nurse practitioner to exchange information. You were able to help the father reduce

D. Sampson, L.C.S.W. • M. Mueller, Psy.D. (✉)
Teleconnect Therapies, P.O. Box 1665, Avalon, CA 90704, USA
e-mail: dsampson@teleconnecttherapies.com; mmueller@teleconnecttherapies.com

© Springer International Publishing Switzerland 2017
M.M. Maheu et al. (eds.), *Career Paths in Telemental Health*,
DOI 10.1007/978-3-319-23736-7_29

277

his anxiety and substance abuse by providing therapy and coordinating care to help him access and enter a residential recovery program. While the father was in residential treatment, you worked with his 17 year old son, your next patient today who will be there for his final session. He has been trying to adjust to his circumstances and manage his own fears and anxiety. The treatment you delivered over the last 12 weeks has been a traditional evidenced-based treatment protocol for anxiety. For your final session, your patient brings with him his father. Together you review his progress in treatment and solidify the gains achieved. You also get a chance to hear first hand how both father and son had renewed hope and optimism for their future and were creating a new chapter in their lives as a result of the integrated care provided and the ability to access mental licensed mental health professionals in their own rural community. As your day comes to a close, you say good-bye to your patients and the clinic staff, complete your progress notes either by entering them into the clinic's electronic health record system or faxing them to the staff to be scanned. And then, you sign off and walk out of the door of your home office. At the end of the month you submit your invoice for that month's services rendered and wait for your check to arrive from TeleConnect Therapies. A day in the life of a licensed telemental health practitioner providing services from her home. With the Health Insurance Portability and Accountability Act of 1996 (HIPPA), the Affordable Care Act of 2010, and constantly evolving and advancing innovative technologies, the landscape of healthcare service delivery is changing in both rural and urban areas across the country. With increased access to affordable care, healthcare settings and providers are being asked to improve both security and privacy, as well as to consider new ways to increase their capacity to deliver primary care, specialty care and behavioral health services. Residents of rural communities, which make up approximately 20 % of the population, or 55 million people in the United States, are at a distinct disadvantage because 85 % of rural areas are also designated as Mental Health Professional Shortage areas (MHPSAs) (Bird, Dempsey, & Harley, 2001). In other words there are not enough professionals to provide the mental health services needed in these communities. In the state of California, there has been a growing shortage of providers in rural communities, where 20 % of all Californians live but only 9 % of the providers practice (Yellowlees, Marks, Hilty, & Shore, 2008). Telehealth is one solution to increasing access to services and improving the quality of care delivered. Research shows that integrating telemental health services into the local mental health care delivery system provides numerous benefits, including improved access to care, higher quality of care without travel to tertiary care centers, more timely and responsive medication management, improved continuity of care, and better facilitation of family support through reduced travel time and expense (Armstrong et al., 2004). It can be as effective as services provided in person in treating many mental illnesses, and consumers perceive these services as beneficial, of high quality and worth continuing (Smith & Allison, 2001). As Americans become increasingly comfortable using electronic means to access health information, the acceptance of telemedicine is expected to increase as well.

Current research indicates that depression, substance abuse, and domestic violence occur at the same rates in rural communities as in urban areas (Cellucci & Vik, 2001; Smalley et al., 2010) and that suicide occurs at even higher rates in rural communities (Singh & Siahpush, 2002). With a demonstrated need for service and a shortage of licensed mental health professionals, we have identified a market. However, there are barriers for individuals living in rural communities to accessing services such as higher rates of poverty, inadequate housing and transportation, lower rates of insurance, poorer health status (Stamm et al., 2003; Wagenfeld, 2003) and long wait lists at county funded community mental health centers. Individuals living in rural communities tend to go to their local health clinics and hospitals as their first resource when they are not feeling well, whether it is due to a physical or mental health condition. Often primary care providers are overwhelmed by the demand and do not have the time to address and link individuals to appropriate behavioral health services. By integrating behavioral health into these primary care health settings, TeleConnect Therapies reduces the barriers that prevent individuals from accessing and utilizing mental health services. By contracting with clinics and hospitals to provide qualified licensed mental health professionals to deliver these services, utilizing hi-tech, secure and confidential videoconferencing technology, we have increased the capacity and quality of care to serve those individuals living in rural communities.

TeleConnect Therapies (TCT), a California based company, started in 2009 as a partnership between a licensed clinical social worker and licensed psychologist on Catalina Island which is located 26 miles off of the Southern California coast. Co-owners, Dawn Sampson, LCSW (formerly Director of Social Services at the Catalina Island Medical Center) and Mindy Mueller, Psy.D. (formerly of The Guidance Center in Long Beach, CA) saw and experienced first-hand the shortage of professionals and barriers for individuals trying to access mental health and primary care services in rural areas. Our goal was to develop a company that would help solve this dilemma for individuals living in rural communities, their rural clinics and hospitals, and licensed mental health providers who had the passion and availability to serve the underserved by using the advancing secure and HIPAA compliant videoconferencing technologies.

In 2009 TeleConnect Therapies began contracting with clinics and hospitals in rural California, offering clinical psychology and clinical social work services to rural residents. We created a HIPAA secured videocommunications channel between practitioners and medical settings using Med-RT, one of the leading telemedicine consulting companies in the field today. We worked with technology experts to purchase, learn how to operate, and troubleshoot potential problems using the necessary videoconferencing equipment (laptops, monitors, high-definition cameras, speakers, etc). Through this technology we have been able to offer secure Internet Protocol connections at minimum transmission speeds of 384 Kbps, typically averaging 512 Kbps or above, providing natural communication for the pace of telemental health visits (at and above the required standard). When there is a technical problem, we have the back-up of the leading experts at Med-RT at our fingertips to step-in and help diagnose and resolve the technology and communication issues.

TeleConnect Therapies researched and used existing practice guidelines to create a solid foundation and operational plan from which to deliver services. Practice guidelines for tele-mental health services were adopted from those published by the American Telemedicine Association, the California Board of Behavioral Sciences, the California Board of Psychology, the American Psychological Association and the National Association of Social Workers. We also structured our business model to align with Medicare and Medi-Cal regulations regarding provision of mental health services through electronic means. For additional training and continued education, we accessed the ongoing opportunities, conferences and workshops available through the California Telehealth Network and the Telemental Health Institute.

TCT negotiates contracts with hospital and clinic administrators to best meet the needs of the facility and rural community by scheduling blocks of time during which mental health services will be provided. Hours are scheduled at the convenience of the clinics, for a minimum of a 4 h block of time. We can direct medical facilities to published Medicare and Medi-Cal reimbursement guidelines, as desired. The rural facility bills third party payers and pays TeleConenct Therapies on a monthly basis for services provided. TCT in turn sub-contracts with licensed therapists who work from their own home offices. TCT owners and interested contracted therapists conduct on-site visits 1–2 times per year to meet with clinic staff and administrators to review how services are being implemented and integrated and discuss ways to improve the quality of care and flow of services and documentation. A highlight of these visits for TCT providers is meeting with the patients we are currently treating and providing services on-site during the visit.

Rural health clinic staff typically fax referrals to the TCT Clinical Director who contacts patients via telephone to set up an initial appointment with a contract therapist who is available on the patient's desired day of the week. Typically an appointment is scheduled within less than 7 business days. A Welcome/Intake packet including an overview of services, consent and other forms to be discussed during the first session, an appointment reminder, and contact information for the assigned licensed practitioner are sent to the patient via postal mail. Welcome/ Intake Packets with required documentation are also available on-site as needed. On the day of the patient's first session, the patient goes to their community health facility and signs in with the reception staff. A telemedicine coordinator then walks with patient to the videoconferencing room/office. The patient enters the room, and the coordinator introduces the patient and leaves the session. (Children are usually seen with a parent or guardian in the room.) The videoconferencing room is usually similar to other office settings (chairs, workbooks for patients, small children's art area). However, the other equipment necessary is typically a large flat screen wall-mounted monitor and CODEC video camera and audio equipment. The initial session begins with reviewing telemental health consent forms, HIPAA, office and emergency procedures. Each session is typically 50 min in length, but may vary depending on the clinic's specific contract. The TCT therapist transmits patient medical records directly to the clinic via fax or through remote access to the clinic's electronic medical record system (at the clinic's preference) at the end of each day of service. Therapists place reminder calls to patients the day prior to scheduled appointments, and follow-up calls for missed appointments. Ongoing scheduling of patients is done by the clinic or by TCT contracted therapists, at the preference of the clinic. For adults, the Schedler Quick PsychoDiagnositic Panel assessment (an assessment instrument developed by Patient Tools) is completed upon intake, and every 6-months thereafter, to monitor patient progress. For minors, 6–18 the Achenbach Inventories (Child Behavior Checklist, Youth Self-Report, and Teacher report Forms) are utilized and administered at the same time intervals. TCT also provides telephone availability for patients to a licensed mental health professional from 8:00 AM to 8:00 PM seven days a week. TCT works with each community's existing system for involuntary psychiatric holds as necessary.

TCT sub-contracts only with mental health professionals licensed in the state of California, with a minimum of 5 years of clinical experience. By doing this, we have been able to provide rural clinics with experienced qualified professionals that operate and deliver services independently. We contract with licensed practitioners who are familiar with and utilize evidence based treatments as a foundation for the delivery of services (i.e., CBT, DBT, TF-CBT, Seeking Safety, IPT etc.). We have found there are several ways to enhance videoconference based services by: (1) including interactive pro-social and therapeutic games (either traditional therapy board games or internet based games); (2) using the interactive presentation feature on videoconferencing software to present patient education information; (3) utilizing patient workbooks available at both the provider and the patient sites, and (4) for children, utilizing puppets or similar play therapy materials to introduce thematic interactive play with the provider.

From the authors' perspective, the benefits for a licensed practitioner using this model of subcontracting with an established telemental health company to deliver integrated behavioral health into a primary care setting are the following: (1) increased flexibility in work schedule; (2) increased access and communication to a multi-disciplinary team of specialists and resources; (3) ability to work from home without having to work in isolation; (4) no overhead costs for marketing or generating referrals; and (5) greater ability to serve rural and underserved communities even when living in large urban areas without incurring the burden of frequent travel. From our perspective, the barriers for implementing and delivering services from home and within this model are the following: (1) learning and staying current with all the advancements in technology and frequent changes in telehealth policies; (2) challenges creating a quiet, private, office setting in your own home that has enough lighting, air conditioning and access to consistent and dependable high-speed internet connections; (3) purchasing a fireproof safe for storage of documents and equipment, and creating backup procedures for electronic files and documents; and (4) troubleshooting computer and equipment challenges when they arise.

From our perspective and from that of our contracted clinics, patients have benefited in the following ways: (1) improved access to specialty mental health services in a more consistent and flexible manner; (2) improved quality of mental health care for patients; (3) improved compliance with medical treatment plans and attendance at follow-up appointments; (4) improved patient satisfaction and outcomes. The manager of one contracted clinic has stated "Since starting our telemental health program the whole feel of our clinic has changed, it is less stressful in the waiting room and at the front desk, knowing there is an easily accessible resource for vital mental health services". From the clinics' perspective some of the challenges have been: (1) Securing, maintaining and enhancing the necessary equipment and information technology infrastructure; (2) finding and training qualified telehealth coordinators to facilitate the flow and delivery of service at the clinic site; and (3) local primary care providers and administrators who are wary of using technology to provide mental health services. As a caveat, and what is demonstrated by the research, patients are often more supportive and comfortable with the telemental health services than providers or administrators.

Under this service delivery model the challenges involved with marketing to, and contracting with rural health facilities in an environment of ever-changing telehealth regulations and reimbursement policies is the responsibility of TeleConnect Therapies owners. Developing your own company takes time, energy, and dedication, not to mention knowledge of the market and industry, and developing relationships with a whole host of experts and consultants to rely on for areas outside of your scope. These essential relationships include technical (equipment, broadband, and security) companies, your state Telehealth Resource Center and state rural health organizations, professional organizations, telehealth associations, legal, accounting, marketing and graphic design professionals.

To be successful and sustainable as a company and private practitioner in telehealth, it is important not only to have a solid understanding of how to generate revenue and balance expenses with the challenges and pitfalls that exist, but even more importantly to have a clear and current understanding of how to navigate the legal, regulatory, reimbursement and ethical issues that are the underpinnings of your success. But the rewards are immeasurable, in developing relationships with patients living hundreds of miles away in rural areas previously unserved by mental health professionals, and helping these rural residents to lead happier, healthier lives.

References

Armstrong, T.M. and Sprang, R. (2004). *Telemental health.* Chapter 9. pp 188–205 .In J. Tracy (Ed.) *Telemedicine Technical Assistance Documents: A Guide to Getting Started in Telemedicine.* Office for the Advancement of Telehealth.

Bird, D.C., Dempsey, P., & Harley, D. (2001). *Addressing mental health workforce needs in underserved rural areas: Accomplishments and challenges.* Working paper No. 23. Portland, ME: Main Rural Health Research Center. Retrieved from http://muskie.usm.maine.edu/Publications/rural/wp23.pdf

Cellucci, T., & Vik, P. (2001). Training for substance abuse treatment among psychologists in a rural state. *Professional Psychology: Research and Practice, 32,* 248–252. doi:10.1037/0735-7028.32.3.248.

Singh, G. K., & Siahpush, M. (2002). Increasing rural-urban gradients in U.S. suicide mortality, 1920-1997. *American Journal of Public Health, 92,* 1161–1167. doi:10.2105/AJPH.92.7.1161. Retrieved from http://ajph.aphapublications.org/cgi/reprint/92/7/1161.pdf.

Smalley, K. B., Yancey, C. T., Warren, J. C., Naufel, K., Ryan, R., & Pugh, J. L. (2010). Rural mental health and psychological treatment: A review for practitioners. *Journal of Clinical Psychology, 66,* 479–489. doi:10.1002/jclp.20688.

Smith, H. A., Allison, R. A. (2001). *Telemental health: Delivering mental health care at a distance, a summary report.* U.S. Department of Health and Human Services, Health Resources and Services Administration. Retrieved from http://www.hrsa.gov/telehealth/pubs/mental.htm

Stamm, B. H., Piland, N. F., Crouse, B., Boulger, J., Davis, G., Ide, B. A., ... Tidwell, K. (2003). Essays from the field. In B. Stamm (Ed.) *Rural behavioral healthcare: An interdisciplinary guide* (pp. 11–20). Washington, DC: American Psychological Association Books. doi:10.1037/10489-000.

Wagenfeld, M. O. (2003). A snapshot of rural and frontier America. In B. Stamm (Ed.), *Rural behavioral healthcare: An interdisciplinary guide* (pp. 33–40). Washington, DC: American Psychological Association Books. doi:10.1037/10489-002.

Yellowlees, P., Marks, S., Hilty, D., & Shore, J. (2008). Using e-health to enable culturally appropriate mental healthcare in rural areas. *Telemedicine Journal and e-Health, 14*(5), 486–492.

Chapter 30
Walking the Wire: Technologies Across an Academic Career

Laura Schopp

> *The only way to make sense out of change is to*
> *plunge into it, move with it, and join the dance.*

Alan Watts

Narrative

It's a snowy Monday morning and it looks like a lively week at the academic medical center. I'll spend Monday morning seeing patients in clinic if they can brave the icy roads and then shift to the telehealth clinic in the afternoon to conduct video teleconferencing follow-up sessions with patients from all over rural Missouri. It's a relief that these patients don't have to risk a long ride on icy rural highways to keep our appointment today. Tuesday is a research day to collaborate with the engineering team I recruited for an NIH grant to improve telehealth systems so they are more usable for persons with disabilities. Wednesday and Thursday I work with a multidisciplinary team on a federally funded project to produce a web-based peer-to-peer system to support persons with disabilities who want to share resources, exchange health information, and improve community accessibility. Friday morning I use video teleconferencing to train rural social workers and counselors in the needs of persons with brain injury so they can provide care for rehabilitation hospital inpatients who will be discharged home to rural areas. Friday afternoon I'm working with educational software to train undergraduate health science majors, uploading information about HIPAA and health ethics to a computer-based distance learning software tool my students access from home. Patient care, technology innovation, community planning, remote professional training, and distance teaching are just a few of the areas in which health technologies expand the reach of what I can do as a behavioral health professional.

L. Schopp, Ph.D., A.B.P.P. (✉)
Department of Health Psychology, University of Missouri,
DC 116.88, 1 Hospital Drive, Columbia, MO 65212, USA
e-mail: schoppL@health.missouri.edu

© Springer International Publishing Switzerland 2017
M.M. Maheu et al. (eds.), *Career Paths in Telemental Health*,
DOI 10.1007/978-3-319-23736-7_30

Training

I've have been something of a Luddite most of my life, and I never dreamed that technologies would play so central a role in my career. I was resistive to the changes technology might bring to health care and imagined that in health care, no change was good change, especially with respect to technologies I imagined would come between me and my patients. I'd assumed that using technologies to deliver and manage patient care and professional training would be at odds with the personal connections needed to support those endeavors.

The needs of my patients, trainees, students, and family convinced me that I would need to embrace a health-care world that would soon have a large place for information technologies in patient-centered care and health education.

I started with the typical arc of training as a clinical psychologist specializing in clinical neuropsychology: 5 years graduate school in Clinical Psychology, a 1-year internship at Duke University Medical Center, and 2 years of NIH postdoctoral training in clinical neuropsychology research.

While on postdoctoral fellowship, I treated many residents of rural communities as inpatients in a rehabilitation hospital. These patients were typically young people who had sustained traumatic brain injury from accidents or car crashes. On discharge, I referred patients back to their communities, where there was a dearth of specialized care to address their brain injury needs. My patients and I both had a sinking feeling that the services they needed would not be available in their rural communities after hospital discharge, and that was generally the case. Often I tried to contact rural mental health providers to recruit them to serve these patients after discharge, but they often told me they lacked the training or background to serve these patients well. It was difficult for patients, their families, rural providers, and specialists like me who wanted to ensure that their patients could access care in their home communities.

During this time, I traveled several hours to see outpatients at rural hospitals each week, which was exhausting because I was the nursing mom of a newborn and was expecting another baby, so circuit-riding was challenging for my family. At the same time, it was difficult for my patients to travel to see me for neuropsychological assessment, and many could ill afford the gas money, time off work for family to accompany them to clinic, or time away from family obligations to spend hours in the car to attend a 1-h appointment with me.

I began to use video teleconferencing to see outpatients with traumatic brain injury and stroke and found to my surprise and somewhat to my dismay that most of my patients embraced this technology wholeheartedly. I became curious about patients' views on the acceptability of telehealth sessions, and the National Institute on Disability and Rehabilitation Research supported our project to learn more about the benefits and limitations of telehealth for persons with neurologic disabilities. In this project, we convinced some colleagues to try using video teleconferencing for patient care. These colleagues and their patients agreed to conduct their standard sessions using teleconferencing and give feedback on what they did and did not like about this technology. When patients and psychologists rated the same telehealth session, patients overwhelmingly supported using these telehealth methods, but the psychologists providing care were more reluctant to do so, citing concerns about not feeling as connected when they were not in the room with the patient. It was also a concern that at that time in the late 1990s, our high-speed telehealth network delivered good video quality but was subject to technology mishaps on the network, leading to delays and frustration on the part of psychologists and patients alike. Clearly if health-care providers were to embrace these methods, the technology had to improve to accommodate smooth patient care.

Another technology challenge arose as I was training a postdoctoral fellow on how to conduct telehealth sessions by video teleconferencing. It quickly became clear that the video teleconferencing system was not usable for my postdoctoral fellow because she had significant hearing loss. The telehealth system's sometimes muffled audio signals, lack of real-time captioning, slight delays between audio and video, and tendency to blur when multiple people were using sign language needed to improve if video teleconferencing was to be useful for all patients and providers with hearing loss. This seemed especially important because many of our patients from rural areas were elderly persons for whom travel was difficult or impossible, making them ideal candidates for using video teleconferencing. At the same time, these older residents often had hearing loss, making it confusing and difficult to use standard video teleconferencing technology. In recognition of this potential and these barriers, we assembled a team of video compression and speech recognition engineers to address these issues. The NIH's National Institute on Deafness and Other Communication Disorders recognized the importance of solving these problems and supported this work with a multimillion dollar investment through an R01 grant, in which our team developed medical voice-to-text captioning for video teleconferencing, synchronous sound and video to support lipreading, and more robust video compression strategies to enable multiple sign language users to communicate simultaneously without the blur that results from overwhelmed video capabilities.

As time went on and my patients and colleagues educated me more in issues related to disability, I realized I would need to "train up" on health information technologies if people with disabilities were to be fully empowered to transform their health care and community climate. With some trepidation and much optimism, I embarked on a 3-year NIH/National Library of Medicine Fellowship in Health Informatics. During this fellowship, the National Institute on Disability and Rehabilitation Research awarded 3 years of funding to support us in creating a peer-to-peer network that allowed persons with disabilities to monitor community accessibility barriers and resources, take collective action, share information, and coordinate goods and services exchange.

I had the opportunity to serve on a committee for the American Psychological Association (APA) to develop guidance for telehealth psychologists, which highlighted the needs of behavioral health clients and providers in navigating the brave new world of telehealth technologies. At the time, telesupport, teletherapy, and other strategies over phone, video, email, and other modalities were only beginning to emerge, and this change required new thinking to ensure safe, effective treatment. That led to a term as a member and chair of the APA's Committee on Rural Health, which shared an interest in the emergence of telehealth to reach rural clients.

These days I am learning how online classroom teaching technologies work as I teach a blended online and in-person clinical ethics course. The learning curve is relatively steep, though the capabilities are extensive. Students can read course materials online, view assigned videos for class, post to virtual discussion boards with classmates, collaborate on Wiki-based group writing projects, receive feedback on assignments, check their grades, watch lectures I have recorded, take online quizzes and exams, and much more.

I have also used course software in a pilot program to engage an entire college campus in a health promotion program that enabled faculty and staff to complete wellness program requirements to earn a cash incentive. With the success of this pilot, we partnered with a major health information technology company to offer health monitoring and wellness program technologies to over 19,000 eligible employees on our campuses statewide. Further partnerships with our medical third-party plan administrator and our national pharmacy benefit vendor help us monitor health screening rates, adherence to medical and pharmacy regimens, and workforce health status and health-care costs.

Nearly two decades after my first introduction to telehealth, I have never been so glad to have been so wrong in my initial skepticism about the place for technologies in clinical care and teaching. I have learned so much, and the new frontiers of on-demand services, health-care apps for smartphones, and other technologies let clinicians provide more individualized care than ever before. Those of us who trained in the 50-min in-person hour model of behavioral health care are facing the challenges and possibility of truly customizing our care to the needs of our clients, with real-time support, 24/7 behavioral health support apps, and a wealth of new resources.

Pros and Cons

With the advent of new technologies in health care, patients, their families, health-care professionals, and students can access the services and training they need. Rural patients, especially the many low-income rural residents, have historically experienced de facto health-care disparities due to paucity of local resources. Telehealth can help bridge this gap and can improve accessibility and frequency of follow-up care.

Many of us who work in behavioral health came to this work because we value the strong bonds shared with our clients. Being separated from clients by many miles can sometimes feel like there is something lacking that might otherwise be present if we were in the same room. This must be weighed against the struggles our clients experience in traveling to keep appointments. For so many families, rural poverty makes traveling for face-to-face sessions a dubious luxury fraught with expense, inconvenience, and family upheaval. While face-to-face care may seem ideal to the behavioral health-care provider, our studies have shown that our clients do not necessarily agree, particularly in light of what clients must sacrifice to accommodate provider schedules. Client-centered care in its highest sense means we take seriously the needs and struggles of our clients as we consider how best to use existing modalities to serve them.

Learning and keeping up with emerging technologies is daunting, particularly for those of us who lack familiarity with the available array of tools. Graduate training needs to adapt to accommodate telehealth strategies and kindle a learning set that will support ongoing inquiry in telehealth.

Benefits aside, it is admittedly frustrating to be on the "bleeding edge" as an early adopter of health technologies, before the bugs of any particular system are worked out. I have on many occasions lost precious time to technology glitches, programming limitations, and lack of common ground between software designers, engineers, and clinicians. However, if behavioral health providers don't participate in developing appropriate technologies, our clients will seek technology supports on their own, and we will lose the chance to bring our training and experience to bear on addressing complex behavioral health needs.

Input from behavioral health providers is crucial in the rapidly evolving client-directed telehealth market. Last week one of my teenagers got the newest, latest smartphone. It is loaded with tools to support health and wellness, including everything from an internal accelerometer that tracks daily steps to relatively sophisticated software that can help compensate for executive skills and memory deficits. I have downloaded software to my phone that helps me set and monitor weekly health behavior goals. Every day on the radio, I hear ads for software that aims to sharpen cognitive skills. I'm inspired to imagine a future where patients have technology-based tools to take charge of their health, including mobile access to their electronic health records, individualized health tracking and goal-setting tools, and partnerships with their health providers that do not depend on office visits. Behavioral health-care providers can contribute on the front end in the development cycle, as well as conducting rigorous evaluation of technologies to ensure that they deliver as promised.

Evidence Base

Behavioral health-care providers are uniquely situated to forge and evaluate telehealth technologies given our backgrounds in learning theory, personality, cognition, motivation, and qualitative and quantitative program evaluation. Indeed, it is hard to imagine a profession better suited to contribute to this mission.

Psychologists have evaluated telehealth processes and outcomes for well over a decade and have developed tools and self-assessments to support emerging behavioral telehealth providers in preparing to enter the telehealth arena (Glueckauf et al., 2003).

A key question has been whether services rendered via telehealth are as effective as services delivered in traditional face-to-face clinical settings and if telehealth delivers potential unique value for patients encountering the health-care system. Telehealth services have proven equally effective as face-to-face services among children treated in a pediatric obesity clinic (Davis et al., 2014). Telehealth strategies have also proven effective among persons with eating disorders (Hay, 2013) and families of children with epilepsy (Davis, Sampilo, Gallagher, Landrum, and Malone 2014). Teleconsultation has been used to facilitate urgent care access among perioperative patients who are assessed via telehealth (Blozik, Wildeisen, Fueglistaler, & von Oberbeck 2012). Telehealth video has been effective in neuro-psychological assessment for persons with traumatic brain injury (Schopp, Johnstone, & Merrell 2000) and for patients receiving rehabilitation psychology psychotherapy after stroke (Schopp, Demiris, & Glueckauf 2006). As home-based telemental health has become increasingly available, systematic investigations of its risks and benefits have recently emerged, giving guidance on the benefits and potential challenges of using telemental health modalities (Pruitt, Luxton, & Shore 2014).

Clinicians would be wise to wade into the telehealth delivery mechanisms with care, as issues of privacy, safety, reimbursement, and licensure remain important in this field. However, for those eager to investigate ways of serving clients better, telehealth offers an important adjunct or alternative for behavioral health care in a rapidly changing world.

References

Blozik, E., Wildeisen, I. E., Fueglistaler, P., & von Oberbeck, J. (2012). Telemedicine can help to ensure that patients receive timely medical care. *Journal of Telemedicine & Telecare, 18*(2), 119–121.

Davis, A. M., Sampilo, M., Gallagher, K. S., Landrum, Y., & Malone, B. (2014). Treating rural pediatric obesity through telemedicine: Outcomes from a small randomized controlled trial. *Journal of Pediatric Psychology, 38*(9), 932–943.

Glueckauf, R. L., Pickett, T. C., Ketterson, T. U., Loomis, J. S., & Rozensky, R. H. (2003). Preparation for the delivery of telehealth services: A self-study framework for expansion of practice. *Professional Psychology: Research and Practice, 34*(2), 159–163.

Hay, P. (2013). A systematic review of evidence for psychological treatments in eating disorders: 2005-2012. *International Journal of Eating Disorders, 46*(5), 462–469.

Pruitt, L. D., Luxton, D. D., & Shore, P. (2014). Additional clinical benefits of home-based telemental health treatments. *Professional Psychology: Research and Practice, 45*(5), 340–346.

Schopp, L. H., Demiris, G., & Glueckauf, R. L. (2006). Rural backwaters or front-runners? Rural telehealth in the vanguard of psychology practice. *Professional Psychology: Research and Practice, 37*(2), 165–173.

Schopp, L. H., Johnstone, B., & Merrell, D. (2000). Telehealth and neuropsychological assessment: New opportunities for psychologists. *Professional Psychology: Research and Practice, 31*(2), 179–183.

Chapter 31
Walking the Unmarked Path: On Developing an Independent Practice

Thomas J. Kim

> *I would not give a fig for the simplicity on this side of complexity, but I would give my life for the simplicity on the other side of complexity.*
>
> *Oliver Wendell Holmes, Jr. "The Great Dissenter"*

Vignette

Perhaps the greatest professional gift I have received was to be cursed at weekly for 6 months.

My first telehealth job was to care for incarcerated juveniles. I remember being initially conflicted given my interest in caring for vulnerable populations, but reluctance to endure the commute, safety issues, and workflow dysfunctions common to correctional environments. When the opportunity was clarified as telehealth and required only a short walk from my teaching hospital, I decided to give it a try.

After just one clinic, I knew that I would devote my professional life to telehealth. I vividly recall recognizing that telehealth was more than a convenient job during fellowship. In stark contrast to this certainty was my inability to clearly articulate what, why, or how I knew this.

In the spring of my fellowship year, a 15-year-old incarcerated female was scheduled to see me. When she entered the treatment room, I was able to observe the fairly common expression, at that time, of surprise at seeing her doctor on television. I began my standard introduction when she cut me off with "f**k you!" and exited the room. Aggressive mistrust is not unique in this population and I replied, as I commonly do, "See you next week." This brief exchange continued every week for months. She would enter the room, curse me out, storm off, and be rescheduled the following week. Three months later during a treatment team meeting, the staff expressed mounting concern about the case. I expressed optimism and felt that

T.J. Kim, M.D., M.P.H. (✉)
Chief Medical Officer, AGMP Telehealth, 4205 Edgemont Drive, Austin, TX 78731, USA
e-mail: thomas@med2you.co

© Springer International Publishing Switzerland 2017
M.M. Maheu et al. (eds.), *Career Paths in Telemental Health*,
DOI 10.1007/978-3-319-23736-7_31

291

progress was being made. Seeing the looks of astonishment and confusion, again through the monitor as I participated remotely, I asked the following question: "Does anyone find it interesting that she has reliably presented herself every week only to curse me out and leave?"

Recognition of this limited but significant engagement swept the room and we agreed to continue our plan of weekly 5-s encounters, a plan impossible to do by conventional means. Approximately 6 months after my first encounter, the young lady presented to my clinic and uncharacteristically sat down. Following a period of silence where she was observed to be notably withdrawn, she finally asked, "Will you please help me?"

This vignette represents my first experience with the transformative value of telehealth that a better way is possible. Given the above scenarios, most conventional models and systems would have either discharged or rescheduled the young lady weeks to months after each refusal. These conventional responses are understandable and reflect an overwhelming service need with limited provider resources. And though understandable, conventional response do little to help these cases. It is more likely to reinforce a history of neglect or abandonment experiences that perpetuate the aggressive mistrust.

I was extremely fortunate to have had the programmatic support to construct my clinic the way I wished to practice. And despite being a naïve trainee or perhaps because of it, I chose to reinvest the time and resource savings of telehealth into a care model that made sense to me. Still sensitive to resource limitations even with telehealth, I carefully reengineered my practice to improve responsiveness, accelerate clinical stabilization, and ultimately maintain care quality while reducing both direct and indirect costs. Had my initial experience been less accommodating, I might have never glimpsed the true value of telehealth and would be on a very different path today.

Training Experiences

I am an independent telehealth provider, developer, investigator, consultant, strategist, and evangelist. I am fortunate to have engaged a variety of organizations in a variety of roles towards determining how best to use technology in healthcare. Like many who seek a rewarding work–life balance, I have also moved around the country a few times attempting to optimize this balance. The result is my working principally from home and selectively choosing projects that are engaging and helpful to populations in need. I have also been able to sustain my practice in environments with historically high attrition. In point of fact, I take great pride in being the longest continually working provider in the history of the facilities that I support. My life and portfolio of work are unconventional in many ways while unlikely that others would seek to replicate it step for step. I believe that more than a few may be considering the same questions I have sought to answer.

For the purpose of this field guide, I believe that it is most helpful to deconstruct my life and experiences into three parts: early, middle, and late. Specifically I will adopt the storyteller's three-act construct of setup, confrontation, and resolution. This is because, as Justice Holmes opined, getting to the substantive part of anything worthwhile requires navigation beyond the initial distracting complexities. At present, I am in the early part of my professional life's second act having walked a largely unmarked path of preparation towards telehealth mastery.

Act 1. Education

On my path to becoming a physician, I can highlight four primary touchstones that continue to support my telehealth career.

1. Having multiple healthcare jobs prior to medical school gave me an appreciation of the costly disconnectedness within our system and virtue of collaborative learning approaches.
2. Majoring in a humanity (philosophy) cultivated a tendency towards questioning the status quo, holding two competing thoughts in my head, and championing the minority opinion.
3. Attending a medical school affiliated with an urban, public hospital possessing high volume and limited resources ensured the development of creative problems solving and adaptive workflow skills.
4. Pursing a concurrent masters degree in public health cultivated a population-based perspective to balance the individual-based approach of medical school.
5. A fifth touchstone that holds uncertain generalizability is my lifelong love of games (e.g., video, strategy, RPG). When I was a child, games were generally thought to be a waste of time and for some developmentally damaging. Today, game mechanics or gamification is garnering evidence supporting the value with positive habit formation (e.g., improving chemotherapy compliance with a first-person shooter game) and complex task completion (e.g., determining protein folding structures). The gamification of telehealth is enormously promising in areas such as mhealth (mobile health) and behavioral health treatment planning. To that end, play more games … it couldn't hurt.

Ultimately my educational touchstones are far from a prerequisite to a career in telehealth. They are but one path towards developing a professional facility for thoughtful questioning, creative problem solving, and consideration of multiple perspectives or competing viewpoints.

Act 1. Training

I elected to pursue a combined residency in internal medicine and psychiatry. This was followed by a general medicine fellowship during which time I studied health services research and discovered telehealth. The value of a combined residency was not to simply achieve more training, but to gain deeper insight into the challenged of care siloes. Given the renewed interest in collaborative, multidisciplinary care models (ACOs), my training background continues to inspire me to refine collaborative telehealth models towards bridging disciplines and finding better ways to care for complex, vulnerable populations.

Whichever training path you may pursue and whether you are an early, middle, or late career provider, being a skilled telehealth provider begins with being a skilled provider. Another training point is the notion that the value of telehealth emerges not from the reductive approach found in residency education and conventional models, but from the more inclusive approach of redefining care models beyond single disciplines or solutions. The implication of this is that one may need to master a new model workflow and exercise creative adaptability.

Act 1. Experience

Becoming a mature telehealth provider first requires the practice of telehealth care. Clinical opportunities to practice telehealth are growing by discipline and environment. Most of the providers today can find a telehealth opportunity to engage in. For early career providers, these opportunities will likely come from their training centers, as I predict that telehealth will become its own training rotation just like community clinics, inpatient wards, and emergency departments. Community-based and later career providers (particularly those approaching retirement age) may have similar opportunities within academic centers, but there is a rapidly growing market of private ventures seeking to deliver telehealth care. These opportunities are a welcome sight with one caveat that I describe as "The Hobbyist Challenge." Whether an organization or individual, a hobbyist approach to telehealth (something less than the full measure of your effort) risks replicating a flawed conventional model or delaying skill mastery that can lead to the erroneous conclusion that telehealth doesn't work rather than simply not being adequately experienced.

A second recommendation is that of advocacy. Beyond practicing telehealth care, involvement in professional organizations such as the American Telemedicine Association and state medical associations will continue to elevate the profile of telehealth and the critical need for system improvements in areas such as reimbursement and licensure. Advocacy work also has the benefit of developing a deeper understanding of telehealth. Understanding will give rise to improved communications skill in offering guidance and leadership to those you work with.

A final area is to consider recruiting a personal advisory board to help mentor and guide your development as a telehealth provider. It was not too long ago when I recall well-intended advice from colleagues and mentors to consider alternatives to telehealth. Their logic and advice were sound and appreciated. Ultimately, I decided to persist and eventually recruited advisors who fully supported my career in telehealth. One note about my personal advisory board that continues to this day is my need to speculate and adapt any offered guidance to my unconventional path. I have yet to find a mentor or opportunity that represents the optimal job for me. I do, however, remain optimistic that this will resolve itself given the pace of telehealth growth and my continued persistence.

Act 1. Technology

I believe that a portion of my professional success can be attributed to circumstances beyond my control. As a result of my birth time, for example, I stand between those who grew up with technology and the Internet, (i.e., digital natives) and those who engaged the digital revolution as adults (i.e., digital immigrants). Falling between these two groups has allowed me to retain the context of first-hand pre-Internet experience without the burden of having to dramatically reprogram myself to adapt to Internet life. The result is a nimble appreciation of my patients and collaborators, how their digital status impacts our work together, and how best to engage them.

Regardless of what your digital status may be, technology will continue to advance at a brisk pace as what's possible continues to close the gap on what's imagined. Having the benefit of sublimating my long-standing technophilia, I would be best described as an early adopter who enjoys visiting new technologies in order to identify potentially beneficial uses. For those interested in telehealth, but who do not share my techophilia or early adopter disposition … all remains well. For good or for bad, the pace of technology integration in healthcare is notably slower than every other industry that uses technology. Because of this, my strategic approach to technology mirrors my parenting style … good enough. There is rarely a need to require the latest generation gadget or solution. Moreover, existing high-end solutions that many consider the foundation of telehealth models are simply no longer required. This assessment has far-reaching economic and operational implications as we move to more mobile and cost-effective solutions to support a redesigned care model.

Act 2. Education

Having finished the 26th grade, I've come to realize that there are a great many things I do not know (yet). This realization has led me and others to consider additional education such as an information degree or MBA. There are equally valid arguments for additional education or simply learning by doing. I believe that the answer to this question is both personal and complex. Put simply, depending on what your professional target might be, additional education may be required or strongly preferred. Short of that, telehealth expertise extends well beyond business acumen and digital information management.

Act 2. Training

Evidence of continued telehealth maturity as a field includes current conversations among experts about the development of a certification pathway for telehealth providers. And while such a certification is unlikely to be a requirement for telehealth opportunities now, that expectation may likely change over time.

Act 2. Experience

The pathway to telehealth expertise begins with simply doing. In time, those dedicated to this field and their careers will begin to optimize and adapt their clinical models in order to fulfill the promise of telehealth as a meaningful solution addressing the complex challenges of limited access, spiraling costs, and insufficient resources. Caring for a few in a better way will develop the needed experience and perspective towards realizing the broader goal of adequately caring for many.

Act 2. Technology

Like Moore's Law with transistors, the pace of telehealth technology development will eventually slow and possibly become more costly, but hopefully not anytime soon. Until then, we can expect a progressive crescendo of telehealth solutions that will make recognizing signal from noise increasingly more difficult. For example, some have speculated that the meaningful use initiative is headed for a period of costly disruption when the incentives dry up, a number of EHRs fail to satisfy state 3, unintended consequences emerge (e.g., penalizing providers for patients who choose not to engage their portal), and a wave of second or third HER implementations will be needed for those who chose a nonviable solution.

That will be a moment when the field of telehealth and healthcare in general will desperately need measured guidance and informed leadership. For those seeking to enter the field … will you be ready?

Act 3. Pending

I predict that the simplicity on the other side of complexity for telehealth will be achieved in my lifetime. No further comment is offered at this time.

Pros

Telehealth's greatest attraction for providers is a viable alternative to the increasingly hostile and onerous employment options today. Rather than being complicit in a flawed and unsustainable care system, providers can recover and meaningfully preserve the therapeutic relationship that drew us into the profession initially.

And just as healthcare has become increasingly more complex, so has life in general. As the worse half of a two-physician family, constructing a work–life balance with my wife has been something more than a challenge through our early career phase. Telehealth has afforded me extraordinary professional reward with a flexibility that no conventional job could match. I remain grateful that my past, current, and future opportunities are anything but restricted by my location (currently in Austin, Texas) or other commitments.

And as I enter my mid-career phase, I anticipate more and more opportunities as more and more organizations and individuals come to see the potential of telehealth. What was once unconventional and restricted to those in dire need will be commonplace and a part of almost everyone's experience with healthcare tomorrow.

A final note on the virtue of telehealth is around the notion of satisfaction. I contend that the efficiencies and benefits of telehealth may extend beyond the domain of satisfaction to that of pleasure. If we can devise a better way to care for people with less cost, less effort, and greater benefit, the result will be a more pleasurable experience for providers and patients alike.

Cons

My vision of telehealth will not be easily achieved. Realizing the simple pleasure of caring for each other well will require resolving many complexities around care delivery. At present, we struggle with pursing alternatives because we continue to hold on to broken systems with both hands. We debate the important issues such as patient safety and privacy, but often do so in an adversarial, distracting way. And we have devised a reimbursement system that has grown overly complex and misaligned with care goals. These complex challenges require thoughtful leadership to make difficult decisions that extend beyond election terms and demand significant resource and priority shifts. The one promising aspect of overcoming paralyzing inertia and the status quo is that our present trajectory for healthcare is simply not sustainable. Change, however scary, is bound to happen at some point.

There will be a moment when the field of telehealth and healthcare in general will desperately need measured guidance and informed leadership. For those seeking to enter the field … will you be ready?

For the individual considering a career in telehealth, the current availability of mentorship and mature opportunities may confine them to academic and large health systems or deter them from pursing telehealth entirely. Others may pursue a hybrid course of both telehealth and conventional options, which is prudent. Still others with sufficient risk tolerance will avoid the Hobbyist challenge and commit fully to telehealth. Whichever course they may purse, challenges with telehealth sill mastery will either be thrust upon them (e.g., HER implementation) or taken up willingly (e.g., learning to establish rapport remotely). And until these skills are mastered, they represent more up-front effort and delayed or absent benefit realization.

For those seeking an independent telehealth practice, mastering the technology component without infrastructure support and the challenges of growing a private practice can be added to the clinical skill demands of pursing telehealth.

A final challenge to a career in telehealth is the recognition that failure is more likely than not and repeatedly being told "no" is a near certainty. And while these challenges can sometimes be mitigated through large health systems, those same systems are likely to be challenged in nimbly optimizing the telehealth program.

Evidence Base

The evidence base supporting telehealth continues to grow more rigorous and persuasive. The insights in this chapter are largely based upon my appreciation of the telehealth literature, buy only indirectly. This chapter is offered as an inductive approach to sharing my personal experiences and those that I have engaged with or observed working in the field of telehealth.

Index

© Springer International Publishing Switzerland 2017
M.M. Maheu et al. (eds.), *Career Paths in Telemental Health*,
DOI 10.1007/978-3-319-23736-7